MONEY LAUNDERING IN CANADA:
CHASING DIRTY AND DANGEROUS DOLLARS

In recent years, law enforcement agencies around the world have increasingly focused on money laundering – the process of converting or transferring cash or other assets generated from illegal activity in order to conceal or disguise their origins – in their efforts to control organized crime and, now, terrorism. To this end, countries have attempted to harmonize their policies and legislation and, to some extent, their policing strategies. In evaluating these new approaches, however, it is important to understand the prevalence and complexity of money laundering in different jurisdictions, as well as the likelihood of success and the costs involved in anti-laundering strategies.

This new work by Margaret E. Beare and Stephen Schneider brings empirical evidence to the study of money laundering in Canada. The authors challenge the dominant, seemingly common-sense notion, fuelled by political posturing and policing rhetoric, that taking the profits away from criminals (proceeds of crime enforcement) is a rational and effective tactic. Using extensive research involving records gathered from police, financial institutions, and legal sources, the authors paint a picture of a dubious enforcement strategy beset by conflicting interests and agendas, an overly ambitious set of expectations, and reliance on an ambiguous body of evidence as to the strategy's overall merits.

MARGARET E. BEARE is an associate professor in the Department of Sociology and director of the Nathanson Centre for the Study of Organized Crime and Corruption at Osgoode Hall Law School, York University.

STEPHEN SCHNEIDER is an assistant professor in the Department of Sociology and Criminology at Saint Mary's University.

MARGARET E. BEARE AND
STEPHEN SCHNEIDER

Money Laundering
in Canada

Chasing Dirty and
Dangerous Dollars

UNIVERSITY OF TORONTO PRESS
Toronto Buffalo London

© University of Toronto Press Incorporated 2007
Toronto Buffalo London
Printed in Canada

ISBN 978-0-8020-9143-7 (cloth)
ISBN 978-0-8020-9417-9 (paper)

Printed on acid-free paper

Library and Archives Canada Cataloguing in Publication

Beare, Margaret E.

Money laundering in Canada: Chasing dirty and dangerous dollars /
Margaret E. Beare and Stephen Schneider.

Includes bibliographical references and index.
ISBN 978-0-8020-9143-7 (bound)
ISBN 978-0-8020-9417-9 (pbk.)

1. Money laundering – Canada. 2. Commercial crimes – Canada.
I. Schneider, Stephen, 1963–   II. Title.   III. Title: Money Laundering
in Canada

HV6771.C3B43 2006   364.16'80971   C2006-905664-1

This book has been published with the help of a grant from the
Canadian Federation for the Humanities and Social Sciences, through
the Aid to Scholarly Publications Programme, using funds provided by
the Social Sciences and Humanities Research Council of Canada.

University of Toronto Press acknowledges the financial assistance to
its publishing program of the Canada Council for the Arts and the
Ontario Arts Council.

University of Toronto Press acknowledges the financial support for
its publishing activities of the Government of Canada through the
Book Publishing Industry Development Program (BPIDP).

Contents

Acknowledgments

The research for this book covered many different sectors and, hence, we have many different groups of people to thank. We received financial support from a Strategic Social Science and Humanities Research Council of Canada Grant, additional support from the Nathanson Centre for the Study of Organized Crime and Corruption at York University, and financial support from both the Canadian Bankers Associations and from the Royal Canadian Mounted Police. We thank these four bodies for their financial assistance. In terms of access to the data, the police and the financial institutions were critically important.

First, we would like to thank the RCMP Proceeds of Crime Branch and all the Integrated Proceeds of Crime (IPOC) Units for providing funding, access to data, and research support. In particular, we thank Mike Cabana, Dave Beer, and Garry Clement for initiating and sustaining the necessary research, and we would also like to acknowledge the tremendous logistical support provided throughout the research by Pat Callaghan. Credit for data collection should also be extended to the Officers in Charge of the IPOC Units as well as Unit members who helped collect data and coordinate the field research. Many thanks are also extended to Peter German, André Rivard, and Dean Buzza, at RCMP headquarters, for their assistance. Likewise, we are indebted to the Seized Property Management Directorate for their labour-intensive work in identifying the monetary values of seizures and forfeitures associated with the proceeds of crime cases examined for this study.

Within the financial institutions there are obviously too many people to list. However we wish to specifically mention Michael Ballard and Gene McLean at the Canadian Bankers Association and in the 'Big-5' banks we wish to thank the heads of Security and Investigations who provided us with wonderful cooperation. This group included Frank Craddock, Sonny Saunders, Gordon Kennedy, Ted Porter, and Wally Kalichuk. In addition to those people we named there were many others who provided valuable money-laundering and bank defalcation information – we thank them all.

We are grateful to Reetu Kholsa, Alicia Lovell, and Jennifer Auciello, who were invaluable when it came to inputting, collating, and calculating the data for chapter 3. In addition, we would like to thank Maury Medjuck of the Edmonton Integrated Proceeds of Crime Section, Mike Waugh of the Kingston Proceeds of Crime Section, and Glenn Hanna of the Combined Forces Special Enforcement Unit for providing us with photos, graphics, and case studies for the research. We would also like to extend our thanks to the staff at the Nathanson Centre, in particular Joanne Rappaport and Joan Shields, for their administrative support, and to York University graduate students May Friedman, Hosh Drury, and Natalie Azzi who worked on the initial editing of the separate chapters. The Osgoode Hall law students who were in the Summer 2002 LLM International Criminal Law and Regulation class did a wonderful job of trying to track down the evidence behind the many anti-money-laundering claims of the international bodies – we thank them for their efforts. In addition to all of these people, there is a host of critical thinking academics whose work has informed our own.

We thank Virgil Duff at University of Toronto Press for his patience with receiving this manuscript, Beth McAuley for the mammoth copy-editing task, and Mary Newberry for her indexing skills. Thank you everyone.

Preface

Our previous study, *Tracing of Illicit Funds: Money Laundering in Canada*, was prepared in 1990 while both of us worked for the Solicitor General of Canada (Beare and Schneider, 1990). The cases that appeared in that report had been identified to us by the police as having a large financial component, but there were not any actual money-laundering cases since the proceeds of crime legislation had only just been passed into law. That report was, and still is, widely referred to within Canada and internationally. At that time, the attempt to seize and freeze illicit proceeds appeared to be a well thought-out strategy that followed on the heels of the realization that 'kicking down doors' had no lasting impact on drug trafficking. Likewise, the 'targeting up' efforts against the so-called kingpins was dubious given both the difficulty of actually convicting these people *and* the realization that the criminal operations could succeed quite well, often continuing to be run by the big shot from his jail cell. The argument then became the too easily tossed-off line, 'The heads of these criminal organizations may not dirty their hands with the drugs, but they do take possession of the cash.' Hence, law enforcement should go after the proceeds of crime. Left as one policing tool among many, taking the profits of criminal activity away from convicted criminals makes sense. It is the priority given to this approach and the international consequences of a 'harmonized' global commitment to the anti-money-laundering strategies that this book questions.

In the 1990 study, money laundering is broadly defined as the process by which one converts or transfers funds or other assets generated from illegal activity in order to conceal or disguise their illegal origins. A comprehensive money-laundering operation satisfies three essential objectives:

- it *converts* the bulk-cash proceeds of crime to another, less suspicious form
- it *conceals* the criminal origins and ownership of the funds and/or assets, and
- it *creates* a legitimate explanation or source for the funds and/or assets

To realize the greatest benefit from money laundering, criminally derived cash should not simply be converted to other, less suspicious assets; the illicit financing of the assets must also be hidden. The final objective, while less frequently satisfied in most money-laundering operations, is no less important than the first two. The effectiveness of a laundering scheme will ultimately be judged by how convincingly it creates a legitimate front for illegally acquired cash and assets. In short, 'money is not truly laundered unless it is made to appear sufficiently legitimate that it can be used openly, precisely what the final stage of the cycle is designed to achieve' (Naylor, 2002: 137). One of the keys to satisfying the objectives of the laundering process is to conduct commercial and financial transactions that appear as legitimate as possible. The more successful a money-laundering operation is in emulating the patterns of legitimate financial or commercial transactions, the less suspicion it will attract.

In order to satisfy these three objectives, the money-laundering process has to go through four stages: *placement, layering, integration,* and *repatriation.* The initial *placement* stage is where the cash proceeds of crime physically enter the legitimate economy, which satisfies the first objective. Once the funds have been placed in the legitimate economy, a process of *layering* takes place. It is during this stage that much of the laundering activity occurs, as funds are circulated through various economic sectors, companies, and commercial or financial transactions in order to conceal the criminal source and ownership of the funds and to obscure any audit trail. The penultimate step of the money-laundering process is termed *integration*, because 'having been placed initially as cash and layered through a number of financial operations, the criminal proceeds are fully integrated into the financial system and can be used for any purpose.'[1] The final stage of the process involves *repatriating* the laundered funds into the hands of the criminal entrepreneur, ideally with a legitimate explanation as to their source, so that they can be used without attracting suspicion.

The placement stage is the most perilous for the launderer as it involves the physical movement of bulk cash, usually in small denominations. It is at this stage that the offender is most vulnerable to suspicion and detection and where the funds can most easily be tied to criminal sources. Most often the money must enter a financial institution, and it is now mandatory for financial institutions, in countries that have complied with the recommendations of the Financial Action Task Force (FATF), to report all suspicious transactions to a central financial intelligence body within their jurisdiction. The financial institutions thus become 'enforcement' bodies in order to detect laundering. Once the funds are placed within the legitimate economy and converted from their original cash form, the opportunities for money laundering are increased exponentially: the funds can be transferred among, and hidden within, dozens of financial intermediaries and commercial investments, both domestically and internationally.

The above description is what a '*good*' laundering scheme should be. Most of the money-laundering literature continues to pay homage to this UN definition, or to a similar description of money laundering, and then continues to ignore what is required in order for criminal proceeds to be actually 'laundered.' In reality, what has become accepted as money laundering is the mere use or deposit of proceeds of crime. In many of the cases examined for this study, the expenditure of illegally derived revenues was so lackadaisical and unimaginative that the money-laundering objectives and processes laid out above were barely satisfied. In other cases, millions of dollars of criminal funds were proficiently cleansed through elaborate operations that involved numerous economic sectors, dozens of professionals, a myriad of illusory guises and techniques, and hundreds, if not thousands, of obfuscating transactions. In short, one should not be overly preoccupied with the term 'money laundering.' For both analytical and law-enforcement purposes, attention should be paid to how the proceeds of crime are disposed of by the criminal element – with particular emphasis on how it enters and circulates within the legitimate economy – regardless of whether these transactions satisfy the definition of 'money laundering. '

In *Tracing of Illicit Funds*, we argued that understanding money laundering schemes has a direct implication for policing and regulatory efforts (Beare and Schneider, 1990: 425–37). Based on the police files that were examined at that time, 'traditional' policing would likely not continue to be successful in building complicated cases and in following paper trails that often wound through numerous jurisdictions, making use of multiple corporations and nominees. It was believed that a different policing structure, different policing expertise, and different working relationships with other police departments, other regulatory agencies, professional associations, and international contacts would all be required.

The analysis of police cases in our 1990 study revealed that the vehicles most often used by criminal enterprises in their laundering activities or to facilitate these schemes included

- deposit-taking institutions
- currency-exchange houses
- securities markets
- real estate
- incorporation and operation of companies
- miscellaneous laundering via 'big purchases' (vehicles, boats, planes, travel agencies, gems, jewellery, etc.)
- white-collar professionals, such as lawyers and accountants (ibid. xii)

We concluded that money laundering in Canada is a thriving industry that has demonstrated it can utilize any number of economic sectors and services offered within. Despite the illegality and underworld connotations of the proceeds of crime, the laundering process itself is not an economic aberration. Indeed, it thrives and survives on the very same commercial transactions that most Canadians utilize to sustain their own economic well-being and which drive the Canadian economy. The Canadian findings were also shown to be true elsewhere. Australia, for example, replicated the study and produced similar results in a 1992 report titled *Taken to the Cleaners: Money Laundering in Australia* (Australia, 1992).

The laundering schemes we identified ranged from the extremely simple to the extremely sophisticated. The majority of the cases that the police identified were drug related, were located in the largest urban centres and tended to make use of nominees to conceal ownership of the proceeds. We attempted a typology of schemes (without a great amount of success). The basic distinctions reflected the degree of seriousness of the schemes – serious in the sense of the amount of money involved and the ongoing nature of some of the schemes. The first category we identified was a *simple-limited* scheme. These cases involved a small amount of money being laundered, possibly on an ongoing basis. This scheme might involve a tavern, restaurant, vending-machine company, or an actual laundry – any business where the inventory is flexible and dirty money can be claimed as legitimate profit. There is obviously a fairly restrictive ceiling on how much money can be pushed through these laundering operations. The business owner would have to pay taxes on these claimed profits, but this amount would be thought of as a business expense and still be worthwhile since the criminal proceeds would have been given the appearance of clean profit.

Some schemes, although similar to the *simple-limited* schemes, are less restrictive. These fell into the second category referred to as *simple-unlimited* schemes. There are businesses that have such large budgets and involve such a high level of technical expertise that it is typically very hard to refute the amounts of money required in their various operations. Dredging, waste, scrap metal, and construction industries are particularly suited for long-term, high-quantity but fairly simple laundering activity.

The next level of schemes becomes harder to trace because, in fact actual 'tracing,' often requiring forensic expertise, is required. We differentiated between *serial-simple* and *serial-complex* cases. We also created a final category that we called *international* schemes. In reality, many of the serial cases, and certainly most of the truly complex schemes involve an international component. The *serial-simple* schemes involve a large number of financial transactions and account manipulations, and the movement of the money through these accounts is designed specifically to deceive the police. In most of these cases, once the police begin to investigate, the schemes will not likely protect the illicit proceeds. The ability to follow an audit trail will reveal the true source of these funds – or at least reveal that there is no legitimate source.

The *serial-complex* schemes are by definition more complex, and usually require the assistance of professionals such as lawyers and accountants. Imaginative real-estate flips, complex invoice manipulations, and penetration of the stock markets may be involved. The movement of dirty money over borders provides a powerful concealing advantage and in our 1990 study, 80 per cent of the cases had an international component. Exporting the illicit funds offshore and then repatriating the profits back to Canada allows the criminals to make use of the proceeds to perpetuate their criminal operations (i.e., purchase more drugs), and then make use of legitimate business opportunities such as the provisions that allow for foreign investment into Canadian businesses to return the money for use in Canada. 'Loan-back' schemes, front companies, and double invoicing are all part of these cases.

Our 1990 study, as well as subsequent research carried out through the Department of the Solicitor General, led directly to the creation of the Integrated Anti-Drug Profiteering Units. In terms of actual policing strategies, the research indicated the need for

- a continuation of the focus on community-based policing with an emphasis on 'knowing your business community.' An awareness of the nature and extent of the businesses in an area would serve to alert the police to peculiar business operations, such as those that are serving as a front for laundering operations;
- police to gain expertise in the cultivation and control of informants and engagement in undercover work;
- the recruitment and/or training of special 'proceeds-of-crime' investigators; and
- the acquisition of specialized skills and equipment such as forensic accounting skills, computer intelligence systems, and analytical work.

Much has changed between 1990 and 2006, in terms of legislation and policing powers and the post–9/11 alleged links between money laundering and terrorism. During the 1990s the pressure from the international community intensified, most specifically due to the momentum and influence of the Financial Action Task Force. The FATF outlined a series of 'recommendations' (which were later enhanced) that specified what the member countries ought to put in place in order to illustrate their commitment to the 'war' against money laundering. Countries that did not comply were criticized and/or 'blacklisted' for failing to put in place provisions such as a mandatory reporting regime for suspicious transactions and for failing to have a central financial intelligence unit to which all such reports could be sent. All of these changes occurred within little over a decade. In the post–9/11 period, additional requirements were introduced when the FATF included fighting terrorist financing as part of its anti-money-laundering mandate. During this period, the Canadian government has been busy passing an array of anti-money-laundering legislation. The specific focus on the proceeds of crime began with the 1989 amendments to the Criminal Code, which made money laundering a criminal offense when it pertained to certain criminal enterprises and designated drug offences. Since that time the range of these offences has been broadened and new legislation has been added to the crusade. This book is, therefore, an attempt to provide a picture of money laundering both in Canada and internationally, in the wake of legislation and international pressures that have compelled most Western nations to join the call to 'fight' money laundering.

THE AUTHORS

Margaret E. Beare, BA, MA (University of Guelph), Diploma in Criminology (University of Cambridge), PhD (Columbia University)

Dr Beare worked for eleven years within the Department of the Solicitor General Canada, and served two years as director of Police Policy and Research before coming to York University in 1995, where she is currently cross-appointed in law and sociology. She served as director of the Nathanson Centre for the Study of Organized Crime and Corruption at Osgoode Hall Law School from 1996 to 2006. In addition to the 1990 report titled *Tracing of Illicit Funds: Money Laundering in Canada*, co-authored with Stephen Schneider, her books include *Criminal Conspiracies: Organized Crime in Canada* (1996), *Critical Reflections on Transnational Organized Crime, Money Laundering and Corruption* (2003), and a co-edited book titled *Police and Government Relations: Who's Calling the Shots?* (2007).

Stephen Schneider, BA (Carleton University), MSc International Development (University of Pennsylvania), PhD Urban and Regional Planning (University of British Columbia)

Dr Schneider is an assistant professor in the Sociology and Criminology Department at St Mary's University, and adjunct professor in the School of Justice Studies at Ryerson University. For the last fifteen years, his research has focused on organized and economic crime, community crime prevention, and policing. Some recent projects include national and international research examining money laundering, contraband smuggling, fraud, and innovative approaches to combating organized crime. He has also worked extensively at the local level, conducting research into and implementing crime prevention programs in poor, inner-city communities. He has recently published *Refocusing Crime Prevention: Collection Action and the Quest for Community* (2007), and is currently researching a book on the history of organized crime in Canada.

MONEY LAUNDERING IN CANADA

1 Canadian Money-Laundering History and Legislative Framework

Money laundering is a tactical imperative employed by cash-intensive criminal entrepreneurs to maximize their ability to use and enjoy the fruits of their illegal activity without attracting suspicion and/or government interdiction. Within the criminal milieu, money laundering has taken on a life of its own and has become an integral component in the operations of criminal organizations, in part because of the dogged pursuit of illicit funds by law enforcement agencies. A distinct criminal career has opened up to provide laundering services. This career choice has its own distinct skill requirements – a law degree, an accounting credential, financial training, or links to the corporate world are all useful. An advantage of this criminal career is that, in some cases, one can maintain the reputation of a legitimate white-collar professional while reaping the high commissions of a professional launderer.

For much of this century, money laundering remained largely undefined and unrecognized as a criminal activity by lawmakers, police, the courts, and researchers. Nonetheless, there is evidence that professional criminals realized the importance of hiding or legitimizing their illicit proceeds during the formative years of Canadian organized crime. Historical literature suggests that the first conscious attempts at money laundering can be traced to the 1920s and 1930s, when strict temperance laws in Canada and the United States prompted a highly profitable underground economy of liquor distilling and distribution. In the Prohibition era, Canadian distillers illegally reaped millions of dollars by supplying American and Canadian organizations, which in turn satiated a thirsty and receptive U.S. market. By the 1950s, gambling overtook bootlegging as the major source of revenue for North American crime groups, but it was not until the late 1960s and beyond that money laundering came into its own due to the unprecedented revenue generated by the drug trade. Today, money laundering is tied to almost all profit-oriented criminal activity and has become an essential tactical component of organized crime.

Below are some highlights in the history of money laundering in Canada. Many of the issues that are raised in this brief chronology will be discussed in greater detail in the following chapters.

The 1920s and 1930s

There is nothing new about money laundering. Even the 'players' may be quite similar – except now we have tended to stereotype various ethnic groups and certain criminal activities as being particularly problematic. In reality, a diverse array of people, who have become very wealthy and 'legitimate,' made their money in criminal activity and managed to hide and retain these illicit proceeds. Several well-known 'respectable' wealthy families gained their economic base during the Prohibition era. For example, the Bronfman family transferred hundreds of thousands of dollars in profits from illegal liquor distribution to a branch of the Bank of Nova Scotia located offshore. This was considered the first large-scale money-laundering operation involving Canadian groups.

This example also provides an illustration of the roles that 'money laundering,' as it is now called, and lawyers have played in the accumulation of wealth by some of the most elite of Canadian and American society. In 1934 charges were laid against sixty individuals for tax evasion relating to smuggling – including four Bronfmans. Saint-Pierre and Miquelon (the French islands off the south coast of Newfoundland) played a starring role, and Al Capone's hat remains on display in the Hotel Robert as a nostalgic reminder of the past. A group of lawyers, referred to as 'a minor Bar convention,' defended the Bronfmans (see Newman, 1978; Hunt, 1988). The intrigue was heightened by the disappearance of all of the records from Seagram headquarters and by the discovery of the body of the last person in charge of these records floating in the St Lawrence River. Over time, the Bronfmans were 'cleansed' of the Mob connections, just as the Kennedy family was cleansed of its links to Frank Costello and became the number one family in 'Camelot.' A number of lessons could have been learned from this history, two of which are that a population committed to wishing to buy an illicit product (in this case alcohol) will find a means to do so, and illegal trade will be facilitated in part by contradictory laws and policies across jurisdictions within Canada and between Canada and the United States.

The 1950s and 1960s

Millions of dollars in profits from gambling, prostitution, loan sharking, drug trafficking, and other criminal activities were laundered through Canadian banks by traditional American and Canadian crime groups. Criminal activity prompted Canadian officials to respond more aggressively to what was perceived to be a U.S.-style-'organized crime threat.' There is some controversy as to which illegal activity produced the greatest amount of illegal wealth to provide the base for future organized crime activities: gambling or the smuggling of alcohol. The reality may be a mix of the two. Mark Haller argues that even before the 1920s, criminal entrepreneurs had built bookmaking syndicates in American cities and that during Prohibition, bootleggers invested their profits in expanding gambling operations rather than expanding their smuggling operations (Haller, 1976). Daniel Bell contributed that after Prohibition many Italian-American gangsters attempted to gain entry into legitimate businesses, but, since few opportunities were open to them, many turned to illegal gambling operations. Criminal activity of any sort was described by Bell as being 'one of the queer ladders of social mobility,' meaning that when other avenues for upward mobility were closed to new immigrants, criminal activity remained an opportunity (Bell, 1965: 138).

It is noteworthy that in the early discussions concerning organized crime, there is much more of a focus on the desirability of moving criminals from the illegal operations into the legitimate businesses rather than a focus on the dangers of having 'dirty' money mingling with 'clean' money. The lead-up to the U.S. publication *The Challenge of Crime in a Free Society* by the President's Commission on Law Enforcement and Administration of Justice, Task Force on Organized Crime in 1967 involved meetings between Canadian and American law enforcement, various academics, and government officials. The emphasis was on the need for a somewhat uniform response to a type of criminal activity that was seen to move freely across borders. Pressure from the United States and the experiences across the border remain critical aspects both in terms of our understanding of organized crime and money laundering and the adequacy of our Canadian enforcement response.

The 1960s and 1970s

The release of the commission's publication in 1967 was an important event in both the United States and Canada. The commission and Donald Cressey's contribution to it provided the framework that was either defended or refuted in the following decades. Critics such as Michael Woodiwiss credit this era for what they see to be a misplaced, or at least too narrow, focus on the 'mafia conspiracy' – hence what Woodiwiss terms the 'dumbing of American discourse' (Woodiwiss, 2001). Robert Kelly argues that the commission forced those interested in understanding organized crime to look beyond the individual criminals and to consider instead the markets, enterprises, and environments – thus the profits became part of this wider governmental and academic focus (Kelly, 1986). These U.S. definitions and perceptions of organized crime directly influenced the Canadian media, politicians, and academics. The U.S. passed the Racketeer Influenced and Corrupt Organizations (RICO) statute in 1970 and began making use of these powers towards the late 1970s and into the 1980s. These provisions allowed the prosecutors to link separate offences and then to impose triple damages as well as long prison sentences – all in an attempt to increase the risks and remove the profit from crimes.

'Professional launderers' became an occupation with lawyers and accountants vying for the job. For example, in the United States, Frank Ragano represented Mafia boss Santos Trafficante. It is claimed that Ragano operated as a 'conduit' between the Mob and politicians, businessmen, and labour leaders. Robert Blakey, as chief counsel to the Senate Permanent Subcommittee on Investigations, testified that Ragano was a 'house counsel' and therefore a 'functional part of Cosa Nostra.' Ragano pleaded guilty to that charge (Ragano and Rabb, 1994: 247, 366). He also worked for New Orleans Mafia boss Carlos Marcello and, in 1961, he defended Jimmy Hoffa against claims that he had plundered the Teamsters' pension fund.

In Canada, as the financial brains behind the Cotroni organized crime family, Willie Obront, who was named in organized crime inquiries as the Canadian equivalent of Meyer Lansky, laundered millions in profits from securities fraud, gambling, prostitution, extortion, and drug trafficking. Not only did he launder the money he also invested it, creating even more revenues. The Quebec crime probe of 1977 revealed how Obront had washed over $89 million in two years for the organization through various schemes (Quebec Police Commission Inquiry, 1977). Recent cases indicate that the training and reputational 'clout' of lawyers remain extremely useful in large-scale laundering operations.

Meyer Lansky recognized Canada's potential as a money-laundering conduit as early as the 1930s, when he began to funnel revenue from the American La Cosa Nostra (LCN) through Canada or through tax-haven countries like Switzerland before it was repatriated to the U.S. In the 1950s, Lansky promoted the idea of transferring part of the Mob's bookmaking and gambling operations to Canada to avoid intensive American enforcement attention and to protect their illicit revenue from the Internal Revenue Service. In February 1970, Lansky convened a meeting in Acapulco, Mexico, which included leading LCN operatives from Quebec and Ontario – including Vic Cotroni, Paolo Violi, and John Papalia – in part to discuss laundering money through Canada. The idea was to send cash generated from criminal activities in the U.S. to Canadian underworld figures who would then invest in U.S. enterprises as a means to return the money south of the border. Other Canadians, in particular John Pullman of Toronto, were identified as key Lansky associates who facilitated his money-laundering interests in Canada, primarily through real estate investments.[1] In 1974, an article appeared in the *Toronto Star*, based on an interview with Inspector Thomas Venner, at the time the head of the RCMP's intelligence unit in Toronto. The article asserted that 'Laundered crime money is invested in every kind of business in Metro,' which includes 'investments in hotels, restaurants, small shopping plazas, and increasingly, in recent months, real estate (Thomas, 1974: n.p.). The focus on money laundering continued with the publication of a 1974 report by the Royal Commission on Certain Sectors of the Building Industry in Ontario, and the public was drawn to the broader topic of organized crime with the airing of two Canadian Broadcast Corporation (CBC) programs, entitled *Connections I* and *Connections II*.[2]

The 1980s

Throughout the 1980s pressures and experiences from the U.S. continued to push Canadian officials to examine anti-organized crime and proceeds of crime legislative options. As the chair of the Presidential Commission on Organized Crime in the United States commented in 1984: 'Money laundering is the lifeblood of organized crime ... without the ability to freely utilize its ill-gotten gains, the underworld will have been dealt a crippling blow' (Presidential Commission on Organized Crime, 1984: 7). In 1980 the Province of British Columbia released a report titled *The Business of Crime: An Evaluation of the American RICO Statute from a Canadian Perspective*. The Racketeer Influenced and Corrupt Organizations (RICO) statute in the United States was being increasingly used to 'go after' criminal proceeds. The ministries of the Solicitor General and Justice Canada hosted a symposium to discuss the best legislation to tackle criminal proceeds. Among other participants, Robert Blakey, the chief drafter of RICO, discussed the merits of the U.S. model.

If there was a catalyst for the final push towards proceeds of crime legislation in Canada, it was the Luis Pinto case in which an American drug trafficker, who admitted to and was convicted for laundering approximately U.S.$40 million, maintained a bank account at a branch of the Royal Bank in Montreal. The RCMP working with the FBI concluded that $400,000 in that account were proceeds of crime. The Supreme Court of Canada determined in 1985 that cash in bank accounts was an 'intangible' and therefore could not be seized under existing legislation. Proceeds of crime were only forfeitable if they were the *actual* goods or money obtained directly from the commission of an offence. Once the cash was mingled with other cash in a financial institution, the illicit proceeds could not be seized.

In 1985, the *Montreal Gazette* ran a three-part series investigating the role of Canadian Caribbean bank branches in laundering drug money.[3] Scotiabank was fined U.S.$1.8 million by the United States Internal Revenue Service, prompting increased measures by the Canadian Bankers Association and individual banks. International pressure in various forms on Canada continued to be a constant incentive for enhanced efforts to combat money laundering. The U.S. State Department's assessment of Canada as an international money-laundering haven was repeatedly echoed by RCMP personnel. In a 1989 *Vancouver Sun* article, former RCMP Assistant Commissioner Stamler stated that international crime groups considered Canada an attractive spot to invest in legitimate businesses. In addition, Canada had an efficient banking system with branches in many Caribbean tax-haven countries. 'You can deposit money in Prince George, B.C., and put it (electronically) into a Grand Cayman account,' said Stamler (Possamai, 1989: A11). This was reiterated by Bruce Bowie, an officer who had long served in the RCMP's money-laundering enforcement program. According to Bowie, Canada had many attractive features for money launderers. Basically, all of the criteria that were beneficial for legitimate businesses were also ideal for launderers. The Canadian currency was stable, as was the political climate.

In 1988, a 'confidential' (but much quoted) study by the RCMP and U.S. Drug Enforcement Administration detailed how millions of dollars of drug money crossed the U.S.–Canada border annually. Even though this report was already dated when it was leaked to the public, the timing of its release was perfect for providing support to the U.S. demands that countries, including Canada, replicate the U.S.-style currency transaction reporting (CTR) mechanisms system. Millions of forms from banking institutions were fed into and soon glutted the U.S. Financial Crimes Enforcement Network (FinCEN), the centralized body that received all of the suspicious and large financial transactions within the United States. Massachusetts Senator John Kerry argued that drug money was being shipped to Canada to avoid U.S. reporting requirements. A compromise form of legislation was passed in Canada, which did not create the U.S.-style CTR system but was adequate enough to satisfy, for the time being, the demands of the United States and the recommendations of the international Financial Action Task Force (FATF) on money laundering. The Proceeds of Crime (Money Laundering) Act was passed by Parliament in June 1991 (with regulations to follow in 1993). The legislation mandated financial service providers to maintain certain types of records to facilitate money-laundering investigations and to *voluntarily* report suspicious transaction to law enforcement.

In 1989, the federal government enacted new legislation creating a distinct criminal offence for possession of the proceeds of crime and money laundering. It also provided police with specific provisions to seize, restrain, and forfeit assets (both tangible and intangible) that were derived from various criminal and drug offences. The RCMP used the new proceeds of crime seizure provisions to freeze $18 million in a Toronto bank account at Banco Occidente, which was tied to the Medellin cocaine cartel.

The 1990s

Various government and policing reports indicated that Canada was being used to launder the profits of major domestic criminal organizations, including those of Italian, Asian, Colombian, and Middle Eastern descent, as well as outlaw motorcycle groups. However, the laundering activities of Canadian crime groups were said to represent only one aspect of the flow of dirty money into Canada. It was claimed that millions of 'dirty' dollars obtained as a result of drug transactions conducted abroad were also being laundered *through* Canada. In the latter case, according to a 1991 RCMP report,

> foreign-based criminal organizations take advantage of Canada's sophisticated financial system to both move and conceal proceeds of crime. Intelligence further indicates that some foreign-based trafficking groups are using Canadian bank accounts to secure multi-million dollar payments for drug deals in which Canada was not involved as a source or consuming country. In such cases, Canada is used, not as a laundering centre, but a clearing house where organizations settle business debts. (Royal Canadian Mounted Police, 1991: 48)

One of the more recent trends claimed to be used in the internationalization of laundering operations was 'the multiplication of links between major drug trafficking organizations worldwide. As they settle debts and secure drug payment transfers, trafficking organizations in Canada and abroad intersect in an attempt to launder proceeds of crime efficiently and to obscure paper trails' (Royal Canadian Mounted Police, 1993: 52). The RCMP had discovered that certain drug-trafficking organizations channelled illicit funds through money pipelines established by other crime groups:

> Larger organizations sold their money laundering services to smaller ones and commingle proceeds as they were transferred into various accounts. Some of the more powerful Canadian trafficking organizations also introduced less prominent ones to major foreign drug suppliers and underwrote the drug purchases on their behalf. By acting in such a way, powerful organizations distance themselves from any actual drug trafficking activity and shift risks onto others. As brokers, they receive a percentage of the profits and most probably handle all laundering aspects of the transaction. (ibid.)

The U.S. State Department designated Canada as a 'primary concern' for global money-laundering activities. At least ten accounts at two New York branches of the Royal Bank of Canada were frozen by the U.S. Justice Department for alleged links to drug money laundering by the Medellin cocaine cartel, and within Canada dozens of currency exchange companies were charged with money laundering following a RCMP sting operation. The U.S. State Department also designated

Canada as a key international money-laundering location for foreign drug operations. The *International Narcotics Control Strategy Report*, published in April 1993 by the Bureau for International Narcotics and Law Enforcement Affairs of the U.S. State Department, stated that 'Canada has a drug money laundering problem that may be as large as (US)$10 billion and possibly increasing ... Canada is considered a significant money laundering threat, because it is a transit point for drugs and money destined for the U.S. from South America, the Middle East and Asia traffic which compounds the money laundering problem created by domestic use.' The report went on to say that South American cocaine cartels had laundered drug proceeds from U.S. sales in Canadian financial institutions, as had a prominent Middle Eastern heroin-trafficking organization (McCarthy, 1993: B1).

These U.S. charges against Canada continued throughout the 1990s. In its 1997 report, the U.S. State Department once again designated Canada as a 'primary' concern for international money laundering. This was because of

> its advanced financial sector, lack of mandatory reporting requirements, and proximity to the US, which makes it an attractive target to money launderers. The Canadian open financial sector and bank branches located in traditional tax haven countries also make the country vulnerable to money laundering. Currency exchange houses, particularly near the U.S. border, are believed to move large amounts of drug money between the United States and Canada. Canada has financial institutions that engage in currency transactions involving international narcotics trafficking proceeds that include significant amounts of U.S. currency. Like other financial institutions, currency exchanges are not required to report large value or suspicious transactions to authorities. (Bureau for International Narcotics and Law Enforcement Affairs, 1998: n.p.)

The Canadian stock market was also seen to be vulnerable during these years. In May 1998, the FBI raided the U.S. headquarters of YBM Magnex Inc., which was listed on the Toronto Stock Exchange, alleging the company was created as a money-laundering vehicle by Russian organized crime. Following the raid, all trading in YBM shares was halted, eventually leading to the company's collapse. More than $100 million was raised from Canadian investors and the firm had a capitalization of almost $900 million.

Equally important as Canada's attractive financial markets were perceptions of relatively light sentences for money-laundering and drug offences. According to one news-story examining the money-laundering operations of a major Canadian hashish importer, 'Canada has a well-earned reputation for letting drug traffickers off lightly when they get nabbed.' Dealers could count on spending four to six years in jail for a serious drug crime in Canada, compared with up to twenty years in the United States. This also meant that there was considerably less incentive for an operative arrested in Canada to roll over and play witness (Noble, 1996: B2). For 'consensual' crimes where there was likely no complaint, the inability to recruit informants was seen to be critical in scuttling police investigations.

Unarguably, the most salient example of a criminal organization that evolved into a money-laundering specialist for itself and other crime groups was the Canadian-based Caruana-Cuntrera organization, which police alleged had been operating for over thirty years in a number of countries worldwide. The police investigation was called Project Omerta. The alleged head of the group, Alfonso Caruana, and his brothers were believed to have controlled a major portion of the cocaine and heroin imported into Canada since the late 1970s. In addition, the group was alleged to have provided extensive money-laundering services to its associates as well as to other criminal organizations. As early as 1981, the RCMP detected $21.6 million that passed through Alfonso Caruana's bank accounts in the course of only a few months. Like many traditional crime groups, this organization was transnational, controlled most elements of the drug distribution ring, and had an intricate division of labour. While the core group was small, they were alleged to have had an expansive network of associates throughout the world, which facilitated both drug trafficking and money laundering (KPMG, 1999).

Their international laundering operation moved drug money from bank accounts in Toronto and Montreal to Miami, Houston, and Mexico City, then on to numbered accounts in Lugano, Switzerland, and from there, to Colombia. At the same time, this criminal organization relied heavily on more rudimentary methods to launder money and pay for drugs on the international market. In particular, millions of dollars of cash were physically transported across North America and through various other countries. Between 1978 and 1984, police estimated that Guiseppe Cuffaro, one of the group's main money launderers, moved more than U.S.$20 million in cash from Montreal to Switzerland. On 27 November 1978, Caruana and Cuffaro arrived in Zurich on a Swiss Air flight from Montreal and were fined for failing to declare U.S.$600,000 discovered in false-bottom suitcases. They both declared the money was derived from the sale of a boat. Alfonso Caruana paid a small fine and was released.

Oreste Pagano, a member of the Camorra Mafia based in Brescia, Italy, and a middleman between Caruana and his Colombian cocaine suppliers, confessed to police that that he had supplied Alfonso Caruana with cocaine from South America between 1991 and 1998. This included two back-to-back cocaine shipments of 4,526 kilograms into Canada and 8,200 kilograms into Italy. Pagano estimated that these shipments netted the organization CDN$36 million and U.S.$36 million, respectively. Cash payments for the narcotics would be transported to Pagano by vehicle from Canada to Miami. In one instance, Pagano told police that Giuseppe Cuntrera Dimora had sent a courier to Cancun via a commercial flight with U.S.$200,000 for partial payment of a shipment. Pagano also told police that he and Alfonso Caruana did not use the banking system but preferred to make cash transactions from 'hand to hand.' The police investigation revealed that the Caruana-Cuntrera organization was extensively involved in foreign investments around the globe. Documents suggested that countries such as Aruba, Belize, and Venezuela enjoyed significant amounts of their assets. The Italian police dubbed them 'The Rothchilds of the Mafia' due to their global financial prowess. However, on 25 February 2000 key members of the Caruana-Cuntrera group pleaded guilty in court and received jail terms for their part in an international drug-trafficking and money-laundering conspiracy.

Ironically, Project Omerta was facilitated by the breaking of 'omerta' – the Mafia's supposed code of silence. The guilty pleas of the leaders of the Caruana-Cuntrera organization were prompted by the testimony of Oreste Pagano, who provided the RCMP with videotaped testimony and agreed to assist Italian police in solving several drug cases and murders. Pagano pleaded guilty on 9 December 1999 to conspiracy to import and traffic a controlled substance. He was sentenced to time served and then was immediately extradited to Italy as a cooperating witness. Alfonso Caruana, whose principal residence was in Woodbridge, Ontario, was sentenced to two concurrent eighteen-year prison terms for masterminding the importation of Colombian cocaine into Canada. His main role was claimed to be a financial one in which he was 'laundering dirty money to make it look clean' by using numerous bank accounts and real estate transactions. His sentence wasn't as long as it sounded. He pleaded guilty in February 2000 and became eligible for accelerated parole in February 2003 after serving one-sixth of his time. After his release in April 2003, he was immediately arrested on a warrant from Italy and was committed for extradition to Italy, where he had been sentenced in absentia to twenty-

Figure 1.1: Tracking the drug and money flow in Project Omerta

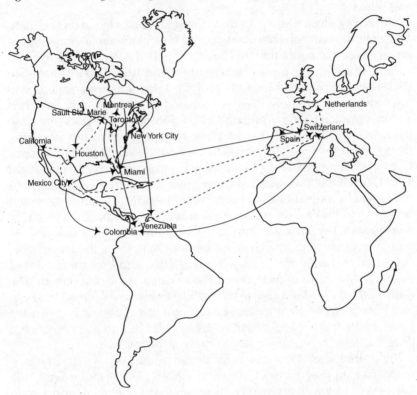

two years in prison for Mob association and drug trafficking. Gerlando Caruana, who had a previous twenty-year drug conviction, was given eighteen years. Pasquale Caruana received ten years for conspiracy and trafficking. Gerlando's son, Guiseppe, was given four years for money-laundering. The convictions are the culmination of a three-and-a-half-year police operation.

Legislative Framework

The development of criminal sanctions and policing powers pertaining to money laundering in Canada can be traced through the following pieces of legislation.

1989 Proceeds of Crime Legislation

The enactment of the legislative initiatives contained in Bill C-61 (the Proceeds of Crime Act, which became law in 1989) was meant to address the Supreme Court decision in the Pinto case and the broader voids that were abundantly apparent in Canada's proceeds of crime laws. This bill resulted in the creation of a new part of the Criminal Code with complementary amendments to Canada's drug enforcement statutes. The new statutes criminalized money laundering and the possession of the proceeds of 'enterprise' criminal offences and designated drug offences. Police were provided with newly created 'special search warrants' and 'restraint orders.' These powers were deemed necessary in order to undertake pretrial seizure of funds and assets (both tangible and intangible) alleged to be funded through the proceeds of criminal activities. Most importantly, the new legislation empowered the courts to force anyone convicted of a proceeds of crime offence to permanently forfeit ownership over any money or assets derived from designated drug and enterprise crime offences (with the potential for fines to be imposed in lieu of or in addition to forfeiture). Bill C-61 also amended the Income Tax Act to grant access to income tax information as part of an anti-drug profiteering investigation and provided civil and criminal immunity to those who voluntarily reported to police any transactions in which money laundering was suspected.

While the legislation was welcomed by law enforcement, critics charged that it was an affront to due process whereby an accused was presumed innocent until proven guilty. 'This law gives police the right to freeze property first and have a trial later,' Toronto lawyer Clayton Ruby was quoted as saying in the media. 'Generally, in democratic countries, we have the trial first' (DiManno, 1989: A3). This concern became even more critical in those jurisdictions, including the Province of Ontario, that introduced civil forfeiture laws, whereby the government could go after assets in a civil court and avoid the much more stringent due process and onus of proof requirements of the criminal courts. Through civil forfeiture, a person would not need to be convicted in order for the goods to be forfeited. Almost immediately after the criminal legislation became law, the RCMP scored an impressive coup when it froze close to $18 million in a Toronto bank account, while restraining real estate valued at more than $2 million. Both the cash and the property were linked to the Colombian-based Medellin cocaine cartel (Moffat, 1991: A2).

Record Keeping Legislation – Enforcement via Banks, Businesses, and Beyond

Throughout the 1990s, proceeds of crime enforcement benefited not only from expanding resources but also from newly legislated tools. Beginning in the early 1990s, a new and controversial chapter in Canadian proceeds of crime enforcement would be written (and rewritten over the next twelve years) with the introduction of Bill C-9, officially titled An Act To facilitate Combating the Laundering of Proceeds of Crime, in 1991. The legislation mandated private-sector financial intermediaries such as banks, trust companies, credit unions, and insurance companies to create and maintain certain records (including client identification information) and to facilitate proceeds of crime investigations. The Act also required financial institutions to maintain records of cash transactions of $10,000 or more for five years. While the legislation did not make it *mandatory* for private-sector companies to *report* large cash or suspicious transactions, in 1993 the RCMP and the Canadian Bankers Association signed a memorandum of understanding that implemented a system of *voluntary* reporting and spoke to the commitment of the banks to assist in enforcement against money laundering.

This legislation was created to reflect a new proceeds of crime enforcement approach that was gaining currency throughout the world, and that was most forcefully advocated by the FATF, the international organization established by the 1989 G7 Paris Summit to enhance and standardize money-laundering enforcement throughout the world. Financial transaction monitoring and reporting consists of policies that mandate the private sector, and particularly the financial services sector, to detect and report suspected money laundering to government agencies. It was designed to expose the money-laundering process at its most vulnerable 'choke' points; that is, when cash entered the financial system, when it was transferred between financial intermediaries, or when it was transported across national borders. By imposing an obligation to report transactions, as well as to provide information on transactions and clients that may be related to profit-oriented criminal activity, a transaction reporting regime could potentially serve a number of important policing and regulatory functions. The theory was that the regime would provide government agencies with a greater capacity to uncover evidence of wrongdoing by creating a central repository of financial information that could identify proceeds of crime and their sources. It also ensured that proper records would be in place within the private sector to facilitate a subsequent criminal investigation. Theoretically, transaction reporting also meant to serve as a deterrent to criminal behaviour for both the original perpetrator of the criminal offence and any financial intermediaries who would capitalize on their position to help launder the illicit funds.

Transaction reporting could be demarcated into two general categories: currency transaction reporting (CTR) and suspicious activity reporting (SAR). A currency transaction reporting system requires that specified financial intermediaries report any currency transaction over a specified threshold (generally $10,000 or its equivalent in the currency of the country implementing the reporting regime). A related type of currency monitoring requires the reporting of currency or monetary instruments above a certain threshold amount when money crosses national borders. The second category of reporting is the suspicious activity reporting (SAR) systems that requires financial intermediaries to report transactions that appear to be suspicious, regardless of the amount. This model provides more discriminate reporting of financial transactions compared to the CTR system. The philosophy behind SAR is that while there are millions of transactions that pass through financial institutions, a certain percentage are irregular in some aspect and warrant greater scrutiny. The most-often cited reason for the implementation of a SAR system is that it is explicitly geared towards identifying transactions that could reveal money-laundering and/or terrorist financing, unlike the CTR system.

From the outset, the new Canadian laws fell short of the international standards advocated by the Financial Action Task Force: the recommended implementation of a *mandatory* cash and suspicious transaction monitoring and reporting system. The Canadian legislation did not force private-sector entities to report large cash transactions or suspicious transactions to law enforcement, and the *voluntary* reporting system was primarily restricted to chartered banks and credit unions. The failure to implement a mandatory transaction reporting system may have been partially the result of intense pressure from the Canadian banking industry, which was part of the working group that drafted the 1991 legislation and adamantly opposed mandatory reporting. However, also working against enthusiasm for a mandatory CTR and SAR system was the lack of evidence that the U.S. reporting mechanism was assisting law enforcement. The U.S. system FinCEN was, at that time, a glut of millions of paper files that in the most untimely manner could only be of limited use to law enforcement, and then only if the police were already alert to a particular individual or crime.

Proceeds of Crime (Money Laundering) Act – Revised and Renamed
the Proceeds of Crime (Money Laundering) and Terrorist Financing
Act (PCMLTFA)

Canada could not long resist the global trend towards mandatory transaction reporting. Given the country's desire to do right by the international community, pressure began to mount to ensure that all of the
Financial Action Task Force's recommendations were adopted, which
meant the implementation of a mandatory transaction reporting regime.
The domestic calls for reform were largely rooted in the international
pressure exerted on the Canadian government and none were more persuasive than the blunt admonitions contained in the Financial Action
Task Force's 1997–98 Annual Report. It reported that Canada's voluntary
suspicious transaction reporting regime

> does not appear to be working effectively and there needs to be an urgent
> resolution of the internal review process which has been continuing since
> 1993. The examiners consider that the most essential improvements are to
> create a new regime, consistent with the Charter of Rights and Freedoms,
> which makes reporting mandatory, and to create a new financial intelli-
> gence unit which would deal with the collection, management, analysis
> and dissemination of suspicious transaction reports and other relevant
> intelligence data. Other measures which would assist are detailed guidance
> on what transactions may be suspicious, a penal or administrative sanction
> for failing to report, and improved general and specific feedback. In
> addition, detailed proposals need to be created and taken forward for a
> system of cross border reporting and ancillary powers for Customs offic-
> ers. The adoption of these measures, when combined with the new IPOC
> units, should lead to a much more effective system. (Financial Action Task
> Force, 1998: 12–13)

This report was preceded by one from an even higher authority: the
U.S. State Department. In their 1997 *International Narcotics Control Strategy Report*, the Bureau for International Narcotics and Law Enforcement
Affairs suggested that Canada's anti-money-laundering regime suffered from a 'fragmented approach' due in part to a lack of 'effective
controls for monitoring and reporting the cross-border movement of
currency and monetary instruments.' The report recommended that
Canada's proceeds of crime enforcement could be 'greatly enhanced by
incorporating effective monitoring and reporting of cross-border controls, reporting of suspicious transactions, and the development of a

strong central financial intelligence unit' (Bureau for International Narcotics and Law Enforcement, 1998).

As a result of these pressures, on 29 June 2000, royal assent was given
to federal legislation that established a mandatory reporting system for
large cash and suspicious transactions as well as the cross-border movement of currency and monetary instruments. Originally called the Proceeds of Crime (Money Laundering) Act, and then revised and renamed
the Proceeds of Crime (Money Laundering) and Terrorist Financing Act,
the legislation mandated all regulated financial institutions, casinos,
currency exchange businesses, as well as other entities and individuals
acting as financial intermediaries to report large-volume cash transactions and any other financial transactions they had reasonable grounds
to suspect were related to a money-laundering offence. The legislation
also required large amounts of funds – including cash, monetary instruments, or wire transfers – being moved across the border to be reported to
Canada Customs. Failure to report could result in the seizure of the cash
or monetary instruments being transported. The maximum penalties for
failing to report designated transactions included fines of up to CDN$2
million and imprisonment for up to five years.

As requested by the Financial Action Task Force, the legislation also
established an independent financial intelligence unit to receive and
analyse the currency and suspicious transaction reports. This new body,
called the Financial Transactions Reports Analysis Centre of Canada
(FINTRAC), was created to become the central repository for cash and
suspicious transaction reports (including cross-border currency reports)
with a view to creating useful intelligence information that could be
used by domestic and foreign government agencies to combat organized crime and terrorism. FINTRAC is mandated to disclose this information to Canadian law enforcement agencies under very specific and
restricted rules. It also has the power to disclose relevant information to
federal taxation officials, Citizenship and Immigration Canada, the
Canadian Security Intelligence Service, and foreign law enforcement
agencies that officially request information pertaining to a money-
laundering investigation. FINTRAC began receiving reports of suspicious transactions in 2001 (FINTRAC, 2003).

Shifting the Focus and Discourse: 11 September 2001 and the PCMLTFA

FINTRAC's mandate, and the focus on the financial underpinnings of
serious crimes in general, would dramatically shift in the wake of the
terrorist strikes of 11 September 2001. Overwhelming attention would

now move away from profit-oriented organized crime to the financing of terrorist activity. While these tumultuous events shifted attention to terrorist funds and represented a whole new set of challenges for those involved in the enforcement of financial crimes, the traditional approaches used in proceeds of crime enforcement – the seize and freeze legislation and mandatory transaction reporting – were unimaginatively adopted as the cornerstone of the financial front in the war on terror.

Most of the amendments to the legislation simply involved adding the phrase 'the financing of terrorist activities' where 'money laundering' was previously the only offence listed. This 'founding legislation' has the following objectives:

- to implement specific measures to detect and deter money-laundering and the financing of terrorist activities and to facilitate the investigation and prosecution of money-laundering and terrorist financing offences, including:
  - establishing record keeping and client identification requirements for financial services providers and other persons that engage in businesses, professions or activities that are susceptible to being used for money-laundering and the financing of terrorist activities;
  - requiring the reporting of suspicious financial transactions and of cross-border movements of currency and monetary instruments; and
  - establishing an agency that is responsible for dealing with reported and other information;
- to respond to the threat posed by organized criminals and terrorists by providing law enforcement officials with the information they need to deprive criminals and terrorists of the proceeds of their criminal activities and funds to support terrorist activities, while ensuring that appropriate safeguards are put in place to protect privacy of persons with respect to personal information; and
- to assist in fulfilling Canada's commitments to participate in the fight against transnational crime particularly money-laundering and terrorist financing.[4]

Program Logic

The culmination of these initiatives is now referred to by the Canadian government as the 'National Initiative to Combat Money Laundering.' Figure 1.2 presents a logic model, prepared by the federal government,

that illustrates the activities, outputs, and outcomes (immediate, intermediate, and ultimate outcomes) of the National Initiatives to Combat Money
Laundering and Related Anti-Terrorist Financing Measures.[5] This logic
model provides a rational, albeit theoretical and highly idealized, dia-
gram that depicts the chain of outcomes resulting from the activities and
outputs of the anti-laundering initiative.

The national money-laundering initiatives represent an attempt by
federal policymakers to fashion a 'strategy' out of a number of dispar-
ate, ad hoc, and incremental policy developments that had been adopted
by (or forced upon) the federal government in recent years. The national strategy is less about creating a comprehensive approach to combating money laundering and terrorist financing than it is about the
federal government adopting and promoting a particular money-laundering enforcement strategy. The title of the model itself is simply a
disingenuous nomenclature for the mandatory transaction-reporting
legislative regime, which resulted in large part from the international
pressure upon Ottawa from groups such as the Financial Action Task
Force. For example, one of the 'Immediate Outcomes' is 'Enhanced
Compliance with FATF recommendations.' If one looks across the range
of 'Activities' in the top line of the model, all but one ('Investigations')
are dedicated to the transaction-reporting approach to combating money-
laundering (and even the investigations aspect is meant to refer to the
investigation of referrals from FINTRAC). As detailed in chapter 4, one
former officer in charge of the Proceeds of Crime Branch at RCMP
headquarters complained that the new emphasis on transaction reporting had come at the expense of the Integrated Proceeds of Crime program. The bottom two lines indicate that the ultimate outcomes are
meant to be a 'Decrease in Money Laundering' (when we have no real
idea how much money-laundering currently takes place); a 'Decrease in
Organized Crime and Prevention of Terrorism' (again, as measured
against no known current amounts), and, vaguest of all, 'Improved
Safety of Canadian Society.'

With that said, the model does succinctly summarize the key principles, strategies, and objectives of a proceeds of crime and terrorist
financing enforcement model that is solely based on transaction reporting and analysis. Likewise, the logic model does accurately articulate
the key activities and principles necessary to make a transaction reporting system successful: *liaison and cooperation* (with other national financial intelligence units); *educating* the private sector (regarding mandatory
reporting requirements); ensuring private sector *compliance* with the

Figure 1.2: National initiatives to combat money laundering and related anti-terrorist financir measures: logic model

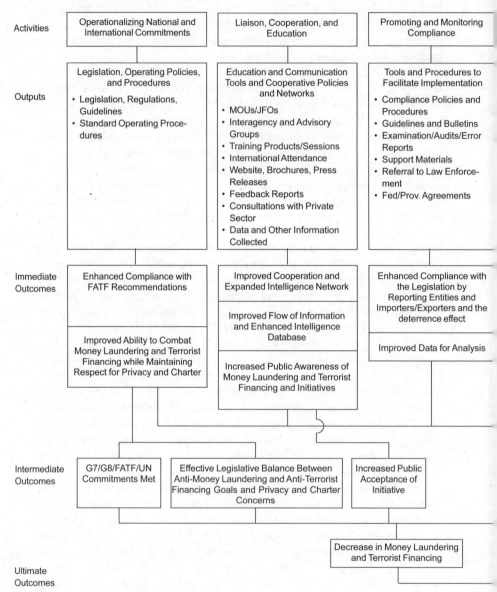

Source: Canada, Department of Finance (2005b), Appendix B.

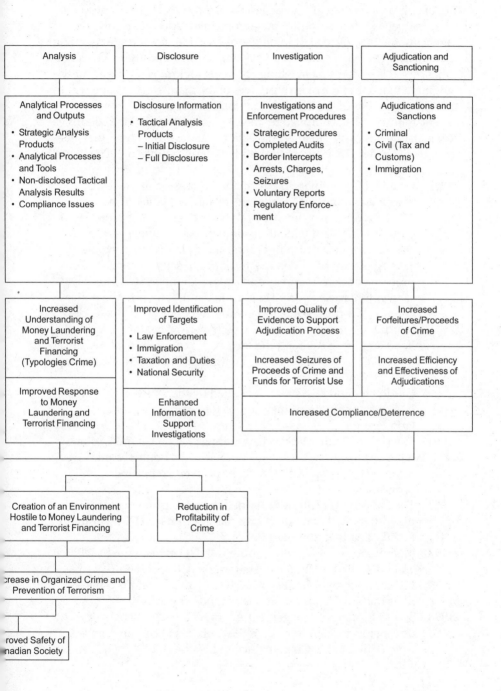

Analysis	Disclosure	Investigation	Adjudication and Sanctioning

Analytical Processes and Outputs
 	
• Strategic Analysis Products
• Analytical Processes and Tools
• Non-disclosed Tactical Analysis Results
• Compliance Issues
	Disclosure Information
	
	• Tactical Analysis Products
	  – Initial Disclosure
	  – Full Disclosures
		Investigations and Enforcement Procedures
		
		• Strategic Procedures
		• Completed Audits
		• Border Intercepts
		• Arrests, Charges, Seizures
		• Voluntary Reports
		• Regulatory Enforcement
			Adjudications and Sanctions
			
			• Criminal
			• Civil (Tax and Customs)
			• Immigration

Increased Understanding of Money Laundering and Terrorist Financing (Typologies Crime)	**Improved Identification of Targets** • Law Enforcement • Immigration • Taxation and Duties • National Security	**Improved Quality of Evidence to Support Adjudication Process**	**Increased Forfeitures/Proceeds of Crime**
Improved Response to Money Laundering and Terrorist Financing	**Enhanced Information to Support Investigations**	**Increased Seizures of Proceeds of Crime and Funds for Terrorist Use**	**Increased Efficiency and Effectiveness of Adjudications**
		Increased Compliance/Deterrence	

Creation of an Environment Hostile to Money Laundering and Terrorist Financing

Reduction in Profitability of Crime

:rease in Organized Crime and Prevention of Terrorism

roved Safety of nadian Society

reporting laws; *analysis* of transaction reports by FINTRAC; the *disclosure* of intelligence information to law enforcement and other government agencies; the *investigation* of intelligence-based leads; and the resulting penalties, *adjudications, and sanctions* emanating from these investigations. What is perhaps most telling about the logic model is its acknowledgment that one of the main objectives of the mandatory system was to meet the demands of the international community.

The following list, compiled by the Department of Finance, identifies the separate pieces of Canadian legislation and other initiatives that were introduced and became part of the anti-laundering enforcement strategy.[6]

1989   Criminal Code amendments made possession of proceeds of crime and money-laundering-related activities criminal offences. The amendments dealt with all aspects of proceeds of crime, including the identification of specific offences, special search warrants, restraint orders, and a confiscation regime. The legislation provided the authority to seize or restrain the proceeds of certain crimes and provided immunity to people who voluntarily reported suspicious transactions to the police. Offences for possession and laundering of proceeds were 'designated substances offences,' which were also added to the Food and Drug Act (and the former Narcotics Control Act since repealed and replaced by the Controlled Drugs and Substances Act).

1990   Guidelines and best practices issued by the Office of the Superintendent of Financial Institutions for combating money-laundering.

1991   Proceeds of Crime (Money Laundering) Act proclaimed. Somewhat of a misnomer, this legislation was the original bank-record keeping legislation with the *voluntary* reporting provisions.

1991   The Canada Drug Strategy funded the establishment of three pilot Integrated Anti-Drug Profiteering Units (IADP) within the Royal Canadian Mounted Police (RCMP).

1993   Memorandum of Understanding (MOU) between the RCMP and the Canadian Bankers Association (CBA) signed. This MOU called for voluntary reporting of all suspicious transactions that might indicate money laundering activities.

1993   Seized Property Management Act proclaimed. Offences of possession and laundering of the proceeds of certain crimes were added to the Customs Act and Excise Act.

1996 Implementation of the Integrated Proceeds of Crime (IPOC)
Initiative, which established ten more integrated units, supple-
menting the three existing IADP units.

1997 Amendments to the Criminal Code (Part XII.2) involving the
and Controlled Drugs and Substances Act (May 1997) and the
1999 Corruption of Foreign Public Officials Act (proclaimed December 1998), which involved two proceeds of crime offences. This
addressed problems associated with corruption of foreign
public officials for business advantage, an issue relevant to the
OECD's Convention on Combating Bribery of Foreign Public
Officials in International Business Transactions.

2000 National Agenda to Combat Organized Crime implemented.
The National Agenda, adopted by federal, provincial and
territorial ministers, recognizes that the fight against organized
crime is a national priority with money laundering being identified as a specific priority in need of attention.

2000 Proceeds of Crime (Money Laundering) Act (PCMLA) enacted,
which established FINTRAC and mandatory client identification, reporting and record keeping requirements for reporting
entities.

2001 Amendments to the Criminal Code (and related statutes) in
respect of provisions dealing with proceeds of crime and of-
fence-related property with the enactment of An Act to amend
the Criminal Code (organized crime and law enforcement) and
to make consequential amendments to other Acts (Bill C-24). It
replaced the 1989 Criminal Code 'listing' of predicate crimes to
all major indictable offences approach to proceeds of crime and
money laundering. The same Act included additional consequential amendments to the Mutual Legal Assistance in Criminal Matters Act, permitting Canada to enforce foreign seizure,
restraint, and forfeiture orders.

2001 An Act to amend the Criminal Code, the Official Secrets Act,
the Canada Evidence Act, the Proceeds of Crime (Money Laundering) Act and other Acts, and to enact measures respecting
the registration of charities, in order to combat terrorism, entitled the Anti-Terrorism Act (Bill C-36), proclaimed. This
amended the PCMLA to include obligations in respect of reporting suspected terrorist financing activities as well as to
enlarge FINTRAC's mandate to include detection, deterrence,
and prevention of financing of terrorist activities. This bill
amended the title of the Act; it was changed to Proceeds of

Crime (Money Laundering) and Terrorist Financing Act (PCMLTFA). A requirement was introduced into the PCMLTFA for reporting entities to send a TPR (terrorist property report) to FINTRAC when they are in possession or control property that they *know* is owned or controlled by or on behalf of a terrorist or terrorist group. If FINTRAC determines that there are reasonable grounds to suspect that the information under its control would be relevant to threats to the security of Canada, designated information is disclosed to the Canadian Security Intelligence Service (CSIS).

2001   Immigration and Refugee Protection Act proclaimed. This act stipulates that a permanent resident or a foreign national cannot be admitted to the country if there are reasonable grounds to believe he or she has, is, or may engage in organized criminal activities, such as money laundering across national borders.

2003   Cross Border Currency Reporting Regulations came into force. The regulations made it mandatory for persons and entities to report the cross-border movement of currency and monetary instruments valued at $10,000 or more.

2004   Public Safety Act (Bill C-7) enacted. This act provides FINTRAC with the ability to collect information relevant to ML or TF that is stored in national security databases, and provides FINTRAC with the ability to share information with supervisory and regulatory agencies for purposes of ensuring compliance with Part 1 of the PC(ML)TFA. The Public Safety Act also allows the Office of the Superintendent of Financial Institutions with the ability to share information on how federally regulated financial institutions comply with the Act.

To this list must be added:

2005   Reverse Onus Forfeiture Provisions (Bill C-53). This Act received royal assent 25 November 2005. The legislation specifies that upon conviction for a 'criminal organization' offence punishable by five years or more, the Crown will identify property that shall be forfeited if satisfied on a balance of probabilities that there had been a pattern of criminal activity for profit in the past ten years; or, legitimate income cannot account for the offender's property. The 'pattern' requirement is satisfied if the offender committed the predicate offence plus one criminal organization offence, or two 'serious' offences (indictable offences, punishable by five years or more). The offender must therefore prove his/her property is not the proceeds of crime. Of note: property interests are not protected by the Charter and forfeiture under this legislation is not considered as an additional 'punishment' since the proceeds are claimed to be illegally possessed and therefore do not 'really' belong to the convicted person. Critics argue that this is a 'legal fiction' that may amount to cruel and unusual punishment.

Like many other Western countries that have declared war on organized crime and terrorism, Canada has witnessed a gradual increase in legislative and enforcement initiatives that target the financial aspects of such crimes. Since 1981, the powers of the Canadian state and its agents to seize and forfeit the proceeds of crime have been continually expanded while law enforcement and prosecutorial resources have been significantly augmented. At the same time, the punitive nature of the government's foray into proceeds of crime enforcement has been gradually intensified. This includes creating substantial penalties for proceeds of crime offences and the replacement of a voluntary transaction reporting system with a mandatory regime (complete with substantial penalties for non-compliance). The adoption of a mandatory system is particularly significant in the context of Canadian criminal law, if not only for the fact that it is the first piece of legislation ever introduced in Canada that legally requires the reporting of suspected criminal activity.

These gradually expanded enforcement measures are the result of both internal (domestic) and external (international) pressures and developments. Internally, the continued escalation and increasingly punitive nature of proceeds of crime enforcement must be placed in the broader context of the intensification of organized crime enforcement in Canada in recent years. The high-profile nature of organized crime in this country – including the ongoing problem of drug trafficking, the emergence of other highly profitable criminal activities such as tobacco smuggling, people smuggling, and the home-grown marijuana industry (not to mention the bloody biker war in Quebec) – resulted in a myriad of legislative and enforcement initiatives that expanded the criminal investigative and prosecutorial powers of the state while signalling a highly punitive approach that is generally uncharacteristic of the Canadian criminal justice system in the post-Charter era.

At the same time, the gradual build-up of proceeds of crime enforcement in Canada, and the mandatory transaction reporting legislative measures in particular, were clearly the result of external pressures from the United States and international bodies, in particular the FATF. These external pressures were rooted in the perceived rise in global organized criminal activities in the 1980s and 1990s, as well as the hegemonic convictions of the U.S. government and the FATF that mandatory suspicious transaction reporting must be a central component of every country's arsenal to combat the financial aspects of drug trafficking and organized crime (despite the absence of any evaluation finding that such systems actually made a significant contribution to organized crime and drug enforcement), as will be discussed in the following chapter.

While the escalating spectre of transnational organized crime and drug trafficking represented the major external impulsion behind the expanding and increasingly punitive enforcement initiatives enacted in Canada, it was the terrorist attacks of 11 September 2001 that solidified, as a policy option, the targeting of the financial underpinnings of major crimes. The attacks upon the United States eventually resulted in the expansion of proceeds of crime legislation to include terrorist financing and a significant shift in enforcement resources toward this new focus. It also brought in some of the most draconian, punitive, and intrusive criminal legislation ever introduced in Canada.

In sum, the contemporary history of Canadian proceeds of crime enforcement can be demarcated into the following causes, effects, and implications. The causes entail domestic and international developments and pressures, including the perceived increase in organized crime activities in Canada and abroad, the 2001 terrorist attacks on the United States, as well as intense international pressure for countries to adopt specific anti-money-laundering and terrorist financing measures. The effects of these developments and pressures were the gradual but unambiguous expansion and intensification of proceeds of crime enforcement as a means to combat organized crime and terrorism in Canada. The implications of these measures included an increasingly punitive approach to combating organized crime and terrorism as well as expanded powers of the state. Moreover, one significant implication of the adoption of the transaction reporting regime in Canada is the partial but unprecedented shifting of legal responsibility for detecting and reporting suspected criminal activity onto the private sector.

Indeed, the rise of transaction reporting is indicative of what David Garland calls the 'responsibilisation strategy' of governance, whereby the state seeks 'to act upon crime not in a direct fashion through state agencies (police, courts, prisons, social work, etc.) but instead by acting indirectly, seeking to activate action on the part of non-state agencies and organizations.' The key phrases of this governance strategy include terms such as 'partnership,' 'inter-agency cooperation,' and 'the multi-agency approach.' The primary concern of this strategy is to 'devolve responsibility for crime prevention on to agencies, organizations and individuals which are quite outside the state and to persuade them to act appropriately' (Garland, 1996: 452). This decentralization strategy, whereby state power is dispersed through institutions and organizations outside of government, is part of a broader neo-conservative governance ideology that now dominates most Western countries. Numerous non-state actors are pulled into 'policing' roles to ensure safety and security through maintenance of order and crime control.

In the next chapter, we look at the responses from the international community, which is followed by an analysis of RCMP money-laundering cases, and, in chapter 4, by an analysis of those enforcement efforts.

2 The Evil that Dirty Money Does: Accusations, Actions, and Evidence

The literature related to money laundering has become vast. However, the empirical base to most of this literature is non-existent. At least three intertwined issues make it hard to generalize about the harm related to money laundering. The first issue, which we have already discussed, is the difference between sophisticated *laundering* schemes versus the spending, investing, or 'pissing away' of ill-gotten profits. Some of the discussion that supports a strong, aggressive anti-laundering regime appears to present an image of all of the profits from one specific market (i.e., drug sales) being delivered into the hands of one criminal operation rather than more modest profits going to hundreds of small entrepreneurs who are involved in criminal transactions. While our police cases reveal some large laundering schemes with large illicit proceeds, the majority of police cases across the country involve profits that are literally 'spent' just as non-criminal citizens might spend their legitimate earnings. Therefore, some of the claimed harms can at most apply to only a small proportion of laundering cases. Research into money laundering must recognize the highly disposable nature of the proceeds of crime, best summed up by the lyrics of the Jimmy Buffett song, 'A Pirate Looks at Forty': 'I've done a bit of smuggling / I've run my share of grass / Made enough money to buy Miami / But I pissed it away just as fast.'[1]

A second issue involves the increasing focus on one particular harm – the harm that involves dirty money mingling with legitimate businesses. This became of particular concern with the passage of the U.S. Racketeer Influenced and Corrupt Organizations (RICO) statute as drafted by Robert Blakey in 1970. Keeping organized criminals out of legitimate business was one of the statute's targets. The stated purpose through much of the debate around this statute was the 'elimination of the infiltration of organized crime and racketeering into legitimate organizations operating in interstate commerce' (Bradley, 1980: 844). Criminal forfeiture, civil forfeiture, and triple damage relief for persons injured by violations that fell under RICO were aimed at financially 'putting the criminal out of business,' be it a legitimate or an illegitimate one.

The majority of the literature today refers to the various 'dangers' to legitimate societal institutions from the laundering of dirty money. There is, however, an alternative literature that questions the priority being given to the fight against money laundering and recognizes that dirty money can interact with legitimate business in an array of different ways, with different consequences.[2] There have been a number of attempts to categorize the various experiences. The creators of these typologies were motivated in part by the rhetoric leading up to the drafting of RICO that spoke, with little evidence, about the threat from what was seen to be an increasing penetration of criminals into legitimate businesses. The Kefauver Commission (U.S. Congress, 1950–51), the McClellan Investigation (U.S. Congress, 1957), as well as the researchers connected with the Presidential Crime Commission (U.S. President's Commission on Law Enforcement, 1967) all elaborated on the 'likelihood of a comprehensive takeover of large sectors of private industry.'

Then, as now, there was disagreement as to the degree and nature of any movement by mobsters into legitimate businesses. Open to debate was the question as to when 'penetration' had actually occurred (reminiscent of a more recent debate). Donald Cressey (Cressey, 1969, cited in Jester, 1974) suggested that the relationship between businesses and criminals could be categorized under the following headings:

1 Businesses legitimately purchased with the fruits of crime and operated:
  a legitimately
  b illegitimately
2 Business illegitimately acquired and operated:
  a legitimately
  b illegitimately

Offering much more detail, Melvin Bers (1970) suggested five categories:

1 legal holdings, legally operated
2 business activity supportive of illicit enterprise and reciprocally
  supported by it
3 predatory or parasitic exploitation
4 monopoly
5 unfair advantage

Dirty Money In – Clean Money Out[3]

Ralph Salerno (1986) and Frances Ianni (1972) disagree as to whether an enterprise owned by organized crime could be run totally legitimately, without calling upon contacts or corrupt officials in times of need to advance the interests of the business. Other writers' research tends to show that some legitimate businesses are bought with dirty money and *are* run totally legitimately (at least as legitimately as other businesses are run). Ianni's study of the Lupollo family found that for over forty years the family had moved gradually into legitimate businesses. In addition to the possibility that the legitimate and illegitimate activities can be kept separate, there is the additional factor that *if* there are other 'interests' that are somewhat less 'legitimate,' the business managers might be particularly keen to be seen running a totally legitimate operation so that suspicions are not raised.

There may also be a generational aspect – some criminals aspire to have their children involved in these legitimate businesses. Academics such as Daniel Bell (1960), Francis Ianni (1974), and Mark Haller (1971–2) have discussed the 'queer ladder of social mobility' whereby new immigrant groups enter the American society at the bottom and use whatever means – crime or boxing are two examples – to gain a foothold for movement up into the ranks of the middle class. While there is no consensus around this theory,[4] there is generally no great dread of the prospect of criminal money mingling with legitimately run businesses.

Much of the pre-1980's literature, in fact, revealed an apathy from businesses and the general public towards the notion of mob-controlled businesses because many of them had excellent reputations, appeared to operate within the law, and offered good services (Jester, 1974). The Chicago Crime Commission in 1970 compiled an extensive list of the legitimately held businesses that were controlled by members of organized crime. It noted the wide range of commercial activities and the ability of these firms to gain government grants and small business administration loans.[5]

Clean and Dirty Money In – Clean and Dirty Money Out

Markets and criminals can enter into mutually exploitive relationships. Whenever concern is expressed about the exploitation of legitimate businesses or legitimate business persons, it is wise to balance these concerns with an awareness of the complicity of many so-called legitimate entrepreneurs. What one must expect in any large commercial operation is a mix of 'clean' and 'dirty' money. The fact remains even today that the public has an ambiguous relationship with organized criminals. In 1983, when the New Jersey public hearings into casino credit practices took place, there was extensive testimony regarding the large amount of credit and 'comps' (complimentary services) that had been regularly given to known members of organized crime. When asked why these comps were being given to known mobsters, the casino officials testified that these men were entertaining and were wealthy 'high rollers' whom the casino management not only tolerated but also tried to attract into their casinos.[6]

Organized cirminals, along with their resources, may be 'invited' in to facilitate an unworkable legitimate operation. Daniel Bell argues that, with our fascination with power and manipulation, we ignore 'the economic fulcrum underneath.' Industrial racketeering and labour unions at various periods in American history would be examples (see Bell, 1960; Landesco, 1968). Some 'legitimate' businesses rely on stolen merchandise or provide shipping, distribution services, and other specialized services whose use would be known to be criminal. Increased profits or maintaining wages or price agreements may be what is 'gained' – at a cost perhaps – from the involvement of criminals.

Dirty Money In – Dirty (Laundered) Money Out

The exploitation is, however, not always 'mutual.' Criminal proceeds may be used to purchase a business that will be run strictly as a 'front' for laundering or legitimation purposes. Legitimately run businesses may rightly feel this results in unfair competition if making a legitimate profit is not an additional intention of the operation. Examples might be cash-based businesses that are operated at a loss in order to launder drug money. In other situations, criminal proceeds can be used to take over legitimate businesses in order to gain an exploitive monopoly over an industry. Negative consequences might be the inflation of prices, displacement of labour, and potential consequences on work conditions and equality of products. Likewise, extortion operations might force legitimate businesses to 'hire' fictitious organized-crime-connected persons in order to provide them with a source of income for tax or 'legitimation' purposes.

Clean Money In – Dirty Operation – Clean Money Out

A legitimate business dealing in a legitimate commodity may choose to operate in a criminal manner. As stated by Robert Blakey: 'The tobacco industry morphed in 1953 from a legitimate industry to an illegitimate industry and it became a front for the selling of a drug, not cocaine, not heroin, but nicotine.'[7] He argues that a criminal tobacco syndicate headed by lawyers operating a bogus scientific research group, shell companies, 'shell' management positions, control by intimidation and a public relations group fraudulently targeted children in order to meet the quota of 3,000 new addicted persons per day. This was before tobacco companies were charged with smuggling and actual money laundering.

Occasionally, a legitimate business does provide a legitimate service to legitimate customers, but the corporation is organized in a criminal manner with the criminal activity targeted mainly at the employees. Blakey provides us with the example of the pyramid-structured Amway Corporation. He compares the 'family structure' of the corporation to that of organized crime groups who use similar forms of intimidation, secrecy, rituals, and enforced loyalty.[8]

Finally, there is the third issue. In addition to the debates over the nature of most laundering schemes and the debate over the degree of harm that is inflicted upon 'legitimate businesses,' there is the blurring of notions of 'harm' between the *predicate offences* (to use an American term) that produced the illicit profits and the actual *profits*. If you take the view that without 'illicit profits' there would be no organized crime, then there is no issue – that is, do away with the potential to use the dirty money and you eliminate crimes. Hence all of the harm from drug trafficking and the harm from money laundering become one. This is the apparent belief behind the rhetoric of money laundering being the 'lifeblood' of organized crime. So the question remains, Does laundering, or more accurately criminal profits, 'cause' people to commit offenses such as drug trafficking (and the harms associated with drug trafficking)?

If taking all of the profits away from criminals were a realistic strategy, the priority given to these profits might be rational. We would argue, however, that other strategies more likely might lead to a greater impact on the criminal activity. While not refuting that people commit crimes mainly for the profit, an array of additional factors can be equally seen to 'cause' drug trafficking, beginning most appropriately with the 'demand' from the public for these goods. Second might be 'opportunity,' not only to commit the offences but also to reap the large, low-risk financial rewards. Finally might be the associations or contacts of the criminals and the desire for the trappings that profits from any source can bring: a desire for the monetary-derived status, lifestyle, and power that are largely shared with the legitimate society. There is a peculiar comparison between the focus on the money gained from criminal activity and the Canadian laws regarding soliciting for prostitution – our laws don't target the act of prostitution or the customer but instead criminalize the exchange of money. Relating the criminal proceeds to the predicate act too closely allows for the claims regarding the ability for the anti-money-laundering regimes to 'fight' crime and eliminate drugs, and now terrorism. Making a statement that 'crime does not pay' and therefore attaching forfeiture to the conviction of criminals eliminates the unrealistic expectations that are wrapped around the anti-laundering crusade.

Unfortunately, the proceeds and the offences that generate the profits get rolled into one. As argued by John Walker (2000a), crime and money laundering have three different types of effects upon the economy: first, there are the losses to the victims of crime; second, there are the gains made by the criminals; third, there is what the U.S. military would probably call 'collateral damage' to the national economy. It is the 'collateral' damage category that dominates much of the current rhetoric. These dangers are usually couched in vague terms such as the potential for the dirty money to pose a threat to the 'fabric of society' or to cause the 'destabilization of the financial system.' In no instance is there data to verify the general threats described – in fact, the 'threats' are seldom described but merely stated. Given the claims made regarding the social, economic, legal, and ethical impact of money laundering, the anti-money laundering movement has taken on a sense of urgency. A number of international agencies have depicted money laundering as constituting an enormous, multifaceted danger, fuelling crime and corruption, undermining financial institutions, destabilizing democracies and free markets, and funding terrorist activities.[9] To demonstrate money laundering's impact, and arguably to justify various legal and regulatory responses, statistics on the magnitude of money laundering have been 'produced.'

The 'war' against money laundering has taken on a moral dimension in the face of the threat to the social, economic, and political well-being of nation states allegedly being undermined by the actions of criminal organizations laundering their proceeds of crime. Among the effects of money laundering cited in the literature, the following claims came up frequently in the reports from various agencies mandated to combat money laundering:[10]

- The amount of money laundered is astronomical and is escalating.
- Money laundering constitutes a worldwide problem.
- Money laundering is threatening financial and monetary stability and integrity.
- Money laundering causes financial, social, and political corruption.
- Money laundering undermines legitimate business, economic growth, and policy.
- Money laundering supports organized criminals, human and fire-arms smuggling, and terrorism.
- Money laundering threatens democracy.
- Only via international cooperation and financial regulation will laundering be curbed, with the notion that international cooperation can in fact control laundering.
- Curbing laundering will curb criminal activity.

Before addressing some of these claims and the evidence or non-evidence in their support, we shall look at the claim-makers.

Bodies Involved in the Anti-Laundering Crusade

There is no shortage of bi-lateral, multi-lateral, and national agencies that have taken as their task the removal of the profit from crime by prioritizing anti-money-laundering initiatives. At least ten major organizations have claimed a mandate to 'fight money laundering.' In several cases, fighting money laundering has become – or always was – the *only* mandate to justify the existence of the agency and the spending of the resources. In the following discussion of some of the major players, the international scope of this crusade is highlighted.

The Financial Action Task Force (FATF)

Perhaps the main organization in this group is the Financial Action Task Force (FATF). It was set up in 1989, specifically identifying money laundering as a considerable threat to the international community. The FATF is a policymaking body, whose purpose is 'the development and promotion of policies, at both national and international levels, to combat money laundering.'[11] The FATF originally had three main tasks (these have since been expanded): first, monitoring members' progress in applying measures to counter money laundering; second, reviewing money-laundering techniques and counter measures; and third, promoting the adoption and implementation of appropriate measures by non-member countries.[12] The establishment of the FATF is claimed to be a result, in part, of the expressed need for a unified response to money laundering – that is, a need for a set of minimum global standards (Morris-Cotterill, 2001: 4). The fact that it was the key individuals central to the FATF who expressed this need gets lost in what is now a fairly long history of the organization. Since 1989 countries have been attending meetings and assigning representatives to FATF, but the total cost for the operation of this group and the related meetings that support FATF activities is unknown.[13] As just one indication of the costs involved in participating in FATF (for one country for one year), the 2000–2001 Annual Report of the Australian Transaction Reports and Analysis Centre (AUSTRAC) reported that they had participated in

- three FATF meetings
- an FATF Typologies Workshop
- an additional FATF ad hoc group meeting with non-cooperative countries and territories
- an Asia/Pacific Group (APG) meeting (assisted with the FATF 'mutual evaluation' process among the Asian countries)
- six FATF/APG coordination group meetings, and
- they represented Egmont Group of Financial Intelligence Units (Egmont is discussed below) at the Asian Pacific Group annual meeting[14]

As of June 2005, the FATF was comprised of thirty-one member countries and territories and two regional organizations, with other international bodies having observer status.[15] The member countries are

Argentina	Hong Kong, China	Russian Federation
Australia	Iceland	Singapore
Austria	Ireland	South Africa
Belgium	Italy	Spain
Brazil	Japan	Sweden
Canada	Luxembourg	Switzerland
Denmark	Mexico	Turkey
Finland	Netherlands	United Kingdom
France	New Zealand	United States
Germany	Norway	
Greece	Portugal	

The two regional bodies are the European Commission and the Gulf Co-operation Council.

The 'global network' that is committed to combating money laundering and terrorist financing includes a number of FATF-style regional bodies. While being technically independent of any other international body or organization and setting their own work, rules, and procedures, they cooperate with other international bodies, notably the FATF to achieve their objectives. In 2005, the first *joint* plenary meeting between the FATF and one of these regional bodies – the Asia/Pacific Group on Money Laundering (APG) with a total of fifty-five member states – was held.[16] The regional bodies as of August 2005 included:

- Asia/Pacific Group on Money Laundering (APG)
- Caribbean Financial Action Task Force (CFATF)
- Eastern and South African Anti-Money Laundering Group (ESAAMLG)
- Eurasian Group (EAG)
- Financial Action Task Force of South America Against Money Laundering (GAFISUD)
- Middle East and North Africa Financial Action Task Force (MENAFATF)
- Council of Europe Select Committee of Experts on the Evaluation of Anti-Money Laundering Measures (MONEYVAL), and
- Offshore Group of Banking Supervisors

The two most recently created regional bodies of MENAFATF and EAG came into existence in 2004. In November 2004, fourteen countries joined together to create their own regional financial action task force for North Africa and the Middle East. Based in the Kingdom of Bahrain, the Middle East and North African Financial Action Task Force (MENAFATF) follows similar procedures as the other FATF bodies. MENAFATF has fourteen member countries: Algeria, Bahrain, Egypt, Jordan, Kuwait, Lebanon, Morocco, Oman, Qatar, Saudi Arabia, Syrian Arab Republic, Tunisia, United Arab Emirates, and Yemen. The EAG was founded in Moscow on 6 October 2004 with six member countries: Belarus, Kazakhstan, Kyrgyzstan, the People's Republic of China, the Russian Federation, and Tajikistan. The EAG held its second plenary meeting on 12–14 April 2005 in Shanghai. Note that during 2004–5, China was accepted as an observer in the FATF and became a member of the EAG.

The cornerstone of FATF efforts – and the efforts of the regional bodies – is the detailed description of appropriate countermeasures for countries to adhere to, set out in the 'Forty Recommendations' formulated and adopted by the group in 1990. In 1996, the original recommendations were strengthened. In 2001, anti-terrorism financing was included as part of the FATF efforts and 'Eight Special Recommendations on Terrorist Financing' were adopted. Further reviews during 2003 resulted in what, as of 2005, has become the comprehensive 'Forty Plus Nine Recommendations' that now form the framework (or, as they say, 'the arsenal') for the continuing work of the FATF and the regional bodies. The original recommendations included

- the criminalization of money laundering and enactment of laws to seize and confiscate proceeds of crime
- obligations for financial institutions to identify all clients and to keep appropriate records
- the requirement that financial institutions report suspicious transactions to competent national authorities and implement a range of internal control measures
- adequate systems for the control and supervision of financial institutions, and
- the need for international treaties/agreements and the passing of national legislation allowing countries to provide cooperation at all levels[17]

More recent recommendations focus on anti-terrorist financing initiatives, including alternative remittance systems (sometimes called informal money transfer systems). The ninth special recommendation requires states to implement measures for the detection of physical cross-border transportation of cash and bearer monetary instruments.[18] The FATF documents now list the following as the organization's tasks:

- Setting international AML/CFT (Anti-Money Laundering and Counter-Terrorist Financing) standards via the FATF 'Forty Plus Nine Recommendations,' as well as through additional interpretation, or guidance, and best practices.
- Monitoring compliance with AML/CFT standards via a peer or mutual evaluation process.
- Encouraging compliance of non-FATF members with FATF standards: via the FATF-style regional bodies (FSRB) and the non-cooperative countries and territories (NCCT) initiative and technical assistance needs assessments (TANAs).
- Promoting worldwide application of the FATF standards: via encouraging the universal implementation of FATF standards by supporting FATF-style regional bodies in all parts of the world and through partnerships with international and regional organizations.
- Studying the methods and trends of money laundering and terrorist financing.[19]

The policies and recommendations established by the FATF are not legally binding, but are enforced to some degree through a graduated system that provides for a variety of sanctions such as the 'blacklisting' of nations that do not comply. The FATF can suspend membership of nations that do not comply. Thus, the FATF may be viewed as a regulatory regime – one that does not seek to control illicit financial movements across borders, but rather seeks to 'bolster the ability of each government to crack down on money laundering activity within its borders' (Helleiner, 2000: 4). The FATF does this in two ways: first, by promoting international harmonization of domestic laws and practices designed to combat money laundering while strongly encouraging governments to introduce these measures; and second, by encouraging extensive international information sharing and legal cooperation between governments regarding the investigation, prosecution, confiscation, and extradition of money-laundering cases (ibid.).

While the FATF literature may sound very consensus oriented, given its original peer-evaluation format, some of the more critical literature questions potential bias in its motivations and its sanctioning of the countries that are 'brought to heel' via the FATF process. Michael Levi (2003) provides an analysis of the 'politics' of the FATF in terms of the international 'spread' of the anti-laundering policy initiatives, and acknowledges some of the scepticism that remains even amid the rush to obtain near-global compliance. The fact is that mainly non-G8 countries are the ones selected for blacklisting while evidence of non-compliance would appear to include the more powerful member countries.

Aside from what can be devastating economic consequences when blacklisted by the FATF, the 'harmonization' demands can also have detrimental consequences to the 'home' communities while possibly serving foreign governments. In one particular case, the Caribbean Financial Action Task Force (CFATF) agreed to implement common counter-money-laundering measures. In an apparent rush to criminalize money laundering (due in no small part to pressure from the U.S.), some Caribbean nations lowered the standard of criminal liability. For example, the issue of intent was diminished (i.e., a person can be convicted based upon negligence rather than clear intent to commit a criminal act). Prior to these legislative changes, countries like the U.S. had expressed difficulty in getting information for prosecution from the Caribbean countries. According to William Gilmore in 'Dirty Money' (1999: n.p.): 'The absence of an established framework for co-operation and strict commercial confidentiality legislation gave rise to difficulties in efforts to secure vital evidence for use in US prosecutions.' Again, one must question the purpose of the legislative changes. Are they to assist the Caribbean nations or to facilitate U.S. prosecutions?

Several other initiatives tumble out of the recommendations and requirements of the FATF process. Complying jurisdictions must create a centralized financial intelligence unit, and these individual FIUs are clustered under a group called the Egmont Group of Financial Intelligence Units.

The Egmont Group of Financial Intelligence Units

The Egmont Group was established at the Egmont Arenberg Palace in Brussels in 1995 to serve as an international organization of Financial Intelligence Units (FIUs)[20] for the stimulation of international co-operation. Comprised of over one hundred entities and led by the U.S.

financial intelligence unit called the Financial Crimes Enforcement Unit
(FinCEN United States), Egmont serves as a network whose purpose is
to foster improved communication and interaction among FIUs in areas
like information sharing (e.g., suspicious activity, transaction reports,
and government administrative data and public record information)
and training coordination. The Financial Transactions and Reports Analysis Centre of Canada (FINTRAC) and the Australian Transaction Reports and Analysis Centre (AUSTRAC) are also members of the Egmont
operation. The City of Toronto in Ontario, Canada, was selected as the
permanent home of the Egmont Secretariat in July 2006 (as we note in
chapter 7).

FIUs meeting the Egmont definition as of June 2006 are listed as
follows:[21]

1 Albania (DPPPP)
2 Andorra (UPB)
3 Anguilla (MLRA)
4 Antigua and Barbuda (ONDCP)
5 Argentina (UIF)
6 Aruba (MOT–Aruba)
7 Australia (AUSTRAC)
8 Austria (A–FIU)
9 Bahamas (FIU)
10 Bahrain (AMLU)
11 Barbados (AMLA)
12 Belgium (CTIF-CFI)
13 Belize (FIU)
14 Bermuda (BPSFIU)
15 Bolivia (UIF–Bolivia)
16 Bosnia and Herzegovina (FID)
17 Brazil (COAF)
18 British Virgin Islands
19 Bulgaria (FIA)
20 Canada (FINTRAC/CANAFE)
21 Cayman Islands (CAYFIN)
22 Chile (UAF)
23 Colombia (UIAF)
24 Cook Islands (CIFIU)
25 Costa Rica (UAF)
26 Croatia (AMLD)
27 Cyprus MO.K.A.Σ.
28 Czech Republic (FAU–CR)
29 Denmark
30 Dominica (FIU)
31 Dominican Republic (UIF)
32 Egypt (EMLCU)
33 El Salvador (UIF)
34 Estonia
35 Finland (RAP)
36 France (TRACFIN)
37 Georgia (FMS)
38 Germany
39 Gibraltar (GCID GFIU)
40 Greece (C.F.C.I.)
41 Grenada (FIU)
42 Guatemala (IVE)
43 Guernsey (FIS)
44 Honduras (UIF)
45 Hong Kong (JFIU)
46 Hungary (ORFK)
47 Iceland (RLS)
48 Indonesia (PPATK/INTRAC)
49 Ireland (MLIU)
50 Isle of Man (FCU–IOM)
51 Israel (IMPA)
52 Italy (UIC/SAR)
53 Japan (JAFIO)
54 Jersey (FCU–Jersey)
55 Korea (Republic of) (KoFIU)
56 Latvia (KD)
57 Lebanon (SIC)
58 Liechtenstein (EFFI)
59 Lithuania (FCIS)
60 Luxembourg (FIU–LUX)
61 Macedonia (MLPD)
62 Malaysia (UPW)
63 Malta (FIAU)
64 Marshall Islands (DFIU)
65 Mauritius (FIU)
66 Mexico
67 Monaco (SICCFIN)
68 Montenegro (APML)
69 Netherlands (MOT/BLOM)
70 Netherlands Antilles
71 New Zealand
72 Norway
73 Panama (UAF–Panama)
74 Paraguay (UAF)
75 Peru (UIF)
76 Philippines (AMLC)
77 Poland (GIIF)
78 Portugal (UIF)

79 Qatar (QFIU)
80 Romania (ONPCSB)
81 Russia (FSFM)
82 San Marino
83 Serbia
84 Singapore (STRO)
85 Slovakia (SJFP
    UBPOK)
86 Slovenia (OMLP)

87 South Africa (FIC)
88 Spain (SEPBLAC)
89 St Kitts and Nevis (FIU)
90 St Vincent and the
    Grenadines (FIU)
91 Sweden (FIPO)
92 Switzerland (MROS)
93 Taiwan (MLPC)
94 Thailand (AMLO)

95 Turkey (MASAK)
96 Ukraine (SDFM)
97 United Arab Emirates
    (AMLSCU)
98 United Kingdom (SOCA)
99 United States (FinCEN)
100 Vanuatu (FIU)
101 Venezuela (UNIF)

Part of the mandate of Egmont is to provide support to member governments in dealing with financial crimes. To facilitate the rapid exchange of this information, it established a secure Internet site, Egmont's International Secure Web System (ESW). The site is used to post and assess information on trends, analytical tools, and technological developments in the area of financial intelligence collection.

The following three organizations are the FIUs from the U.S., Australia, and Canada. Below we provide some background information since these three FIUs play a key role in our analysis.

THE FINANCIAL CRIMES ENFORCEMENT NETWORK (FinCEN)
UNITED STATES

The Financial Crimes Enforcement Network is the major agency behind of the U.S. anti-money-laundering effort. FinCEN is responsible for establishing, overseeing, and implementing policies to detect and prevent money laundering, both domestically and internationally. FinCEN's mandate to combat money laundering also includes efforts to encourage interagency and global cooperation through information collection, sharing data and analyses, providing technological assistance, and implementing Treasury initiatives regarding counter-money-laundering programs. FinCEN sees itself accomplishing this mandate in two ways:

1 by using counter-money-laundering laws (e.g., the Banks Secrecy Act) to require reporting and record keeping by banks and other financial institutions in order to preserve financial trails for investigators to follow criminal assets suspicious transactions; and
2 by providing intelligence and analytical support to federal, state, local, and international law enforcement agencies using state of the art technology to assist law enforcement to build investigations and plan new strategies to combat money laundering.[22]

AUSTRALIAN TRANSACTION REPORTS AND ANALYSIS CENTRE
(AUSTRAC)
Australia has taken a lead position in international anti-money-
laundering efforts since the mid-1980s. For example, Australia was a
founding member of the FATF, and played a large role in drafting its
'Forty Recommendations,' which have been widely accepted internationally as the world's 'best practices' policy guidelines. Australia has
also been influential in encouraging and promoting anti-money-laundering initiatives in the Asia Pacific region. In 1989, the Australian
Transaction Reports and Analysis Centre was established. AUSTRAC
plays a regulatory role in overseeing compliance with the Financial
Transactions Reporting Act (which requires cash dealers to identify
customers and report certain transactions, and which requires the public to report cross-border currency movements of $10,000 or more), and
a significant role in the collection, analysis, and dissemination of financial transaction reporting information, providing large quantities of
significant financial intelligence to national law enforcement and revenue agencies. It is also party to a number of agreements to disseminate
financial intelligence information to and from a range of overseas FIUs.
AUSTRAC is an active participant in national and international law
enforcement committees, task forces, and other forums to provide opportunities for the exchange of information and discussion of issues regarding money laundering, tax evasion, and major criminal activity.

THE FINANCIAL TRANSACTIONS AND REPORTS ANALYSIS CENTRE
OF CANADA (FINTRAC)
In 1997, the FATF concluded that there were serious weaknesses in
Canada's approach to reporting, analyzing, and investigating suspi-
cious transactions and cross-border currency movements. For example,
Canada's reliance on voluntary reporting was deemed ineffective and
Canada was criticized for not having a central financial intelligence
unit, among other problems.[23] In response to these concerns and pressures, on 31 May 1999, the Government of Canada tabled Bill C-81 – an
act designed to facilitate anti-money-laundering initiatives and which
established the Financial Transactions and Reports Analysis Centre of
Canada (Desjardins, 2002). Bill C-81 became Bill C-22 and received
royal assent on 29 June 2000, becoming the new Proceeds of Crime
(Money Laundering) Act. Since then, four amendments have been made
to the Act, the most significant occurring during the enactment of the

Anti-Terrorism Act. Since 24 December 2001, it has been known as the PCML&TFA – the Proceeds of Crime (Money Laundering) and Terrorist Financing Act. The legislation has changed existing money-laundering practices used to combat organized crime.[24] Below are three major changes the government has made to this practice:

1 Implement specific measures to detect and deter money laundering and the financing of terrorist activities and facilitate investigation and prosecution of money-laundering offences and terrorist-activity financing offences. These include the following: establish record keeping and client identification requirements for financial services providers and others susceptible of being used for money laundering or the financing of terrorist activities; require reporting of suspicious financial transactions and cross-border movements of currency and monetary instruments; establish an agency responsible for dealing with reported and other information.
2 Respond to the threat posed by organized crime by providing law enforcement with information they need to deprive criminals of the proceeds of their criminal activities while ensuring that appropriate safeguards are put in place to protect the privacy of persons.
3 Assist in fulfilling Canada's international commitments to participate in the fight against transnational crime, particularly money laundering, and fight against terrorist activity.[25]

Under the PCML&TFA, the mandate of FINTRAC now includes the following tasks:

- collect, analyse, assess, and disclose information to assist in the detection, prevention, and deterrence of money laundering and the financing of terrorist activities
- ensure the protection of personal information under its control is not improperly disclosed
- enhance public awareness and understanding of matters related to money laundering
- ensure compliance with new suspicious transaction reporting requirements
- act as a central repository for information about money laundering activities across Canada
- disclose information to law enforcement agencies in money-

laundering cases where it is concluded that there were reasonable grounds to suspect the information was relevant
- provide the disclosed information to Revenue Canada, Citizenship and Immigration, and the Canadian Security and Intelligence Service should they believe it is relevant to those organizations
- grant statutory authority to 'spot-audit' organizations obliged to report transactions[26]

The United Nations Global Program Against Money Laundering

To address the problem of money laundering, the UN's Office of Drugs and Crime (ONODC) (formerly the UN Office of Office of Drug Control and Crime Prevention, ODCCP) created the Global Program Against Money Laundering (GPML). The goal of the GPML is to increase the effectiveness of international action against money laundering by offering comprehensive technical expertise to member states. The GPML focuses on three main areas: first, the promotion of cooperation through training, institution building, and awareness raising; second, understanding money laundering through research and analysis (e.g., on bank secrecy, offshore financial centres, etc.); and third, raising the effectiveness of law enforcement through the establishment of financial investigation services (FIS) that advise countries on training specialized FIS managers and staff on money laundering while facilitating cooperation between national law enforcement agencies through technical advice and non-partisan mediation.[27]

The International Monetary Fund

The International Monetary Fund (IMF) is a collaborative institution with near-universal membership devoted to promoting macroeconomic stability and growth through operational activities of surveillance and technical assistance (International Monetary fund, 2001c). In terms of policy and enforcement, the IMF defers to the FATF, Interpol, national financial intelligence units, and the UN. The IMF views the key set of standards in money-laundering policy to be the FATF's 'Forty Recommendations.' The IMF also explores ways to augment the work of these other agencies. For example, the IMF carries out the following: works closely with major international anti-money-laundering groups (e.g., participating in meetings and joint workshops and exchanging information, particularly on compliance with financial standards); increases the provision of technical assistance to achieve greater efficiency and effectiveness in anti-money-laundering activities; includes anti-money laundering concerns in its surveillance and other operational activities when relevant to macroeconomic issues; and undertakes additional studies and publicizes the importance of countries acting to protect themselves against money laundering (International Monetary Fund, 2001a: 33).

The Council of Europe

The Council of Europe is an intergovernmental political organization founded on 5 May 1949 and is comprised of forty-one countries. The Council acts as an advisory body and is mandated to promote awareness and consider solutions to problems facing European society, including organized crime and money laundering. The Council is also comprised of non-member observers such as Canada, the U.S., and Mexico. The Council contributes to conventions, which member states have adopted nationally by incorporating parts of these conventions into national laws. In so doing, there is greater harmonization of laws in Europe.[28] The Council can strongly recommend policies, but has no power to enforce these recommendations.

The Council addressed the issue of money laundering in its *Convention on Laundering, Search, Seizure and Confiscation of the Proceeds from Crime* (1990), which aimed to achieve greater unity between members in the form of a common criminal policy.[29] During the late 1990s, calls to broaden the scope of the convention were made due to fears that when countries converted national currencies to the Euro in 2002, the change would allow underground national money to be laundered into legal Euros.[30] The 'PC-R-EV' (Council of Europe Selected Committee of Experts on the Evaluation of Anti-Money Laundering Measures) formally changed its name in 2002 to MONEYVAL. In essence, this group operates as the European regional Financial Action Task Force for countries that are not members of the FATF (member countries can participate as observers). The recommendations of the FATF serve as an essential aspect of MONEYVAL's evaluations. As of 2005, the member countries in MONEYVAL included the following countries; each country is entitled to appoint three 'experts' to attend the meetings:

Albania	Estonia	Russian Federation
Andorra	Georgia	San Marino
Armenia	Hungary	Serbia and Montenegro
Azerbaijan	Latvia	Slovakia
Bosnia and	Liechtenstein	Slovenia
Herzegovina	Lithuania	The former Yugoslav
Bulgaria	Malta	Republic of Macedonia
Croatia	Moldova	Ukraine
Cyprus	Poland	
Czech Republic	Romania	

SEARCHING FOR THE EVIDENCE

Those are the key agencies, organizations, and international 'clubs' whose mandate it is to target money laundering. The question must be asked: What positive results and indirect consequences have their energies and resources produced? These groups meet and bring recommendations to others. The activity is 'process oriented' rather than 'impact oriented.' What is missing from every one of these groups is any empirical evidence of the size of the money-laundering 'problem'; the success of any of their recommendations – aside from the process measurements (i.e., files, surveys, perceptions); and the relationship between the laundering of money and adverse impacts on the society. Having no notion that the amount of laundering has been decreased in any way, there is no possibility of determining whether the focus on laundering has had an impact on the amount of crime. We will look at several of the claims in turn.

The Amount of Money Laundered is Astronomical and is Escalating: Estimates from Nowhere

In this book, we do not provide an 'estimated' figure on the amount of laundered money because there is no credible figure. This is contrary to the traditional approach whereby the authors state that there is no reliable figure and then proceed to supply one with the inadequate disclaimer that the figure is unverifiable. In this manner, made-up figures have entered and remain current by being arbitrarily enlarged with each telling in the 'common-sense' rhetoric of money-laundering experts. Most of these authors admit that estimates of the extent of money laundering are very speculative and almost impossible to verify.

Despite this, there is no shortage of claims of the vast amounts of money being laundered globally. The three most frequently mentioned bases for estimates are the FATF's and IMF's estimates, the Quirk estimate, and the Walker estimate.[31]

Financial Action Task Force (FATF) and the
International Monetary Fund (IMF) Estimates

Despite reference from other agencies to FATF estimates on the magnitude of money laundering, the FATF has *not* generated its own reliable data estimating the size of the world's money-laundering problem.[32] Amazingly, for an organization that was created to focus specifically on money laundering, the estimate that FATF uses is from the IMF – and if the story is correct, from a figure scribbled on a dinner napkin. In a speech at the plenary meeting of the FATF in Paris on 10 February 1998, the managing director of the IMF, Michael Camdessus, while questioning the accuracy of this estimate, indicated that the 2 to 5 per cent estimate has come to be regarded as the general consensus:

> I hardly need to say that the IMF regards the anti-money laundering actions advocated by the FATF as crucial for the smooth functioning of the financial markets. While we cannot guarantee the accuracy of our figures – and you have certainly a better evaluation than us – the estimates of the present scale of money laundering transactions are almost beyond imagination – 2 to 5 percent of global GDP would probably be a consensus range.[33]

The FATF generally adopts the IMF's rough estimate that the extent of money laundering in the world is 2 to 5 per cent of the world's gross domestic product (GDP), which amounts to roughly between U.S.$590 billion and U.S.$1.5 trillion (CDN$700 billion and CDN$1.8 trillion). No empirical evidence supporting this estimate is given in documents or in reports issued by these agencies. Regardless of the lack of evidence to support claims of the extent of money laundering, estimates repeated by the WCO, the Council of Europe, and the UN[34] are drawn directly from the IMF and indirectly from the FATF sources.

In several documents produced by various agencies, the difficulty generating valid and reliable estimates of the extent of money laundering has been expressed. For example, an IMF paper by its Monetary and

Exchange Affairs and Policy Development and Review Departments recognized the difficulty generating accurate statistics given the concealed nature of money laundering:

> Activities underlying financial system abuse and financial crime are, by definition, concealed and therefore their direct observation by the macroeconomist or statistician is not possible. In the absence of hard statistical data and appropriate methodology, indirect methods have been used to estimate the potential volume of such activities. Estimates have used two different types of information – inference based on available macroeconomic data and direct information collected by law and tax enforcement agencies. Both approaches have problems and neither is particularly robust. Thus, an adequate measure of financial system abuse remains illusive.[35]

In its 'Basic Facts About Money Laundering,' the FATF claims that the scope of money laundering is difficult to determine since it takes place outside the range of normal economic statistics (DiLuca, 2002). According to the IMF (2001c), 'the empirical evidence on the magnitude of financial abuse, financial crime and money laundering is limited.' The explanation for the lack of data given by the IMF recognizes the difficulties facing empirical measurement given the nature of money laundering: 'Activities underlying financial system abuse and financial crime are, by definition, concealed and therefore their direct observation by the macroeconomist or statistician is not possible.'[36]

A review of the literature does not reveal a concrete methodological approach used to generate estimates. Rather, what is found is some guess work based on indirect measures and an interest expressed in one day developing a methodology to produce accurate estimates of money laundering. In the 1990 *FATF-I Annual Report*, three methods of indirect estimation to assess the scale of financial flows from drug trafficking are described:

1 estimates based on the United Nations estimate of world drug production and profits that different drugs generate
2 estimates based on consumption needs of drug abusers (surveys that are of doubtful reliability)
3 the use of data from actual seizures of drugs and projections generated by taking the total amount of drugs available for sale and then applying a multiplier

Based on such indirect estimations, the FATF concluded that sales of cocaine, heroin, and cannabis were approximately U.S.$122 billion. With deductions for expenses, the net profit available for possible laundering would be roughly U.S.$85 billion per year.[37] This finding is reiterated in a 2001 IMF report:

> Another approach to estimating the magnitude of financial abuse uses information about expenditures and prices involved in criminal activity that has been collected in the course of law enforcement (micro-data). The most publicized of such estimates have been for global money laundering by the FATF. On the basis of information about final sales of some illegal drugs (about US$120 billion a year in the United States and Europe in the late 1980s) and extrapolating worldwide and generalizing to include all drugs, and subsequently assuming that 50-70 percent of that amount would be laundered, the FATF estimated that money laundering could reach about 2 percent of the global GDP.[38]

However, the (FATF 1990: 6) did candidly observe that this method 'raises significant methodological concerns.'

In another effort, described in the 1996 Typologies Exercise Report, members of the FATF were each asked to provide data on the amount of money laundering in their countries in order to compile an estimate for all FATF members. This methodology also leads to a lack of credible estimates, particularly given that members employed different methods, each with their own limitations, to generate national estimates (FATF, 1996: para. 4–9). The FATF recognized the shortcomings of this method, as 'these numbers cannot sustain a defensible estimate of laundered funds. In most cases, authorities have not been confirming that the funds were of illegal origin' (ibid: para. 7). In this and other estimates, such difficulties render any estimate problematic.

While the difficulties of generating accurate estimates are noted, an IMF/World Bank document/policy paper encourages efforts to continue research on the effects of money laundering:

> Because the scale and consequence of financial sector abuse in general, and money laundering in particular, are not well understood (for the obvious reason that illegal activities are difficult to measure) such additional research would be difficult. At a minimum, however, the research would review effects of financial crime on the macro economy and would aim at providing an indication of the significance with which crime im-

pacts industrial and developing country markets. The output of such research could be brought together in 2002 in a paper for both the Fund and Band Boards. (IMF/World Bank, 2001: 15)

In summary, the evidence used to generate the IMF estimates has been viewed as problematic guesswork (Levi, 2001a: 1, 3). Others might more bluntly apply the term 'SWAG' – scientific wild-assed guesses. The FATF's objective to generate a reliable process of estimating the extent of money laundering has not yet been achieved. Rather, evidence of money laundering in FATF reports generally comes in the guise of anecdotal accounts of specific money-laundering transactions (FATF, 1997: para. 9) that are then generalized to indicate, in common-sense terms, that money laundering is a vast and growing problem.

As noted earlier, those agencies making grandiose claims about the vast, staggering, and devastating effects of money laundering themselves recognize the difficulty in measuring the phenomenon. The FATF, in its 1996 *Report on Money Laundering Typologies*, echoes this sentiment and concludes the report by noting the following: 'It is difficult at the present time to assess the scale of the money laundering problem. Although the experts generally agree that it amounts to hundreds of billions of dollars annually, they also acknowledge that previous attempts at a precise estimate have been empirically flawed' (FATF, 1996: 2–3).

While the FATF's 1997 *Report on Money Laundering Typologies* notes continuing efforts by the agency towards quantification, its 1998–99 report makes only passing reference to attempts by member countries to generate estimates, and its 2002 report makes no reference to any attempts to quantify the money laundering 'problem.'[39] This diminishing interest in quantifying money laundering lends credence to the notion that the extent of money laundering (particularly high-end estimates) has come to be viewed as *common-sense knowledge* that need not be proven. The *Annual Report 2004–2005* is preoccupied with 'process' issues: widening the reach of states involved in the FATF process; identifying states found to be in non-compliance; and sanctioning those deemed to be non-cooperative. In other words, it is presupposed that we know money laundering is a vast problem (both *vast* and *a problem*), so there is no further need to invest resources to determine just how vast a problem it is or whether the FATF activities have an impact on reducing the amount being laundered.

FinCEN (FINANCIAL CRIMES ENFORCEMENT NETWORK)

FinCEN, while citing trillion-dollar estimates in money laundering globally, also recognizes the lack of an empirical foundation for such figures.[40] For example, FinCEN recognizes that data collected from required reports under the Bank Secrecy Act, commercially available databases, and databases of other law enforcement organizations are inadequate.[41] FinCEN, in its Strategic Plans Report, also acknowledges the need to understand the magnitude of the money-laundering problem. It was not until August 2000, after the U.S. Treasury Department granted a contract to commission an estimate, that FinCEN took its first step towards realizing this objective. This effort was, however, limited to the development of a methodology for estimating the magnitude of money laundering rather than an attempt at calculating the actual figure.[42]

THE UN

Dolgor Solongo, an economist and a staff member on the Global Program against Money Laundering (GPML) of the United Nations Office on Drugs and Crime (UNODC), summarizes efforts to estimate the extent of money laundering as follows:

> As far as UNODCCP [now UNODC] is concerned the figure of $400 billion was suggested in 1995 as an annual turnover of illegal drugs. Illegal drugs proceeds are relevant to money laundering, but how much is actually laundered is difficult to say. The figure $500 billion derives from the assumption that money laundering is equivalent to 2 or 3 percent of the world's GNP. If I am not mistaken it was first mentioned by IMF. Overall, any numbers suggested on global money laundering could be only considered as a crude guess rather than a calculation based on the relevant data sources. Therefore, today as far as ODCCP (and many others, including IMF) is concerned no numbers are usually quoted as global money laundering ... The report of the FATF ad hoc group on Estimating the Magnitude of Money Laundering on Assessing Alternative Methodologies for Estimating Revenues from Illicit Drugs, concluded that 'because prices for each drug vary so much among countries, there is no alternative but to construct the global expenditure figure as the sum of national estimates.' It also concluded that 'current data sets on prevalence of use, consumption per user and purity only support very rough estimates of either national or global revenues' ... Overall, I

would like to say that there are no reliable even rough estimates of global money laundering.[43]

Walker's Estimate

In a 1995 report commissioned by AUSTRAC, John Walker, an independent consultant, attempted to estimate the extent of money laundering in Australia. Slightly sceptical of taking on such an endeavour (and acknowledging the uncertainty that surrounded the state of knowledge regarding the true scope and extent of money laundering), Walker offered the following caveat:

> there is more than a whiff of paleontology about the study of money laundering ... while I embarked upon this project hoping at least to put a substantial amount of flesh on the bones of the animal ... like most paleontologists, I have only been lucky enough to dig up a few scattered clues to its size and shape, its habitat and its lifestyle. So, like the paleontologist, I have tried to speculate intelligently on the basis of these few bone fragments. The process involves a great deal of lateral thinking and the juxtaposition of a variety of possibly unconnected facts, to create what might be a plausible scenario. If what I came up with seems plausible then I've probably done a good job, because others can dig for more and better clues in the areas that seem to provide promise and eventually we may get to know the full story of money laundering.[44]

Walker argued that the task was important – if possible – because 'efforts to combat it are costly and need to be properly targeted and in proportion to the real size of the problem.' Walker began his attempt to measure the extent of money laundering in Australia with a review of official statistics and followed this with a survey of expert opinion on money laundering (e.g., operational police serving on specialist squads, police statisticians, crime researchers). Walker found official statistical data most unhelpful, arguing that agencies – including police forces, the Australian Customs Service, Australian Taxation Office, the National Crime Authority (whose mandate is to counteract organized criminal activity and reduce its impact), the Australian Bureau of Statistics, and others – should compile comprehensive statistics on the extent of money laundering. Most of these agencies at the time compiled no such statistics, which hampered the efforts of AUSTRAC.

Among the sources that figured into Walker's estimate were the following:

- official statistics from various agencies
- a survey of law enforcement entities
- a questionnaire sent to all federal, state and territorial police services
- information from the Australian Bureau of Statistics on the Understatement of Income Data
- data from AUSTRAC regarding reports of suspect financial transactions and the flow of finance through Australian banks and international transfers

Drawing on these sources, Walker concluded that between $1 and $4.5 billion of 'hot money' was generated in Australia and laundered in Australia and overseas. More specifically, Walker concluded that the most likely figure was $3.5 billion.[45] Walker did, however, recognize limitations in his study, in particular the need for statistics on money laundering from other countries. He states:

> There is no doubt that the estimates contained in this report cannot be used in isolation with absolute confidence. The methodology is one which appears to have converged on a credible figure for money laundering from the proceeds of crime in Australia, but it would be considerably enhanced if it could be measured with equivalent figures from other countries ...[46]

Walker went on to estimate the global extent of money laundering, in response to the need expressed by Stanley Morris (retiring chair of the FATF) to generate such an estimate. Walker's model was, at one point, relied upon by the UN in their estimates of the amount of money laundered globally. According to Walker, the quantity of money laundering generated in each country is dependent on such factors as

- the nature and extent of crime in that country
- the estimated amount of money laundering per reported crime for each type of crime, and
- the economic environment in which the crime and the laundering takes place

The quantity of money attracted to each country is dependent on

- the presence or absence of banking secrecy provisions
- government attitudes to money laundering

- levels of corruption and regional conflict, and
- geographical, ethnic, or trading proximities between origin and destination countries

Countries with secretive banking practices or poor government controls over banking would see higher levels of money laundering.[47]

While Walker took crime statistics from the UN Centre for International Crime Prevention database (which contains the number of recorded crimes per year in almost 100 countries), he began his model with a 1995 AUSTRAC report that estimated the amount of money laundered in Australia. In that report, Walker estimated the total amount of laundered money for each type of crime and divided the amount by the number of those types of crimes recorded per year in Australia (e.g., $50,000 per recorded fraud offence; $100,000 per recorded drug trafficking offence). He then took these figures and applied them to the estimated numbers of crimes recorded in each country (from the UNCJ database) for preliminary estimates of 'hot money' in each country. These numbers were then factored up or down, depending on the GNP per capita of each country. Proceeds per crime in any given country were assumed to be proportional to that country's GNP per capita. A figure was then generated that estimated the amount of money generated by crime in each country and made available for money laundering. The model then estimated the proportion of money laundered in the country with the remainder being laundered in other countries. Walker compared his findings with estimates from news clippings and found few discrepancies. He concluded by recommending that more research be conducted in countries where little data exists in order to improve the accuracy of his estimates.[48]

Based on this model, the U.S. acts as an origin country for 46.3 per cent of the world's laundered money. In terms of the flow of laundered money, including within the U.S., the U.S. ranks first with 18.5 per cent. Walker suggests that the global output of money laundering is as high as U.S.$2.85 trillion per year, most of which is concentrated in the U.S. and Europe.[49]

Quirk's Estimate

Peter Quirk completed his research as an adviser to the IMF's Monetary and Exchange Affairs Department. His 1996 study of the amount of money being laundered globally is often cited in IMF documents. Quirk concedes that 'large variations in estimates have led to reliance on "consensus" numbers, like the undocumented assertion in 1994 by the *Financial Times* that the amount of money laundering worldwide annually was roughly $500 billion' (Quirk, 1997: 8). Quirk thus relied instead on a different type of 'consensus estimates' – those created by law enforcement (including Interpol) and other institutional officials rather than economists ('built up estimates by crime category based on street knowledge; sampling; detailed medical, social and financial / tax records') (ibid.: 2). The result of this exercise was the 'consensus' of 2 to 5 per cent of the GDP.

Quirk presents the impacts of money laundering by looking at both microeconomic and macroeconomic levels, although he admits that the IMF figures related to money laundering as a function of GDP are not precise, and he admits that the impact he alleges and the figures he reports are, to some extent, speculative.

While many attempts at securing reliable estimates abound, perhaps the most useful source is the review of both macroeconomic and microeconomic estimates that pertain mainly to the U.S. and that were published by Peter Reuter and Edwin Truman (2004). Peter Reuter had been involved in the FATF efforts to produce reliable estimates, which, he acknowledged had 'failed.' Pertaining to the numerous other attempts, of both types (macro and micro), the authors state:

> ... neither yields estimates of the volume of laundered money that can be considered as anything more than an indicative order of magnitude. Such figures are useful to confirm that the phenomenon of money laundering is of sufficient scale to warrant public policy attention, but their quality is not good enough to provide guidance for policy. (Reuter and Truman, 2004: 10)

Canadian Estimates

THE SCOPE AND IMPACT OF MONEY LAUNDERING IN CANADA
Canadian data on money laundering is no better and no worse than information elsewhere. A review of the literature reveals a number of occasions where estimates of the scope of money laundering in Canada have been attempted. In 1989, Rod Stamler (at that time an assistant commissioner with the RCMP who was instrumental in initiating proceeds of crime enforcement in Canada), estimated that CDN$10 to $13 billion was laundered in this country (Possamai, 1989: All). The RCMP

state in their 1993 drug intelligence report, 'in fact, no accurate statistical base is available to evaluate with any precision the overall value of laundered proceeds in Canada. The full extent of money laundering in Canada remains unknown.' However the RCMP report continued on to say that 'some estimates suggest that the total sum of drug proceeds laundered in this country could well exceed $10 billion' (RCMP, 1993: 52). The following year, no estimate was provided due to controversy over the lack of verifiability.

In the *Organized Crime Impact Study*, compiled by Sam Porteous for the Solicitor General of Canada in 1998, $7 billion to $10 billion in sales of illicit narcotics in Canada is estimated. Of that, it is estimated that 50 to 70 per cent is available for laundering and subsequent investment. The report concludes that the amount of funds laundered (drug money plus other illicit proceeds) in Canada annually is between $5 and $14 billion. While this ridiculously wide range renders the estimate irrelevant – similar to the $1 to $4.5 billion range estimated in Australia – one remains puzzled by its source. As is the case with other estimates, no detailed methodology or precise format for reaching these figures is supplied. Like the aforementioned RCMP estimates, this total has been derived in the absence of any scientific or statistical method; instead, it relies on an amalgam of previously culled opinions by RCMP experts, including a calculation of a percentage of the estimated value of drug trafficking proceeds in Canada (50 to 70 per cent of an estimated $7 to $10 billion illegal narcotics industry plus an unknown 'additional' amount).

Even in the absence of reliable indicators, Porteous contends that money laundering has an enormous impact on Canadian society, primarily in the support it provides to the continuation of destructive criminal activity, such as drug trafficking, fraud, extortion, and smuggling. The impact is therefore seen to stem from the profits rather than from the criminal activity that produced the profits. His argument is that because criminals are motivated by profit, 'the direct impact of money laundering encompasses all of the impacts of the other organized crime-related activities (assessed in his report)' (Porteous, 1998b: 20). This appears to be a reversal of the causal ordering of events. Instead, a more accurate sequence would be for the crime of drug trafficking to lead to money laundering (in part due to the enforcement strategies that target the proceeds of crime).

Porteous argues that money laundering has a negative impact on the basic values of society because, to the extent that it is allowed to continue, it is a clear signal that crime does indeed pay. One might argue that the basic values of most Western countries are capitalistic values that, in fact, value and reward success – almost regardless of how it is achieved, as is evidenced by our ability to 'forgive' some of our wealthiest citizens the origins of their bounty. However, rule of law is important and, according to Porteous, 'money laundering must be controlled not because it causes significant economic distortions (in many cases it may not) but because it is recognized as morally unacceptable that individuals profit from criminal activities' (ibid.: 20).

If anyone was to question the methodology, then an alternative methodology could be offered: the application of the equally unscientific IMF estimate (ibid.: 18). Using the IMF estimate that the total amount of money laundered in the world is 2 to 5 per cent of the global GDP, Porteous generates a statistic for the amount of money laundered in Canada that is 2 to 5 per cent of Canada's GDP. He states:

Another simpler method to estimate the amount of money laundering taking place is to employ a 'rule of thumb' advocated by some money laundering authorities, which estimates that the amount laundered in a country is on average equal to approximately 2% of that country's GDP. This calculation is drawn from International Monetary Fund estimates that global money laundering is equal to approximately 2% of global GDP. Using this rule of thumb, the estimate of the amount of money laundered in Canada annually would be approximately $17 billion. Combining the two approaches results in a rough estimate of the amount of illicit funds laundered in Canada per year of between $5 billion and $17 billion. (Porteous, 1998b: 18)

Making an accurate assessment of the amount of money laundered in Canada more confusing are figures posted by the Montreal-based Integrated Proceeds of Crime Unit, which places the amount of money laundered in Canada annually even higher (between $20 and $30 billion)! In one of the most extreme estimates, a 1997 Canadian Press Newswire story stated that the United Nations estimates that at least U.S.$750 billion in dirty money is laundered every year and that as much as $50 billion of that flows through Canada.[50]

Like their counterparts in other nations, Canadian counter-money laundering agencies report difficulties in getting an accurate quantitative picture of the extent of money laundering in Canada. This appears to be of little concern, however, as it is generally believed by these agencies (and then passed on to the public as 'objective' truth) that the money laundering problem is vast, expanding and poses a significant threat to us all. We are reminded that accurate figures are not necessary because we all know that the amount of money involved in drug trafficking alone is huge. As the RCMP claim: 'Drug trafficking alone generates billions of illegal dollars for criminal organizations every year. Although it is difficult to pinpoint the exact amount, it is clear that the problem is vast.'[51]

A complicating factor is that this rhetoric tends to assume that all drug trafficking money is corporately owned and funnelled into one destination – stacked on one board-room table ready for laundering – rather than being 'pissed away' by combinations of innumerable small-time and large scale drug trafficking entrepreneurs. Recognizing there is little empirical data to support such estimates, Daniel Murphy, senior counsel of Strategic Prosecution for the federal Department of Justice, maintains that a more pressing issue than searching for a figure that is impossible to prove is to understand how various governments will combat money laundering. He states, 'I take the phenomenon [the magnitude of money laundering] as a truism and the magnitude issue is less important than the ability to investigate and prosecute civilly or criminally.'[52]

Again, the argument is that while we only assume the problem is large, it still warrants an intensive response. Tom Naylor is bolder in his assertion that attempts to quantify money laundering and, on the basis of these estimates, to develop anti-money laundering initiatives have not been successful:

> The bald fact remains that, after 15 years of progressive escalation of its use, no one has been able to determine with any remote degree of confidence whether or not the proceeds-of-crime approach to crime control has had any discernable impact on the operation of illegal markets or on the amount, distribution and behavior of illegal income and wealth. The entire exercise rests on a series of inaccurate or, at least improvable, assumptions. (Naylor, 1999a: 51)

Money Laundering Corrupts and Undermines Financial Institutions, Economies, and Currencies and Leads to Unfair Competition with Legitimate Business

Significant among the purported effects of money laundering is the economic devastation that money laundering will leave in its wake –

threatening economic and financial systems in many countries, as well as corrupting[53] and undermining confidence in the integrity of financial institutions.[54] Among these economic effects, money laundering is thought to create changes in money demand, produce greater prudential risks to bank soundness, produce contamination effects on legal financial transactions, and produce greater volatility in international capital flows and exchange rates due to unanticipated cross-border asset transfers.[55] The United Nation's Global Program against Money Laundering (GPML) echoes these sentiments, arguing that the presence of laundered money in an economy will drive out legitimate business, undermine the legitimate private sector as well as the integrity of financial and banking systems, lead to the loss of control over economic and monetary policy, and undermine economic stability in general. As Ian Carrington points out on behalf of the GPML,

> One clear risk in circumstances in which bad money is introduced into a system that was previously clean, is that the good money will very often seek other domiciles leaving the system in question with only the bad money, a bad reputation that will keep out new bonafide investors and a regulatory system that is inadequate to cope with the challenges with which it is now faced. (Carrington, 2000: 2)

John Walker has labelled this impact of money laundering the 'bad money drives out good money phenomenon' and describes the process as follows:

> Money Launderers will be very keen to purchase an asset such as a business or some real estate because possession of the cash is much more potentially incriminating while possession of the business or the land enables them to build apparently legitimate wealth. In order to purchase the business or the land, they need not be too discriminating in the price they pay. They will outbid other potential buyers with more realistic and honest reasons for buying, not caring if they pay more than the true worth of the purchase. This may drive up the purchase prices of equivalent businesses or parcels of real estate to unsustainable levels, so that only other crime-resourced purchasers can afford to buy. Furthermore, if the launderer buys and operates a business, while simultaneously conducting the criminal activities, which generate additional funds, they may integrate these funds into the business, effectively subsidizing the business – possibly to the point where they drive out legitimate competitors. Finally,

they may be tempted to ensure the success of their venture by corrupting public officials or other business colleagues. So, even when the overall effects on the economy are benign or even positive, there may be significant adverse effects arising from the take-over of legitimate businesses by illegitimate operators.[56]

A press release outlining the money-laundering problem since 11 September 2001 and the initiatives of the GPML summarizes these anticipated negative financial effects:

> Left unchecked, money laundering can erode a nation's economy by largely increasing the demand for cash, making interest and exchange rates more volatile, and by causing high inflation in countries where criminal elements are doing business. The siphoning away of billions of dollars a year from normal economic growth poses a real danger at a time when the financial health of every country affects the stability of the global market. The consequences of money laundering are bad for business, development, government and the rule of law.[57]

No evidence is provided to prove the assertions made in this statement. Against all of those 'negatives,' John Walker acknowledges that the evidence to support those potential consequences is weak:

> The effects this money laundering has on the Australian economy cannot be assessed accurately with the information available ... When illicitly gained money is spent on lavish real estate there is probably a net loss to the economy, but where it is turned into legitimate businesses the net effects can be quite positive to the economy ... When money is brought into Australia from overseas for laundering, one might conclude that from a purely economic view the effect on Australia economy is an entirely positive one. (J. Walker, 2000a: 1)

Money Laundering Destabilizes Democracies and Free Markets

With these economic effects collectively threatening to corrupt whole economies and currencies, the fear has been expressed (for example, by FinCEN) that money laundering has the potential to not only destabilize free markets, including the commercial and trade systems, but also to destabilize democracies.[58] In particular, the fear has been expressed that money laundering may have the most profound effects on smaller countries that may be more easily corrupted and destabilized (Camdessas, 1998). The United Nations General Assembly, in its 'Political Declaration and Action Plan Against Money Laundering,' summarizes this perception of the political and social decay that money laundering may create: the 'sheer magnitude of money laundering is such that it now ranks as one of the gravest criminal threats to the global community, capable of corroding international financial systems and corrupting entire democracies.'[59] Such hyperbolic rhetoric, *without substantiation*, requires a substantial challenge and receives little response. In his Canada-based study, under the heading of 'Sovereignty and Threat to National Stability,' Porteous shifts the focus and argues that 'Canada's performance in combating money laundering will continue to impact on its relations with the US, [and] other FATF members' (Porteous, 1998a: 101) Hence, the threat to security is not from money laundering but rather from how Canada's response to this 'crisis' is perceived by foreign jurisdictions. He acknowledges that money laundering involves no violence, no direct health and safety issues, no environmental impact and, from a macroeconomic perspective, neither Canada nor the international financial system as a whole is threatened. Furthermore, he questions the FATF's concern with an impact related to tax collection: 'It is still not clear how moving funds from the illicit economy where they would not be taxed into the licit economy where by definition they would be declared and liable for taxes would result in tax losses' (ibid.: 99).

A second, more recent 2002 government report, also completed for the Department of the Solicitor General Canada (now called the Department of Public Safety and Emergency Preparedness Canada), looked at four main categories of 'harm' caused from money laundering: (1) lost tax revenue, (2) instability to the economic system, (3) reputational impacts on financial institutions, and (4) unfair competition (TCI Management 2003). Again, the preoccupation with tax loss is puzzling. Criminal proceeds that remain hidden are tax free; if they are laundered, they generally are not. As stated above, laundering the proceeds may in fact result in taxes that otherwise would not be paid. One can only guess what citizens might spend their money on if they did not purchase illicit goods or services. Those alternative purchases *might* generate GST (goods and services tax) or PST (provincial sales tax). However, once the money is laundered, most likely these funds will then be used to purchase goods and services with all of the appropriate taxes paid. Again, the real issue is crime and/or a large underground economy.

While the authors of this 2002 report state that the most likely area for a significant amount of hidden economic activity is in the unreported income of organized criminals, one needs only to interact with the building/construction trade, service industry, or even sales to realize that there is a vibrant underground economy within the so-called legitimate business world that has little to do with organized crime. The authors of the 2002 report acknowledge that the present-day economy already includes a significant level of hidden economic activity and the Canadian monetary and fiscal policies already take this into account. They conclude that it would require an unlikely rapid increase in unreported income levels to affect an impact on the economic system as a whole.

Canadian financial institutions claim to monitor the impact of money laundering on the reputation of their organizations but only in an 'informal way.' There seems to be more concern about how the international community would see Canadian financial institutions if there were to be large scandals involving money laundering. Of greater concern have been the large financial frauds – which may have a laundering component – but again, the predicate offence is the one that harms the investors and destroys companies.

The final 'impact' the report looks at is unfair competition. The evidence consists of a number of plausible anecdotal scenarios. It states that a number of experts have reported that competitors 'sensed' that something was strange about the dirty businesses. For example, the prices charged might be too low if profit is not an objective, and the prices paid for properties or assets might be too high if the real profit is elsewhere. What remains unknown is the frequency with which the businesses run for the purpose of laundering, or those acquired with 'dirty money,' are run any differently from businesses acquired and run legitimately.

There are, however, countries where the impact from illicit proceeds, laundered or not, may be more serious. Colombia serves as an example, and the detailed research by Francisco Thoumi (2003) illustrates the complexity of the issues. Thoumi describes several ways the reinvestment of drug revenues into Colombian society and the presence of the drug trade affect the country:

- drug money funds presidential campaigns, resulting in collusive ties between government and criminals
- funding of candidates is given with assurances for very specific 'understandings and assurances,' including assurances regarding the legal status of the traffickers

- funding from drugs increases the warring capacities of both the guerrillas and the paramilitary
- the drug industry has the capacity to change the country's economic power structure
- while the funds have a short-term benefit on the society, it is argued that there is a long-term negative effect on the economy in terms of criminality, violence, and delegitimation of the regime that results in a loss of trust leading to stagnation
- environmental destruction is caused by the cultivation of drugs on vulnerable land and the defoliation campaigns used in the 'war on drugs'

All of these impacts are 'real' and, *if* anti-laundering strategies influence the amount of drug trafficking, then a closer link could be made between money laundering and these outcomes. That link cannot, or at least has not, been made. As Thoumi concludes: 'Successful anti-drug strategies must recognize that profits are an important factor, but also that the competitive advantage in illegal drugs is based on a weak state and tolerant institutions' (Thoumi, 2003: 370).

Anti-drug strategies must recognize the complex social, economic, and political factors; to apply universal anti-laundering requirements when the societal 'equipment' to demand compliance is lacking becomes a pointless or sheer political exercise.

Laundered Money Fuels Further Crime

A further category of literature broadens the base of concern by linking the laundering of criminal proceeds to the 'sponsoring' of other forms of organized crime and now, of course, to terrorism. According to FinCEN, money laundering fuels the engine of crime, providing the means by which criminals may operate and expand their operations.[60] Thus, money laundering is viewed as constituting the 'life blood' of profit generating criminal activity,[61] facilitating corruption,[62] trade fraud, other fraudulent activities, tax evasion,[63] and terrorism, all of which are viewed as producing negative macroeconomic effects. This argument is based on the distorted belief that the *illicit profits* from previous criminal conduct, rather than the original *criminal activity*, are to blame for ongoing criminality. Eliminating criminal 'predicate' conduct would obviously eliminate the illicit profits, but without the more attractive prospect of successful state forfeitures.

Efforts to evaluate the extent and precise impact of money laundering are increasingly being seen as too laborious and too resource intensive. According to some anti-money-laundering agencies, the dangers of money laundering should be clear, even to the untrained eye. In contrast, according to John Walker, the overall effects of money laundering on economies *can only* be determined when there is precise, detailed information:

> Without good data on how much money launderers have to invest or data on how they invest it, we can only speculate on how the economy might be affected. As a body of information is built up, our speculations may become more and more realistic and accurate. At this point in time, it would appear to be impossible to do better than to float a few ideas using hypothetical examples. (J. Walker, 2000a)

Impact of the Anti-laundering Strategies on Crime

We can accept that quantifying the amount of money laundering is at this time impossible – but what about the impact of the anti-laundering strategies on society? Surely, the impact is the *reason for* the activity of these agencies. However, the lack of reliable methods for quantification of the extent of money laundering renders it very difficult to properly evaluate the efficacy and success of counter-money-laundering measures. Needing to have some impact, the anti-laundering agencies have resorted to secondary measurements to gauge the effectiveness of counter-money-laundering agencies. Claims of success tend to be based on industry compliance with regulations *versus* any reduction in money laundering or more importantly any evidence of a reduction of profit-generating criminal activity.[64] Officials list off the 'successes' brought about by the anti-laundering initiatives:

- the adoption of anti-money-laundering laws
- the creation of anti-money-laundering institutions
- new skills acquired by the officials in this field
- greater understanding of the subject around the world, which promotes up-to-date measures against this crime[65]

Peter Reuter and Edwin Truman (2004: 124–6) have made the most concerted effort to measure the performance of anti-laundering efforts, most specifically in terms of the reduction of predicate crime. In reference specifically to illegal drugs, they look at the volume of predicate offences, the price of drugs, and the number of dependent drug users.

They conclude that while performance measurement is an increasingly important component of public policy, it remains difficult to find credible measures of these anti-laundering measures actually reducing crime.

Therefore our conclusions, based on all of the available evidence, can be stated as follows:

- The size of laundering activity is totally unknown, but figures continue to be repeated with increasing sound and fury.
- The references to the impact of laundering on many societies serves mainly as rhetoric and there is some information that laundered money in certain circumstances can actually contribute to the economy. There are, however, countries like Colombia where the amount of drug money impacts directly and negatively on society.
- The impact of anti-laundering efforts on laundering activities yields seizure statistics and process 'evidence' of compliance with no evidence of a reduction in laundering activity. There is possibly some evidence of greater sophistication in laundering schemes conceivable due to enforcement efforts.
- The impact of anti-laundering efforts on predicate crimes provides no evidence of anyone being 'driven out of their criminal activities' nor any reduction in criminality.
- There is evidence that some of the anti-laundering record-keeping systems provide the police with additional intelligence when they are engaged in an investigation; there is less evidence that these systems alert the police to unidentified criminal activity.

Consequences Flowing from the Anti-Laundering Strategies

While the various agencies described above have been instrumental in establishing worldwide anti-money-laundering regimes, they have done so in the absence of quantitative data that accurately estimate the extent of the problem or the impact, if any, on the criminal activity that they are mandated to combat (neither money laundering nor the predicate offences). This is problematic given that such high-end estimates have been employed to justify often intrusive and extensive policies and questionable forms of legal, political, and economic regulations. If the problem of money laundering were not framed in such terms, securing continued funding for the various anti-money-laundering agencies would be hampered, as would the enactment of legislation to expand the powers of these agencies. The FATF, in particular, has been increasingly aggressive in its bids to enforce global anti-money-laundering strategies. In what follows, some of the social, economic, and political implications of the estimates are explored.

Blacklisting Non-Compliers

In response to the slow adoption of the FATF standards or recommendations, especially among non-member nations, the FATF undertook a non-cooperating countries and territories initiative in 2000 (known as the *name and shame* list) (Mitchell, 2002). As mentioned earlier, such recommendations, while not legally binding, strongly encourage financial intermediaries and agents to be subject to strict obligations regarding the prevention, detection, and punishment of money laundering (FATF, 2000: para. 1–3). The report sets out twenty-five criteria for determining if a non-member nation is cooperative and mandates a country-by-country review resulting in the compilation of a list identifying non-cooperative nations. Among the consequences that flowed from being on this list were requirements that financial institutions pay special attention to, or report, financial transactions established in non-cooperative jurisdictions. Furthermore, the initiative specified the 'conditioning, restricting, targeting or even prohibiting financial transactions with non-cooperative jurisdictions' (ibid.: para. 44–55). To be classified among the non-cooperative countries and territories (NCCT), therefore, had significant financial consequences for a country in that it discouraged foreign investors.

In the country-by-country FATF review, released in June 2000, fifteen nations were listed as sufficiently non-cooperative to merit the imposition of economic sanctions. Nations failing to adhere to these regulations were subject to scrutiny, as banks adhering to these regulations were instructed to exercise caution to ensure transactions with blacklisted nations were legitimate. In a subsequent June 2001 FATF review of non-cooperative countries, four countries were removed from the list (but still subject to FATF monitoring), six new countries were added to the list, and it was recommended that members apply countermeasures to three nations which were identified as non-cooperative or which had not made adequate progress in adhering to FATF regulations and recommendations (FATF, 2002: para. 1; Levi, 2001a: 208). By July 2004, six countries remained on the list.

This move to blacklisting reflects a shift in the FATF's 'operation' and nature: '[w]hat had begun as a peer-evaluative, consensus-building exercise became a black-listing regime' (Beare, 2001: 12–13). Such a shift has also afforded powerful FATF members the ability to monitor and control the economic activities of non-members: '[The shift] raises the prospect of financial movements involving non FATF members being not just monitored but also controlled. This raises the prospect of Western financial powers forming a kind of "zone of exclusion" within which capital movements take place freely but which is open only to those states which have agreed to police money laundering' (ibid.: 9).

The IMF has remarked on the negative economic implications for some nations resulting from allegations of non-compliance with anti-money-laundering recommendations established by organizations like the FATF. However, in the fall of 2002, an agreement among the FATF, the IMF, and the World Bank resulted in most of the reviews and evaluations being done, not by the FATF but rather by the World Bank and the IMF (Reuter and Truman, 2004: 87). These blacklisting practices have been criticized as rigid and unfair, especially given that there is no formal appeal process for listed nations. Listed nations must comply with the recommendations to be removed from the list. The review process is generally viewed as being unfair in not adequately recognizing the efforts of listed nations' attempts to improve regulatory oversight (Peel, 2000). It is also pointed out by critics that some of the small, lesser developed states, moved into financial services at the prompting of their 'former or present colonial powers' in order to reduce their dependence on aid – those industries that are now categorized as money-laundering operations (Levi, 2003: 9). In addition to the 'blacklisting' initiated by the anti-money-laundering evaluators, some of these nations were faced with being 'blacklisted' by the OECD stemming from the initiative on harmful tax competition. At issue in this latter initiative was the sovereign right of countries to develop their own distinct tax regimes (Delaney, 2002: 7).

Offshore Havens for Money Laundering?

Offshore financial centres have frequently been highlighted as money-laundering havens (due in part to differences in taxation regimes). Among the regions considered havens is the Caribbean basin. According to the UN, criminals find financial offshore centres that do not have rigid anti-money-laundering-strategies and are therefore attractive for money laundering: 'The major money laundering cases share a common feature; criminal organizations are making wide use of opportunities offered by financial havens and off shore centers to launder assets thereby creating roadblocks to law enforcement organizations.'[66]

This construction of offshore financial centres as money-laundering havens has been criticized by those who argue that these low-tax jurisdictions have taken on an unfair burden when one considers that a considerable amount of money laundering also occurs 'onshore' in high-tax jurisdictions (Mitchell, 2002: 1). The United States, in particular, has been cited as a suitable and frequent site for money laundering. For example, in a March 2001 U.S. Senate sub-committee report, a number of U.S. banks (The Bank of America, Chase Manhattan, Citibank, and The Bank of New York) were linked to money laundering, tax evasion, and fraud (Morris-Cotterill, 2001). That a nation that has led blacklisting efforts also has several of its major financial institutions involved in such illicit activities has led to criticisms that the FATF is a puppet of economically strong nations like the United States.

Based on research by John Walker, the *origins* and the twenty top *destinations* of laundered money are as follows:

Top 20 Flows of Laundered Money

Rank	Origin	Destination	Amount ($/yr)	% of Total
1	United States	United States	528,091	18.5%
2	United States	Cayman Islands	129,755	4.6%
3	Russia	Russia	118,927	4.2%
4	Italy	Italy	94,834	3.3%
5	China	China	94,579	3.3%
6	Romania	Romania	87,845	3.1%
7	United States	Canada	63,087	2.2%
8	United States	Bahamas	61,378	2.2%
9	France	France	57,883	2.0%
10	Italy	Vatican City	55,056	1.9%
11	Germany	Germany	47,202	1.7%
12	United States	Bermuda	46,745	1.6%
13	Spain	Spain	28,819	1.0%
14	Thailand	Thailand	24,953	0.9%
15	Hong Kong	Hong Kong	23,634	0.8%
16	Canada	Canada	21,747	0.8%
17	United Kingdom	United Kingdom	20,897	0.7%
18	United States	Luxembourg	19,514	0.7%
19	Germany	Luxembourg	18,804	0.7%
20	Hong Kong	Taiwan	18,796	0.7%
Total		All Countries	2,850,470	100.0%[67]

It is interesting again to note how much of the laundered money, using these assumptions, flows to already developed countries, particularly the United States and Europe. The potential of money laundering to widen the gap between rich countries and poor countries is another important issue that can be tested using a model of this kind. Related to concerns over blacklisting non-compliant nations, the FATF has been criticized for unduly placing too much attention on 'tax havens,' while turning a blind eye to the conspicuous practices of its members. According to Nigel Morris-Cotterill (2001: 4): 'Unfortunately, the FATF has taken on a hugely political role the last three years, attacking non-members that fail to comply with its demands and constraining the activities of small countries that depend on financial services, not just agriculture and tourism for their livelihoods ... the FATF also has a deplorable tendency to place too little weight on its own members' failings.'

One implication of the characterization of the Caribbean basin as a haven for money laundering is that, in response to treaties and the fear of being blacklisted by the U.S. and organizations like the OECD and FATF, most Caribbean nations have passed legislation to criminalize money laundering and seize criminal assets. As R.T. Naylor (2002: 5) points out: 'The US run FATF blacklists countries that fail to do so (comply with its standards) [are threathening] them with flight of capital that could spell ruin to their economies ... in response, country after country has been coaxed and cajoled to pass US-style laws that criminalize money laundering, allowing governments to find and freeze tainted funds and enable their forfeiture.' For example, Jamaica created the Forfeiture of Proceeds Act in 1994 that allows enforcement officials to apply to the Supreme Court for forfeiture of property from persons convicted of drug-related or money-laundering offences where it can be established that the property was used in conjunction with the offence. These proceeds are then deposited in a consolidated fund. Fears have been expressed that such legislation raises the possibility that these funds may be used as incentives for overzealous law enforcement agencies to lose their focus and emphasize confiscation of assets over due process.[68]

Also, by emphasizing deficiencies in 'offshore' countries, the FATF opens itself up to criticisms that it is acting with the OECD to protect the tax dollars of rich member nations. Margaret Beare writes that the 'international consensus building may be designed to begin to lay the collaborative framework for an international focus on tax evasion. Some critics believe that: "the hidden agenda behind the attack on money laundering is for big countries to make it much harder for their citizens to evade taxes by cutting off those offshore centres that offer low taxes.'''[69]

A related concern is that the campaign by industrialized countries to eliminate money laundering in offshore countries may be viewed as an attempt to capture lost revenues now available to offshore countries in the Caribbean: 'The fear on the part of the onshore countries of loss of revenue as a direct result of offshore activity is not one to be dismissed. The enrichment of offshore coffers at the expense of those onshore provides a powerful economic motive for the legal offensive on the offshore sector' (Antoine, 2001: 7).

Big Brother: U.S. Dominance in Anti-Money-Laundering Efforts

The United States, particularly through FinCEN and its steering of FATF policy, has played a significant role in creating a worldwide network of financial intelligence units (e.g., the Egmont Group) as part of the U.S. strategy on fighting transnational crime.[70] With its role in creating and regulating such multi-lateral agencies, the U.S. has played a significant part in both making claims about the extent of money laundering and initiating the most imperative anti-money-laundering policies. Some, like Michael Woodiwiss (2001: 245–55, 270–71), have argued that the inflated statistics on the magnitude of the money-laundering problem have unnecessarily led to empire building by law enforcement agencies (especially U.S. agencies) through requests for increased power and funding to combat money laundering. R.T. Naylor (2002: 133) has argued that the American FIU, FinCEN, is part of the Americanization of international justice and the drive to compel other nations to adopt U.S. practices. This trend continues despite the lack of evidence of the efficacy of these practices and in the absence of accurate estimates of the extent of money laundering in the U.S. and around the world.

Key among the U.S. demands is that each country assemble its own FIU, preferably one affiliated with the Egmont Group.[71] As noted previously, those countries that resist complying face international blacklisting (with member nations notifying other member nations' financial institutions that to accept financial transactions from non-cooperating countries runs the risk of facilitating the transfer of illicit funds).[72] The United States' pressure tactics on other countries to spend money to track financial transactions (e.g., through the establishment of FIUs) has had some negative international effects beyond the high financial costs of compliance. For example, political instability, including armed rebellion and other violence, in countries are conditions that are seen to be exacerbated by American foreign policy.[73]

National and international politics and power prove to be key components in understanding this war on organized crime rhetoric. The political entwining of money laundering, the war on drugs, and now terrorism has lead to the enthusiastic adoption of money-laundering policies, investigations, and sanctions (Beare, 2002). Given the lack of empirical evidence of negative impact, the question must be asked, Who is driving the international focus on anti-laundering and why? Critics speculate that the term money laundering is being used as a 'selling concept' to advance legislation and policies regarding capital flight and tax evasion. Evidence supporting this perspective may be found in the U.S. State Department's policy documents where a loss of government revenue is one of the enumerated consequences of money laundering (McDowell and Novis, 2001). The significant pressure on the international community, largely generated by the U.S., to get tough on money laundering is summarized by Beare: 'Various black-listing strategies make it essential for countries such as Canada to appease the international community in their various campaigns to harmonize laundering regulations, legislation and policies – a campaign initiated and largely driven by the United States. [Claims of] "Justice" plus financial gain is a powerful combination in state policy-making!' (qtd. in Townsend, 2002: 6).

The Cost of Compliance

Threats of reprisal (e.g., to those nations that do not 'cooperate' with FATF guidelines by not establishing an FIU) have had unintended consequences. For example, many countries are not equipped to establish U.S.-endorsed regulatory mechanisms without the requisite resources or knowledge. This problem is noted by Morris-Cotterill: 'In a rush to avoid criticisms, some governments have created FIU's (financial intelligence units) without any realistic idea of how these agencies deal with the information they receive and without allocating the financial, technological, or human resources necessary to support or launch investigations' (qtd. in Diluca, 2002: 22).

In addition, the cost to the financial services industry of complying with the regulations produced by FinCEN has been reliably estimated to exceed $100 million annually.[74] Specifically, financial institutions must initiate detailed training programs and have rigorous procedures for identifying their customers and for monitoring their accounts, transactions, and procedures. They must also establish and maintain internal auditing of their own departments and personnel. Financial institutions are also encouraged to have free-standing anti-money-laundering units.[75] The most widely circulated estimate of the cost of compliance is $10 billion,[76] a figure always attributed to the American Bankers Association (ABA): the ABA, however, denies ever publishing any such statistic.[77]

With such high costs of compliance, the concern has been expressed that increased banking and business costs associated with compliance, as well as the costs of establishing FIUs, will be passed on to consumers/taxpayers. The Canadian Bankers' Association, in a written submission to the House Committee, noted the following: 'The large and intrusive state apparatus being proposed and the cost to taxpayers for the establishment of the Financial Transactions and Reports Analysis Centre to address a problem that we believe reflects a relatively minor portion of business activity in Canada leads us to conclude that the possible salutary results of Bill C-22 [now the Act] are outweighed by its predictable deleterious effects.'[78]

To understand financial institutions' commitment to the war on money laundering, one must understand these efforts in the context of their main goal of delivering profits to their shareholders. Financial business's interest in making a profit (not acting as social service/law enforcement agencies) often does not sit well with anti-money laundering efforts. The business of financial institutions is the business of making money. There is no intermediary commodity, the production of which can be 'negotiated' to meet labour or environmental sensitivities. While regulators and best practices guidelines and other compliance mechanisms pressure financial institutions to assist with enforcement, the banks see themselves as being in a situation of increasing competition with the one objective being to attract funds. As Beare states:

> The amount of 'dirty' money that moves around through international banks is obviously huge ... However, the rhetoric suggests that turning down 'dirty' money might actually be good for business because of the enhanced reputation of the banks. Having a good reputation is claimed to generate more 'clean' profits. The difficulty is in verifying this claim. The

evidence that does exist tends to favour the opposing view. Banking is highly competitive. There would need to be real evidence of a detrimental impact from dirty money before accepting the claim that there is any redeeming corporate advantage to ethical behaviour aside from the sense of being a 'good corporate citizen' – and of course under a mandatory system, being law abiding. (Beare, 2005: 185)

Thus, there may be little real incentive for financial institutions to crack down on money laundering despite claims about the magnitude and impact of the 'problem.'

In the face of these allegations, reviews of the literature provide little to no evidence to support the claims made by the various agencies hailing money laundering to be a multifaceted danger or that the control efforts are having success. In *Wages of Crime*, Tom Naylor sees little, if any, evidence of the pervasiveness and multi-faceted danger posed by money laundering: 'Stripped to its fundamentals, money laundering consists of a set of acts that are harmless in themselves; indeed, they add up to little more than usual financial practices, even if sometimes undertaken for unusual reasons. Furthermore every rational assessment indicates that the sum of criminal money involved is grossly exaggerated.'[79]

3 Money-Laundering Cases: The RCMP Study

Aside from law enforcement and government rhetoric, what we know about money laundering *empirically* is derived from police cases that are defined by the Royal Canadian Mounted Police (RCMP) to be 'proceeds of crime' cases. While this may speak to some selection bias as to who is targeted for enforcement purposes, the data are the best that we have. Potential 'offenders' who are not detected or are not treated as such continue to operate without benefit of the analysis of researchers. Commenting on a researcher's dependence on police data to study organized crime, Pierre Tremblay and Richard Kedzier opined, 'What documentary sources are pertinent for the analysis of the organization of crime? It is generally agreed that police statistics, while now standardized and fairly reliable, tell us more about the organizational qualities of the police than about crime as such.'[1]

Police investigations cannot always identify the full range of laundering vehicles and techniques used by offenders. This is especially true of more sophisticated money-laundering operations and those that successfully transfer the proceeds of crime and related assets offshore. Due to the intrinsically secretive nature of money laundering (which can be pursued with a high degree of sophistication and stealth), there is no guarantee that the proceeds of crime (POC) investigation – let alone this study – was able to identify all of the assets and laundering vehicles associated with a particular criminal conspiracy.[2]

The goal of this chapter is to examine how the proceeds from profit-oriented (organized) criminal activities are disbursed through the legitimate and underground economy in Canada. Particular emphasis has been placed on discerning the processes and techniques used to launder the proceeds of crime through legitimate financial and commercial sectors. Specifically, this chapter identifies, examines, and quantifies:

• the types of illegal activity that generate criminal revenue invested into the legitimate economy
• how illicit funds enter the legitimate economy
• the sectors of the economy into which criminal proceeds are placed
• specific assets or services purchased with the criminal proceeds in each sector
• transactions and processes used in each sector for money-laundering purposes
• specific guises and/or techniques employed to facilitate the money-laundering process, and
• the linkages between different economic sectors, transactions, and techniques that are forged through money-laundering operations

Methodology

The findings and analysis summarized in this chapter have been taken from a national study into money laundering in Canada that was conducted between 2000 and 2003 (Schneider, 2004). For the purpose of this text, these primary data are complemented with the results of a similar study published in 1990 (Beare and Schneider, 1990) as well as secondary information extracted from government reports, the media, and other literature.

The source of much of this data is RCMP proceeds of crime case files. Beginning in 1999, research was undertaken based on a random sample of cases, which was drawn from the RCMP Management Information System (MIS), a database of cases investigated by the RCMP. The population of POC cases was refined through the application of criteria intended to maximize the relevance and quality of the cases included in the final sample. The most important criterion for the inclusion of a case in the sampling frame was that the legal definition of 'possession of the proceeds of crime' or 'money laundering'[3] must have been satisfied. To this end, the two initial criteria for the inclusion of cases in the sampling frame were as follows: the file was *successfully* closed between 1993 and 1998[4] (i.e., the file was closed by the RCMP following the forfeiture of assets resulting from either a conviction or plea bargain), and at least one proceeds of crime seizure or restraint had been made, or at least one possession of proceeds of crime or money-laundering charge had been laid.

Based upon the application of these criteria, the MIS database produced a total of 371 proceeds of crime cases. An additional set of criteria reduced this number to 149 cases. The additional criteria – which were used to ensure that all qualifying cases contained sufficient information on how the proceeds of crime were disbursed by offenders – were threefold. First, the monetary value of the property that was the target of the seizure or restraint had to be above $10,000. Second, the case could not simply involve a cash seizure. In other words, if a file was initiated by the seizure of cash by police, to qualify for inclusion in the sample a proceeds of crime investigation must have subsequently been undertaken (POC files initiated by cash seizures, but where no subsequent investigation took place, generally have insufficient information on how the proceeds of crime are laundered). Third, the case had to have involved more than forty person-hours of investigative time. The application of this additional criteria resulted in a final sample of 149 cases.

Using a standardized coded questionnaire, data from the eligible 149 cases were initially collected by members of the Proceeds of Crime Sections who were part of the Expert Witness Program.[5] In addition, Stephen Schneider conducted site visits among most of the POC Sections and IPOC (Integrated Proceeds of Crime) Units to collect original data and to check the accuracy and completeness of the questionnaires filled out by police members. The objective was to identify as much information as possible on the predicate criminal conspiracy, how the criminal proceeds were disbursed by offenders, and to detect for analysis any money-laundering techniques used during the process of hiding or disposing of the illicit proceeds.

This data generally came from documents prepared to obtain judicial authorization to execute certain police powers, such as an 'Information to Obtain a Search Warrant,' an 'Application for a Part VI Authorization' (electronic surveillance), or a 'Restraint Order.' In order to obtain these powers from a judge or justice of the peace, police in Canada must include on an affidavit an extensive amount of detailed information on the accused and the alleged criminal conspiracy. In the context of a proceeds of crime investigation, these documents provided invaluable data for an in-depth analysis of money laundering. Other police documents that proved useful for this study included court transcripts, investigative progress reports, court briefs, intelligence reports, and 'statements of facts.' Documents obtained by police during an investigation and contained in the case files (such as banking statements, real estate contracts, and correspondence), also proved to be useful sources of primary data. Personal interviews were also conducted with police investigators and prosecutors to corroborate or elaborate on information contained in these documents or to provide any information that may have been absent from the case file.

Based on a pilot-test survey, the questionnaire was revised and then sent to all police members assigned to collect data. The police members were instructed to return the completed questionnaires to the Proceeds of Crime Branch at RCMP headquarters where they were reviewed by designated personnel to ensure that sensitive information was not disclosed. All completed questionnaires and accompanying documentation were then reviewed for accuracy, completeness, and to ensure the case satisfied the aforementioned criteria for inclusion in the study. Field research was then carried out at most of the POC Sections and IPOC Units to corroborate the data that was collected and/or to collect any outstanding information. As one would expect, some jurisdictions responded with more complete information and more enthusiasm to participate than others. Overall, the support across the country was extremely good.

Distribution of Cases Across the Country

This study was national in scope in that the final sample included proceeds of crime cases drawn from every province (except Prince Edward Island), from all of the major Proceeds of Crime Sections, and from each of the Integrated Proceeds of Crime Units within each province. In general, the sample of cases included in this study is representative of the distribution of POC cases investigated on an annual basis across the country. The one exception is Quebec, where the number of cases included in this survey is disproportionately under-represented. Figure 3.1 shows how the proceeds of crime cases included in the study are distributed across the country.

Offences Generating the Proceeds of Crime

While there are a number of illegal activities that produce substantial revenues, according to this survey, drug trafficking represents the

Figure 3.1: Distribution of survey cases across Canada

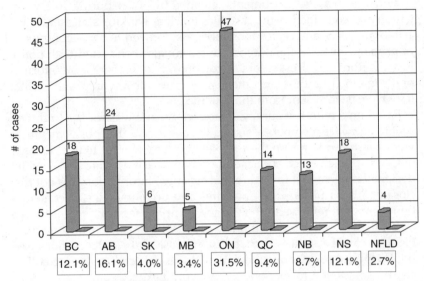

Proportion of cases from each province included in the survey

single largest source of the proceeds of crime. This finding is both a reflection of the prominence that drug trafficking has assumed in the repertoire of most criminal groups, as well as the priority that the RCMP Proceeds of Crime Program has placed on anti-drug profiteering enforcement. Of the 149 POC cases, 111 (74.5 per cent) involved a designated drug offence as the predicate criminal activity. Of these 111 cases, 60 (54 per cent) involved cannabis, 59 (45 per cent) involved cocaine, 9 (8.1 per cent) involved heroin, and 4 (3.6 per cent) involved synthetic drugs. The second most common predicate offence was committed against the Customs Act and/or the Excise Act, which primarily consisted of the highly profitable trade in contraband tobacco and liquor products. The survey included 23 cases (15.4 per cent) where the substantive offence was committed against either of these acts. Of these 23 cases, 20 involved cigarettes and 16 involved liquor. Offences involving theft or fraud accounted for 11 cases (7.4 per cent of all predicate offences).[6]

Figure 3.2: Guises and techniques used to facilitate money laundering

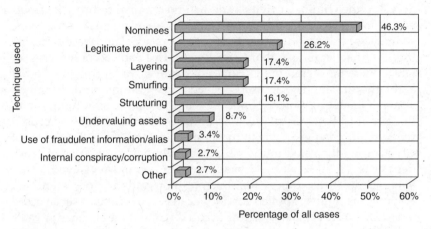

Techniques Used to Facilitate Money Laundering

In many of the police cases, a number of guises and techniques were used to facilitate the laundering process. In particular, attempts were made to hide the true source and ownership of illegally-acquired cash and other assets (e.g., through the use of nominees and layering), to avoid suspicions that may stem from transacting in large amounts of cash (e.g., by using smurfs and 'structuring' transactions), or to create the perception that the funds were derived from a legitimate source (e.g., by claiming the criminal proceeds as revenue from a legal business). As indicated in figure 3.2, the most prevalent money laundering techniques used were nominees, smurfing, layering, structuring, and claiming that the criminal proceeds were generated from legitimate sources.

Nominees

The most common technique used to help expedite the laundering process was the use of nominees. Of the 149 cases, 69 (46.3 per cent) involved some attempt by the accused to obscure a direct connection between themselves and assets they owned, primarily by registering legal title to the asset in the name of another individual, usually a

relative, a friend, or a lawyer. In most cases, the nominee was uncon-
nected to the criminal activities and had no criminal record. The assets
most often placed in the name of nominees were real estate, cars,
companies, and banks accounts. In one case, a Calgary-based cocaine
trafficker had signing authority for twenty-five bank accounts, most of
which were registered in the names of relatives, favouring his mother
and father-in-law. The accused opened bank accounts in their names,
while maintaining power of attorney and sole signing authority over
the accounts. Between 10 July 1995 and 8 September 1996, the accused
wrote eight cheques payable to his mother totalling $182,050, all of
which were deposited into bank accounts in her name. A single cash
deposit of $162,182 was also made into an account registered in her
name. Despite deposits of hundreds of thousands of dollars into her
account, his mother applied for and received government social assistance. On 20 November 1996, the accused wrote three cheques payable
to his father-in-law worth $68,500, all of which were deposited into the
latter's personal bank account. In a one-year period, the accused deposited almost $1.4 million into a bank account registered in the name of
his father-in-law. The accused also wrote several cheques to nominees
from accounts registered in the names of other nominees. For example,
a cheque for $53,000 payable to the brother-in-law of the accused was
drawn on an account registered in the name of the mother of the
accused.

Disguising the Proceeds of Crime as Legitimate Revenue

The second most common laundering technique is to claim the proceeds of crime as legitimate revenue from a legal business, which attempts to satisfy the third objective of the laundering process: creating
the perception that the criminal proceeds were derived from a lawful
source. Once this 'legitimate' source of revenue has been established,
criminal proceeds can be deposited into bank accounts under the guise
of this business. In some cases, the proceeds of crime will be commingled with revenues generated from legal businesses and deposited
into bank accounts.

   To avoid suspicion associated with depositing large amounts of cash
in small denominations, the type of company used as a guise should
typically generate a high volume of cash in small denominations, such
as grocery stores, restaurants, nightclubs, movie theatres, or video arcades. In one RCMP file, a Saskatchewan-based cocaine trafficker named

Tom Luey operated two businesses, Florida Imports and Moose Lumber, both of which were based in Saskatoon. Florida Imports was a sole proprietorship that imported high-end used vehicles for resale in Canada. Most of the vehicles that were imported were supplied by a wholesaler in Miami, who was also Luey's cocaine supplier. When a shipment of cocaine was purchased, a car was also provided and both were transported to Canada. Luey used the business to rationalize his need for American cash (stating to banks that American wholesalers wouldn't accept cheques drawn on Canadian banks) and to legitimize the cash deposits being made into the company's bank account (which he stated were the proceeds from the private sale of the vehicles in Canada). By the end of the police investigation, Luey was in the process of obtaining commercial lines of credit at a local bank, which would have allowed him to transfer funds into a U.S. line of credit account, and then wire the money south to his 'lumber supplier' in the United States.

Layering

Within the context of money laundering, layering involves separating the illicit proceeds from their source and obstructing any audit trail by creating several 'layers' of financial and commercial transactions and/ or assets. Layering is accomplished by either conducting multiple transactions with the illicit funds or by setting up complex hierarchies of assets in order to put as much distance between the laundered assets and their original source of funding and beneficial ownership. In many respects, the layering stage is the backbone of the money-laundering process. For example, tobacco smugglers in British Columbia deposited $112,000 in an account at a Vancouver branch of a major Canadian bank. A GIC was purchased with the funds, which in turn was cashed to help finance the purchase of a home. The real estate was then sold and a solicitor's cheque was issued for the proceeds. This cheque was cashed at another bank for large denominations of cash as well as bank drafts. The bank drafts were then cashed at yet another bank and the large denominations of cash received were smuggled out of Canada to Hong Kong.

Smurfs

A money-laundering technique closely associated with the use of nominees is 'smurfing,' which involves spreading cash deposits across dif-

ferent accounts (and, in some cases, different branches or deposit institutions) by using a number of money couriers (who may also pose as
nominee account holders). In the context of money laundering, the term
'smurf' was derived from the blue cartoon characters, all of whom are
innocuous in appearance (a characteristic of nominees that is highly
valued by money launderers). Used primarily during the placement
stage of the laundering process to circumvent mandatory reporting
requirements and avoid suspicion associated with large amounts of
cash, each smurf is instructed to deposit less than $10,000 at a time.
Larger criminal organizations may utilize a number of smurfs as part of
an elaborate money-laundering effort. The objective of this laundering
technique is to avoid transactions involving large amounts of cash by
spreading the funds among a sizeable number of individuals, financial
institutions, and accounts. In one case, a cocaine wholesaler in Ontario
used a number of friends and relatives, including some as young as
sixteen, to make cash deposits into bank accounts. At least fourteen
accounts, spread across seven banks were registered in the names of
these nominees, who were instructed to make several deposits each
week. Police were able to connect all of these accounts to the drug
trafficker.

Structuring

Structuring refers to a process whereby large cash deposits and other
transactions are broken down into smaller amounts to avoid suspicion
associated with large amounts of cash. Structuring is most commonly
practised at banks and similar financial service providers and is an
integral part of smurfing. The need for structuring as part of the money-
laundering process will be heightened in Canada as new legislation
requires the financial services sector to record and report all cash transactions over $10,000. In one case, a drug trafficker conducted more than
140 cash deposits at a bank in Richmond, BC, over the course of a single
month. The vast majority of these cash deposits were between $3,000
and $5,000. The highest amount was $8,000. In one ten-day stretch,
eighty-six cash deposits were made into the bank account. On one day
alone, fifteen deposits were made to this account through various
branches and automated teller machines.

Undervaluing Assets

Undervaluing assets is a laundering technique whereby a property
seller agrees to a purchase price below the actual value and then ac-

cepts the difference under the table. This laundering technique is most often used in relation to real property and requires the collusion of the seller, including the completion of the legal land-title transfer documents that list the price of the real estate as less than for what it was actually sold. This technique allows the money launderer to conceal the actual amount that was spent (the less money that official records show a criminal entrepreneur has spent, the easier it is to hide illegally derived and non-reported revenue). By using this technique, the launderer can claim that he/she purchased an asset for a price that falls within his/her legitimate financial means. This transaction also allows the criminal entrepreneur to dispose of cash, which is provided under the table to the seller. In one case, a drug trafficker in Fredericton, New Brunswick, purchased a home as a dwelling for himself and his wife. Rental properties and vacant land for future development were also purchased at prices under their fair market value. He then paid cash under the table for the difference. Mortgages were obtained and then quickly repaid with the proceeds of crime.

Internal Conspiracies

One of the most effective ways to satisfy the laundering process is either to engage the cooperation of corrupt professionals or for a criminal enterprise to place operatives within financial institutions. By doing either of these, an offender can bypass scrutiny, falsify documents, and avoid mandatory transaction reporting requirements. Internal conspiracies and corruption were identified in four cases. In one case, Marcus Browning, a multi-kilo importer of cocaine, conspired with a number of professionals, including bank staff, mortgage brokers, and insurance agents, to help launder the proceeds of his drug trafficking. A mortgage broker named Penelope Avente was particularly active in facilitating the laundering process. Through police surveillance, it became clear that she was well aware of the source of the funds. Intercepted telephone communications revealed that Browning made two separate $25,000 cash deposits into a bank account in Toronto. Avente obtained the services of Claudio Villa, who in turn recruited an accomplice working at the branch to deposit the funds into the account of a shell company. Police learned that Avente paid bank branch employees to accept large cash deposits on behalf of Browning without filing transaction reporting forms. The funds were then moved through another bank with the help of two other insiders, Ian Browning and Natasha Hamilton (Mark's brother and his girlfriend).

Figure 3.3: Economic sectors and other assets used for money laundering

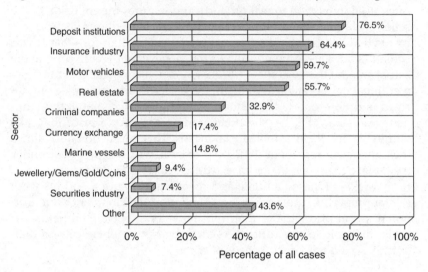

Sectors of the Economy Used: An Overview

The survey findings indicate that criminal proceeds find their way into a number of different economic sectors in Canada. Figure 3.3 identifies these sectors and the frequency with which each was the recipient of criminal proceeds. Deposit institutions, the insurance industry, motor vehicles, and real estate are the four most frequent destinations for the proceeds of crime. Deposit institutions are the single largest recipient, having been identified in 114 of the 149 POC cases (76.5 per cent). While the insurance sector was implicated in almost 65 per cent of all cases, in the vast majority, the offender did not explicitly seek out the insurance sector as a laundering vehicle. Instead, because motor vehicles, homes, companies, and marine vessels were purchased with the proceeds of crime, it was often necessary to purchase insurance for these assets. In a smaller number of cases, the insurance sector was used as a financial service provider to launder the proceeds of crime. In these cases, mortgages, investment certificates, life insurance policies, and mutual funds were purchased from an insurance company or broker. Motor vehicles were purchased or financed with the proceeds of crime in 89 cases (59.7 per cent). Real estate transactions were identified in 83 cases (55.7 per cent). In 49 cases (32.9 per cent), companies were established or purchased by an offender to facilitate the laundering process. Currency exchange companies and cheque cashing businesses were implicated in 26 of the cases (17.4 per cent),[7] and the purchase or sale of securities was implicated in 11 cases (7.4 per cent). Other assets purchased with the proceeds of crime were marine vessels (22 cases), jewellery, precious gems, or gold (13 cases), rare coins (1 case), art work (3 cases), and livestock, including race horses (6 cases). Legalized gambling, in particular in casinos and lotteries, were used to launder funds in 5 cases.

The police cases show that the proceeds of crime were expended in the legitimate economy, not only for personal consumption and laundering purposes but also to purchase equipment necessary for the continuation of predicate criminal conspiracies. Among the purchases made with criminal proceeds were marijuana cultivation equipment, weigh scales, slot machines, generators, mobile phones and pagers, boats, tractor trailers, and computers.

In 130 of the 149 cases (87.3 per cent), it was the individual(s) accused of the substantive offence(s) who originally placed the cash proceeds of crime into the legitimate economy. However, other individuals or entities – nominees – were involved in placing the proceeds into the legitimate economy in 53 cases (35.6 per cent). The route into the legitimate economy involved a company (10.1 per cent), a lawyer (10.1 per cent), or another professional (4.0 per cent). In 122 of the 149 cases (81.9 per cent), the currency of the cash criminal proceeds originally placed in the legitimate economy was Canadian, while American currency was initially used in 29 cases (19.5 per cent). Other currency generated from criminal activity placed in the Canadian economy was the Belgian franc and the British pound.

Deposit Institutions

Deposit institutions[8] are used more frequently to launder the proceeds of crime than any other single sector of the Canadian economy. By their very nature, banks and similar deposit institutions are effective at satisfying the inherent objectives of the laundering process. First, they can be used to convert the cash proceeds of crime into less suspicious assets, both tangible (e.g., a cheque, bank draft, money order) and intangible (e.g., bank accounts, term deposits, GICs, RRSPs). Second, these instruments can be used to access other laundering vehicles such as wire transfers, real estate, and motor vehicles. Third, money-laundering techniques intended to conceal the criminal origins of illicit funds can be used in tandem with banking services (e.g., registering accounts in the names of nominees). Deposit institutions can also be used as part of a laundering scheme that creates the perception that illicit funds are derived from legitimate purposes, primarily by establishing commercial accounts registered in the name of shell companies and then depositing the proceeds of crime under the guise of legitimate business revenue.

Deposit institutions are not only the ultimate destination of dirty money, but they frequently serve as an integral link in a money-laundering chain. In fact, deposit institutions often represent the essential first step in accessing other laundering vehicles. Typically, the cash proceeds of crime are deposited into bank accounts and electronic funds are used to purchase a bank draft or to access other banking services or financial instruments (e.g., wire transfer, mortgage), which are then used to access other economic sectors or even other countries. The conversion role played by deposit institutions in the money-laundering process helps criminal entrepreneurs avoid suspicion that may be aroused if expensive assets, such as cars or real property, are purchased with large amounts of cash.

Types of Deposit Institutions Used

While all types of deposit institutions are susceptible to money laundering, police cases indicate that chartered banks, and particularly Canadian-incorporated banks, were used in more cases than all other types of deposit institutions combined. As figure 3.4 shows, of the 114 cases that involved deposit institutions, 100 (87.7 per cent) included at least one transaction conducted at a Schedule 1 chartered bank – Canada's 'Big Five' banks. Credit unions and caisse populaires were implicated in 32 cases (28.9 per cent), with trust companies and foreign-incorporated chartered banks being used in 17 and 9 cases, respectively. Provincial government savings institutions were implicated in 2 cases. There are several reasons that account for the preponderance of banks as a laundering conduit. Chartered banks in Canada – in particular the 'big banks' – dominate the financial services industry in this country and thus, criminal entrepreneurs, like legitimate customers, tend to gravitate to these institutions. As of 2006, there were twenty-one Schedule 1 banks in Canada. Chartered banks offer an unparalleled range of services that are conducive to money laundering and have an international reputation

Figure 3.4: Types of deposit institutions implicated in POC cases

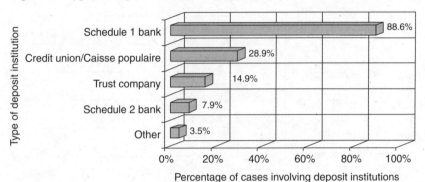

for efficiency, fast clearing systems, and customer confidentiality. The extensive international network of Canadian bank branches facilitates the international transfer of funds, especially to the so-called safe-haven countries of the Caribbean basin, where Canadian financial institutions are dominant.

Our original money-laundering study conducted in 1990 speculated that as internal anti-money-laundering controls tighten at the major chartered banks, there might be a tendency for the criminal proceeds to gravitate to smaller institutions with fewer security measures. A comparison of the latest research findings with the results of the 1990 study, however, suggests that the anticipated exodus of illicit funds from chartered banks to other deposit institutions has not materialized. Schedule 1 chartered banks continue to be the preferred choice of criminal entrepreneurs over all other types of deposit institutions.

Form in Which the Proceeds of Crime Entered the Deposit Institution

As figure 3.5 shows, cash was the principal form by which the proceeds of crime entered deposit institutions: in 94 of the 114 cases (82.5 per cent) involving deposit institutions, the proceeds of crime were introduced as cash. Combined with the frequency with which they are used to launder the proceeds of crime, this statistic indicates that Schedule 1 chartered banks continue to constitute the most significant entry point for the proceeds of crime into the legitimate economy.

Figure 3.5: Form in which the proceeds of crime entered the deposit institution

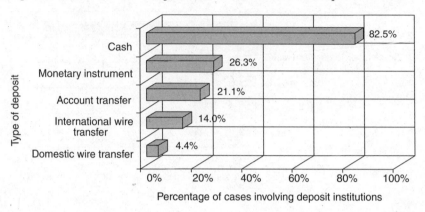

Percentage of cases involving deposit institutions

Banking Services Used

There is a wide range of banking services used to launder money (see fig. 3.6). The most frequently used service is a regular savings or chequing account – 91 of the 114 cases used a savings or chequing account, or a term deposit (79.8 per cent). Monetary instruments were a distant second, with 47 cases (41.2 per cent) using a monetary instrument, in particular, a bank draft. In many other cases, a number of different services were used, often as part of the layering process to distance the illicit proceeds from their criminal source. Once cash is deposited into an account, a number of transactions or services can then be used, such as purchasing monetary instruments, making account transfers or wire transfers, opening safety deposit boxes, and buying mortgages.

Savings/Chequing Accounts

Simply depositing the cash proceeds of crime into a bank account is frequently the first step in the money-laundering process and is used to access other laundering vehicles within the deposit institution or other sectors. Using bank accounts relieves the criminal entrepreneur of cumbersome amounts of cash while allowing the funds to be spent, invested, or transferred without attracting suspicions that may be associated with large volumes of cash. As such, a savings or chequing account presents the most common portal through which illegally de-

Figure 3.6: Banking products and services purchased/used with criminal revenues

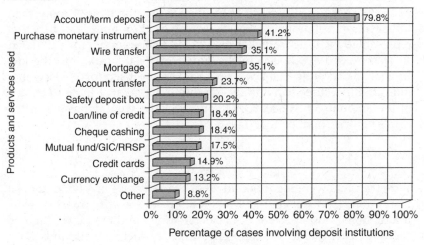

rived cash enters a deposit institution and, by extension, the legitimate economy. In one case that was examined, a cocaine trafficker in Ontario had signing authority for thirty-two bank accounts, including at least eleven foreign accounts and twelve commercial bank accounts in Canada. All thirty-two accounts were active, with large numbers of cash deposits, withdrawals, account transfers, and wire transfers taking place. From 1994 to 1997 the accused deposited more than $2 million into his Canadian bank accounts.

Monetary Instruments

Once the cash proceeds of crime are deposited into a bank account, the funds are frequently withdrawn in the form of a monetary instrument – usually a bank draft – which satisfies a primary money-laundering objective: converting cumbersome amounts of cash into less suspicious assets. In 47 of the 114 cases involving deposit institutions, bank drafts, money orders, certified cheques, and traveller's cheques were purchased either directly with cash or with funds drawn from an account containing the proceeds of crime. The greatest advantage of a negotiable instrument as a laundering tool is that it represents a more convenient and inconspicuous means to move large amounts of funds or to purchase a big-ticket asset like a car or real estate. A typical case in-volved a drug trafficker in Manitoba who bought four bank drafts with cash, which he then used to help finance the purchase of more than forty acres of real property. A police search of a Winnipeg law office that represented the drug trafficker discovered a series of receipts, all dated 13 December 1993, issued to the trafficker for deposits into the law firm's bank account. The law firm's bank deposit slip for 13 December indicated that three bank drafts – each purchased at a different bank – in the amounts of $4,600, $3,800, and $4,400 – were deposited in the firm's bank account on that day.

Wire Transfers

Wire transfers were identified in 40 of the 114 cases involving deposit institutions (35.1 per cent). Of this total, 22 of the wire transfers were international and 18 were domestic. Wiring funds is tantamount to sending cash instantly to a different branch, a different bank, and even a different country. Indeed, one of the advantages of a wire transfer for money-laundering purposes is that it is the most efficient way to spirit money out of a country. In one case, the operator of a prostitution house in Paris deposited cash into a local bank account. The funds were then wire transferred to an account established at a credit union in Montreal. In total, $750,000 was deposited to the latter account through several wire transfers conducted over a period of months. The funds were eventually withdrawn to purchase and renovate a $275,000 cottage in Quebec.

Account Transfers

In twenty-seven of the cases involving deposit institutions, funds were transferred between accounts. In the context of a money-laundering operation, transferring funds between different bank accounts is often used as part of the layering process to hide the criminal source and ownership of the funds and to obscure the audit trail. In one case, thirteen individuals involved in a BC-based interprovincial drug traf-ficking network (most of whom were family members related by blood or marriage) made numerous account transfers to one another between various banks, credit unions, and currency exchange companies. These transactions took place primarily among accounts in BC, but accounts in other provinces were involved as well. In addition, the thirteen individuals made deposits into accounts registered in the names of one another. According to the RCMP, the primary purpose of the account transfers was to distribute profits and to pay for drug supplies and other expenses.

Safety Deposit Boxes

Safety deposit boxes were used in twenty-three cases, primarily to store cash, precious gems, jewellery, or coins purchased with criminal revenue. In addition to providing a secure place to store valuables, for the purposes of money laundering, a safety deposit box leaves a minimal paper trail, at least as far as the contents of the box are concerned. However, police cases show that individuals using safety deposit boxes to store the proceeds of crime are often conspicuous by their frequent requests to access the contents. In one case, police surveillance of a cocaine trafficker established that the majority of his cash proceeds were placed in safety deposit boxes at one trust company and two chartered banks. The safety deposit boxes were in his name as well as the name of an associate. The trafficker would frequently add and remove the cash – which was a mixture of American and Canadian currency – based on his cocaine sales and purchases. At one point, the total amount of Canadian cash held in two safety deposit boxes at the branch of the trust company was $385,595. A search of safety deposit boxes rented by the drug trafficker also turned up a large amount of jewellery, including gold and diamond-encrusted watches, gold chains, gold and diamond bracelets, gold and diamond-studded earrings, and gold rings (as well as a gold-plated license-plate holder that read 'crime pays').

The Real Estate Market

Real estate has many attributes that make it an attractive destination for criminal proceeds. It provides a home in which the offender can live and work (homes and rural properties are often used for the cultivation of marijuana and the manufacture of synthetic drugs). As a money-laundering vehicle, a host of mechanisms commonly used with real estate transactions can frustrate efforts to unearth the criminal source of funds, such as nominees, fake mortgages, real estate lawyers, and legal trust accounts. The criminal proceeds can be funnelled to the real estate market through a number of legitimate transactions such as deposits, down payments, mortgages, as well as construction and renovations

Figure 3.7: Types of real estate purchased with criminal proceeds

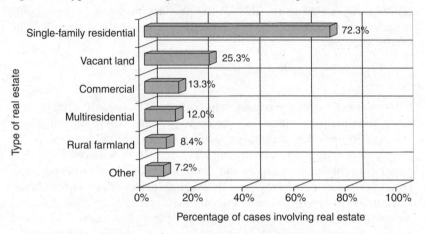

Percentage of cases involving real estate

expenses. Real estate investments can also be used to create the perception of a legitimate revenue stream; rental property can be purchased which allows the criminal entrepreneur to deposit the proceeds of crime into bank accounts under the guise of rental income.

Types of Real Estate Purchased

Police cases show that the type of real estate most frequently purchased with the proceeds of crime is single-family residential property. As figure 3.7 shows, of the eighty-three cases where criminal revenue was invested in the real estate market, sixty (72.3 per cent) involved the purchase of one or more single-family residential properties. In the vast majority of these cases, the accused purchased a home in which to live. In numerous cases, homes and rural properties were also purchased explicitly for use as sites for marijuana grow operations, which have recently emerged as a billion-dollar industry in Canada. In a Canada-wide series of police raids targeting marijuana grow operations that took place in January and April of 2002, 417 people were arrested on 877 drug charges, and police seized 116,329 marijuana plants worth approximately CDN$116.2 million. The vast majority of the sites used for the grow operations were rental residences (Criminal Intelligence Service Canada, 2002: 3–4). Marijuana grow operations have become so lucrative that new homes are being customized for the sole purpose of housing marijuana operations, according to RCMP officials in Surrey, British Columbia. The custom homes are bare of carpeting or standard appliances to allow more growing room and are equipped with power-ful air conditioning units to deal with the high temperatures caused by heat lamps, extensive venting systems to dissipate telltale odours, and high-capacity electrical outlets. In one Surrey home raided by police, an underground bunker had been built to house an extensive marijuana grow operation.[9]

Forms in Which the Proceeds of Crime Entered the Real Estate Market

According to the police cases, the proceeds of crime entered the real estate market in a limited number of forms. In 65 of the 83 cases involving real estate (78.3 per cent), a mortgage was obtained, (the payments of which were often made with criminal proceeds). In 64 cases (77.1 per cent), cash was used as a deposit, a down payment, or a mortgage payment. In a small number of cases, cash was exclusively used to finance the purchase of real property. In some police cases, the amount of personal funds used as financing was unusually large, espe-cially when compared with typical real estate purchases where per-sonal financing typically does not exceed 25 per cent of the total purchase price. Monetary instruments, in particular cheques and bank drafts, were used as part of a real estate purchase in twenty-eight cases (33.7 per cent). In one typical case, a marijuana grow operator purchased a number of properties throughout Ontario, financing his acquisitions with cash and through mortgages. One rural property was purchased through a single cash payment of $325,000 and a mortgage of $215,000. Six years later, the accused purchased another property worth $450,000, which was paid in full with cash.

While large amounts of cash have been used to purchase real estate, a more common approach is for an offender to use bank drafts, which are often purchased directly with the cash proceeds of crime or from a bank account into which illicit cash has previously been deposited. In order to avoid large cash reporting requirements at banking institutions, a number of bank drafts, each with a value less than $10,000, will be purchased. Unfortunately for the drug traffickers, because the average cost of residential real estate runs into the hundreds of thousands of dollars, they are often forced to turn over multiple bank drafts to their lawyers or real estate agents. In some cases, the use of multiple bank drafts to finance real estate reaches ridiculous proportions. For ex-

Figure 3.8: Techniques used to launder money through real estate

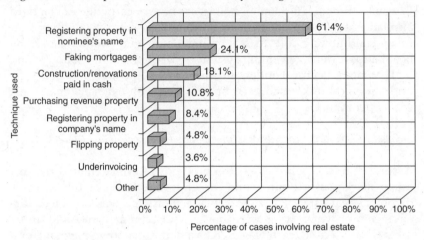

Percentage of cases involving real estate

ample, between February and September 1998, more than 130 trans-actions were conducted through a trust account of a law firm that represented a drug trafficker named Carl Singer in the purchase of a $600,000 Vancouver home. Between 19 and 27 February, seventy-eight bank drafts, purchased from eight different banks or credit unions, were deposited on behalf of Singer in the law firm's trust account. On 19 January alone, seventeen different bank drafts were deposited into the account. The amounts of the bank drafts were between $3,000 and $5,000 in value, with the highest amount being $9,000.

Techniques Used to Launder Money through Real Estate

Laundering money through real estate ranges from the simple to the sophisticated. At one end of the scale, the accused simply buys a home and registers the property in his/her name. At the other end of the spectrum are the more intricate approaches, which include various techniques used expressly to satisfy the objectives of the laundering process. These techniques, and their frequency of use in proceeds of crime cases involving real estate, are summarized in figure 3.8.

REGISTERING PROPERTY IN NOMINEE'S NAME
The most prevalent technique used to facilitate the laundering process in the real estate market is to register property and/or mortgages in the

name of a nominee in order to obscure the criminal ownership and source of financing for the property. In 51 of the 83 cases involving real estate (61.4 per cent), real property and mortgages were often registered in the names of relatives, friends, business associates, lawyers, and shell or legitimate companies. In one case, a British Columbia drug trafficker told a police informant that he owned twenty-five homes throughout the province that were used for marijuana grow operations. The houses, almost all of which were mortgaged, were rented out to individuals who were hired to oversee the grow operations in return for a percentage of the profits. Four of these properties were registered in the name of the sister of the drug trafficker, while seven were registered to companies of which he was listed as a director. Police could not find one property in British Columbia that was directly registered in the name of the trafficker.

FAKING MORTGAGES

While many criminal entrepreneurs certainly have no shortage of cash to invest in real property, police cases indicate that mortgages are nonetheless obtained, either to avoid suspicion associated with large personal financing or because the purchaser genuinely requires a mortgage. There is also some evidence that offenders seek out a mortgage to limit their equity in a home, which in turn minimizes their personal financial loss if the property is forfeited to the Crown. In some cases, the mortgage (as well as title to the property) was registered in the name of a nominee. In other cases, a criminal entrepreneur personally financed a mortgage for a property that he controlled, but which was registered in the name of a nominee. This laundering technique provides the bogus owner with a seemingly legitimate source of funds to purchase the home, while hiding the true criminal ownership of the property. Alternatively, mortgage financing was provided by a nominee, such as a family member or a business associate, for property registered to an accused (in these cases, the mortgages were a fake and the funds were ultimately traced to the accused). Police cases show that mortgages are also financed by criminally controlled companies incorporated in Canada or offshore. In total, the survey included twenty cases that involved fake mortgages.

A Canadian proceeds of crime investigation into Frederick Tatum, a convicted New York City cocaine trafficker and ex-professional boxer, found that a sizeable portion of his cash revenue was physically transferred to Canada where it was used to finance the purchase of more than forty properties in the Greater Toronto Area over a nine-year period. The total cost of the properties was $1,385,969 spent over the course of six real estate transactions and, of this total, $950,693 was allegedly financed by various family members. In addition to personal equity financing, family members or their companies would be listed as the source of mortgage financing for homes registered in the names of Frederick Tatum's parents or siblings. For example, on 12 November 1995, title to one home was transferred to Moe Tatum (Frederick's father) for $129,500 and, on the same day, a mortgage was registered against the home. The source of the mortgage financing was Rachel Tatum, Frederick's mother. On 30 November 1995, title to another property was transferred to Lucy Browne (Frederick's sister) for $186,500. Four mortgages were registered against this property in July 1998, March 1999, May 2000, and September 2001. The last mortgage was registered for $187,000 in the favour of Tom Donnoly Investments Ltd., a company whose president was Susan Hograth, Frederick's sister. On 9 September 1995, another home was purchased in the name of Rachel Tatum for $185,000. On 22 October 1995, a mortgage was registered against this property for $65,000. The source of this financing was Moe Tatum. Police were able to prove that all of the above mortgage and personal equity financing were funded through revenues generated by Frederick Tatum's drug trafficking activities. Most of the homes were forfeited to the Canadian government as the proceeds of crime.

PURCHASING REVENUE PROPERTY

Another technique used is to purchase income-generating property and then commingle the legitimate rental income with criminal revenue, which is deposited together into a bank account. This technique is used primarily to provide a seemingly legitimate source of revenue for a criminal entrepreneur. In one case, a cigarette and liquor smuggler in eastern Ontario would deposit his cash revenue into a local bank account. Over a five-year period, the funds were used to purchase four apartment buildings, financed in part through mortgages secured from the same bank. The revenue from the rental properties was combined with the profits from the sale of contraband and deposited into various personal and commercial bank accounts.

FLIPPING PROPERTY

In some cases, the accused or a nominee will purchase real estate with criminal revenue and then quickly sell it, claiming a legitimate source of revenue. In a few of these cases, the sale was, in fact, bogus since the property was sold to nominees. This technique allows the offender to claim legitimate revenue while maintaining ultimate control over the property. Another money-laundering technique used in conjunction with flipping property is to pay for the construction/renovation of a home with the proceeds of crime. The property is then sold at an increased value. The added benefit of this technique is that it takes advantage of the sizeable underground, cash-based home-renovation industry. Cash is paid under the table to contractors, thereby benefiting both parties: the criminal entrepreneur profits because he has acquired an asset, while relieving himself of cumbersome cash, while the contractor has received undeclared and untaxed income. In one case, a convicted drug trafficker purchased hundreds of acres of farmland in Ontario with a one-time cash payment of $305,000 and a mortgage for $200,000. Fifteen months later, the trafficker sold the property for $600,000. Police surmised that a substantial amount of interior renovations were made to the 3,500-square-foot home. Based on a net worth analysis conducted on the accused, police determined that revenue from cocaine sales was used to finance the improvements. According to the RCMP's Report to Crown Counsel, 'his intent was to sell the property at a profit, therefore showing gain on paper.'

Currency Exchange Dealers

There is considerable evidence that currency exchange companies have long been used for money laundering. Retail-currency exchange dealers are especially popular as laundering vehicles because, like deposit institutions, they offer services that are desirable to the criminal element, especially the conversion of Canadian cash into American currency. Other services frequently used for money laundering purposes include converting small denominations of cash into larger denominations, purchasing negotiable instruments, and electronically transferring funds abroad. Recognizing the attractions of these types of businesses for money laundering, the Proceeds of Crime Sections in Montreal and Vancouver established their own retail currency business as part of an undercover operation targeting the proceeds of crime (see chapter 4).

Cash is the form by which the criminal proceeds most frequently enter the currency exchange company, and the majority of funds are revenue from drug deals conducted in Canada. Accordingly, much of the money laundering that occurs at these businesses involves changing

Canadian cash into American currency. This type of exchange is common given the necessity of converting the Canadian proceeds of drug trafficking to American funds, the principal currency used in the international drug trade. In one case, police executed a search warrant at the business of a courier company in Montreal that shipped goods and facilitated the transfer of American funds to destinations in South America and the United States. Police suspected that the American funds being transferred abroad were the proceeds of cocaine trafficking in the Montreal area and that the purpose of the international transfers was to purchase cocaine. Because the revenue from the cocaine sales in Montreal was in Canadian currency, it was necessary that the cash be exchanged before it was sent out of the country. Between 24 January 1996 and 19 March 1999, four individuals linked to this drug trafficking operation exchanged approximately CDN$3.2 million into American currency through a covert police-run currency exchange business operated by the Proceeds of Crime Section in downtown Montreal. In total, individuals associated with this courier company conducted approximately 158 separate transactions at the currency exchange business. The smallest amount of Canadian cash converted in one transaction was $135. The largest single transaction was the conversion of $96,625.

Police cases also show that in recent years there has been an increase in the conversion of American funds to Canadian currency. This increase is primarily the result of the sale of Canadian-grown marijuana in the United States, the proceeds of which are often smuggled back into Canada for laundering purposes. For example, in March 1994, a money launderer well known to police introduced an associate named James Dublin to an undercover police officer working at a covert currency exchange business in Vancouver. Over the next seven months, Dublin and three co-conspirators visited the undercover business on more than a dozen occasions, converting a total of U.S.$290,852 into CDN$398,590. By his fifth visit, Dublin admitted that the cash was from the sale of British Columbian pot in the United States. The American cash was often turned over to the currency exchange staff in highly suspicious circumstances, including producing tens of thousands of dollars – mostly U.S. twenties – from the pockets of jeans, coats, plastic bags wrapped in duct tape, and gym bags. The denominations of Canadian currency with which he left the store were generally $1,000 bills (which are not produced any more). Dublin volunteered to one undercover officer why he favoured using the currency exchange houses for obtaining the large bills in his laundering activities: 'they are easier to carry' and the volume of $20 bills was 'hard to explain to banks.' Exchange houses were obviously less 'suspicious.' As Dublin took one undercover officer in his confidence, the amount of cash brought into the currency exchange began to increase. The police officer suggested another special arrangement to gain the confidence of Dublin: he would personally have the cash proceeds transferred from the United States into Canada. Dublin would then simply have to pick up the converted Canadian currency at the store. Dublin enthusiastically agreed to this plan, declaring, 'You guys think of everything!'

Criminal entrepreneurs will attempt to avoid suspicion associated with transactions that involve large amounts of cash, and will use 'smurfs' to exchange small amounts of cash at a wide range of currency exchange outlets. For example, on 10 November 1996, an individual attended a money exchange kiosk at the Halifax Airport and attempted to exchange $3,900 in U.S. currency. The employees at the kiosk contacted the RCMP as they suspected the individual might be related to a money-laundering ring operating in the Halifax area. An RCMP member attended the office and spoke with the suspect, who provided a variety of reasons for how he came to be in possession of the money. He initially said the money was from friends in New York who were contributing to a movie that he was making. He then changed the story and stated that the money came from his winnings at a casino in Bangor, Maine. According to notes made by police, throughout his interview, the suspect became more and more evasive and nervous and began to sweat profusely. He eventually agreed to accompany the police officer to a Halifax police station. Even after a specially trained drug-detection dog indicated the presence of cocaine on the cash, the suspect continued to deny that the money had any criminal connections. Despite these admonitions, he advised police that he was prepared to relinquish the money. Although he was advised of other options, the suspect insisted on giving up the cash. Police then had the suspect sign a Relinquishment of Claim form and on the Disclaimer of Ownership of Currency form, which he also had to sign, he wrote 'the money was given to me as an investment for a video in New York.... They can keep their stinking money.' No other attempts were made to reclaim the cash.

Finally, police cases indicate that money launderers are also using other types of unregulated financial service providers to exchange currency. In particular, cheque cashing operations have become popular destinations for money launderers looking to avoid the scrutiny of banks and currency exchange operations. When Tad Lowe first started trafficking cocaine in Regina he had no need to exchange funds as he had left a large amount of cash in safety deposit boxes in Los Angeles, where he purchased much of his cocaine. As this reserve of American currency was depleted, however, he sought out the services of a cheque cashing operation in Saskatoon that sidelined as a currency exchange. Lowe would drop off a satchel containing Canadian currency and then pick up the American cash two or three day later. Each transaction was between U.S.$85,000 and $115,000. For each transaction, Lowe paid a 5 per cent premium on top of the usual fees charged by the cheque cashing company for the exchange services.

In a report to Crown counsel, the Vancouver IPOC Unit outlined some potential indications of laundering through a currency exchange business. The report advises that suspicions should be raised if a customer

- trades just under the CDN$10,000 threshold
- demonstrates a knowledge of relevant money-laundering laws and displays a conscious effort to circumvent these laws
- brings in money in a suspicious manner (e.g., all small bills, money carried in brown paper bag or other unorthodox packaging)
- brings in cash that has a strange smell (if U.S. dollars, it may smell like marijuana; if Canadian currency, it may smell like mothballs)
- arrives with several packets of money, each in pre-counted amounts, but only trades one bundle (the others are being saved to be exchanged elsewhere)
- asks if it is possible to exchange larger – sometimes much larger – amounts of cash in the future
- conducts multiple transactions, sometimes over the course of one day, or requests to conduct several smaller transactions in lieu of one large transaction
- says he/she is conducting the transaction for an unnamed third person
- acts suspiciously (e.g., looks nervous, watches the door, won't carry on a conversation)
- questions whether the staff of the currency exchange are police
- admits that the cash is the proceeds of crime, either directly (e.g., 'This is dope money') or indirectly (e.g., 'I'm going to Jamaica for twenty-four hours')

- admits or even brags about his/her involvement in criminal activity
- demonstrates a comprehensive knowledge about currency exchange rates, or attempts to obtain a better rate of exchange
- talks about converting currency as a regular line of business

Criminally Controlled Companies

Criminal entrepreneurs have long been involved in establishing and operating companies within the legitimate economy. Beginning in the nineteenth century, the Sicilian Mafia became dominant in the production and distribution of artichokes, olive oil, wine grapes, and other necessities of Italian life. In the United States, enterprising loan sharks became silent partners in companies owned by recalcitrant debtors (Richard, 1989). During the 1930s, and for decades after, members of criminal groups in North America had considerable interests in the transportation industry, a natural outgrowth of their involvement in trucking during Prohibition. Indeed, by criminalizing the production and consumption of alcohol during the 1920s and early 1930s, governments in the United States and Canada laid the foundation for an unprecedented involvement of organized crime figures in related industries, including those involved in the production of spirits, commercial transportation, entertainment, importing and exporting, hotels, restaurants, bars, and legalized gaming. Drinking establishments, restaurants, and retail stores have long been popular investments for crime groups due to their utility as headquarters, meeting places, 'booze cans,' gambling halls, and as venues to launder the proceeds of their illegal activities. Between the 1940s through to the 1980s, criminal entrepreneurs – in particular, Italian-American crime families – had a controlling interest in many of the casinos of Las Vegas. In the late 1980s, U.S. District Attorney Rudolph Giuliani convinced a federal judge that New York City's Fulton Fish Market – which supplied much of the seafood in the metropolitan area – was so dominated by organized crime that it was said to operate as a 'sovereign entity' where 'the laws of economic power and physical force, not the laws of New York City, prevail[ed].'[10] Throughout North America, criminal groups continue to be active in industries as diverse as construction, real estate, waste disposal, entertainment, food production and distribution, garment manufacturing, automobile sales, legalized gaming, and telemarketing, to name just a few.

In some of the cases included in this study, multiple companies were established to satisfy different objectives of the criminal organization, such as drug smuggling and money laundering. In chapter 1 we discussed the Canadian-based Caruana-Cuntrera crime group – one of the world's longest-running cocaine and heroin trafficking groups. Police discovered that they had set up dozens of companies spread throughout the world, including Canada, Venezuela, Switzerland, Thailand, Italy, and the Netherlands Antilles. These businesses included import-export companies, fitness clubs, night clubs, restaurants, supermarkets, auto leasing and sales companies, a tanning parlour, a car cleaning company, a pool hall, a decorating company, a real estate firm, a travel agency, a meat packing company, a record distribution company, and a hotel management business. The cartel had also established numerous numbered and holding companies, most of which carried out no legitimate commerce.

Companies established by the Caruana-Cuntrera group can be divided into two categories. The first consisted of companies that were used as fronts for international shipments of drugs. The RCMP in Montreal were first alerted to the Caruana-Cuntrera organization in 1984 when the British Customs and Excise Agency discovered a 250-kilo hashish shipment concealed in furniture sent by Shalimar Enterprises of Kashmir, India. British Customs took control of the shipment and controlled-delivered it to its destination, a warehouse in London rented by a company called Elongate Ltd., where two Canadian nationals of Sicilian origin were arrested. Police found that this pair was tasked with relabelling cargo filled with hashish to be reshipped to a Montreal company called Santa Rita Import-Export Ltd (Nicaso and Lamothe, 2000). The second category of companies established by the cartel were those created expressly for money laundering purposes, many of which were numbered companies based in Ontario and Venezuela that existed only on paper. The various shell and operating companies were also used to create an air of legitimacy for family members, in part by providing seemingly legitimate business revenue and salaries. Figure 3.9 provides an overview of Toronto-based companies set up by the Caruana-Cuntrera organization.

While companies are established by organized criminals for a number of reasons, arguably the greatest single motive for the infiltration of crime cartels into the private sector in the last twenty years has been to launder the proceeds of their illicit activities. Especially attractive to money launderers are businesses that customarily handle a high vol-

Figure 3.9: Toronto-based companies of the Caruana-Cuntrera cartel

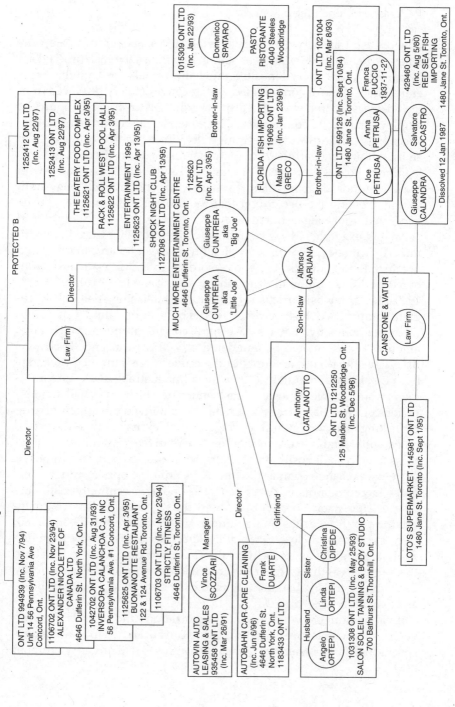

ume of cash transactions – such as retail stores, restaurants, bars, currency exchange dealers, and gas stations – because the cash proceeds of illegal activities can be deposited into bank accounts as legitimate revenue (either alone or commingled with revenue actually produced from the business). Companies also provide criminals an apparent source of employment in the community, which helps cultivate an image of respectability and invents a seemingly legitimate source of income. In short, criminally controlled companies help create an effective guise to legitimize both the proceeds of crime and individuals associated with the illicit funds, thereby satisfying an essential objective of money laundering: creating the perception that the proceeds of crime have been generated from a legal source.

A vivid example of how companies can effectively be used to legitimize dirty money involves Gary Hendin, a lawyer for an Ontario-based organized crime syndicate, who, according to RCMP estimates, laundered CDN$12 million in drug money during the late 1970s and early 1980s. Hendin was particularly adroit at establishing shell and legitimate companies, which became the backbone of his laundering activities. One company that was a central conduit through which large amounts of cash would be laundered was M&M Currency Exchange. By establishing bank accounts in the name of the currency exchange business, Hendin maintained an almost impenetrable pretence for numerous and sizable deposits of cash, much of which was small denominations of Canadian currency that had been derived directly from drug trafficking. The very nature of the currency exchange business, combined with Hendin's upstanding reputation in the community, ensured these large cash deposits avoided suspicion and scrutiny. In addition, a currency exchange company afforded Hendin the opportunity to purchase large amounts of American cash under a seemingly justifiable visage. The American cash purchased through banks was eventually used to purchase drugs on the foreign market. During 1979 and 1980, Hendin purchased close to $9 million in American currency from one bank in Buffalo. The majority of the Canadian cash used to purchase these funds was drawn from an account in the name of M&M Currency Exchange at a Canadian bank branch in St Catharines, Ontario (Beare and Schneider, 1990: 317–18).

As a medium between criminal organizations and other laundering vehicles, companies are very flexible and can be tailored to a launderer's specific needs. For example, to facilitate access to real property, criminal organizations can incorporate realty companies, mortgage-brokerage firms, and development or construction companies. During the investigation into Gary Hendin, police discovered that he incorporated a number of shell companies and trust accounts in Canada and abroad through which he would funnel drug proceeds to purchase real estate in Canada. To further legitimize his real estate transactions, Hendin incorporated construction and development companies, through which properties would be purchased with mortgages financed by other shell companies he had established. In one such transaction, he used construction, development, and mortgage finance companies to purchase property already owned by another shell company he had established. One of the purposes of purchasing property that Hendin already de facto owned was to repatriate money to Canada (in the form of a mortgage) that was located in the account of an offshore shell company.

One specific example of this complex laundering method, illustrated in figure 3.10, involved the purchase of real estate in Canada by a shell company incorporated by Hendin, called Rosegarden Construction. Mortgage financing for this property came from Cencan Investments, a credit company also incorporated by Hendin. A payment of CDN$330,000 came in the form of a certified cheque issued through a bank account in the name of M&M Currency Exchange and payable to Cencan Investments. This cheque was converted into a bank draft and deposited 'in trust' to a bank account registered in the name of Hendin's law practice. Another mortgage was then registered against the property in favour of Gary Hendin 'in trust.' The source of this mortgage was the Antillean Management Company, which was incorporated in a tax-haven country and controlled directly by Hendin's criminal client. The funds in this offshore account were, in fact, the proceeds of drug sales that had been wire transferred from Canada. No payments were ever made against the fictitious mortgage (Beare and Schneider, 1990: 317–18).

Criminally controlled companies also have the added benefit of producing legitimate revenue for their owners that can be maximized by applying tactics traditionally associated with organized crime, such as intimidation, violence, extortion, corruption, and labour racketeering. At the peak of their power during the 1960s and 1970s, the Cotroni crime family of Montreal controlled a number of legitimate businesses throughout the city, including those involved in construction, food wholesaling, hotels, restaurants, bars, vending machines, and hotels,

Figure 3.10: Flow chart of a Gary Hendin money-laundering operation

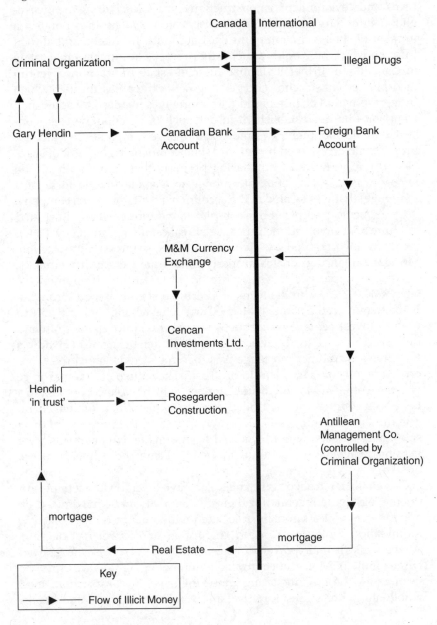

which were used to carry out both legitimate and illegitimate commerce, including money laundering. Willie Obront, the financial brains behind this criminal organization, was an executive or officer of thirty-eight different companies and, along with two associates, he supplied 500 vending machines to the 1967 Montreal World Exposition, while managing the only on-site meat storage facility (a monopoly that allowed them to sell spoiled meat to concessionaires) (Edwards, 1990). Evidence gathered through the Quebec Police Crime Commissions of the 1970s indicated that the Cotroni family used intimidation and the corruption of government and labour union officials to help obtain this monopoly (Quebec Police Commission Inquiry on Organized Crime, 1977).

The influx of illicit revenues into legitimate businesses also provides criminally controlled companies with a marked business advantage over their competitors. In one case, a New Brunswick drug trafficker started a masonry business with the proceeds of his drug sales. Due to the ongoing injection of drug revenues into the company, its value was artificially inflated. The constant cash flow also meant that the company was able to underbid competitors on construction contracts. Revenue from both the drug trafficking and masonry businesses were commingled and deposited into bank accounts registered in the name of the latter.

Types of Companies Used to Launder Money

Of the forty-nine proceeds of crime cases identified in this research that involved criminally controlled companies, no one type of business predominated; the companies operated (or purported to operate) various lines of commerce, including currency exchange, importing/exporting, retail fish sales, masonry, paving, painting, auto wholesaling, auto financing, lumber supplies, courier services, marine craft sales, office supplies, restaurants, bars, hotels, marinas, real property development, retail tire sales, construction, pool halls, pinball arcades, car washes, tanning salons, and fitness clubs. Numerous other businesses were established as numbered or holding companies and had no declared line of business. In some cases, the nature of the company's business was not chosen haphazardly; it pursued a trade that attempted to maximize the appearance of legitimacy and normalcy that would help shroud its criminal intentions. For example, in certain cases,

- restaurants were established to provide a locale for the sale of drugs and as a guise under which the cash proceeds of these sales could be deposited into bank accounts
- a currency exchange company was established by a drug trafficking group to convert Canadian to American cash which was then transferred internationally to purchase drugs
- an auto theft ring incorporated companies that specialized in auto wholesaling, which made possible the sale of stolen cars to automobile dealerships
- an auto importation company was established by cocaine traffickers in Canada to legitimize their need to purchase American currency (which in fact was used to purchase cocaine); in addition, cocaine was exported from the U.S. to Canada concealed in cars 'sold' by an American auto export company that was, in fact, operated by the U.S.-based cocaine supplier

Police cases show that many criminally controlled companies carry out no legitimate business; they exist only on paper and are established explicitly to facilitate the laundering process. One purpose of a shell company is to create a conduit through which illicit money can be funnelled to other laundering vehicles, in effect providing a means to obscure any trail that would lead from the company to a criminal enterprise. In many of the police cases studied, the investments, properties, and assets controlled by a criminal enterprise were legally registered as being owned by shell companies.

Money-Laundering Techniques Associated with
Criminally Controlled Companies

Companies allow the criminal an effective guise to access other laundering vehicles and utilize different laundering techniques. As discussed above, companies produce (cash) revenue and it is under this guise that illegally derived cash can be deposited into bank accounts. In addition, once a company is established, a wide range of techniques can be used to further the laundering process, such as using nominees as owners and directors, establishing a hierarchy of companies, lending money between criminally controlled companies, selling a company artificially inflated with the proceeds of crime, purchasing a company already owned by the criminal enterprise, paying out fictitious expenses or salaries, disguising the transfer of illicit funds under the veneer of payment for goods or services, offering public shares in a company, or purchasing real estate with proceeds of crime disguised as mortgages granted by criminally controlled companies.

CONCEALING CRIMINAL OWNERSHIP

Companies can also be quite effective in concealing criminal ownership of the company itself as well as concealing other assets purchased with the proceeds of crime. To maximize the air of legitimacy and to distance a criminally-controlled company from its unlawful sources, nominees will be used as owners, shareholders, directors, or officers. In one case, a cocaine trafficker based in Edmonton was the owner, operator, and financier of at least six restaurants during the period he was under investigation. Not only was the cocaine sold out of the restaurants, but these businesses were also used to launder the profits of the illegal sales. Although it was clear that the accused had ultimate control over these restaurants, he was not registered as the official owner of any of them. Instead, title was placed in the names of his nominees, who included his wife, his niece, his mother, his father-in-law, sisters, brothers-in-law, as well as business associates, two of which were convicted of narcotics trafficking offences that occurred at his restaurants. Commercial bank accounts were opened for each restaurant, and cocaine revenue was deposited into the accounts under the guise of legitimate sales from these restaurants.

Criminal ownership can also be concealed by incorporating domestic companies as subsidiaries of corporations based in tax-haven countries with strict secrecy and disclosure laws. In one case, Basil Rolfe, a Vancouver-based lawyer, incorporated numerous shell companies in Canada and in offshore locations on behalf of George Burden and others involved in a large-scale drug importation conspiracy. One shell company incorporated by Rolfe, and of which he was the sole director, was used to channel more than CDN$6 million in drug money to other assets, including bank accounts, real estate, cars, stock portfolios, and other shell companies. Rolfe also represented Burden in the purchase of homes in the Greater Vancouver Area, including Burden's principal residence that Rolfe registered in the name of a Bahamas-based shell company called Taipei Trading Corp.[11]

ESTABLISHING A HIERARCHY OF COMPANIES

In some police cases, a number of companies were established, many of which were connected through a complex hierarchy of ownership. In addition to concealing criminal ownership, establishing a labyrinth of different companies facilitates the transfer of illicit funds between different companies, which contributes to the essential money-laundering process of layering. In other cases, efforts were made to ensure that there was no evidence of a common ownership among the different companies established. This allows companies to purportedly conduct business with each other using fraudulent transactions (such as fake loans or the purchase of products or services) to transfer illicit funds between themselves (in some cases expediting the international transfer of funds). Holding companies are particularly attractive to money launderers because the sole purpose of this type of business is to own other companies, assets, and financial portfolios. As such, a holding company becomes an effective intermediary between the criminal organization and other laundering vehicles. In the 1980s, an RCMP investigation of a Toronto-based criminal organization revealed that it controlled over sixty companies in Canada, all of which were financed either in whole or in part by the proceeds of crime. Over CDN$40 million in drug revenues was funnelled through an elaborate matrix of companies that was so complex police investigators referred to it as the 'Spaghetti Jungle' (Beare and Schneider, 1990).

FAKE LOANS OR INVESTMENTS

Criminal proceeds can be laundered by transferring funds disguised as loans or investments between two criminally controlled companies, a method that is often used to repatriate to Canada illicit funds that had previously been sent to another country (usually a tax-haven country where a shell company has been established). In one case, a Toronto drug trafficker invested $1 million into a chain of Canadian restaurants he already controlled. A down payment of $50,000 was made and properly declared. A $450,000 mortgage was then negotiated from a bank and the remaining $500,000 was 'borrowed' from a shell company also controlled by the trafficker. The $500,000 was 'repaid' with interest to avoid suspicion.

SELLING A COMPANY

Flipping companies, which consists of purchasing or starting a business and then selling it, has also been used as a money-laundering technique. Selling a criminally controlled business provides the criminal entrepreneur with a seemingly legitimate source of capital. The added benefit of selling a business through which illicit cash has been invested is that it will ostensibly exhibit a significant cash flow and, as such, will appear as an attractive business venture and realize a high selling price. In a case out of Calgary, a cocaine importer owned and operated several businesses, including grocery stores, ice cream parlours, and jewellery stores. Proceeds from drug sales were recorded as revenue on financial statements and, on the basis of the apparent profitability of these businesses, the owner was able to sell them at inflated prices.

PURCHASING A COMPANY ALREADY OWNED BY
THE CRIMINAL ENTERPRISE

Another laundering technique is to 'purchase' a company already owned by the criminal enterprise. According to a 1980 report by the now-defunct Coordinated Law Enforcement Unit of British Columbia, a common scenario is for criminal proceeds, previously sent to an off-shore tax-haven country, to be used to buy a company in Canada that is already owned by the criminal enterprise. In this way, the launderer successfully returns a large sum of money to Canada. The business may be purchased at an artificially inflated price and the difference between the artificial and the real market value is deposited in the bank account of a foreign subsidiary company in a tax haven country (BC, Ministry of the Attorney General, 1980).

FICTITIOUS BUSINESS EXPENSES/FALSE INVOICING

Once a criminal enterprise controls corporate entities in different jurisdictions, it can employ a corporate fraud technique that involves fake business transactions, the claiming of fictitious expenses, and the creation of falsified invoices. This common fraud practice is often used to transfer illicit funds internationally and can be a part of the layering process. This method can also be used as a cover to pay for illegal drugs being purchased on the international market. At its most basic, at least two companies are established: one in Canada and one in another country. The Canadian company purchases fictitious goods or services from the offshore corporation, fake invoices are created by the foreign company, and the payment is made by the former to an offshore bank account in the name of the latter. Both companies are owned by the same criminal enterprise and the 'payment' is actually a way to spirit the illicit funds out of Canada to the safer confines of a tax-haven country or to a country where drugs are being purchased. To repatriate funds previously spirited out of Canada, this technique is simply reversed.

PAYING OUT FICTITIOUS SALARIES

In addition to claiming the proceeds of crime as legitimate business revenue, criminally controlled companies can help to legitimize participants in a criminal conspiracy by providing them with salaries. In some cases, salary cheques were signed back to the company by the 'employee' as part of the laundering operation. In one case, video stores, which were registered in the name of a holding company, were used to launder the proceeds of drug trafficking. Personally, or through a courier, cash would be picked up from drug traffickers and then deposited into bank accounts as revenue from the stores. The funds would then be returned to the criminal clients as paycheques. The manager of the video stores even completed the appropriate taxation documentation for his 'employees.' The maximum amount of money a drug trafficking client was allowed to run through the stores annually was $60,000, which was seen as a credible salary ceiling to avoid suspicion. For his service, the manager of the video stores received a 25 per cent commission on all funds laundered through the stores.

The Securities Market

Organized crime has infiltrated the capital markets for two reasons. The first is to make money, primarily through fraud, share manipulation, insider trading, as well as deceitful and coercive telemarketing. The second reason is to launder money that is generated from drug trafficking and other profit-oriented crimes.

From the 1950s to the early 1970s, traditional crime groups in the United States and Canada masterminded schemes to steal millions of dollars worth of securities certificates from the vaults of brokerage houses and banks.[12] To facilitate these thefts, criminal groups relied on corruption and intimidation of industry insiders. During the 1950s, the Papalia crime family of Hamilton, Ontario, used intimidation tactics to extort money and insider information from securities brokers. From then on, the markets became increasingly vulnerable to manipulation and fraud by criminal groups. In the 1960s and 1970s, Willie Obront was charged with over 400 counts of fraudulently manipulating stock market shares over a fifteen-year period (Quebec Police Commission Inquiry on Organized Crime, 1977: 148). A 1977 report of the Quebec Police Commission examining organized crime in the private sector dedicated an entire chapter to the securities industry. A 1974 intelligence report on commercial crime by the Coordinated Law Enforcement Unit (CLEU) of British Columbia documented the involvement of organized (and unorganized) criminals in the Vancouver Stock Exchange (BC, CLEU, 1974: 27).

In 1997, police began investigating the possible role of outlaw motorcycle gang members in manipulating the publicly traded stock of Montreal-based BioChem Pharma. This investigation was intensified after four bombs exploded outside the company's Quebec headquarters on 24 and 25 November of that year.[13] One media article reported that over those two days, an unusually large number of BioChem 'put options' was purchased through the Montreal Exchange. The intent of the bombings may have been to destabilize the stock, causing it to drop rapidly and allowing speculators to make a substantial profit.[14] In April 1997, Claude Duboc, who was arrested and convicted in Florida for his part in masterminding one of the world's largest hashish trafficking empires, agreed to pay his lawyer, F. Lee Bailey, in BioChem stock, then worth U.S.$5.8 million. Soon after making the transfer, the stock shot up in value to over U.S.$20 million. When U.S. authorities tried to claim the stock as the proceeds of crime, Bailey refused to give it up. He relented only after a judge jailed him for contempt.[15]

By the late 1990s, U.S. federal law enforcement agencies and securities regulators began investigations into allegations that members of Italian-American crime families, in cooperation with Russian crime groups, had established a network of stock promoters, securities dealers, brokerage firms, and 'boiler rooms' that sold stocks nationwide through high-pressure sales tactics and intimidation. A 1996 *Business Week* article reported that Philip Abramo, a high-ranking member in the New Jersey-based DeCavalcante crime family, controlled at least four brokerage firms through front men and exerted influence upon still other investment dealers. Other securities dealers and traders were reported to have paid extortion money or 'tribute' to Abramo.[16] Four years after this article was published, federal prosecutors brought indictments against eighty-five people, including brokers and suspected members and associates of the DeCavalcante organization as well as New York's Colombo, Bonanno, and Genovese crime families. The indictments alleged that the defendants stole more than U.S.$100 million from investors using threats, bribes, pension-fund raids, and 'pump-and-dump' market manipulation tactics. It was later shown in court that the conspirators were secretly controlling large blocks of shares in approximately twenty companies, which they pushed onto investors through high-pressure sales calls. They also paid their own brokers hefty kickbacks to get outside investors to buy shares at inflated prices. Mafia enforcers were employed to ensure none of the brokers would sell on behalf of their clients, thereby keeping the price of the stocks artificially high. Once the stock value reached its zenith, the conspirators sold their secretly held shares.[17]

Abramo's market manipulation activities were not confined to the United States. Stockbroker Jean Claude Hauchecorne, who worked at the Vancouver-based Pacific International Securities until 1999, told police that Abramo and two other Mafia-connected figures, placed dozens of orders to buy and sell U.S. stocks, many of which had been identified by *Business Week* as Mob-manipulated. At one point, Abramo demanded that Hauchecorne return U.S.$1.75 million he had transferred to Switzerland on the instructions of another Mafia operative who had had a falling out with Abramo. If he did not heed their demands, they threatened to have him killed.[18]

In the vast majority of proceeds of crime cases that implicate the securities industry, the source of funds was from drug trafficking, a reflection of the sheer volume of drug cash that circulates within the legitimate economy (relative to other criminal sources), as well as the RCMP's emphasis on anti-drug profiteering enforcement. While the RCMP Proceeds of Crime Program rarely focuses on securities infractions, it is safe to assume that much of the revenue that is generated through such breaches as insider trading is at least initially or partially 'laundered' through the capital markets, taking advantage of the same processes and vehicles utilized in the original crime. A particular challenge is determining when the securities offence ends and the money-laundering offence begins.

Two RCMP cases from the 1980s demonstrate how the revenues from securities infractions are laundered through the capital markets. In the first, the principals of a publicly listed company in Canada were involved in the manipulation of its stock as well as the theft of company assets. As owners of a large amount of the company's stock, these individuals benefited greatly from the manipulation of stock prices. The stock was then sold at an artificially high price, and the proceeds invested into other public companies through the same trading accounts used for the share price manipulation. The police investigation also revealed that the companies into which the proceeds of these infractions were invested were indirectly controlled by those behind the original securities infractions (Beare and Schneider, 1990: 121–2). In another high-profile case, Edward Carter and David Ward manipulated the shares of nineteen public companies listed on the Vancouver Stock Exchange (VSE) during the mid-1980s. The two also paid secret commissions to Carl Lazzell, the portfolio manager of United Services Funds' Prospector Fund, an American-based mutual fund, to purchase CDN$27-million of stock in fifteen VSE-listed companies controlled by Ward and Carter. It was estimated that the pair reaped more than CDN$15 million in profits through the manipulation of these shares. This profit was in turn laundered through various trading accounts and the purchase of securities and other commodities. In the end, police counted more than 100 trading accounts distributed among fifteen brokerage firms in Canada, the U.S., and the Cayman Islands. Many of the accounts were registered in the names of beneficial owners and numbered companies incorporated in the Cayman Islands. Carter sold stock to the mutual fund from one account located at the Cayman Island branch of the Canadian brokerage firm Richardson Greenshields Ltd., which was in the name of the Cayman Island branch of the Royal Bank of Canada. This account was also used to purchase silver and gold bullion, Government of Canada bonds, U.S. Treasury bills and a number of blue chip stocks. By funnelling the illicit proceeds of their fraud into commodities and other securities, this trading account was utilized as an important money-laundering conduit (ibid.: 121–53).

The Form in Which the Proceeds of Crime Enters the Capital Markets

Unlike the proceeds of securities infractions, which are initially realized as electronic credits in trading and bank accounts, revenue from drug trafficking or other organized crime offences can enter the securities market in a number of forms, including cash, monetary instruments, and account transfers. In one case, a cocaine trafficker in Ottawa walked into a brokerage firm with a gym bag containing $25,000 in cash that he used to invest in certain stocks. In another case, two drug traffickers used family members as nominees for bank and trading accounts. Drug cash would first be deposited into a bank account, often in small denominations. The funds would then be transferred into trading accounts at brokerage firms established in the names of the nominees. Alternatively, the nominees would purchase bank drafts, which were subsequently deposited into their trading accounts.

Brokerage Firms and Money Laundering

As indicated above, criminals laundering money through the securities market will more often than not gain access through a brokerage firm. There are two advantages of using a brokerage firm for money-laundering purposes: its position as a chief point of entry into the stock market for investors, and its ability to operate as a quasi-deposit taking institution, where funds can be converted into account credits, securities, or monetary instruments. Brokerage firms can also be used to electronically transfer funds between accounts and between countries.

In 1982, Vincent Patrick Smith was arrested in Amsterdam for drug-smuggling offences. The subsequent investigation uncovered more than $30,000 in cash and security certificates in a safety deposit box. The investigation also revealed that Smith utilized a Merrill Lynch office to wire transfer money from Canada to Miami. In another case, the Canadian Imperial Bank of Commerce reported to police that a customer had walked into a Winnipeg branch with a suitcase full of $50 and $100 bills and purchased a bank draft for CDN $81,500 made payable to himself. Bank employees, suspicious of this transaction, notified the police who followed the customer to the brokerage firm Richardson Greenshields. He emerged from this office with a cheque payable to himself for $59,467.35 in U.S. funds. He then took the cheque to a branch of the Royal Bank and 'converted' it to U.S. cash. A subsequent investigation revealed the accused performed the same transactions the previous week with CDN$25,000. It soon became evident that the subject was acting on behalf of a close friend who was known to be an active drug trafficker.

Establishing Multiple Trading Accounts

One of the common denominators in both fraud and money laundering offences that take place within the securities market is the use of multiple trading accounts. In the context of money laundering, multiple accounts are used for 'layering.' In their book *Fleecing the Lamb*, David Cruise and Alison Griffiths show how a long-established technique to manipulate a stock's price can also be used to launder money. First, a 'master' trading account is registered in the name of the individual who is to receive the laundered money. Only legal funds with an easily verifiable source, such as money borrowed from a bank, should enter this account. Nominees then open other trading accounts with the proceeds of crime at a number of other brokerage firms. The master account slowly makes blocks of stock available, which are purchased by the nominees through their various trading accounts. The aim of the master account is to remove a dollar of clean money for every dollar of dirty money used by the nominees. A one-for-one trade between clean and dirty money is considered excellent in the laundering business, and any profits are a bonus (Cruise and Griffiths, 1987: 216).

Money Laundering Through Derivatives

The *1998–1999 Report on Money Laundering Typologies* by the Financial Action Task Force highlights the use of derivatives[19] to launder the proceeds of crime. 'Compared to banks,' states the report, 'the derivatives markets and associated products represent perhaps a better opportunity for laundering because of the ease with which audit trails can be obscured.' The high volume of trading activity and a high degree of liquidity of the derivatives market, combined with the numerous brokers who trade the products, muddies the connection between each new participant and the original trade. As a result, 'no single link in the series of transactions will likely know the identity of the person beyond the one with whom he is directly dealing.' In addition, when compared to banker's derivatives, brokers 'tend to be less familiar with anti-money laundering efforts' (FATF, 1999: 19, para. 52, 53).

According to the FATF, money laundering through derivatives begins with the deposit of criminal proceeds into a trading account. The broker uses the proceeds to purchase 100 derivative contracts, trading at an offer price of $85.02, with a 'tick' size (which determines the value of each 'cent' of a contract) of $25. At the same time, the broker sells 100 contracts of the same commodity at the bid price of $85.00. The activity provides two legitimate contracts. Later in the trading day, the contract price, through normal market fluctuations, has changed to $84.72 bid and $84.74 offered. The broker closes both open positions at the prevailing prices and then assigns the original purchase at $85.02 and the subsequent sale at $84.72 to account 'A.' The percentage difference between the two prices is 30 points or ticks (the difference between $84.72 and $85.02). The loss incurred in the trade is $75,000, which is determined by multiplying the tick size ($25) by the number of contracts (100) and by the difference in price (30). The other trades are allocated to account 'B,' which, by following the same calculations, results in a profit of $65,000. Thus the launderer pays out $75,000 to receive $65,000 in laundered funds (a $10,000 'fee' is not uncommon in money laundering). The transaction has created no false documentation and has been conducted transparently in full sight of the market (FATF, 1999: 19).

Money Laundering Through Initial Public Offerings of Criminally Controlled Companies

Instead of purchasing securities, a criminal enterprise may take the opposite route to launder its illicit proceeds: offering shares in a public company, previously injected with criminal proceeds, which allows a criminal organization the opportunity to raise capital and thus a seemingly legitimate source of funds. Under this method, a private company is incorporated or an existing one is bought by a criminal organization. The registered owners, directors, and officers of the company are nominees such as a lawyer or an offshore shell company. The company may not carry out any legitimate business but can appear to be highly profitable through the injections of the proceeds of crime, which are made to appear as the legitimate revenue. Shares are then issued to the public in conjunction with a respectable underwriter. The actual laundering occurs after shares are purchased and the 'capital financing' is received by the original criminal owners of the company. The objective of this method is to generate a clean dollar through the issuing of shares for every dirty dollar invested in the company before its initial public offering. Because these shell companies can appear to be highly profitable through the injection of criminal profits, the original investors can actually make a substantial profit on their investment through the initial public offering.

One of the most infamous examples of this laundering technique involved YBM Magnex International Inc., a public company once listed on the Toronto Stock Exchange. In May 1998, the FBI raided the U.S. headquarters of YBM Magnex Inc. as part of an investigation into suspicions that the company was used by Russian organized crime as a money-laundering vehicle. Following the raid, all trading in YBM shares was halted, eventually leading to the company's collapse. Before the trading was halted, more than $100 million was raised from Canadian investors and the firm had a capitalization of close to $900 million.

YBM was formed in 1991 by its parent company, Arigon Co. Ltd. One of YBM's original shareholders (and a director of Arigon) was Semyon Mogilevich, reported to be a leading Russian organized crime figure. Arigon was established in the Channel Islands in 1990 and was Mogilevich's original conduit for laundering money, according to a 1995 British criminal intelligence report. A 1999 *New York Times* report describes Mogilevich as 'one of the world's top criminals' who used YBM 'purely to legitimize the criminal organization by the floating on the stock exchange of a corporation which consists of U.K. and US companies whose existing assets and stock have been artificially inflated by the proceeds of crime' (qtd. in Beare, 2000: 6). Arigon also reportedly had ties to Sergei Mikhailov, a former KGB agent and a suspected leader of the Solntsevo group, which, at the time, was reputed to be one of the most powerful crime groups in Moscow, involved in drug trafficking, extortion, smuggling, auto theft, and prostitution. A private forensic investigation into YBM claimed that its six original investors, including Mogilevich, were all members of the Solntsevo group.

A few months later, Arigon established a subsidiary in Moscow known as Arbat International Ltd., which was also used as a laundering vehicle for Mogilevich and Mikhailov, according to the 1995 British intelligence report. In 1991, Arigon bought another Hungarian manufacturing company for $1.8 million. This company was renamed Magnex and started producing industrial magnets from a plant in Budapest. According to U.S. court documents, the factory was set up in part with stolen equipment and also sold embargoed items such as weapons and enriched uranium to customers in Pakistan and the Middle East.[20] On 16 May 1991, law enforcement authorities in Britain raided the London offices and homes of Mogilevich's lawyers and his former girlfriend and seized files relating to Arigon. British police charged that U.S.$50 million in proceeds of crime passed through the Arigon accounts at the Royal Bank of Scotland over a three-year period.

By the early 1990s, Mogilevich and Mikhailov began to expand into North America. In 1993, an associate of Mogilevich contacted Joseph Bogatin, a Russian academic who lived in the U.S. and specialized in magnet technology. In February 1994, Bogatin left his employer and formed YBM Magnex Inc. in Hatboro, Pennsylvania. YBM then merged with Arigon. In April 1996, Bogatin created Pratecs Technologies Inc., a company incorporated in Alberta and listed on the Alberta Exchange. In October 1996, Pratecs formally acquired YBM Magnex, and changed its name to YBM Magnex International Ltd. By that time, Mogilevich and five of his associates owned just under one-third of YBM's outstanding shares. In 1996, YBM moved onto the Toronto Stock Exchange, and on 20 November 1997, the Ontario Securities Commission approved a $53-million equity issue at $16.50 a share.

From the outset, police alleged that Mogilevich and his co-conspirators routinely fabricated and destroyed accounting and other financial records, sold products that they knew didn't work or didn't exist, and misled investors and regulators about nearly every aspect of YBM's operations. Court documents suggest that Mogilevich deposited illegal revenues in YBM-related bank accounts in Philadelphia, which were then disbursed to co-conspirators. The forensic investigation raised serious questions about the firms with which YBM supposedly did business, suggesting that dozens of shell companies were established to act as YBM customers. In Britain, for example, 'all companies [are] in the Channel Islands and Isle of Man; many are shells, some are shells within shells; no way to know to this point who real buyer is,' according to a briefing note prepared by the investigators. In the U.S., the private investigators checked out two supposed magnet buyers and instead 'found offices of an attorney. No sign of [either firm].'[21] Private forensic investigators also found approximately U.S.$2 million in cash at the Budapest factory, which YBM officials explained was for salaries.[22]

In their indictment of Mogilevich, U.S. attorneys estimated that he made more than U.S.$12 million through the sale of 2.1 million YBM shares held in an account at First Marathon Securities between 1996 and early 1997. The proceeds were then transferred to an overseas bank account he controlled. The indictment also alleged that Mogilevich personally made another U.S.$6 million from bonuses and other compensation from YBM, including sales commissions.[23]

By December 1998, the company was in receivership and, in 1999, YBM officers pleaded guilty to conspiracy charges in U.S. Federal Court, admitting the company was conceived as a vehicle for fraud and money laundering. The company eventually went bankrupt. According to court documents filed by U.S. government attorneys, Mogilevitch intentionally used Canadian stock exchanges to orchestrate his laundering activity because he felt Canada had lax regulations. Assistant U.S. Attorney Suzanne Ercole was quoted in the media as stating, 'One of the concepts behind the [money laundering] plan, and the formulation of the plans to take [YBM] and make it a public company and to initiate trading, was to initiate trading on the exchanges in Canada,' because they believed that the regulations were more lenient.[24]

Concealing Criminal Ownership

One of the necessary components in any successful laundering process is to conceal any association between the criminal owner and the laundering vehicle. Police cases involving the laundering of illicit monies through securities reveal various means to satisfy this essential prerequisite, including the use of nominees, shell companies, and numbered companies. Pierre LaPointe, a Windsor, Ontario, drug trafficker, invested $37,000 in the stock market by establishing a trading account at a local brokerage firm. The account was, in fact, registered in the name of a nominee, who also delivered cash to the brokerage firm for investment. Further investigations revealed that Lapointe used nominees for all his laundering activities.[25] In another case, a member of a Calgary-based organization that trafficked in cocaine and marijuana laundered his illegal revenue through various banks, real estate, and stock market investments. Along with $113,930 in cash, police seized the following documents from the truck of the accused:

- An account statement from a brokerage firm for the period ending June 30, 1996. The account was registered in the name of a numbered company that was eventually traced to the accused. The Canadian dollar account showed a net value of $7,938.94.
- A receipt from the same brokerage firm for a different account (but registered in the name of the numbered company) in the amount of $10,000.
- A mutual fund account statement from a major chartered bank dated 2 July 1996 and addressed to the numbered company, showing a balance of $3,024.17.

Criminally Controlled Investment Dealers

Police cases show that criminal groups will establish their own 'investment firms' to further both their money-making and money-laundering ventures in the securities market. Controlling a business that purports to facilitate financial investments also opens up an endless stream of money-laundering possibilities. Fake clients, shell companies, and nominees can be used. Paperwork can be forged or destroyed. A myriad of obfuscating trades and other transactions can be created. Criminal proceeds can be claimed as start-up capital for both the investment firm and for other criminally controlled, publicly listed companies that are underwritten by the investment firm. Unscrupulous traders and criminal conspirators can be hired and high-pressure sales tactics can be used to sell stock in these companies, thereby generating a source of clean money.

International Transactions and Safe Haven Countries

The ongoing internationalization of securities markets parallels a similar development in money laundering: the increased transborder movement of illicit money. Sophisticated laundering techniques are increasingly taking advantage of the integration of the world's securities community by conducting transactions that cross national borders and using safe-haven countries to obstruct any paper trail. The first step in many international laundering operations is to send the illegal funds offshore, often to a safe-haven country with strong bank-secrecy laws. Police cases demonstrate a persistent connection between Canada and such safe-haven countries in the laundering of illicit proceeds generated from securities infractions and other criminal offences. The directors and officers of a public company in Canada accused of insider trading utilized accounts at a brokerage firm located in a Caribbean country to launder the proceeds of their activities. The trading accounts were registered in the name of shell companies and hundreds of thousands of dollars of stocks and government bonds were purchased and sold through these accounts. Legitimate loans from Swiss banks were often deposited directly into these accounts in order to justify the large securities transactions.[26]

Securities, Money Laundering, and the Internet

There is a growing fear about the new possibilities for fraud and money laundering offered by electronic commerce, in particular online trading and Internet banking. Police and prosecutors in Italy are on record as saying that organized criminals are laundering their proceeds through e-commerce transactions, sending electronic cash to cyber accounts located all over the world, which then reappear as stocks and shares. The Internet provides anonymity and facilitates international transactions, which are critical to fraud and money laundering. Criminal organizations have the financial resources to buy almost any kind of technological resource or expertise. The Hells Angels, for example, are known to have their own Internet service provider, an effective way to block attempts by police to monitor their activity on the Internet. Law enforcement authorities in Italy are convinced that the Sicilian Mob is convulsing world stock markets by laundering hundreds of millions of dollars through Internet-based investing services. Surges in stock markets are being attributed to online trading and banking by Italian criminals, Italian police say. Police in Palermo uncovered what they said was a U.S.$528 million fraud, which they believe is part of a global money-laundering scheme. The money was electronically spirited between a U.S. company incorporated in New Zealand, the Cayman Islands, and brokerage accounts in Israel and Spain. It was then deposited into Swiss bank accounts. A Sicilian prosecutor was quoted in the media as saying, 'Investigations have highlighted an unregulated and borderless financial market open to anyone with the capacity, for whatever reason, to exchange stocks and money.' Mob experts agree that new technology is boosting criminals' coffers while minimizing the risk. 'The Internet is a powerful weapon. It eliminates the middleman. There's no need to find corrupt bankers,' stated Mario Centorrino, a professor at Messina University in Sicily.[28]

Utilizing Multiple Laundering Techniques

The following case demonstrates how a number of techniques employed by criminal entrepreneurs can be used in tandem to launder the proceeds of crime through capital markets.

On 17 December 2001, Lance Boyle was arrested at the Winnipeg Airport in possession of $115,050 in Canadian cash. The next day, members of the Winnipeg Integrated Proceeds of Crime Unit and the RCMP Drug Section executed a search warrant at a home owned by Boyle and an associate, identified as Willie Van Houghton. During this search, approximately $19,870 in Canadian currency, $9,045 in U.S. currency, $25,000 worth of anabolic steroids, and two pounds (1 kilogram) of cannabis were seized. By the end of the investigation, a total of eighty-nine drug and proceeds of crime charges were laid against twenty individuals involved in this drug trafficking network. A forensic audit conducted as part of the investigation estimated that between 1996 and 2000, Boyle had unexplained income of approximately $775,000. The proceeds of crime investigation into Boyle and Van Houghton revealed that both were active investors in the stock market and had amassed impressive portfolios, although neither had declared any income over the past several years.

Police were able to connect fifteen investment accounts to Boyle. These accounts were located at eleven different banks, brokerage firms, and fund managers, and while some were registered in the names of relatives, Boyle was authorized to trade through all of them. Police ultimately proved that funds in accounts registered in the names of Boyle's mother and brother were derived from criminal activity. In addition, Van Houghton managed a company called Investing Networks Ltd., which police described as operating in a manner similar to a mutual fund. Through the course of their investigation, the RCMP determined that Boyle and Van Houghton had established accounts at ten brokerage firms in Canada, including some of the largest in the country. Shortly after the arrest of Boyle and Van Houghton, money and securities were transferred among a number of brokerage accounts in the names of the two accused, their relatives, and other nominees. Accounts were also registered in the names of shell companies established by Boyle. One such company was BSE Investments, which opened an account with a major brokerage firm on 25 June 2000. From that day until 30 June four deposits totalling $67,500 were made into this account. In addition, $17,000 was transferred from Boyle's account at another brokerage firm to that of BSE Investments.

Following Boyle's arrest, there was a dizzying movement of funds from bank and investment accounts he directly or indirectly controlled. Shares in a public company called Edusoft Inc. were transferred from a BSE Investments' account to the account of Boyle's brother. An additional $27,000 was withdrawn from the brother's investment account and transferred to Boyle's bank account. The funds were then moved to the mother's account at another bank and subsequently transferred to her account at Investing Networks Ltd. She also opened an account at another investment firm with a deposit of $17,000. The source of these funds was two cheques, which were drawn from two investment accounts in the name of Lance Boyle (one of which was opened after he was arrested). The mother also wrote a $25,000 cheque to Investing Networks Ltd. from a bank account in her own name, which was deposited into another account at the same bank in the name of Investing Networks. The $25,000 cheque was preceded by a deposit of $25,000 on the same day from a bank account in the name of Boyle's brother.

The source of the funds appeared to be a $25,000 cheque drawn from the brother's brokerage account a month earlier. The funds in this account were from the sale of Edusoft shares, which were transferred to the brother from a BSE Investments' account (Schneider 2004: 54–55).

The Insurance Sector

While a quantitative analysis of RCMP files indicates the insurance industry was implicated in 64.4 per cent of all cases included in the sample, an important caveat should be applied to the this statistic, and by extension, the use of the insurance industry to launder the proceeds of crime. Unlike those sectors of the economy that predominate as money-laundering vehicles – such as deposit institutions or real estate – in most of the police cases the insurance sector was not expressly sought out by criminals to launder their illicit revenues. Instead, insurance policies were purchased because big-ticket items that require coverage – such as cars, homes, marine vessels, and businesses – were acquired with criminal proceeds. As such, in most cases the insurance sector was somewhat tangential to the actual money-laundering objectives and processes.

With that said, police cases and other research reveal the use of traditional personal insurance services, in particular, life insurance policies, as destinations for criminal proceeds. In a 1998 report entitled *Money Laundering Typologies*, the Financial Action Task Force identifies the purchase and redemption of single premium insurance bonds as a key laundering vehicle. Under this scenario, insurance policies can be purchased and then redeemed prior to their full term, less a fee, which provides the launderer with a 'sanitized' cheque. The FATF report cautions insurance industry officials that the following transactions should raise suspicions of potential money laundering by a client:

- cash payments on insurance policies
- refunds requested during a policy's 'legal cancellation period'
- policy premiums paid from abroad, especially from an offshore financial centre
- a policy calling for the periodic payment of premiums in large amounts
- changing the named beneficiary of a policy to a person with no clear relationship to the policyholder

- lack of concern for significant tax or other penalties when cancelling a policy, and
- redemption of insurance bonds originally subscribed to by an individual in one country by a business entity in another country

In one Canadian case, a New Brunswick drug trafficker purchased a life insurance policy with a value of approximately $75,000. The policy was purchased through an agent of a large Canadian life insurance company using a cashier's cheque. The customer made it known that the funds used to purchase the policy were the proceeds of drug trafficking, which prompted the agent to charge a higher commission. Three months following this transaction, the drug dealer cashed in his policy for its full value. In another case, an insurance broker in Alberta accepted large amounts of cash from known criminals, which was then invested under his own name. For a fee, he would issue his clients an insurance policy document, which could be redeemed at their request. As part of an undercover operation, the broker took $35,000 in ($100 bills) from an RCMP undercover operator. The insurance broker then filled out a 'Whole Life Policy' with a specified cash surrender value of $35,000 plus interest. The broker stated that he could put the policy in any name and would even hide the existence of the policy. He then offered to funnel the cash into the insurance company account through his own commercial bank accounts on a monthly basis so as not to attract suspicion.

Canadian police cases also show that the insurance sector has been used as a financial investment intermediary to launder the proceeds of crime by facilitating investment opportunities increasingly offered by insurance companies (such as RRSPs and mutual funds), as well as establishing client accounts, accepting cash deposits, offering term deposits, and providing mortgage financing. Like any other sector that can be used to launder the proceeds of crime, corruption and internal conspiracies within the insurance field can be of considerable benefit to the offender seeking to convert criminally derived cash into other assets. In one file, a $90,000 mortgage was obtained from a major life insurance company to finance a home purchase for a multi-kilo drug trafficker. In the course of their investigation, police also found that the drug trafficker had almost $130,000 invested into short-term investments (GICs) through the same company. The investments were facilitated by a co-conspirator working within the insurance company who siphoned the funds through another unwitting insurance broker to avoid detection.

Motor Vehicles

Motor vehicles are generally purchased for personal use by offenders, although in some cases they are also employed as part of the criminal conspiracy to illegally transport drugs, contraband, or people. In many of the cases examined, cash was used to purchase motor vehicles. Monetary instruments, such as bank drafts or personal cheques were also prevalent. In some cases, instead of purchasing a car, a lease would be obtained, which helped avoid possible suspicions associated with large cash transactions and also limited the amount of equity an offender had in a vehicle, in the event that it was seized by police.

Two predominant money-laundering techniques used in conjunction with the purchase of motor vehicles are registering ownership and insurance in the name of nominees, and 'flipping.' The flipping technique involves purchasing a car with cash, quickly re-selling it, and obtaining a cheque or bank draft for payment. Another associated laundering technique is underinvoicing, whereby a seller of a motor vehicle agrees to a purchase price below the actual value and then accepts the difference under the table. Police cases show that this technique has been used in both private sales and through automobile dealerships and requires the collusion of the seller, including the completion of fraudulent sales invoices and ownership transfer documents that list the price of the car as less than it was actually sold for.

In one investigation involving Francois Savard, a long-time drug trafficker in Quebec, police discovered the extensive use of motor vehicles to help launder his illegal proceeds. Enquiries conducted by the RCMP with the provincial motor vehicle branch indicated that twenty-one motor vehicles had been registered in Savard's name over a period of five years. Savard used a number of laundering techniques in conjunction with his numerous purchases and sales of motor vehicles. One technique was to avoid transferring ownership of an automobile upon purchase (the collusion of the seller was often obtained through financial incentives). Savard also registered cars and their insurance policies in the names of nominees, including friends, family members, and business associates. For example, on 5 November 1997, police interviewed the owner of a Plymouth Chrysler dealership regarding the purchase of a 1996 Dodge Caravan by Savard. Invoices indicated that he purchased the vehicle on 7 December 1997 at a cost of $29,206.65. A payment of $10,000 in cash was made by Savard at the time of purchase, with the balance of $19,206.65 being financed by the Chrysler Credit Corporation. Six months after the purchase, Savard traded in the van. The balance owed at the time of trade-in was $8,607.29, which Savard paid with cash.

While under surveillance, police noted that Savard was driving around town in three different vintage cars. One of the cars was registered to another known drug dealer, although Savard appeared to be the only person who drove the vehicle. The individual who sold the cars to Savard stated that he received $1,000 for each. Police later obtained an estimate from an insurance broker specializing in vintage cases who placed the retail value of two of the vehicles at $10,500 and $9,800 respectively. On 23 October 1996, Savard purchased a 1994 Ford Ranger in a private transaction. Provincial motor vehicle branch records indicated that the purchase price was $11,500. A voluntary written statement obtained from the seller claimed that he was paid $11,500 in $20 bills. The Red Book value for the car at the time of the sale was approximately $19,000. On 11 May 1995, Savard purchased a 1992 Chevrolet Chevette in a private sale. Although the motor vehicle branch information indicated that the purchase price was $1,000, police obtained a written statement from the seller that he had sold the vehicle to Venerante Savard (Francois's mother) for $8,000. The vehicle registration was transferred from Francois to his mother on 15 December 1995 as a gift, however, the vehicle was insured in the name of Francois. On the insurance forms, Francois reported the purchase price of the car at $3,500.

Gold

Safe from currency fluctuations and unpredictable capital markets, gold is a readily recognized and highly convertible form of wealth. Police cases show gold is often simply purchased with illegal funds in its physical form (bars, wafers, and coins). As part of a bankruptcy fraud, police found that Kenneth Gillis, the owner of Gillis Oilfield Construction Ltd., sold the assets of his business and left the country leaving creditors empty-handed. Using funds generated from the sale of these assets, Gillis purchased CDN$400,250 worth of gold in one-, two- and five-ounce gold wafers. The wafers were purchased with cheques from a Calgary-based coin dealer.

Private bullion dealers, coin dealers, and chartered banks are the most common source of gold in its physical form. Jewellers, pawnbrokers, coin collectors, and watchmakers will also buy and sell small amounts of bullion. Some of the larger multiservice currency exchange houses will also perform this role. Police cases indicated that coins or ingots are perhaps the most sought after form of gold for laundering purposes. In one case, a long-time marijuana importer approached a currency exchange office in Montreal to facilitate the purchase of US$1 million worth of maple leaf gold coins. He then arranged for the transfer of U.S. funds from his bank in Switzerland to the Toronto bank account of the currency exchange.

Police cases indicate that the proceeds of crime are also invested into precious metal accounts or trading accounts at brokerage firms to buy and sell precious metals. Similarly, gold can also be purchased in the form of a 'certificate,' a legal document indicating that an individual has title to a specified quantity of a precious metal. Certificates can be purchased at chartered banks, trust companies, bullion dealers, and larger foreign currency exchange dealers. The RCMP discovered that between 1979 and 1986, a convicted Calgary drug trafficker purchased more than 300 ounces of gold in certificate form.

Precious Gems and Jewellery

As a laundering vehicle, precious gems and jewellery possess similar attributes to gold. Most importantly, they satisfy the conversion requirement of the laundering process; that is, illicit cash is transformed into a less conspicuous asset, expensive jewellery. Especially appealing to launderers is the physical compactness and portability of gems and jewellery. A large amount of cash can be converted into a small amount of jewellery or gems that can then be easily concealed and transported – a valuable attribute for the transborder movement of criminal proceeds. Precious gems can also be easily converted back into cash almost anywhere in the world. Jewellery is also attractive to launderers because purchases can be made in cash and do not require identification.

The lack of identification combined with the use of cash means that retailers maintain few records that could assist a police investigation. Moreover, many jewellery retailers will purchase jewellery, allowing the launderer to convert precious gems back into cash. Finally, jewellery can be purchased for private consumption, satisfying the personal tastes of the consumer. Police cases reveal that launderers take advantage of the difficulty in accurately determining the true worth of gems. The difference between a diamond worth $1,000 and one worth $10,000 or even $100,000 is not readily apparent to most people, including customs agents. A valuable piece of jewellery can be brought into Canada and declared at a value substantially below its actual worth, thereby avoiding suspicion. The services of a professional gemologist are engaged only when there is a large discrepancy between the declared purchase price of a gem and the assessment of a customs agent. Once gems have been imported, they can be resold at their true value.

In most proceeds of crime cases where precious gems were identified by police, jewellery was simply purchased with the cash proceeds of crime from a retail vendor. For example, a police search of the home of a cocaine trafficker detected more than sixty separate pieces of jewellery, including gold and diamond-encrusted watches, gold chains, gold and diamond bracelets, gold tie clips, gold and diamond-studded ear rings, and gold rings. The estimated value of the jewellery was $50,000. A search of safety deposit boxes rented by the accused also turned up jewellery. In another case, a police search of the Ontario home of the head of an international drug trafficking network discovered jewellery with a retail value of $304,229. Another search conducted on a safety deposit box also found jewellery and coins, which were later appraised at $314,592. From 1980 to 1984, Montreal was home to the wife of a former Mexico City chief of police accused of embezzling millions of dollars from municipal fines levied in that city. She used much of the embezzled funds to purchase valuable jewellery. After being notified by Mexican authorities, the RCMP seized more than CDN$1 million worth of jewellery from her home.

Legalized Gambling

Police cases show that legalized gambling – in particular, casinos, lotteries, and race tracks – have been used for money laundering purposes.

Money laundering through a casino involves purchasing chips with the cash proceeds of crime, and then eventually cashing in the chips for larger denominations of cash or a cashier's cheque.[28] In addition to converting a large amount of cash into a less suspicious asset, an added benefit of this technique is that the proceeds of crime can be claimed as legitimate casino winnings. In one case, a cocaine and hashish trafficker based out of Ontario attempted to launder the proceeds of his illegal activity through a casino. After providing $8,000 in cash to his son as well as $22,000 in cash to a friend, he advised them to go to a casino, purchase chips, play a few games, and then cash out, requesting a cheque for the amount of the chips. This laundering scheme might have been successful had it not been that the friend, unbeknownst to the accused, had a serious gambling problem and lost the entire $22,000 at the craps table. A further complication, however, is the government requirement for casinos in Canada to keep records and in most cases the criminals would be given their cash back rather than a casino cheque, and hence would not have 'laundered' the money.

In a few cases, criminal entrepreneurs have purchased winning lottery tickets from the real winners (before the prize is claimed) and then claim the prize, which provides them with a seemingly legitimate source of funds. To entice the sale of the winning ticket, the real winner may be offered cash that exceeds the value of the prize. These types of conspiracies are also attractive to the real lottery winner as they do not have to pay taxes (in those jurisdictions where there are taxes on lottery winnings) on the cash provided to them as part of this underground transaction. In one investigation into a Newfoundland drug dealer, police interviewed the owner of a car dealership located in that province. The purpose of the interview was to inquire into the sale of a 1998 Chrysler Intrepid to the accused on 15 June 1999. The invoice indicated a purchase price of $35,246.81. Police established that the vehicle was originally won in a lottery operated by a local charity. Police were able to track down the lottery winner, who stated that she had sold the winning ticket to the accused for $37,000 in cash, most of which was given to her in $20 bills contained in plastic bags. Police determined that following this transaction, the accused proceeded to the car dealership, winning ticket in hand, to claim the prize.

In another case, individuals involved in laundering the proceeds of a massive hashish importation operation purchased a number of winning lottery tickets as a means to claim a legitimate source of revenue. During the investigation of a Vancouver-based lawyer who was alleged to have been involved in the money-laundering conspiracy, police discovered that the lawyer cashed $225,000 worth of winning lottery tickets in Toronto. In total, there were more than seventy winning lottery tickets cashed by the lawyer, the average prize valued at under $5,000.

Horse racing has also come under scrutiny over allegations that criminal groups are using the sport to launder money. There are essentially three ways to launder funds through horse racing. The first is for a drug trafficker or other professional criminal to purchase a race horse with the proceeds of crime. Arrangements can be made to purchase the horses with large amounts of cash and the winnings can be claimed as legitimate revenue. For example, a Toronto cocaine trafficker purchased seven harness race horses for more than $180,000, the cost per horse ranging from $14,000 to $41,000. Although two of the horses were reasonably successful on the racing circuit, the trafficker lost close to $160,000 from this investment. (One of the trainers was permanently suspended from harness racing in Ontario, as some of the horses he trained tested positive for cocaine.)

A second method that can be used to launder money through race tracks is to simply convert small denominations of cash generated from criminal activities into larger bills through pari-mutuel wagering. Alternatively, large bills can be exchanged for smaller ones. While suspicions would be raised if a bettor simply requested to exchange currency at a pari-mutuel betting wicket, one case that police investigated in New York indicates that this method can be facilitated through corrupt pari-mutuel clerks. In the fall of 2000, New York state police went through the cash boxes of scores of betting clerks at the Belmont Park race track. The investigation was part of a response to allegations that individuals with links to organized crime had been colluding with pari-mutuel clerks to launder money.[29]

The third and most common way to use race tracks for money-laundering purposes is simply to place bets using small denominations of cash, which can then be parlayed into larger denominations or even cashier's cheques that are paid out to a winning bettor. Of course, the bettor would not win on every race, but the losses would simply be counted as a necessary expense. To avoid suspicion, the money launderer would always bet on the favourite.[30] Even if he won only as much as he bet, he succeed in exchanging dirty money for clean. To minimize the risk of losing large amounts of money through unsuccessful bets, organized crime figures rely on a long-time tradition of corruption and race-fixing. One jockey in the U.K., who spoke to the media on a condition of anonymity, claimed that as many as one in ten jockeys have been corrupted by criminal syndicates operating in Britain to facilitate money laundering by rigging horse races. The informant jockey admitted to involvement in race-fixing, and said that before one race, his life had been threatened by a gangster who told him not to finish in the first six. The jockey ensured his horse was held back.[31]

Figure 3.11: Professionals coming into contact with the proceeds of crime

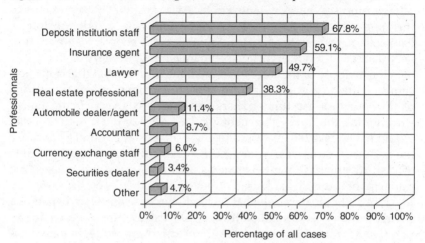

Percentage of all cases

Professionals and Money Laundering

Because most of the cases under discussion in this survey involved the use of at least one sector of the legitimate economy to launder money, it was inevitable that the accused or an accomplice came into contact with a professional. As figure 3.11 shows, the professionals that were predominately used to facilitate the laundering process in the police cases examined are deposit institution staff (101 cases), insurance agents or brokers (88 cases), lawyers (74 cases), real estate professionals (57 cases), automobile dealership staff (17 cases),[32] accountants (13 cases), currency exchange staff (7 cases), and securities dealers and portfolio managers (5 cases). The 'Other' category includes travel agents, notaries, and real property managers.

In general, professionals that come into contact with the proceeds of crime can be divided into two broad categories that correspond to the type of services and expertise provided. This first group includes those with specific technical skills who can provide a criminal entrepreneur with specialized services, advice, and access to industry insiders who can add legitimacy to transactions conducted with criminal revenue. Within this category, lawyers and accountants are the most sought-after professionals, with notaries, financial advisers, and mortgage brokers also being favoured. The second category includes front-line staff of retail businesses that come into contact with criminal entrepreneurs in the course of their day-to-day money-laundering activity, including bank tellers, real estate agents, automobile sales people, insurance brokers, staff at currency exchange companies, and jewellery dealers.

In the majority of the cases examined, the professional that came into contact with the proceeds of crime appeared to have had no knowledge of the source of the funds. There were not any overt circumstances surrounding the funds, the client, or the nature of the transaction that would have raised suspicions. However, in a smaller number of cases, the transaction was clearly suspicious, such as the use of large amounts of cash to purchase big-ticket items, including cars and houses; the purchase of multiple bank drafts from different banks on the same day to pay for a home; requests that lawyers purchase assets on behalf of a client through cheques issued from legal trust accounts; and the incorporation of numerous companies that carried out no legitimate businesses, yet had significant amounts of cash deposited into corresponding bank accounts. In most of the cases involving suspicious transactions, no reports were made to police, which indicates that the professional was either uneducated on suspicious transactions or was wilfully blind to the suspicious circumstances.

Details involving the role of professionals working in the financial services sector, real estate, automobile dealerships, currency exchange companies, and the securities industry have been explored throughout much of this chapter. The following section explores the role of two professional groups that come into contact with the proceeds of crime but which have not been separately addressed thus far: lawyers and accountants.

Lawyers

Police cases demonstrate that, in general, lawyers were not consciously sought out by an offender to launder money, nor was there an explicit attempt by the offender to utilize legal services as a means of satisfying the objectives of money laundering. The services provided by lawyers used for money laundering are frequently part of a series of commercial and financial transactions conducted by criminal entrepreneurs. More specifically, in the police cases examined, lawyers came into contact with the proceeds of crime mainly through their role in facilitating a real property transaction by a drug trafficker or accomplice. In conducting these transactions, lawyers physically handled the cash proceeds of crime or monetary instruments provided by an offender or nominee, deposited these funds into bank accounts in trust for clients, and issued cheques on behalf of clients for the purchase of real estate.

However, there are also police cases where the services of lawyers were explicitly sought out and, in some cases, repeatedly used by criminal offenders to launder their criminal proceeds. Lawyers are highly desired by criminal entrepreneurs because they can satisfy the inherent objectives of the money-laundering process: they can convert the cash proceeds of crime into other less suspicious assets by facilitating the purchase of real estate, depositing illicit funds into bank accounts, or purchasing monetary instruments. Canadian police cases also show that lawyers are used to conceal the true source of funds provided to them by offenders through the use of legal trust accounts and the invocation of solicitor-client privilege, which can place stringent restrictions on the ability of law enforcement to gather information from law offices.[33] Lawyers have also helped to conceal criminal ownership of assets by registering titles in the names of nominees and, in some cases, their own names; they have been involved in transferring funds derived from criminal activities to 'tax-haven countries,' including establishing shell companies in these countries; and have been used to satisfy the third objective of money laundering, creating a seemingly legitimate source of revenue for criminal offenders. This last objective is largely accomplished by establishing shell and active.companies, selling assets on behalf of offenders, and purchasing revenue-generating rental properties.

In the majority of POC cases involving lawyers, they appear to have been unaware of the criminal source of funds provided by an offender and hence were unknowingly used to facilitate money laundering. A minority of cases strongly suggest that the lawyer was either knowledgeable about the criminal source of the funds for which transactions were conducted on behalf of a client or, at the very least, turned a blind eye to the suspicious circumstances surrounding the client, the requested transaction, or the alleged source of funds provided by the client. Moreover, some lawyers appeared to offer services that were tailored expressly to satisfy the objectives of money laundering. This included converting substantial amounts of cash into less suspicious assets, concealing the true ownership of assets, incorporating numerous companies that carried out no commercial activities, fabricating or falsifying financial or legal documents, and transferring funds between bank accounts or between multiple trust account files established on behalf of the client or companies beneficially controlled by the client, for no apparent commercial reason or financial gain.

The services of a lawyer are especially essential in large-scale money-laundering conspiracies. Indeed, in the largest money-laundering operations uncovered by the RCMP to date, all have identified the persistent involvement of one or more lawyer in conducting suspicious transactions for clients. One such example is that of a Montreal lawyer named Giuseppe (Joseph) Lagana who was sentenced in 1995 to thirteen years in prison for masterminding a $47-million money-laundering operation.[34] Another is Basil Rolfe, a Vancouver-based lawyer who admitted to handling at least $8 million in drug proceeds between January 1993 and June 1994.[35] Lawyers are often required as part of large-scale money-laundering operations because the greater the quantity of cash generated by the criminal enterprise, the greater the need for increased sophistication in the laundering scheme. In turn, this increased sophistication requires the expertise of white-collar professionals working to construct and navigate the laundering operation through the complexities of the legitimate business and financial world.

In short, the nature of the involvement of lawyers in money laundering is dictated by the complexity and sophistication of the laundering operation itself. In rudimentary schemes such as those involving the simple purchase of a home, a lawyer is not sought out by the money launderer but becomes involved out of the necessity to involve legal professionals in real property transactions. In these cases only a limited range of services are offered by the lawyer, who is generally not in a position to detect a suspicious transaction or client (especially given the lack of due diligence conducted on clients). In larger, more complex laundering schemes, there appears to be a concerted effort by criminal offenders to seek out and involve lawyers. In these cases, lawyers are more actively involved in providing a wide range of services specifically tailored to money laundering and often appear to be in a position where there is a greater chance that they are cognizant of the criminal source of the funds.

Lawyers and Real Estate Transactions

The instances where lawyers came into contact with the proceeds of crime are mostly the result of the popularity of real estate as a money-laundering vehicle, combined with the necessary role of lawyers in real estate transactions. Typical services provided by lawyers to clients purchasing real property include conducting lien searches, obtaining property tax information, calculating property tax payments for the buyer and seller, obtaining information on insurance requirements, preparing title transfer and mortgage documents, registering the transfer of title, and receiving and disbursing funds through the law firm's trust account as part of the real estate deal, including deposits, down payments, 'cash-to-close,' and mortgage financing.

In a case we have previously discussed, Frederick Tatum, a principal player in a New York-based Jamaican drug trafficking group, arranged to have large amounts of cash physically smuggled into Canada by family members who then laundered the money through financial institutions, law firms, and real estate transactions in Toronto. The drug cash was often taken directly to D. Charles English, a real estate lawyer who was frequently involved in facilitating real estate transactions by family members with tainted funds. A ledger seized from English's law office indicated that the amounts of cash provided to him on any single transaction ranged from U.S.$11,000 to $65,000, much of it in $100, $50, and $20 bills. Most of the real estate purchases made by Tatum family members were immediately preceded by large cash deposits into their lawyer's bank account. Between 1995 and 2000, the period in which Tatum was most active in the drug trade, family members purchased and sold more than forty homes in the Greater Toronto Area. Title to most of these properties was registered in the name of family members or companies controlled by them. In addition to facilitating the purchase and sale of these properties, English was also involved in drafting mortgage contracts, which in many of the property purchases were purportedly between members of the families, but which police ultimately traced to Frederick Tatum's drug revenues. In six real estate transactions, the total cost of the properties was CDN$1,382,696 and of this total, $940,396 was allegedly financed by various family members. English was also a registered owner of three properties, co-owned by two of Frederick Tatum's sisters.

The lawyer's role was significant. A vast number of real estate transactions conducted by family members involved the family's lawyer. On 15 August 2001, a search warrant was executed at English's law offices and in response, the lawyer asserted a claim of solicitor-client privilege on behalf of his clients. However, on 19 December 2001, a judicial order was issued that the documents seized from the law office be turned over to the RCMP. These documents became essential evidence in the proceeds of crime investigation. Although homes registered in the names of family members were forfeited as the proceeds of crime, the lawyer was never charged.

Incorporating Companies

Lawyers are often used in a number of capacities to facilitate launder-ing schemes involving criminally controlled companies. First, they are used to incorporate companies, which includes completing all the nec-essary paperwork, filing the appropriate incorporation and tax docu-ments with government regulatory bodies, setting up bank accounts, and establishing a board of directors. Second, a lawyer may act as a director, officer, trustee, and, in some cases, the owner or a shareholder of the company. Third, if the company operates a legitimate business, the lawyer may manage its ongoing legal, administrative, and financial affairs. Fourth, lawyers have been involved in fabricating accounting and legal documentation. Fifth, a law office may be used as the corpo-rate address for a company controlled by a criminal entrepreneur. Sixth, lawyers have been used in some cases to deposit the cash proceeds of crime into bank accounts, including legal trust accounts, under the guise of legitimate revenue derived from a company.

During one proceeds of crime investigation into three Alberta-based cocaine and marijuana traffickers, named Jake Dowling, Mark Shields, and Sam Zimmerman, police identified three lawyers who helped the accused in setting up and operating companies which were eventually proven to be nothing more than money-laundering vehicles. Docu-ments seized by the RCMP indicated that Sherry Howell acted as legal counsel on behalf of Dowling in the incorporation and preparation of annual returns for DowlShields Investments Inc., a public company in which Dowling and Shields each held 50 per cent voting shares. The corporate address listed for this company was Howell's law office. Documents seized by police from the law office of Howell also showed that she represented Dowling in the purchase of real estate, the title of which was registered in the name of DowlShields Investments Inc. Among the documents were letters from Howell addressed to the com-pany, including certificates of incorporation, bank statements for com-mercial accounts, and documents showing that Dowling and Shields were directors and shareholders of the company. Another lawyer acted on behalf of Dowling in incorporating a numbered company, conducting real estate transactions on behalf of Dowling or numbered companies he controlled, purchasing a car wash, and preparing lease agreements between Dowling and the tenants of a home that was used for a marijuana grow operation. Finally, documents seized by police indicated that Gordon Hoffner, a partner in a local law firm, acted on behalf of Mark Shields and Sam Zimmerman in the incorporation of three other Alberta companies.

Legal Trust Accounts

Criminal revenue is often placed in a law firm's bank account in the name of the offender, a nominee, or a company associated with the offender. In the majority of the police cases, trust accounts were simply used as part of the normal course of a lawyer's duties in collecting and disbursing payments for real property on behalf of a client. Regardless, the significance of a legal trust account in the context of a money-laundering operation should not be underestimated: it can be used as part of the initial first step in converting the cash proceeds of crime into other less suspicious assets, it can serve to help hide criminal ownership of funds or other assets, and it is often used as an essential link between different money-laundering vehicles and techniques, such as real estate, criminally controlled companies, nominees, and the deposit and transfer of illegal revenues. In short, a legal trust account can be used in all four stages (placement, layering, integration, and repatriation) of the money-laundering process.

In one case, Peter Humber used the proceeds from the sale of cocaine, marijuana, and steroids to purchase several homes throughout British Columbia. He admitted to an undercover police officer that he regularly provided cash to his lawyer who would then deposit the funds into his law firm's bank account, $4,000 to $5,000 at a time. When the balance of the account reached a certain level, Humber would use the funds to purchase property. The same lawyer represented Humber in the purchase of most of these properties. Police were able to prove that many of the homes were purchased with the proceeds of crime and used as locations for marijuana grow operations. When asked about his money-laundering operations by an undercover police officer, Humber explained that he purposely used legal trust accounts to help block access to information about the true ownership of funds in the account. Humber boasted to the police officer that legal trust accounts are 'safe havens' because the police, taxation officials, or the 'bar association' could not readily access them.

Lawyers Handling Cash

In some of the police cases, a lawyer or a delegate within a law firm physically handled cash directly generated from criminal activities. In most of these cases, the cash was provided to a lawyer in the context of a real estate transaction and these funds were deposited in trust for the client. However, in other cases, there was no real estate transaction involved and, in fact, no rational explanation why the client was providing large amounts of cash to his/her lawyer.

For example, on 2 October 2000, Rob Cheney was convicted in Edmonton for drug trafficking and received an eighteen-month sentence. The proceeds of crime investigation showed that Cheney had amassed considerable assets over the years, despite the fact that he had no legitimate source of income. Cheney laundered his drug profits through banks, companies he established, legal trust accounts, and real estate. Real estate purchases would often be financed in part through funds from legal trust accounts filled with deposits of cash directly generated from drug sales. Cheney used different lawyers and law firms to facilitate his laundering activity, including Ron Day of Day and Company, Barristers and Solicitors, and Lester Barry of Barry, Egbert, Krauss (and formerly of Day and Company).

The services provided to Cheney by the law firms included facilitating the purchase of real estate, setting up and maintaining shell and active companies, and accepting large sums of cash from Cheney. Ron Day personally made many of the cash deposits in trust for Cheney. Police seized a number of deposit slips, dated between 17 July 1993 and 18 April 1998, indicating that Day had deposited $285,000 (ranging from $19,000 to $70,000, mostly in Canadian $100 bills) on behalf of Cheney. All of the deposit slips included the signature or initials of either Ron Day or Lester Barry. Police intercepted a phone conversation in which Cheney described how he once visited his lawyer with a suitcase containing $150,000 in cash, which was subsequently deposited for Cheney in trust. In another phone conversation, Cheney was heard to say that his lawyer accepted a suitcase with $60,000 in cash, which was also deposited into the trust account. These funds were then used to purchase a Porsche 911 for Cheney. In another phone conversation, Cheney directed an accomplice to deposit $35,000 in cash into Cheney's lawyer's trust account.

Accountants

Like a legitimate company, criminal entrepreneurs must keep track of their revenue and expenses, as well as assets and liabilities, and ideally this job is best carried out by someone possessing accounting or book-keeping skills. Although criminal organizations parallel legitimate businesses in many ways, they are unique in that few businesses purchase millions of dollars in product using cash. The principal job of an accountant working for a successful criminal enterprise is to keep track of the volumes of cash generated by drug trafficking and other profitable crimes. In police cases where accountants were implicated in laundering money, they were used to provide accounting services for both the personal and company-related finances of criminal entrepreneurs.

The need by large-scale criminal operations for accountants was made vivid during a trial of Hells Angels' members and associates in Quebec. Stephane Sirois, a former member of the Rockers – a biker gang affiliated with the Nomads Chapter of the Hells Angels – testified in court that the Nomads purchased as much as 1,000 kilograms of cocaine at a time, which would then be distributed to members of the Nomads and other Hells Angels' chapters for wholesale distribution. The drug revenues were collected by couriers who carried bags of cash to nondescript apartments where they would be counted. By the end of their investigation, police had seized $5.5 million in cash from safes located at various apartments. Police also confiscated accounting spreadsheets which indicated that in one eight-month period in 2000, the Nomads made $92 million from the sale of cocaine. In one recording taped secretly by Sirois, he is heard asking another Rocker named Jean-Guy Bourgoin if he knows of a good accountant. Bourgoin replies with the name of Georges Therrien in Laval. 'He's one hell of a good guy,' Bourgoin responds. 'He worked twenty-five years for the government. And he was Rizutto's accountant – he's always worked for that Italian clique. You give him cold cash – 'Here, wash this for me' – and he will play with your money.' Bourgoin was most likely referring to Vito Rizzuto, described by police as the head of Montreal's leading Mafia family.[36]

Other than the necessity of tracking large amounts of cash in small denominations, police cases show that the tasks performed by accountants for criminal entrepreneurs are no different than that which they perform for legitimate clients. Large-scale criminal entrepreneurs require accountants to help not only with their own personal finances but also with the companies that have been set up to clean their illegal revenue. The work for an accountant in these situations is even more challenging when the company has no legitimate line of business.

Peter Humber, the aforementioned BC drug trafficker, kept two chartered accountants, Norval Reading and Ralph London, busy almost full-time tending to both his personal finances as well as to the many businesses he used to launder his criminal proceeds. Documents seized by police included correspondence between the two chartered accountants and Humber, much of which was in regard to work performed by the accountants for businesses Humber had purchased with the proceeds of crime. The nature of some of the correspondence is summarized in table 3.1. All of these companies were controlled by Humber, including PAH Holdings, which was the registered owner of a number of other legitimate companies.

In an affidavit for a search warrant, one police investigator noted that he examined the reports and other correspondence to and from the two accountants. He concluded that both accountants had prepared comprehensive financial statements on companies owned by Humber and that these statements detailed the income of and disbursements by those companies. Based on this review the investigator intimated that the accountants must have been aware of Humber's true source of wealth, writing, 'It was my belief that in order to prepare those reports, it would be necessary for each accounting firm to be provided by Humber a thorough disclosure of his financial transactions.'

In their quest to legitimize revenue from unlawful activities, criminal entrepreneurs take advantage of a wide range of sectors, services, transactions, and professionals in the legitimate economy. Despite its underworld connotations, the money-laundering process itself is not an economic aberration; it thrives on the very same commercial and financial transactions that are conducted by most Canadian citizens and companies. Indeed, a fundamental tenet of money laundering is to ensure that the transactions used to clean criminal proceeds appear as legitimate as possible.

While this chapter has demarcated its analysis of money laundering into different economic sectors, the research shows that in many cases, a number of different sectors will be used in the context of a single money-laundering operation. This is especially true of the larger, more sophisticated schemes. When used for money-laundering purposes, the different economic sectors are not mutually exclusive but critically interconnected; one sector of the economy (such as deposit institutions)

Table 3.1: Correspondence of accounting firms

Date yr/mo/day	Correspondence	Accountant
94.08.22	Cheque for $500 payable to Reading	Reading
94.09.14	Cheque for $1,000 payable to Reading with the memo 'for accounting'	Reading Reading
95.01.21	Balance sheet of Hummer Appliance Rebuilders	Reading
95.03.22	Cheque for $3,000 payable to Reading with the memo 'for accounting'	Reading
95.04.09	Letter from Revenue Canada to Reading regarding Humber's income tax returns for 1989 and 1991	Reading
96.01.25	Financial statement as of 92.07.31 for Hummer Appliance Rebuilders drafted by Reading	Reading
96.02.11	Cheque for $1,000 payable to Reading on Hummer Appliance Rebuilders account	Reading
96.06.12	Statement prepared by Reading regarding the purchase by Humber of four properties in Peachland, BC	Reading
97.03.11	Letter to a drug-trafficking accomplice of Humber regarding his 1994 income tax returns	Reading
97.03.19	Letter to Reading from Humber's lawyer regarding a mortgage held by N.B. Golf and Tennis on a property owned by PAH Holdings Ltd.	Reading
97.06.02	Revenue Canada notice of assessment regarding Beverly Humber (Peter's wife) sent to Reading	Reading
98.02.31	Financial statement of High Times Developments Ltd.	London
98.04.14	Letter from Reading to a drug-trafficking associate of Humber regarding personal income taxes	Reading
98.06.03	Financial statement as of 96.04.30 for PAH Holdings Ltd.	London
98.08.19	Balance sheet of PAH Holdings Ltd.	London
99.01.24	Facsimile transmitted to a registered director of High Times Developments	London
99.03.17	Letter from Humber's lawyer to London regarding money held in trust for PAH Holdings Ltd.	London
99.05.29	Financial statement as of 97.04.30 for PAH Holdings Ltd.	London
99.10.08	Letter from an employee working for London regarding a mortgage owed by PAH Holdings Ltd.	London

will often be used as a first step in accessing others (such as real estate). Nonetheless, deposit institutions continue to be the most frequently used medium through which the proceeds of crime are laundered. They also constitute the common thread running through the myriad of money-laundering schemes used by criminal enterprises. This sector is especially significant because it represents the single largest portal into the legitimate economy for cash generated in the underground economy.

A number of techniques – some rudimentary, some more inventive – are used to facilitate the money-laundering process. Nominees, smurfs, structuring, and claiming criminal proceeds as legitimate revenue are commonly employed to conceal criminal ownership and avoid suspicion associated with large amounts of cash. Given the new mandatory transaction-reporting regime in Canada, it is inevitable that these techniques will increase in the future in order to circumvent the filing of large cash and suspicious transaction reports by the private sector. One should also anticipate an increase in efforts by criminal organizations to corrupt industry professionals in order to bypass or manipulate the transaction reporting requirements.

4 Enforcement: Assessing Proceeds of Crime Enforcement and FINTRAC

The previous chapter provided an analysis of police cases involving the proceeds of crime. However, it presented little information as to the efficiency or effectiveness of the law enforcement efforts that produced the cases. Evaluating law enforcement units, especially those concerned with the notoriously immeasurable activities associated with organized crime, is a precarious and uncertain endeavour. With that said, this chapter will wade into these murky methodological waters by offering an assessment of the two main 'enforcement' initiatives that are the focus of Canadian enforcement against money laundering. First, proceeds of crime enforcement will be examined with particular attention paid to the Integrated Proceeds of Crime Units (IPOC) and, its predecessor, the Integrated Anti-Drug Profiteering Units (IADP). Following this, the recently created Financial Intelligence Transaction Analysis Centre (FINTRAC) will be discussed.

Proceeds of Crime Enforcement: A Conceptual Overview

Over the last 15 years there has been a quiet revolution in the theory and practice of law enforcement. Instead of simply closing rackets that generate illegal income, the central objective has become to attack the flow of criminal profits after they have been earned. Prodded on first by the U.S., then by the Financial Action Task Force of the G-7 countries, then, in more recent years, by the United Nations, a new crime – money laundering – has been put on the books of many countries. Furthermore many law enforcement agencies now host special units responsible for pursuing not malefactors, but bank accounts, investment portfolios, houses and cars; while officials of the justice system are made responsible for managing such sequestrated assets until they can be forfeited and sold. The law enforcement apparatus therefore has ventured onto territory and begun using methodologies formerly the preserve of revenue authorities. Given the current zeal, it sometimes seems as if what criminals do has ceased to be as important as how much they earn by doing it. (Naylor, 1999a: 1)

The logic of proceeds of crime enforcement is simple, yet it is seductively attractive to governments and law enforcement doing battle with organized crime and, more recently, with terrorism. As an enforcement strategy targeting criminal entrepreneurs and organizations, confiscating the proceeds of crime is meant to achieve three overlapping objectives. First, it punishes offenders by depriving them of the fruits of their trade. Second, it strives to remove the incentive for an offender to engage in profit-oriented criminal activities. Third, it is meant to reduce the financial power base from which criminal organizations can operate. While we might be able to assert that the first objective is achieved, the other two remain dubious. 'Deterrence' theory in relation to any form of criminality lacks credibility – perhaps even more so with organized criminals or persistent career criminals of any sort. Such criminals speak of the 'cost of doing business' and, short of an all-out enforcement assault culminating in massive imprisonments and near-total confiscations, the criminal operations appear to take most seizures in stride. It must also be asked whether the most serious and most sophisticated criminals are even suffering these minor enforcement successes. Do the statistics merely reflect law enforcement successes against the most vulnerable of criminals? While our RCMP cases revealed some large-scale criminal operations among the proceeds of crime cases that were analysed, what the federal government, the RCMP, and the numerous annual evaluations of the IADP and IPOC programs have been unable to empirically establish is the actual impact (if any) on criminal operations from proceeds of crime enforcement efforts.

Proceeds of crime enforcement can be demarcated into two broad and overlapping categories. The first includes the so-called freeze and seize legislation, which allows the state to take possession of cash and assets generated from criminal activities. The second category includes transaction reporting laws, which mandate individuals and organizations operating in the private sector (or crossing the border) to detect and report transactions over a certain monetary threshold or to report those that appear to be associated with criminal or terrorist activities.

The two are not mutually exclusive, but are meant to be complementary: 'Anti-money laundering rules that require extensive reporting on financial transactions help to create a paper trail to facilitate the subsequent tracing and seizing of criminal money, and create new offences that help justify such seizure' (Naylor, 1999a: 1).

Despite a relatively laggard adoption of these enforcement approaches, an abounding optimism among Canadian politicians, government officials, and law enforcement agencies accompanied the introduction of each new proceeds of crime legislative or funding initiative. Federal law enforcement and justice department officials argued that proceeds of crime enforcement represented one of the more innovative and effective tools to target organized crime. Proceeds of crime enforcement also engendered the added benefit of producing revenue for the state; revenue that some optimistically predicted would exceed enforcement costs, thereby generating a net profit for the government. The $18 million Canadian police seized during the year before the introduction of this country's seize and freeze legislation would, as the theory went, represent only 'a drop in the bucket' compared with that which could be confiscated following the new legislation.

This hypothesis was put forth by the RCMP's national proceeds of crime supervisor in 1988. Due to the anticipated increase in proceeds of crime seizures that would result from the new legislation, he wrote, '[i]t's conceivable that drug enforcement will not cost the taxpayer a nickel.'[1] The deputy minister of health at the time of the creation of the Canadian national 'drug strategy' spoke of the resources required to set up the integrated proceeds of crime units as being similar to 'priming the pump' from which riches would flow towards the government! These riches were to be delivered to the Canadian government in part through the enhanced enforcement efforts of the highly touted and distinctive law enforcement units created in 1991 to implement the anti-money-laundering legislative provisions: the three pilot RCMP-led Anti-Drug Profiteering Units.

The significance of these units reaches far beyond money-laundering enforcement. Their multi-agency composition (complete with a interdisciplinary approach that complements traditional police investigative resources with on-site forensic accounting and legal advisers) have become a prototype for major crime investigative units in Canada, in-cluding those targeting drugs, white-collar crime, smuggling, and terrorist groups. Yet despite its groundbreaking status, key questions continue to revolve around proceeds of crime enforcement in Canada, such as:

- Has proceeds of crime enforcement lived up to all the potential and hype that has surrounded it?
- Has the theory of proceeds of crime enforcement been adequately and effectively applied in Canada?
- To what extent has the joint force approach contributed to proceeds of crime enforcement?
- To what extent has proceeds of crime enforcement increased the effectiveness of organized crime and drug enforcement in this country?
- Has proceeds of crime enforcement had any impact on drug trafficking and organized crime in general in Canada?

Our research benefits from annual evaluations of federal proceeds of crime enforcement in Canada that stretch as far back as 1993. In addition to these evaluation results – which we secured through Canada's Access to Information Act[2] – this book is informed by original research conducted with current and former members of the proceeds of crime units. The book also draws on enforcement information that was collected as part of the survey of proceeds of crime files described in chapter 3.

Integrated Anti-Drug Profiteering/Integrated Proceeds of Crime Units

The genesis of proceeds of crime enforcement in Canada can be traced to the creation of the RCMP Anti-Drug Profiteering (ADP) Units in 1981. As a part of the RCMP Drug Enforcement Directorate, the ADP units were charged with 'tracing drug money flows [and] identifying and seizing criminally obtained assets through investigation' (RCMP, 1998: 96). Initially, the ADP program received only spartan resources. For much of the 1980s there were fewer than sixty regular RCMP members dedicated to anti-drug profiteering investigations for the whole country. Few drug investigations incorporated a financial focus due to inadequate resources, a reluctance by drug enforcement units to embrace this new investigative focus (primarily because of the perception that it unnecessarily prolonged drug investigations), and, as equally important, the absence of laws that specifically empowered police to seize the proceeds of crime.

Until 1989, when money laundering was made a criminal offence in Canada, the legislated powers of the Anti-Drug Profiteering Units to seize and forfeit criminally derived funds and assets were limited to section 312 of the Criminal Code, which prohibited the possession of money or property knowingly obtained by or derived from the commission of an indictable offence in Canada or abroad. This Criminal Code section, however, was primarily concerned with providing police the power to confiscate stolen property. The limitations placed on the power of police to seize and forfeit criminal proceeds through this legislative provision culminated in a 1985 Supreme Court decision that denied the RCMP the ability to seize U.S.$700,000 held in a Royal Bank account in Montreal that belonged to Luis Pinto, a Colombian business-man arrested by the FBI in the United States in 1983 for his part in a massive conspiracy to launder cocaine profits. The rationale provided by the Supreme Court was that the definition of this Criminal Code section was not broad enough to allow for the seizure of assets that existed in an 'intangible form,' in this case a bank account credit.[3]

Throughout the 1990s, the resources, powers, and statutes targeting the proceeds of crime and money laundering continued to accumulate. The police still argued, however, that their filing cabinets were full of important cases that they did not have the resources to investigate. Officials at the Department of the Solicitor General asked police forces across Canada what they needed in order to successfully target orga-nized crime. In 1991, the federal cabinet, as part of the renewal of Canada's Drug Strategy, provided $33 million to fund the creation of a five-year pilot project: the Integrated Anti-Drug Profiteering Units. The resources and services provided within these IADP Units represented their 'wish-list.' Designated Crowns, forensic accountants, clerical staff to help with the paper work, and resources committed to long-term complex investigations were what was requested and what received funding. Implemented in Montreal, Toronto, and Vancouver, the multi-agency units combined the resources and expertise of federal, provin-cial, and municipal police personnel, customs officials, Crown counsel, forensic accountants, and support personnel to target the profits of drug-trafficking conspiracies.

The RCMP was designated as the lead agency for the IADP Units and managed their day-to-day operations, and RCMP members made up the vast majority of operational personnel. In addition, for the first time on any sustained enforcement unit in Canada, federal Department of Justice lawyers were physically situated with police, primarily to provide pretrial legal advice and support, such as helping to prepare affidavits and warrants, and providing pre- and post-charge legal guidance.

While drug trafficking was the initial focus of proceeds of crime enforcement and the integrated units, the Canadian government also applied this enforcement strategy to the fight against a rapidly emerging federal priority: cigarette smuggling. The problem had grown so great that by 1994, according to a statement made by the prime minister in the House of Commons, contraband products constituted approximately 40 per cent (roughly 90 to 100 million cartons) of the $12.4 billion Canadian cigarette market (Chrétien, 1994). As part of the National Action Plan to Combat Smuggling, which was announced in February 1994, legislation was passed that applied proceeds of crime and money-laundering offences to tobacco and alcohol smuggling-related crimes. In addition, 116 of the 390 new RCMP positions funded by this national strategy were dedicated to investigating and seizing proceeds of the contraband tobacco trade (Solicitor General Canada, 1997: 4).

In 1996, the federal government not only renewed the IADP initiative, but also expanded it from three to thirteen cities: Vancouver, Toronto, Montreal, Edmonton, Calgary, Ottawa, London, Halifax, Fredericton, Winnipeg, Regina, Quebec City, and St. John's. The geographical expansion was accompanied by a broadening of the units' focus beyond drug trafficking to include other profit-oriented criminal offences, including smuggling, immigration offences, as well as fraud and white-collar crime offences (although the emphasis continued to be placed on drug trafficking and, to a lesser extent, on other federal enforcement priorities like smuggling and immigration offences).[4] Beginning on 1 April 1997, thirteen of the twenty-two Proceeds of Crime (POC) Sections across Canada became integrated units, which were mandated to 'vigorously pursue criminal organizations by virtue of national and international partnerships in government and in the private sector, by detecting, seizing, and restraining illegally gained assets' (RCMP, 2001a: 15).

The expanded Integrated Proceeds of Crime (IPOC) Program was provided with $180.5 million in federal financing over a five-year period (1996–97 to 2000–01), with the RCMP once again receiving the lion's share. However, in an unprecedented and highly contentious move, the federal government officially recorded the funding for the integrated proceeds of crime units as an advance/loan arrangement that was to be 'repaid' through the cash and other assets forfeited to the government as a result of the enhanced proceeds of crime program. This example of 'creative government bookkeeping' (no doubt motivated in part by a sense of fiscal restraint across the federal government and in part by the inviting lure of proceeds of crime enforcement's revenue-generating nature), created considerable consternation and unease among those within and outside the law enforcement community. The police, while welcoming the continuation of the integrated proceeds of crime initiative, feared that the primary mandate of the IPOC Units (a contribution to the dismantling of major criminal networks and organizations) would now be usurped by attempts to maximize seizures and forfeitures in order to 'repay' the loan.

The arrangement was such that the RCMP and the Department of Justice would bear the greatest financial risk; however, they felt (quite reasonably) that the success of the proceeds of crime initiative, in terms of the revenue that was generated, relied on other partners – especially the Seized Property Management Directorate. As the Integrated Proceeds of Crime Evaluation stated in its 1999–2000, 2000–01 report: 'While the advance/loan mechanism purportedly has provided visibility into the efficiency of the initiative, it has also resulted in a significant emphasis on gross financial performance data at the expense of other performance and financial data' (Solicitor General Canada, 2002). Some non-police critics looked to the negative consequences in the United States where police had gained directly from seized assets but where, in too many cases, budgets were then reduced by governments who took these 'likely' seizures into account. The results were thought to include

- a biasing of justice as cases were selected on utilitarian grounds (i.e., easy seizures with no victims with whom the proceeds would need to be shared)
- an unwillingness to work collaboratively with other agencies due to a desire to hold on to all of the criminal's proceeds, and
- violations of citizens' rights as vulnerable targets were 'robbed' by the police and forced to fight to retain their legitimate earnings

In 1998, a long sought-after piece of the integrated proceeds of crime puzzle was put into place when, for the first time, tax investigators from the Canada Customs and Revenue Agency were seconded to the Integrated Proceeds of Crime Units across the country to intensify the application of powerful taxation laws – including the collection of unpaid taxes and significant penalties – against the unreported, taxable profits of criminal entrepreneurs. The addition of tax officials on the Integrated Proceeds of Crime Units, which razed a long-standing barrier between proceeds of crime and taxation enforcement, was yet another signal of the federal government's determination to combat organized crime and the primacy that proceeds of crime enforcement assumed in this battle. Although Canadian police forces could always share information with Revenue Canada, Revenue Canada remained restricted as to what could be divulged to the police.

As part of the funding requirements for the original Integrated Anti-Drug Profiteering (IADP) pilot units as well as the expanded Integrated Proceeds of Crime (IPOC) initiative, the federal department of the Solicitor General was mandated to evaluate the effectiveness of proceeds of crime enforcement in Canada. Particular emphasis was placed on the contribution made by the IADP/IPOC special program funding and task force approach. The broad objectives of this evaluation were to determine whether the provision of adequate funding and coordinated resources resulted in improved proceeds of crime investigations, more successful prosecutions, and a more effective application of the proceeds of crime legislation.

Evaluations were conducted on an annual basis beginning in fiscal year 1993–4. In addition to summarizing the results of these annual evaluations, original research was undertaken for this book that included a review of the raw data collected for the government evaluations, interviews with current and former IPOC Unit members, as well as an analysis of specific cases and other data collected as part of the survey of RCMP proceeds of crime files. In collating and summarizing the results of these data sources and methodologies, four levels of inquiry are used to assess proceeds of crime enforcement and the IADP/IPOC initiatives:

1 Inputs: The quantity and quality of the *resources* provided to the Integrated Anti-Drug Profiteering and Integrated Proceeds of Crime (IADP/IPOC) initiative and the deployment of these resources (including legislation).
2 Process: The contribution made by the IADP/IPOC initiative to proceeds of crime enforcement *capacity.*
3 Outputs: The *intermediate enforcement objectives* of proceeds of crime enforcement: the value of its financial outputs, including seizures/ restraints, forfeitures, fines, and referrals.

4 Outcomes: The *ultimate objectives* of proceeds of crime enforcement: reducing money laundering, depriving offenders of the fruits of their trade and financial power base, dismantling or disrupting criminal organizations and networks, and reducing the number of predicate criminal offences, such as drug trafficking, contraband smuggling, fraud, and so on.

Inputs: The Quantity, Quality, and Deployment of Resources

Canada must be strongly commended for the willingness to apply significant resources into tackling the problem of proceeds of crime – a measure which will undoubtedly result in many more prosecutions and forfeited proceeds. (FATF, 1998: 12)

Proceeds of crime enforcement in Canada would be a relatively insignificant aspect of policing were it not for the resources provided through the IADP and IPOC initiatives. Ignoring for now the perpetual demands made by all law enforcement agencies for increased resources, the rationale underlying the substantial injection of federal dollars into proceeds of crime enforcement in Canada was twofold. First, proceeds of crime enforcement represents what was seen to be an effective strategy to combat drug trafficking and organized crime in general, especially when combined with traditional investigative and interdiction strategies. Second, proceeds of crime investigations, especially those targeting large, sophisticated criminal conspiracies, can often be complex and labour intensive, especially since the inherent objective of money laundering is to hide criminally derived revenue and assets. More funds were required if the police were to commit to these types of investigations.

During the 1990s, there were few specialized enforcement functions that received the level of government financial largesse that proceeds of crime enforcement enjoyed. From 1993 to 2001, the IADP and IPOC initiatives received more than $213 million in direct federal funding. In addition, between 1994 and 1998, proceeds of crime enforcement was allocated a further $116 million from the National Action Plan to Combat Smuggling (primarily by financing an additional 100 RCMP proceeds of crime investigators). This special program funding was in addition to the RCMP's base budget for the Proceeds of Crime Sections.

The success of an enforcement function is not simply determined by the *quantity* of resources. The *quality* of the resources – in particular, the quality of the investigative personnel – is also a significant factor in ensuring effectiveness and success. This is particularly true of proceeds of crime enforcement. This area of law enforcement requires individuals to be trained and experienced in general investigative techniques, drug enforcement, commercial crime enforcement, as well as financial investigations. Money-laundering investigations have an inherent complexity. At one level, these investigations concentrate predominately on financial aspects of crime and, as such, they require a detailed knowledge of financial accounting and commerce, an area of investigative technique not traditionally associated with most Criminal Code offences and not a traditional element of police expertise. Moreover,

> because laundering operations are not confined to any one segment of the business and financial communities, investigators must be familiar with the intricate details of many divergent areas of the private business sector ... in the context of larger enterprise crime and designated drug cases, money laundering investigations must incorporate all aspects of traditional police investigative techniques and resources, including: street-level enforcement; undercover operations; surveillance; search warrants; sophisticated intelligence gathering and analysis; the use of informants and referrals; and criminal as well as financial investigative experience.'
> (Beare and Schneider, 1990: 350–51)

There was an explicit recognition among federal policymakers and law enforcement officials that the personnel hired with IADP/IPOC funds had to be experienced and effective investigators, with a background in drug and commercial crime enforcement. In general, the evaluation findings of the IADP/IPOC initiative acknowledge that most of the personnel working within the new units were competent, experienced, and motivated investigators with broad policing experience conducive to investigating proceeds of crime.

While annual evaluations generally acknowledged the high quality of personnel assigned to proceeds of crime enforcement, the IADP/IPOC Units are not immune to staffing problems common to most law enforcement agencies. These 'handicaps' include the dumping of inexperienced, unmotivated, or incompetent personnel within the units. RCMP staffing policy has also been criticized for undermining the ability of the IADP/IPOC Units to maintain a core group of investigative personnel for a long-term period. Multijurisdictional police forces such as the RCMP engage in a wide range of federal policing duties (drug enforcement, contraband smuggling, national security investigations, immigrant smuggling, commercial crime, etc.) as well as provincial and municipal policing. One of the implications of this multijuris-dictionality is that transfers of personnel across functions, sections, detachments, divisions, and provinces is constant. And while high turn-over certainly contributes to the development of well-rounded police officers, it also has the negative effect of limiting any long-term resi-dency of a police officer within a particular section or area of expertise. Moreover, RCMP promotion policies generally mean that individuals receiving a promotion are often transferred to a new section. The result is that when Proceeds of Crime Section members reach a level of exper-tise and qualify for a promotion, they are most likely transferred to wherever there is a vacant position at the higher rank.

An evaluation report documenting the findings of four 1995 focus groups held with IADP investigators, ADP investigators, Crown coun-sel, forensic accountants and prosecutors, and the management of par-ticipating agencies, summarized the agreed-upon staffing problems experienced by the Montreal Integrated Anti-Drug Profiteering Unit. All of the groups agreed that it is extremely difficult to ensure that individuals stay with a unit over a five-year period, given frequent organizational changes and career requirements. Moreover, the indi-viduals assigned to a special unit such as the IADP are often recruited from among the best an organization has to offer; they are therefore likely to be rapidly promoted and transferred. The Proceeds of Crime Section has nonetheless managed to promote some of its members within its units, thereby ensuring a minimum level of continuity (Schneider and Sauvageau, 1996: 13–14).

These staffing problems were documented by Consulting and Audit Canada in a 2002 internal evaluation of the final two years of the IPOC initiative. According to the *National Post,* which secured a leaked copy of the confidential study, the report states, 'There is a shortage of highly skilled investigative, legal and financial personnel in the various IPOC units.' The evaluation report goes on to say:

> The RCMP promotion and transfer system exacerbates the situation be-cause, in a majority of cases, members must accept positions outside of IPOC to receive promotions. This is particularly disturbing when it is generally accepted that individuals take about three years to gain the experience needed in IPOC to operate efficiently and effectively. (Consult-ing and Audit Canada, 2002: 56)

Despite these challenges, it is arguable that RCMP management has been more supportive of the needs of Proceeds of Crime Units than other areas of RCMP policing. The unit heads have claimed some ability to recommend the assignment of specific individuals into their Integrated Proceeds of Crime Units and have had the support of senior management for these selection methods. Likewise, attempts have been made to increase the number of key positions within the units in order to allow for promotions *within* the units rather than *out of* the units.

What the RCMP cannot 'fix' is the marketability of IPOC members. IPOC Sections have become fertile grounds for poaching by the private sector. The experience of these members as well as their expertise in financial investigations means they are in great demand from the growing industry of private forensic investigation firms. These firms can offer significantly greater annual incomes to ex-police employees. However, with this increase in salary comes greater job insecurity as, unlike in public police forces, each member must perform in an extremely uncomplicated 'performance evaluation' environment where the *bottom-line* takes precedence over any other consideration.

While this book is particularly concerned with anti-money-laundering policing, the same difficulties arise in all areas of police work that require the accumulation of a very specialized body of expertise. Until the promotional system endemic to hierarchical, paramilitary organizations begins to change, good people will be moved out of their areas of expertise. The Consulting and Audit Canada report also identified insufficient training in complex areas such as money laundering, international criminal operations, and foreign legislative and investigative approaches. These training problems 'will be exacerbated by the new need to include training on terrorism networks and operations.' The report contends that the IPOC program has been given 'limited investigative and legal resources' to counter organized crime and political extremists (Bronskill, 2003: A7).

Despite these ongoing personnel problems, the allocation of IADP/IPOC resources by the RCMP and other partner agencies was highly strategic, focused, and consistent with the federal mandate to target organized criminal operations. While the majority of funds were allocated to investigative positions filled primarily by RCMP members, other areas deemed essential to innovative and effective proceeds of crime enforcement also benefited. These areas included the financing of undercover operations, technology purchases (including surveillance equipment and X-ray machines used to detect outbound drug cash at airports), informant and agent funding, as well as the more mundane, but necessary purchases, such as photocopiers and software for managing the hundreds of thousands of pages of documentary evidence gathered by the Proceeds of Crime Sections.

The joint force, multidisciplinary philosophy underlying the IADP/IPOC units was also a guiding factor in how funding was allocated. This multidisciplinary approach was almost universally praised in increasing the effectiveness and productivity of proceeds of crime enforcement in Canada and overcoming an obstacle that had longed plagued organized crime enforcement: a lack of coordination and cooperation among different enforcement agencies. The evaluation findings indicated that the units became increasingly integrated, albeit slowly. This integration was evidenced by annual increases in the number of agencies taking part in the initiative, an increase in the sharing of intelligence information among participating agencies, and a team approach that utilized the respective expertise of the different agencies and professionals on the units. This increased cooperation, coordination, and communication among participating agencies in turn facilitated access to a wide range of resources, expertise, and source intelligence. According to *The Year Four Evaluation Report* of the three IADP units prepared in November 1996, the IADP 'model stresses the importance of integration and the operational value of all partners working together in close proximity on the unit. This has been cited as a strength of the initiative in each of the previous annual evaluation reports and will be confirmed once again in this document' (Walker, 1996: 1).

The multidisciplinary approach of the units was exemplified by the presence of forensic accountants, who are instrumental in providing financial advice and analytical support to investigators, conducting net-worth analyses of targets, piecing together financial paper trails for investigations, and providing expert testimony in court. In the 1996 evaluation report for the IADP Units, 'the accountant's value as an expert witness and as an educator, teaching the investigators what to look for in files and banking records' was cited as the major contribution of the forensic accountant serving on the Vancouver unit (Walker, 1996: 29).

Another positive aspect of the integrated units was the placement of federal Crown counsel. The initial annual evaluations of the IADP Units revealed an almost giddy appreciation among police investigators and management of the on-site Crown counsel, who were also extremely positive about this new relationship. The stationing of Crown counsel on the IADP Units – which was a first for a criminal investigative program in Canada – served to break down many of the barriers that obstructed a productive working relationship between Crown counsel and police. The physical presence of Crown counsel also helped create efficiencies by drastically reducing the turnaround time for the preparation of affidavits and warrants, which were once the sole domain of law enforcement. Police investigators sought the advice of Crown counsel much earlier in an investigation, which helped circumvent any problems in obtaining pretrial judicial warrants or in the prosecution of the file. Special search warrants and affidavits were also better prepared, 'resulting in a more expeditious approval process by the courts.' The on-site lawyers ensured that evidence and cases were better prepared by the enforcement units for prosecution purposes and 'were often able to mediate and resolve situations when differences arose between the police and the Regional Office Crown Counsel assigned to prosecute a case.' The end result was a 'greater percentage of successful outcomes' (Walker, 1996: 20, 30).

However, this new-found relationship was not without problems. The *Year Four Evaluation Report* of the three IADP units noted, 'unfortunately, the past year has seen a gradual movement away from of [sic] the integrative aspect of the initiative across the three units. This has ranged from: a breakdown in the communication among IADP partners; to questions of leadership and cooperation; to the point where partners have physically removed themselves from the units.' Indeed, in the fiscal year 1995–6, the Crown counsel assigned to the Toronto IADP Unit decided not to move to the unit's new location in Newmarket, Ontario, while the Crown lawyers in Montreal and Vancouver also decided to relocate back to the Department of Justice regional office (Walker, 1996: iv, 1). A 1995 focus group with ADP investigators in Montreal summarized the deteriorating situation as such: 'According to most of the investigators, there is an obvious lack of communication among the investigators and counsel, and the outcome is negative. The presence of Counsel has had the perverse effect of delaying the preparation of legal documents. The benefits of having Counsel on staff are becoming less and less obvious' (Schneider and Sauvageau, 1996: 17).

Despite additional resources and their efficacious deployment, the annual evaluations painted a picture of the IADP and IPOC Units as continuously overwhelmed by a growing backlog of files due to an increase in internally generated cases, which were made possible by the additional resources, and a rise in the number of referrals from other enforcement units and the private sector. The focus on large criminal organizations meant that considerable investigative resources were con-sumed by a few large operations. One RCMP supervisor of the Vancouver Proceeds of Crime Section who was interviewed as part of the evalua-tions estimated that between 1994 and 1996, approximately 95 per cent of the IADP Unit's personnel in that city were tied up with two large-scale investigations: Project Eyespy and Project Exceed.[5] RCMP man-agement in Montreal also indicated that by February 1996, nine of the eleven IADP investigators had been assigned to the unit's major file, Project Cervelle (Schneider and Sauvageau, 1996: 13). According to the evaluation report for the fourth year of the IADP units, a total of 151 new cases were opened in fiscal year 1995–96. This represented a 59 per cent decrease from the previous year, which was partially blamed on the resource-intensive nature of the investigations targeting large-scale criminal organizations (Walker, 1996: v).

A number of external events and developments have also conspired to offset the increased funding provided to proceeds of crime enforce-ment. One of the most significant trends in organized crime during the 1990s was the proliferation of well-established criminal groups and networks, representing a diverse range of ethnicities and nationalities and operating at the national and international level. There is also considerable evidence that organized criminal conspiracies have be-come more sophisticated and larger in scope: while a 15-kilo drug shipment was considered large during the 1980s, in recent years, law enforcement in Canada has consistently seized drug shipments that total hundreds of kilos.[6] Globalization and technology have also in-creased the international reach and the number of victims of criminal groups. Fifteen years ago, consumer fraud was limited to the available communication mediums, such as word of mouth, telephone, fax, and letter. Today, the Internet and email help criminal groups peddle vari-ous fraud scams to tens of millions of people on a daily basis, while computers, digital colour printers, and photocopiers have allowed cur-rency counterfeiters to proliferate in a field once confined to those with access to expensive offset printing technology. By the end of the century, there appeared to be a steep rise in the scope, variety, and frequency of (predatory) crimes carried out on an ongoing and organized basis.

There have not been any radically *new* predatory crimes introduced in recent years, simply a reemergence and 'repackaging' of traditional crimes that are more technologically astute and international in scope, including various types of government tax fraud, consumer and corpo-rate fraud (credit card theft, identify fraud, deceitful telemarketing,

Figure 4.1: Per cent of cases by drug type

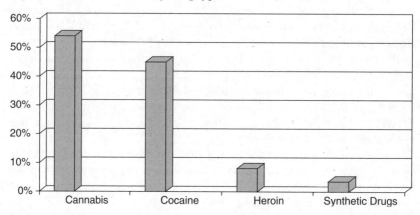

stock market manipulation, advance fee fraud, fake lotteries, etc.), counterfeiting (currency and commercial products), auto theft (which has
become increasingly organized and transnational in scope), and human
trafficking (including organized prostitution).[7] Another unanticipated
trend that began to overwhelm proceeds of crime enforcement – as well
as drug enforcement and municipal and provincial police forces all over
the country – was the explosive growth of the indigenous marijuana
trade, which has become an enormous and highly lucrative industry in
Canada, while attracting international attention for its highly potent
'BC Bud' or 'Canadian Gold.' Proceeds of Crime Units across the country have been besieged by marijuana 'grow-op' files, which became a
priority for the units, especially in British Columbia.

As figure 4.1 illustrates, of the 149 proceeds of crime cases surveyed
for this research, 111 cases (74.5 per cent) involved a designated drug
offence, and of this total, 60 (54 per cent) involved cannabis, while 59
(45 per cent) involved cocaine. Only 9 (8.1 per cent) of the cases involved heroin, and only 4 (3.6 per cent) stemmed from trafficking in
synthetic drugs.

Another issue that has come back to haunt proceeds of crime enforcement in Canada is that of the original funding arrangements devised for
the IPOC Units in 1996. There are a number of disturbing aspects to the
'loan' agreement that underwrote the IPOC's funding, the most perni-
cious of which is the potential that this pact could influence the nature
of proceeds of crime enforcement itself. The loan arrangement is a

quintessentially Canadian compromise to the highly contentious debate over whether law enforcement agencies should benefit financially from the proceeds of crime they have confiscated. Critics charge that these asset-sharing schemes turn police into bounty-hunting, revenue-generating, self-financing entities that can greatly skew priorities and promote the misallocation of seized funds, not to mention police corruption.[8] While the Canadian government had long resisted any policies that permit federal law enforcement agencies to benefit directly from confiscated assets, the loan arrangement certainly contains the most contaminating aspects of asset-sharing policies. Police were, during this period, motivated not simply by their ultimate enforcement objectives – the dismantling of criminal organizations – but also by the self-serving goal of maximizing the value of seizures and forfeitures, regardless of the impact on criminal enterprises.

It is difficult to ascertain the impact these funding arrangements have had on proceeds of crime enforcement in Canada, although concerns have been raised by individuals both within and outside the Proceeds of Crime Sections that maximizing the financial value of seizures and forfeitures became a goal in itself. In the statistics-driven world of law enforcement, it would be naive to assume that maximizing the monetary value of asset forfeitures was ever *not* a priority for the Proceeds of Crime Sections. As noted in *The Year Four Evaluation Report* of the three IADP Units, 'unit staff are beginning to think more in terms of economic outputs, given the shift in emphasis with the new IPOC units to generate revenue to ensure that the annual loan from Treasury Board is paid off' (Walker, 1996: 8). A summary of a 1995 focus group held with Montreal proceeds of crime investigators noted that,

> during the past year, the inspector in charge of the Proceeds of Crime Section suggested that small seizures be made to improve the statistics. According to the investigators, this can easily be done by means of systematic searches at airports, without having to invoke proceeds of crime legislation. (This approach goes against the philosophy of proceeds of crime legislation, which focuses on taking the proceeds of crime away from drug traffickers and not on randomly seizing money.) (Schneider and Sauvageau, 1996: 11)

One can argue that a preoccupation with maximizing the value of forfeited assets is actually antithetical to what had become a major priority of federal law enforcement in Canada: dismantling large organized criminal conspiracies. Successful proceeds of crime investigations into large criminal conspiracies generally result in larger asset seizures; however, they are also much more complex, resource-intensive, and time-consuming. Moreover, the pricey legal counsel hired by well-heeled criminals can drain a sizeable portion of the forfeited assets. It is important to note that proceeds of crime legislation in Canada allows criminal defence lawyers to be paid through the liquidation of assets seized from the defendant. The lawyers therefore profit from the proceeds of crime. Given the potentially small bounty that accrues from targeting large criminal conspiracies, the goal of maximizing the accumulated monetary size of forfeitures may induce the Proceeds of Crime Sections to increase their efforts on smaller files, because these 'quick hits' can be investigated more efficiently. Collectively, small seizures may produce a greater financial value in seizures, relative to the investigation of a smaller number of large criminal conspiracies.

An unfettered emphasis on maximizing the value of forfeitures may also result in a greater temptation for police and prosecutors to plea bargain with defendants to avoid lengthy trials or offshore investigations. The tacit assumption underlying these plea bargains is that the offender agrees to consent to forfeit the assets already seized by police while the government agrees not to pursue any further investigations into other potential assets held by the offender. The incongruity between innovative proceeds of crime undercover work that targets the upper echelons of large criminal organizations and the efficient accumulation of seized assets was summarized by the RCMP member in charge of a Toronto Integrated Anti-Drug Profiteering reverse sting operation during a 1995 interview:

> It was tremendously successful in terms of infiltrating a number of organizations and working our way up to a rather high level of several criminal organizations. In terms of asset recovery, it was not as successful as we would have liked. We spent a lot of time dealing with substantive offenses and supporting the substantive offenses with actually some very good success. But with assets, it was limited. (Schneider and Sauvageau, 1996: 38)

A report prepared for the RCMP and the Solicitor General referred to the government becoming 'the newest Schedule 1 bank handing out advances, taking in deposits, and subsequently turning outstanding advance amounts into loans with payments matched against future forfeitures' (ABCsolutions, 2002: 5). The press release at the time of the report quoted the Honourable Herb Gray, then Solicitor General, as stating:

> Experience has shown that these special units can effectively use the Proceeds of Crime laws to cripple organized crime efforts. And this is a law enforcement effort that will generate revenues for government, through the court-ordered forfeiture of criminally obtained assets. The success of the three pilot units shows that more such units located across the country could make a much greater impact on organized crime.[9]

Like Herb Gray, the deputy ministers had high expectations. They fantasized about the IPOC 'pump' that would flow with money that could be used in diverse ways throughout government. In reality, however, the results were disappointing. By the end of the original IPOC advance/loan funding initiative in fiscal year 2000–01, it became clear that the units would not come close to repaying the $180.5 million 'loan' through the forfeitures generated from proceeds of crime enforcement.

According to the evaluation reports and other RCMP estimates, between fiscal years 1996–7 and 2000–01, IPOC investigations led to only $71 million in forfeitures (RCMP, 2001b: 19). This financial shortfall was not completely unexpected. However, by the end of fiscal year 2000–01, the shortfall contributed to one of the worst crises that proceeds of crime enforcement had faced in Canada since the inception of the ADP Units some twenty years earlier. According to the Consulting and Audit Canada evaluation of the final two years of the IPOC initiative, the 1996 loan arrangements 'seriously impair[ed] the effectiveness of the initiative or even [made] it impossible to continue,' mainly because revenues from proceeds of crime were 'much lower than anticipated,' resulting in a substantial deficit (Bronskill, 2003: A7). At the end of fiscal year 2000–01 – the final year of that cycle of IPOC funding – there was no indication from the federal government on whether it would continue to fund the integrated program. For the next two years, the IPOC units were held in abeyance, forced to exist on a patchwork of interim and substantially reduced funding.

The lack of an operating budget resulted in a significant level of instability and uncertainty for proceeds of crime enforcement in Canada. The reduction in funding and uncertainty over the future of the IPOC program had grave effects. The reduction meant that some units were operating at half their usual capacity, ongoing investigations had to be shelved, the backlog of pending cases grew even larger, the number of seizures began to drop, source intelligence imploded due to a lack of funds for informants, and strategic planning was greatly curtailed. The Consulting and Audit Canada evaluation found that the lack of dedicated funding following the end of the original IPOC initiative in 2001 exacerbated staffing problems by creating a level of instability that undermined the effort to attract and retain qualified staff. According to the report, retaining staff in the IPOC Units was an 'ongoing concern' because of the uncertain nature of the program's funding, which did 'not encourage individuals to try to build a career in the initiative' (Bronskill, 2003: A7).

In the federal budget tabled in February 2003, the government allocated $46.6 million over the next two years to continue the integrated proceeds of crime initiative, which reduced annual funding from approximately $36 million to $23 million.[10] The advance/loan arrangements were terminated.

The uncertainty over ongoing funding and the eventual decrease in IPOC funding arose during a period when increased federal attention was being paid to the government's newest weapon in its battle against money laundering and terrorist financing: transaction reporting and the creation of the federal financial intelligence unit. It was during this time that the Financial Transactions Reports Analysis Centre of Canada (FINTRAC) was established. A former officer in charge of the Proceeds of Crime Branch at RCMP headquarters, who was interviewed for this research, complained that the new funding provided to FINTRAC at a time when funding to IPOC Units was being dramatically reduced was tantamount to 'robbing Peter to pay Paul.' In effect, he argued that limited anti-money-laundering program financing was shifted to FINTRAC from the RCMP. In turn, this contributed to an ongoing fragmentation of proceeds of crime enforcement as more federal agencies were created, including, in addition to FINTRAC, new RCMP branches such as the RCMP Financial Intelligence Branch (dedicated to terrorist financing), the Seized Property Management Directorate, and the Forensic Accounting Management Directorate. While these comments may be merely reflective of the oft-encountered 'Mountie mentality' that all enforcement functions should be centralized in the RCMP (and more specifically within the RCMP section where the spokesperson is positioned), all of these new units and organizations do in fact compete for a limited amount of funds dedicated to proceeds of crime enforcement in Canada.

Process: Proceeds of Crime Enforcement Capacity

Due to the IADP and IPOC funding, Proceeds of Crime Units in Canada were able to undertake innovative, albeit controversial, enforcement techniques that were previously unfeasible in this country. Almost immediately following the launch of the IADP, the RCMP embarked on a national sting operation targeting retail currency exchange businesses, which had long been considered a highly desired conduit for money laundering, due in part to the lack of any industry regulation or supervision. Undercover police officers, posing as drug traffickers, carried large sums of cash into the targeted businesses and confessed to the operators that they were the product of drug trafficking. At the conclusion of the seven-month operation in June 1994, 190 charges were laid against 36 companies and 65 individuals in 7 cities across Canada (Marsden, 1994: A4).

The three original IADP Units also embarked on an even more ambitious undercover operation, this time with police posing as the money launderers. This operation marked the difference between 'sting' operations whereby the police purchase or use the services of criminals and 'reverse sting' operations whereby the police offer the criminal goods or services. The Montreal IADP Unit implemented Project Compote, which involved establishing a retail currency exchange business called the Centre International Monétaire de Montréal (CIMM) on de Maisonneuve Boulevard in the downtown core. The business was officially incorporated on 17 August 1990, and began exchanging money in September 1990. It was officially terminated in 1994. Likewise, based on the Montreal model, the Vancouver Proceeds of Crime Section launched Project Eyespy, which also involved the launch of a fake retail currency exchange operation staffed by undercover police personnel. The Vancouver version was called the Pacific Rim International Currency Exchange and was located at 818 Burrard St. in the financial district of downtown Vancouver.

These undercover operations, which would not have been possible without the funding provided through the IADP initiative, were instrumental in identifying a number of money-laundering operations. These were mostly small-time criminals but also included some very large criminal operations. The undercover operations were the primary technique used to infiltrate large criminal organizations while targeting their principals. When asked if Project Eyespy was able to target larger criminal organizations and their upper echelons, one RCMP member involved in the project and interviewed in 1995 had this to say:

> Very, very much so. We knew that 90 per cent of people who came into the store were not people who were of real interest to us. But those people, through statements, through surveillance led us to other individuals and the operators within the store always tried to step through the people who came into the store and work their way up ... The objective was to work our way up the ladder as high as we could to identify individuals or groups and to target those higher-level individual or groups through successful seizures, forfeitures and prosecutions ... As far as identifying major criminal organization and meeting the objectives of why the project was initially established, we certainly were successful in doing that. (Schneider and Sauvageau, 1996: 86)

According to the RCMP, Project Eyespy ran from 1993 to 1996 and identified 430 people in the Vancouver area who laundered money through the undercover currency exchange business. In the end, ninety people were charged with more than 1,000 criminal counts related to the laundering of approximately $40 million in criminal proceeds. The proceeds were mostly revenue from cocaine and marijuana and, to a lesser extent, contraband liquor and tobacco. Sixty per cent of the cash brought into the Vancouver retail operation was in Canadian currency (mostly from local cocaine sales), all of which was converted into American currency. The exchange was also attractive to those selling British Columbian marijuana in the United States, which typically involved converting American dollars smuggled back into Canada into Canadian currency. The undercover operation also led to the seizure of 222 kilograms of marijuana, 815 kilograms of cocaine, $2.5 million in cash, and several handguns, and led to the dismantling of at least three marijuana grow operations in the Greater Vancouver Area.[11]

The undercover operations also generated source intelligence that led to the identification of several drug importation conspiracies and the seizure of multi-kilo shipments of cocaine and heroin in Canada and abroad. These shipments were linked to major criminal enterprises including Colombian cocaine trafficking networks, the Hells Angels, and the Montreal-based Rizzuto crime family. At the culmination of the Montreal undercover operation on 30 August 1994, fifty-seven people were arrested and charged with hundreds of counts of money laundering and drug offences. Of particular note was the arrest and conviction of Montreal lawyer Giuseppe (Joseph) Lagana, who had strong ties to Vito Rizzuto, the reputed head of Montreal's Italian Mafia. In 2006, Rizzuto was deported to the U.S. to face murder charges (see also Lamothe and Humphreys, 2006). In 1995, Lagana was sentenced to thirteen years in prison for organizing a $47-million money-laundering operation that relied extensively on the services of CIMM (Centre International Monétaire de Montréal). Undercover RCMP officers staffing the bogus currency exchange business accepted millions of dollars in cash delivered personally by Lagana and other employees of his Montreal-based law firm Barza and Lagana (his law partner was not implicated in any of Lagana's money-laundering operations).

According to court testimony, Lagana concocted the laundering strategy and recruited two other junior lawyers, Vincenzo Vecchio and Richard Judd. All three were involved in picking up and transporting drug money to CIMM and ensuring that the large volumes of small denominations of Canadian currency were converted into larger denominations of Canadian or American currency. Other CIMM services availed by the lawyers included purchases of monetary instruments and arranging for overseas wire transfers. In the end, Lagana was personally responsible for laundering more than $15 million in Canadian funds over four years through CIMM, including drug proceeds provided by members of the Hells Angels.[12]

The investigation into the lawyer uncovered a substantial cocaine importation conspiracy by members of the Hells Angels (reputed associates of Rizzuto) and Jorge Luis Cantieri, a Montreal businessman who ran numerous import-export companies that were a front for the Colombian Cali Cartel. The clients of the Montreal undercover currency exchange business had built up so much trust with the police operatives that they asked for their assistance in smuggling cocaine into Canada. As a result, the RCMP chartered a freighter and, with help from U.S. customs agents, sailed it to Colombia, picked up 558 kilos of cocaine and brought it back to Montreal where it was seized (Marsden, 1994: A4). Among those arrested was Cantieri, who eventually received a fifteen-year prison term for orchestrating the cocaine shipment.

In Toronto, the most significant ongoing money laundering undercover operation did not involve establishing a retail currency exchange as in Montreal and Vancouver. Instead, the Integrated Task Force set up a covert 'financial investment house' called Inter-Cay Financial Investment Limited. Physically located in a private office in a commercial tower within Toronto's financial district, the covert operational strategy focused specifically on attracting the criminal element. According to Chris Mathers, a former RCMP officer and lead undercover operative for Inter-Cay, a private financial investment approach was deemed more effective at screening out legitimate money and transactions, which were common in the Montreal and Vancouver operations due to their retail services, high traffic locations, and competitive exchange rates. Through a strong informant base, and in close cooperation with undercover agents operating out of substantive enforcement units in Canada and the United States, Inter-Cay became the recipient of numerous referrals of drug traffickers and other criminal entrepreneurs looking for confidential money laundering services. Indeed, to its targets, the undercover officers who staffed this private investment company made no pretence about the raison d'être of this business: to help criminal entrepreneurs invest and launder their proceeds of crime. The exorbitant rates levied by Inter-Cay for its services, as well as the additional commissions charged for each transaction, were also meant to send a clear signal to targets of the high-risk and illegal financial investment services offered by the company. The high expenses also helped to establish criminal intent necessary for successful prosecutions.

The undercover work of the Toronto Integrated Task Force also proved to be an effective back-door route to gathering evidence on substantive drug trafficking and criminal code offences. As such, the Integrated Task Force (ITF) became increasingly involved in investigating not simply the proceeds of crime offences but also the predicate offences that gave rise to money laundering (e.g., drugs, fraud, smuggling). For example, in 1995, evidence identified by the Integrated Section led to the seizure of 40 kilos of cocaine, the take down of a 'large' marijuana hydroponic grow operation, and the dismantling of an illegal telemarketing organization (Schneider and Sauvageau, 1996: 50). In 1996, the ITF contributed to the seizure of 400 kilos of cocaine and 125 kilos of heroin (Schneider, 1997b: 2).

In Projects Once and Once More, the ITF undercover operation worked in close concert with drug enforcement units in Canada and the United States to target large-scale international drug trafficking operations. In Project Once More, which targeted a large-scale Guyanese drug trafficking operation that operated out of New York and Toronto, drug enforcement units focused on the middle level of the criminal organization while the ITF undercover operation was able to successfully target the organization's upper echelons through the covert money-laundering sting operation. In commenting on the use of the reverse

sting operations, and more specifically the operation of currency exchange bureaus by police, one long-time crime reporter for the *Montreal
Gazette* wrote, 'Even if the full extent of the planning and security
measures are never revealed, on the face of it, the sting demonstrates a
new willingness at the RCMP to launch elaborate, imaginative and
expensive operations to snare illicit money and the money movers'
(Marsden, 1994: A4).

Despite their apparent success, the reverse sting operations were
controversial. At the time they were implemented, it was illegal for
anyone to have in their possession the proceeds of criminal activities.
As the courts pointed out in later decisions, there was no exemption for
police officers conducting criminal investigations (although the laws
have since been changed to grant police such exemptions). Moreover,
the RCMP was faulted for not requiring its customers to complete
transaction reporting forms or to show identification, thereby contra-
vening the 1991 Proceeds of Crime (Money Laundering) Act. When a
Montreal client of the covert RCMP currency exchange was charged
with possessing the proceeds of crime and money laundering in 1995,
he challenged the legality of the police-run operation. While a Quebec
court judge ruled the undercover operation was legal, two years later, a
BC Supreme Court judge declared the RCMP's reverse sting operation
in Vancouver to be illegal. In a judgment handed down in January 1998,
Madam Justice Humphries said that 'the police knowingly possessed
proceeds of crime and agreed to operate in such a way that would
necessitate handling those proceeds. Generally, those actions, if done by
anyone else, would be criminal acts' (Ouston, 1998: B1; McIntosh, 1998d:
A1).

In a decision rendered on 30 June 1995, Madam Justice Eileen Nash of
the Alberta Queen's Bench assessed the legality of a similar RCMP
money-laundering scheme conducted in Ontario in 1990 and 1991,
called Project Mercury. Justice Nash, in response to a submission by the
federal justice department that the Criminal Code does not apply to the
RCMP if they are engaged in a bona fide investigation, stated:

> That submission is novel and creative, but it is not the law in Canada ... I
> am satisfied that the provisions of the *Narcotic Control Act* and of the
> *Criminal Code* apply to the RCMP regardless of whether they are engaged
> in a bona fide investigation. There must be legislation that specifically
> exempts the police before such an exemption applies, or a grant of immu-
> nity. (Martin, 1996: A17)

In a scathing critique of the undercover operations, Vancouver lawyer David Martin wrote in a 13 February 1995 op-ed piece in the *Vancouver Sun* that 'it appears that the RCMP and the Justice Department ignored this ruling when they continued to run *Eyespy* here in Vancouver after June 30' (Martin, 1996: A17).

The issue of police immunity for criminal conduct during a police investigation was decided in *R. v. Campbell and Shirose* (April 1999, Supreme Court of Canada [1999] 1 S.C.R. 565 File #25790). This Supreme Court case confirmed that 'neither the *Narcotic Control Act* nor its regulations authorized the police to sell drugs' (para. 15).

The RCMP also came under fire when the *Ottawa Citizen* published a series of articles in June 1998 that accused the covert exchange business in Montreal of helping drug traffickers get away with laundering more than $140 million in drug proceeds in a four-year period. Because the Montreal Proceeds of Crime Section was so overwhelmed with the volume of cash processed through the exchange, only a small fraction of the suspected drug trafficking clients could be investigated (McIntosh, 1998e). One of the *Citizen* articles stated that the Montreal Proceeds of Crime Section seized only $16.5 million from the $141.5 million that passed through the operation, while helping to move more than $94.7 million in drug money to Colombia in 1992 and 1993 (McIntosh, 1998c). Citing an internal RCMP report, a *Citizen* article published on 11 June 1998 article accused the undercover operation of facilitating drug purchases. The article alleged that the conversion of Canadian to American currency allowed traffickers to purchase cocaine in the United States, while the conversion of American to Canadian cash allowed purchases of high-grade hydroponic marijuana in British Columbia. The *Citizen* articles asserted that the RCMP-led operation was undermined by

- a chronic shortage of police human resources as well as technical resources, such as specialized computers needed to perform wiretap operations
- missed drug seizures, and
- internal security breaches by two or more corrupt RCMP officers (McIntosh, 1998b: A1)

According to a newspaper article published on 13 June 1998, 'There were too few investigators and surveillance teams, there was too little money and not enough technical resources to investigate all the criminals who walked in off the street to use the currency exchange.' Police personnel shortages were so bad that two years into the undercover operation one incensed RCMP investigator, Constable Mike Cowley, complained in writing to his superiors that 'without the necessary resources and personnel to do proper and complete investigations, it seems like all we are doing is offering a money laundering service for drug traffickers' (McIntosh, 1998d: A1).

The same article went on to assert that once police converted Canadian cash into U.S. currency or bank drafts in U.S. dollars and handed it over to their drug world 'clients,' they had no control over what happened to the money as soon as the traffickers walked out the door. Without a sufficient quantity of surveillance teams and investigators, police often failed to discover where the drug money came from and where it went (McIntosh, 1998d: A1). In a 24 June 1998 report addressed to the Solicitor General, then-RCMP commissioner Phil Murray admitted that the Montreal reverse sting operation suffered from 'a critical lack of investigative resources,' due to emergency policing responsibilities for a stand-off with armed Aboriginal protesters in Ontario (the Oka Crisis) and the Gulf War that occurred about the same time (McIntosh, 1998g: A6).

While the RCMP claimed that resource shortcomings were a factor, there are other issues that cannot be ignored. Reverse sting operations are intoxicating in terms of the power and invisibility that is granted to the police who run them. One imagines the sense of theatre attached to even the process of setting up the offices and dressing the part of high-roller launderers. These operations require at least as much, and likely more, oversight than the normal degree of supervision that is required in all undercover operations. We know how badly wrong a small-scale undercover operation can go. How much greater harm can be done as a result of badly managed, ill-monitored, and out-of-control reverse sting operations? A 14 June 1998 *Ottawa Citizen* article revealed that, based on a review of classified federal documents, the Montreal undercover operation ran for five months in 1990 before obtaining the required approval from the Solicitor General of Canada. Even when the Solicitor General's approval was later obtained, 'it appears that the RCMP never told the minister about the full extent of its covert operation: that police officers were changing Canadian currency into U.S. funds for suspected drug traffickers, and that such transactions would facilitate the importation of drugs' (McIntosh, 1998e: A1).

Moreover, despite the program's inception in September 1990, it was not until February 1992 that the RCMP formally told U.S. drug enforcement authorities that, as part of its covert operation, it was using a U.S.-

dollar account at a New York City branch of a Canadian bank. Quoting a confidential internal RCMP memo, the newspaper reported that police officers operating the Montreal currency exchange business came 'precariously close to being prosecuted by a U.S. Attorney's office for money laundering.' The RCMP disclosed its covert operation to the U.S. Drug Enforcement Administration and U.S. District Attorney in New York during a meeting in the United States in early February 1992 (McIntosh, 1998f: A1).

By the beginning of the IPOC initiative in 1996, there was a marked reduction in the use of standing reverse sting operations, especially those as ambitious as Projects Compote in Montreal and Eyespy in Vancouver. Adverse court decisions were a major factor. The diminution in proactive, innovative enforcement may also be attributed to the various problems that emerged during the operations, the increasingly risk-adverse mentality of senior RCMP officials, and the substantial resources consumed by such undercover operations. One can also speculate that the 1996 funding advance/loan arrangements may have helped to sound a death knell for undercover operations. The increased emphasis placed on maximizing the monetary value of seizures and forfeitures meant that greater resources would be dedicated to traditional investigations where the potential for fast and substantial seizures could be better estimated and realized, relative to reverse sting operations that had to be carried out for years before arrests and seizures could be made.

Outputs: Intermediate Enforcement Objectives

The most oft-cited indicator used to assess proceeds of crime enforcement – and one that is certainly unique among criminal investigative units – is the monetary value of seizures and forfeitures. The reliance on this criterion for evaluation purposes by law enforcement management, policymakers, and government evaluators is unfortunate because these objectives are not necessarily reflective of the objectives or the ultimate success of proceeds of crime enforcement. Moreover, the reliance on these statistical indicators and any emphasis on maximizing seizures and forfeitures may be pursued at the expense of other more important objectives, particularly the dismantling of criminal conspiracies. From a research and evaluation perspective, an added problem is that in Canada, one is hard-pressed to find reliable and consistent estimates of these enforcement outputs. Anyone inquiring into proceeds of crime statistics will be inundated with a plethora of different figures that have been churned out to estimate the monetary value of seizures and forfeitures, none of which are particularly accurate due to both the inherent difficulty of estimation and the largely unscientific method used by federal agencies in estimating the value of assets that have been seized.

With this preface in mind, some estimates of the monetary values of proceeds of crime seizures and forfeitures released by the federal government and the RCMP are as follows.

- In the first four years of the IADP initiative (1992–3 to 1995–6), $87.2 million in cash and assets were seized and $25.04 million was forfeited. In addition, the units referred approximately $240 million in seized cash, assets, and stolen properties to other domestic and foreign law enforcement agencies for action. (Solicitor General Canada, 1997: 4)
- Between fiscal years 1996–7 and 1999–2000, IPOC investigations resulted in $53 million in seizures and almost $60 million in forfeitures. (Schneider, 2000: 67)
- According to the *2000/2001 Performance Report* of the RCMP, the outputs of the Proceeds of Crime Program resulted in $23.6 million in seizures by all IPOC and satellite units, $10.7 million in revenue collected, $353,433 imposed in fines, and $55 million in referrals to other law enforcement agencies. (RCMP, 2001b: 19)
- The *2001/2002 Performance Report* of the RCMP states that the Proceeds of Crime Program seized $46 million in assets, collected $13.7 million in revenue, imposed $1.7 in fines, and referred $59.4 million for investigation to other law enforcement agencies. (RCMP, 2002: 19)
- Briefing notes prepared for the Solicitor General dated 5 February 2001 state that 'to date, IPOC units have seized over $170 million and over $117 in forfeitures and fines have been realized.' (Solicitor General Canada, 1999)
- One web-based edition of the *RCMP Fact Sheets 2000/01* reads, 'The RCMP has enjoyed considerable success since Proceeds of Crime legislation was first passed in 1989, and has seized/restrained approximately $221 million dollars worth of assets.' (RCMP, 2001a: 15)
- In response to a question in the House of Commons on 24 February 2003, the Solicitor General announced that the IPOC program 'has contributed to seizures of criminal assets of more than $215 million and forfeitures of more than $86 million. It has referred cases worth $89 million to other jurisdictions in Canada and abroad.'[13]

For evaluation purposes, these inconsistent figures are almost meaningless, especially since the Proceeds of Crime Program and the IADP/IPOC initiatives never set specific goals for the value of its seizures and forfeitures. To judge the success of the IPOC Units based on their ability to pay back the loan through forfeitures is also highly arbitrary. A more illuminating method of judging the success of proceeds of crime enforcement, at least on a fiscal basis, is to calculate two sets of ratios. The first of these ratios compares 'recoveries' (seizures and restraints) to 'revenues' (forfeitures and fines), which is a determinant of the ability of police and prosecutors to ensure that all property seized by the Proceeds of Crime Sections is permanently confiscated. The second ratio compares the costs of operating the Proceeds of Crime Sections with its financial outputs (recoveries and revenues, respectively).

Seizure versus Forfeiture Statistics

Some estimates of the first ratio for the IADP and IPOC pilot units, as well as the RCMP Proceeds of Crime Program in general, include the following:

- In the first four years of the IADP initiative (1992–3 to 1995–6), the pilot units' forfeitures were 28.7 per cent of seizures ($87.2 million in seizures compared with $25.04 million in forfeitures). (Schneider, 1997a)
- Between fiscal years 1996–7 and 1999–2000, forfeitures were 113 per cent of seizures ($60 million in forfeitures compared with $53 million in seizures). This percentage included the forfeiture of seizures from a previous year. (Schneider, 2000: 67)
- In fiscal year 2000–01, 'revenues' (which include forfeitures and fines) were 46 per cent of seizures ($11.05 million and $23.6 million. respectively). (RCMP, 2002: 19)
- In fiscal year 2001–02, 'revenues' were 33.5 per cent of seizures ($15.4 million in forfeitures and fines compared with $46 million in seizures). (RCMP, 2002: 19)

Proceeds of crime enforcement is considered most successful when the difference between the monetary value of recoveries and revenues is small because this means that the government has been successful at maximizing the permanent confiscation of proceeds of crime seized by police. As indicated above, on average, forfeitures were less than half of seizures, which could be interpreted as a negative reflection of the ability of the Crown to maximize forfeitures. This may result from a judge ordering a defendant to forfeit only a portion of the seized money or assets, which may result from the inability of the Crown to prove that such assets were derived from criminal activity. Alternatively, prosecutors may plea-bargain with a defendant, whereby some of the assets are returned to the offender. Another reason why the value of forfeitures are much smaller than that of seizures is due to section 462.34 of the Criminal Code, which allows the use of seized assets to pay a defendant's legal fees (a fact which causes no small amount of consternation among proceeds of crime enforcement personnel).

In acknowledging the differences between the monetary value of seizures and forfeitures in its 2000–01 annual report, the RCMP tacitly shifts the blame for such differences to the Department of Justice and the judiciary, 'There is a difference between seizures by the police and forfeitures decided later on by the courts (often down by 25 per cent). In general, seizures represent police enforcement results while forfeitures are a performance indicator of the prosecution and the courts' (RCMP, 2001b: 58).

There are also a number of inevitable and unavoidable valuation issues that account for the differences between the monetary value of forfeitures and that of seizures, and which should not reflect poorly on government efforts to maximize the former. The most common scenario is that at the time of seizure, an asset may be appraised at an estimated *gross* value, yet when it is eventually forfeited, payments from the liquidated asset must often be made to legitimate third partners, including mortgage-holders and other creditors. Finally, it should be noted that comparing forfeitures and seizures for the same period is misleading as forfeitures generally take place months and even years after the cash or asset was originally seized. During the years when forfeitures were greater than seizures, the explanation would be that previously seized proceeds had worked their way through the courts and had finally been forfeited.

Enforcement Costs versus Financial Gains

Comparing the operational costs of proceeds of crime enforcement with the financial benefits accruing from this enforcement strategy has also been used as an evaluation yardstick. According to a 1997 document that outlines the evaluation framework for the IPOC Units prepared by the Department of the Solicitor General,

A total of $33.02 million in [Canada Drug Strategy] resources were assigned to the IADP over the five years. In the first four years, the new resources resulted in $87.2 million in seizures and $25.04 million in forfeitures. The total amount of forfeitures reflects 96.6 per cent of the costs of the initiative during the same time period. Factoring in the initial 'growing pains' of such an initiative, it is clear that the three IADP units have met their expectations from a cost return perspective. Furthermore, if one were to add in the eventual return on the seizures at a fairly conservative rate of 40 per cent, the total value of forfeitures for the same time period would increase by a further $34.88 million. Cumulatively, this would show a return of $59.92 million on a four-year investment of $25.93 million, a 131 per cent increase. (Solicitor General Canada, 1997: 4)

This paragraph was taken from a proposal for more special program funding for proceeds of crime enforcement (eventually leading to the formation of Integrated Proceeds of Crime Units). The image of great success and even greater expectations were obviously part of the intended message. However, the original calculations upon which this exultant assessment was based (Schneider, 1997a) did not materialize in the actual operations of the IADP pilot units. A cost-benefit analysis of the three IADP Units conducted in 1997, based on a cost-revenue ratio and compared with their previous un-integrated ADP operations, indicated that they had not necessarily become more efficient. In their first four fiscal years of operation (1992–3 to 1995–6), the IADP Units 'recovered' $327 million over a four-year period (including seizures, restraints, and referrals). In addition, the three units accounted for over $26 million in total revenue. While these totals represented a substantial increase over those accumulated during the four-year period immediately preceding the IADP initiative – seizures increased by 95 per cent and revenues by 427 per cent – the cumulative *seizure to cost* ratio of the three IADP Units declined from 8.86 to 2.31 from the four-year period prior to the start of the IADP initiative. There was also a drop in the revenue to cost ratio: from 0.88 to 0.70.

A comparison between the IADP Units and a control group of ADP Units also showed that the former were less efficient than the latter: both the seizure to cost ratio and revenue to cost ratio were higher for the control group of ADP Units. As such, from a purely financial standpoint, during their first four years, the IADP Units were generally more productive but less efficient than their pre-IADP structures. While costs rose substantially, they were not accompanied by a commensurate rise in either seizures or revenues.

For example, total costs for the Proceeds of Crime Units rose from $5.5 million (during the fiscal years 1988–9 to 1991–2) to $38.9 million (during the period 1992–3 to 1995–6), an increase of approximately 594 per cent. However, seizures increased by only 95 per cent. These figures should give pause to anyone who believes that every dollar invested in proceeds of crime enforcement will automatically generate $2 dollars or more in recoveries or revenues. At some point the level of resources invested in proceeds of crime enforcement will meet with diminishing returns, as far as recoveries and revenues are concerned.

Outcomes: Ultimate Enforcement Objectives

This aspect of the 'evaluation' exercise is the critical one. The monetary value of seizures and forfeitures is meaningless unless the enforcement actions statistically represented by these figures can actually contribute to the ultimate objectives of proceeds of crime enforcement: reducing money laundering, depriving criminal entrepreneurs of their assets, stopping drug trafficking, and controlling organized crime in general.

While an objective of proceeds of crime enforcement is to stem the tide of dirty money into the legitimate economy, the incalculable uncertainty over the actual amount of criminal proceeds in circulation makes it next to impossible to assess the impact of government policies and law enforcement on this total. *Basically – in the bleakest of terms – there are no reliable estimates that can accurately gauge the extent to which proceeds of crime enforcement has deterred, denuded, or reduced the amount of dirty money injected into the legitimate economy.*

The annual evaluations of the IADP/IPOC initiatives rely largely on anecdotal evidence provided by interviews and surveys with law enforcement personnel. And what these data tell us is that proceeds of crime enforcement has done little to stem the tide of criminal revenue or money laundering; instead, at best, proceeds of crime enforcement has simply influenced the way many criminal entrepreneurs expend and launder their illicit funds. In other words, one modest indicator of the success of proceeds of crime enforcement is that criminal organizations are increasingly worried about this enforcement technique and are taking greater measures to conceal their ill-gotten gains. When asked about the impact that the Toronto Proceeds of Crime Section had on money laundering by criminal organizations, the RCMP officer in charge had this to say:

> We have irritated them. We've made them sit up and take notice. They are adjusting their ways. I mean in '88, '89, '90, the currency exchanges, the banks were overflowing with dirty money. It is not happening as much now. They are much more careful about how they do it. They have had to change their methods. They are certainly very nervous about dealing with people in the financial sector because they don't know if it is going to be a sting or not. You hear them talking on the wires saying they better start liquidating because the police are coming after everything they own. That was never heard before. And they are taking elaborate steps to hide it. I think that is the result of enforcement. (Schneider and Sauvageau, 1996: 42)

In short, proceeds of crime enforcement has simply forced the bad guys to be more cautious and sophisticated in their laundering activities. Like all innovation in law enforcement, the once novel proceeds of crime approach and the numerous pioneering techniques that accompanied the IADP and IPOC Units were eventually stripped of their potency. This was due in part to the indefatigably resilient and adaptive criminal mind, and in part by court-imposed disclosure requirements that mandated the Crown to provide details on investigative techniques to an accused during the pretrial stage.

Another key criterion in assessing proceeds of crime enforcement is the extent to which it has been successful in identifying and confiscating the full complement of the financial wealth and assets of criminal targets. Once again, there is no conclusive evidence regarding the impact of proceeds of crime enforcement on the actual financial and property holdings of criminal entrepreneurs, simply because no government agencies bother to address this issue. Even if they did, there are few reliable methods to collect such data. However, what the police cases do reveal is that the wealth of the relatively small number of large-scale criminal entrepreneurs and organizations is so vast and so internationally dispersed, and the laundering methods so complex, that the likelihood of Canadian law enforcement identifying, let alone seizing, the complete wealth of such individuals and groups is unlikely.

Moreover, as previously mentioned, the plea-bargains that conclude many of the proceeds files may incorporate the tacit and unspoken agreement between the accused and the Crown that if the former agrees to forfeit much of the property already identified, the latter will forego any further attempts to pursue and seize any unidentified assets.

While there are major criminal operations, our research also reveals that many other criminal operations are small; the actual amount of criminal proceeds is not only limited but is in fact spent in the same manner that law-abiding citizens spend their income. One must remember that the sampling for our case analyses excluded many of these smaller criminal cases that would still have absorbed policing resources. Do these amounts of criminal proceeds entering the legitimate economy hurt the economy? No evidence is available to support the oft-sited horrors of dirty money mingled with the legitimate economy.

Even though these smaller cases exist, there is reliable evidence that the IADP and IPOC initiatives have provided the Proceeds of Crime Sections with a greater capacity to target larger criminal organizations and more sophisticated money-laundering operations. The pilot projects provided the necessary resources to dedicate the time for labour-intensive investigations that are necessary to successfully target large criminal organizations and the upper echelons within those operations. Prior to the IADP pilot project, the Proceeds of Crime Sections simply did not have sufficient resources to undertake the type of investigations and undercover operations required to target larger criminal organizations. The increased resources allowed the Proceeds of Crime Sections to, as one Toronto RCMP officer put it, 'run with the big boys.' However, what the 'big boys' accomplished is still under debate.

Almost immediately after the IADP pilot project was implemented, the Proceeds of Crime Sections in Toronto, Montreal, and Vancouver began to dedicate additional resources to taking on larger criminal conspiracies. The initial evaluations of the IADP Units touted the early successes of the enhanced Proceeds of Crime Sections in infiltrating major criminal organizations and charging the principal players connected with these organizations. The covert money-laundering operations implemented by the Proceeds of Crime Sections in the three cities and funded almost exclusively by the IADP initiative were cited as a particularly successful approach to infiltrating larger criminal organizations by allowing undercover operators the ability to work their way to the top of the Canadian cells of these organizations. A memorandum to the Solicitor General dated 14 March 1997 concerning year four of the

IADP evaluation noted that 'all three units continue to work towards their prime objective of attacking the proceeds generated by major organised criminal groups through their illegal activities ... individually, each unit continues to focus on those criminal organisations predominant in their region.'

Examples of large criminal conspiracies targeted by the Proceeds of Crime Sections included

- Canadian cells of Colombian cocaine cartels
- a major hashish-importing network whose various members are reputed to be worth over $100 million
- Canadian-based Eastern European crime groups
- one of the largest tobacco and liquor smuggling operations in Ontario
- members of the Hells Angels, and
- the Ontario-based Caruana-Cuntrera crime family, renowned as one of the largest and longest running international drug trafficking syndicates in Canadian history

According to Tim Killam, a senior RCMP officer formerly in charge of the Proceeds of Crime Branch, 'There is no question that government, the RCMP and policy departments in general recognize that the way to the top of criminal organizations' is through proceeds of crime investigations (Marsden, 1994: A4). During the same 1995 interview, an RCMP supervisor in the Vancouver IADP Unit added:

> This is the only direction we can go in ... It is the only way to attack organized crime and drug traffickers. You look at *Compote* in Montreal in four short years, they were operating at the upper echelons of the Mafia and they did it through the back door through the financial end of it. Now if you had gone the traditional approach to that problem they would have entered through the contraband side and it would have taken twenty or thirty years to obtain that kind of success ... for some reasons they seem to trust outsiders more with their money than they do with their contraband. That's gotta be where the future is. (Schneider and Sauvageau, 1996: 87)

Yet despite the immense hopes that continue to be pinned to proceeds of crime enforcement, one must acknowledge that the ultimate impact of this enforcement approach is no different than the myriad of other strategies employed to combat organized crime in Canada or any country: a few battles may have been won, but the war has effectively been lost. The impact of proceeds of crime enforcement is commensurate with law enforcement's overall battles against organized crime: there are measurable successes, but the problem is a constant and remains largely undisturbed. Historical and contemporary case studies from Canada and other countries demonstrate that early successes in enforcement are often followed by diminishing returns as criminal entrepreneurs adapt to increased or new enforcement efforts. An understanding of the history of organized crime in North America reveals that enforcement efforts ultimately result in its mere displacement, not its eradication.[14] The demand for illegal services or illicit goods must be reduced before there will be a significant reduction in the supply. On one level, the police appreciate this argument. In discussing the potential consequences of decriminalization of drugs, the argument is often made by the police that organized crime would simply switch to another commodity. This sense of futility does not, however, extend to the futility of decades of drug enforcement with the availability, the accessibility, the purity, and the price on the street remaining essentially constant – or even becoming cheaper with more choice.

In an interview conducted for the IADP evaluations, a Vancouver Police Department officer who supervised his department's participation in the joint force initiative in that city succinctly summarized the negligible long-term effects of proceeds of crime enforcement on organized crime:

I don't see at the moment this legislation and this system having a major impact on organized crime, yet ... We have had this system in place for five years and organized crime is stronger than it was five years ago. We are chipping away at it through this, but it hasn't had the effect that we wanted to see. (Schneider and Sauvageau, 1996: 97)

This was echoed in a 1994 report submitted to the Federal Treasury Board that summarized the early evaluation results for the IADP units:

[the] IADP units have demonstrated clearly that they have an impact on [criminal] organizations actively involved in money laundering within Canada. Unfortunately, their efforts are minuscule in comparison to the extent of this practice ... current proceeds of crime investigations are seizing only a small percentage of the estimated billions of dollars being laundered in Canada annually. (Solicitor General Canada, 1997: 4)

These ambivalent responses reflect the difficulty of determining what impact can possibly be derived from enforcement of any sort. Curtailment of all organized criminal activity? Likely not. A more realistic objective might be the reduction of the amount of criminal activity to some notion of a tolerable level – while at the same time actually eliminating those few forms of criminal activity that are deemed 'intolerable' to society. There therefore needs to be a distinction made among forms of criminal activity. The 'objectives' that supported the integrated proceeds of crime units, however, made no such distinction. While one problem seemed to be that each of the diverse agency or departmental partners involved in the Integrated Proceeds of Crime Units had their own slightly different objectives, all the objectives were still of the 'removal of the financial incentive of crime' sort. These sorts of objectives are too unverifiable to be of any real use in a true evaluation.

Did anyone want a 'true' evaluation, if there actually could be such an exercise? Amid IPOC claims of limited resources, the department responsible for policing seemed to be mired in a endless process of attempting to 'buy' results that might actually ensure a continuation of what had become an extensive initiative. This would have had considerable resource implications for both the Department of the Solicitor General and the RCMP – very positive resource implications if resources were extended and expanded, and significantly negative implications if resources were terminated. In the midst of debates as to whether or not the IPOC initiative should continue to be funded, the Department of the Solicitor General spent $99,900 in engaging Consulting and Audit Canada to complete what was called a 'Comprehensive Evaluation of the Integrated Proceeds of Crime Initiative.' This contract might well have been justified except that this new report was due in October 2002 – the same year that the same firm had submitted a previous evaluation report. The report titled *IPOC Evaluation Report, Years 4 and 5* had also been completed by Consulting and Audit Canada and had been submitted to the Department of the Solicitor General in February 2002 – only two months prior to the second evaluation contract to the same firm.

In addition, in January of the same year, ABCsolutions (2002) was contracted to provide the Department of the Solicitor General with a commissioned study entitled *The Future of IPOC: Progress or Peril*. Likewise, during March 2002 – once again, the same year – the Department of the Solicitor General contracted with a firm to complete another report entitled 'Review of the Impacts of Organized Crime-Related

Money Laundering Activities on Canada.' This was a fairly small $20,000 contract with an amazingly short turn-around time. The final report was to be due in May 2002. Given what we felt was an absence of empirical 'impact' data, we were anxious to obtain a copy of this last document. Three years later, we were still unsuccessful, although we eventually obtained a copy through Access to Information. As antici- pated, this report did not fulfill the expectations of the Department of the Solicitor General in revealing the horrors of the impact of money laundering on society.

One important criterion by which proceeds of crime enforcement should be evaluated is its ability to facilitate drug enforcement, given that anti-drug profiteering has been the central focus of the Proceeds of Crime Sections. As documented in earlier sections, in addition to assisting drug enforcement generally, the Proceeds of Crime Program i n Canada has been directly involved in identifying and interdicting drug-trafficking conspiracies. At the same time, undercover money- laundering operations have been touted as the most effective way for law enforcement to infiltrate cash-intensive drug-trafficking networks. Despite these successes, proceeds of crime enforcement, like drug en- forcement in general, has had a minimal impact on drug trafficking in Canada. This is corroborated by evidence that, in recent years, illegal drugs are more readily available at the street level where purity has increased and prices have dropped, indicating an expanding market.[15] When commenting on the contribution that proceeds of crime enforce- ment made to a large drug bust in British Columbia in 1996, Bruce Bowie, then the RCMP officer in charge of the Vancouver Proceeds of Crime Section, acknowledged that the seizure of approximately 220 kilograms of marijuana, 815 kilograms of cocaine, and $2.5 million in cash wouldn't make much of a dent in the illegal drug trade in that province:

> We're talking about a problem that is very large and I don't subscribe to the notion that a single enforcement action and the arrest of a number of people is going to have a dramatic impact on the overall problem ... But it's going to keep some people off balance and anything we can do to make it more difficult for drug traffickers meets our enforcement objec- tive. (Steffenhager, 1996: A12)

This last sentence has become the new mantra for proceeds of crime and, more generally, for organized crime enforcement in Canada. While political and even upper-police-management rhetoric might sound different, for officers involved in the operational work there is no longer any pretence of ridding the legitimate economy of illicit funds or completely relieving organized crime figures of their assets. Moreover, there is no lingering belief that proceeds of crime enforcement – or any type of enforcement for that matter – can sufficiently stop or even slow down drug trafficking or other organized criminal activities. Proceeds of crime and organized crime enforcement in general is now implicitly couched in terms of a risk management approach, where the ultimate objective is not eradication but simply keeping the bad guys 'off balance' and making their illegal activities 'more difficult' to conduct.

Annual evaluations of the IADP and IPOC initiatives have consistently concluded that proceeds of crime enforcement in Canada since the early 1990s has achieved a number of successes, including greater cooperation among all levels of law enforcement, innovations in investigative and undercover techniques, and an improved ability to target larger criminal organizations and the higher echelons within. These successes would surely not have been achieved without the special program funding, and to a lesser extent, the integrated, multidisciplinary approach of the IADP and IPOC units. Added financial and human resources have allowed the Proceeds of Crime Sections to take on a greater number of files, as well as more complex files that target large criminal conspiracies. Moreover, the added resources have been the principal factor in promoting innovation and proactive investigations. They have brought together different law enforcement agencies from the federal, provincial, and municipal levels, as well as collaborators from the private sector. These partners have worked together in a cooperative, coordinated, and integrated manner. Annual evaluations indicate that law enforcement agencies participating in the IADP and IPOC initiatives appear sincerely committed to the joint force approach and most have sought ways to increase their representation on the units in recent years.

There is arguably no federal law enforcement function in Canada during the pre–9/11 period that has received more attention, resources, legislative support, or the addition of new agencies and units than proceeds of crime enforcement. However, like any other high-profile criminal activity that has attracted intensive government attention, proceeds of crime enforcement has done little to contain drug trafficking and other organized criminal activity in Canada; it has simply forced criminals to be more cautious, sophisticated, and inventive in their laundering activities. The experience of those working within the integrated units supports the old adage, 'No sooner is a law made than the way around it is discovered.' As far as the objectives of proceeds of crime enforcement are concerned, the bar seems to have been lowered to the level where causing nervousness among the criminal element is trotted out as a sufficient accomplishment. At the same time, the IPOC Units seem to have abandoned many of the more ambitious and innovative (and in some cases possibly illegal) undercover techniques employed in their early years.

Many proceeds of crime personnel interviewed for the annual evaluations singled out current criminal laws (and their judicial interpretation) as the most significant impediment to effective and efficient organized crime and proceeds of crime enforcement. More specifically, they blame what they see as weak criminal penalties and limited court-imposed sentences for the perpetrators of large-scale criminal conspiracies, especially those involving large-scale marijuana grow operations. The arguments are familiar enough: weak penalties and sentences do not provide any type of deterrence and they undermine law enforcement efforts to use the threat of stiff penalties to coerce those arrested into providing evidence that can be used against co-conspirators and those in the upper echelons of large criminal operations.[16] As one Proceeds of Crime Unit member put it in a 1995 focus group conducted for the IADP evaluation,

> We do not have the hammer. The drug and anti-drug profiteering laws ... are too weak. The majority of cases we get in Canada are referrals from the U.S. where somebody rolled over because of the threat of stiff sentences ... There is nothing in the legislation which motivates people to cooperate ... There is no motivation for people to talk. And without them talking we can't make the charge and we can't get to the top of the upper echelons of the organization. (Schneider, 1997a: 33)

Our more recent *criminal associations* legislation (Bills C-95 and C-24) does allow for stiffer jail sentences. Nonetheless, when compared to the U.S. multi-hundred-year jail sentences, which obviously serve largely as an expression of outrage from the courts, our sentences may still appear weak.

Another consistent complaint revolves around the requirement that investigators must link suspected proceeds of crime to both an offender and a specific designated drug or other serious offence, which they argue is extremely difficult to establish in many cases. The need to establish this triumvirate relationship stems from the nature of the legislation that attaches forfeiture to the result of a criminal conviction of an offender, thereby placing a heavy onus of proof upon law enforcement officers and Crown prosecutors. The inability to satisfy this onus results from the inherent characteristics of sophisticated criminal enterprises whose laundering techniques, division of labour, and multinational operations make it difficult to establish the nexus between all three elements.

As a result of these criticisms, there have been numerous calls, particularly from the law enforcement community, for legislation that allows the Crown to confiscate criminally derived property through a civil process rather than within the criminal courts. When forfeiture is pursued through the civil courts, the burden of proof placed on the state is reduced from 'beyond a reasonable doubt' to a 'balance of probabilities' and the Crown can confiscate money or assets where only a reasonable suspicion exists that the cash or assets constitute the proceeds of crime. In addition, the onus of proof is now shared between the state and the defendant; that is, unlike a criminal trial where there is no obligation on the defendant to prove his innocence, in a civil forfeiture process the defendant must often prove that the assets in question were derived through legal and legitimate means.

While the Canadian government has long resisted the adoption of civil forfeiture laws to combat organized crime and terrorism in Canada, on 12 April 2002 new legislation was enacted by the Provincial government in Ontario that would allow police in that province to confiscate cash or any other assets suspected of being purchased with the proceeds of crime without a criminal conviction. When Ontario passed their civil forfeiture legislation they boasted that the benefit of these powers was that 'the government didn't ever need to charge or convict the person.' The Remedies for Organized Crime and Other Unlawful Activities Act would allow a civil court judge to authorize the seizure of assets once the Crown has proven on a 'balance of probabilities' that the assets were obtained with the proceeds of crime. The bill also gave the province the power to file civil suits against two or more people who conspire to commit unlawful activities that harm the public.

The legislation has met with stiff opposition from the legal community in Canada. John Rosen, a noted criminal lawyer in Toronto, said in a media interview that the law 'presumes guilt ... It's contrary to our whole history of criminal justice in our country.' The legislation will almost certainly prompt a constitutional challenge based on the premise that it is designed to influence criminal law, which is the exclusive domain of the federal government. Furthermore, the legislation may be deemed to contravene due process as enshrined in the Charter of Rights, based on the fact that the standard of proof involved in civil processes are applied to criminal offences. However, the Ontario government argues that the legislation is not criminal in nature (it is based on civil laws, and is therefore well within the jurisdiction of provincial government) and that the legislation focuses on criminally derived property, and property rights are not protected in the Charter of Rights (Selick, 2000: C19).

The application of civil sanctions against organized and economic crimes has been most vigorously (and controversially) applied in the United States. The federal Racketeer Influenced and Corrupt Organizations (RICO) Act makes it unlawful to acquire, operate, or receive income from an enterprise through criminal means. RICO allows the government or a private citizen to file a civil suit requesting the court to order sanctions or to provide injunctive relief against an individual or organization involved in a 'pattern of racketeering.' Civil RICO injunctions can, for example, prohibit individuals from owning or becoming involved in certain legitimate or illegitimate businesses or activities. RICO also allows for the state or private victims to sue civilly to recoup 'treble' damages (i.e., the defendant must pay to the plaintiff three times the amount of damages that have been determined by a court). A criminal conviction is not a prerequisite for injunctive relief or asset forfeiture under RICO and no person need be charged; the civil asset forfeiture provisions of RICO focuses on property, not people (National Governors' Association et al., 1998: 73–7).

However, civil forfeiture together with the policy in the U.S. of returning forfeited proceeds directly to police forces turned out to be a seductive combination. The 'poetic justice' that saw the criminals effectively having to pay for their own prosecutions – or paying without a prosecution in the case of civil forfeiture – has in the opinion of the critics, turned into an enterprise that took precedent over any objective of pursuing justice. Michael Zeldin, former director of the U.S. Justice Department's Asset Forfeiture Office states: 'We had a situation in which the desire to deposit money into the asset forfeiture fund became the "reason for being" of forfeiture, eclipsing in certain measures the desire to effect fair enforcement of the laws' (Nkechi, 1994: 108; see also

Levy, 1996: 153, and Cheh, 1994: 4). As quoted in the *New York Times* (31 May 1993: 1), Zeldin accused his successor, Cary Copeland, of putting the maximization of seized funds ahead of good law enforcement. Zeldin characterized his department's orders as 'Forfeit, Forfeit, Forfeit. Get Money, Get Money, Get Money.'

Despite the implementation of civil forfeiture in the United States and Australia, both countries continue to experience significant levels of organized criminal activity and money laundering, which do not appear to be slowed by the more 'efficient' civil forfeiture laws. Indeed, during the last twenty years there has been considerable evidence of a growing pluralism of crime groups in Canada, the United States, and abroad, many of which greatly surpass the scale of the ethnic Italian criminal organizations that predominated in North America and Europe for much of this century. Accompanying this pluralism has been an ever-increasing diversification and sophistication of criminal activities carried out by these groups. Even more daunting is evidence that inter-group competition has given way to greater cooperation and coordination at the international level. While there have been notable examples of success in law enforcement efforts to contain organized crime in North America and globally (notably, the incarceration of major drug 'kingpins,' the large-scale seizure of drugs, contraband, and criminal proceeds, and the dismantling of criminal organizations), it is generally acknowledged that the 'war' against organized crime has effectively been lost.

There are myriad reasons why organized crime continues to persist in society. First and foremost is its inherent nature, a defining characteristic of which is a continuity sustained by the ability to replace members, partners or suppliers; the use of corruption, intimidation, and violence to shield criminal members from arrest and prosecution; the insulation of the upper echelons of criminal groups, the threat-imposed adherence to secrecy; and the sophistication of some dominant crime groups. Of course, organized crime also continues to exist and prosper because of its pivotal role in catering to the indefatigable demands that Western society has nurtured for certain (prohibited) products and services.

Law enforcement in Canada operates under significant constitutional constraints. In any democratic country with strong human rights protections, there is a trade-off for law enforcement. The right to remain silent, the right to legal counsel, the right to be speedily tried, the right to confront witnesses, the right to refuse to provide self-incriminating testimony, and the rights of the people to be secure against unreasonable searches and seizures are all entrenched in the Charter of Rights and Freedoms. While one certainly does not want to characterize these quintessential human rights as constraints, the fact is that they have served to place some limitations on the powers of law enforcement, and the police will argue that this affects combating organized crime, perhaps more than some other targets of law enforcement.

In recent years in Canada, there have been dozens of Charter challenges launched by criminal defendants that have had significant (and often negative) implications for organized crime enforcement. Two recent Supreme Court decisions resulting from Charter challenges launched by criminal defendants had significant (negative) repercussions for organized crime enforcement in Canada. *R. v. Campbell and Shirose* limits the use of undercover operations by law enforcement, and *R. v. Stinchcombe* defines the extent to which law enforcement must disclose intelligence and evidentiary information to defence counsel. A 1998 report by the Evaluation Section of the Department of Justice examining proceeds of crime prosecutions revealed that, in 46 per cent of all cases, the disclosure requirement was more than 1,000 pages, with 24 per cent of the cases requiring more than 5,000 pages (Department of Justice, 1998a: 9). Numerous cases have been dismissed and charges stayed due to the inability of police to collate and disclose evidence to defence counsel.

In one case, thirty-nine-year-old Roman Paryniuk was charged with shipping 7,680 kilograms of hashish into Canada. Paryniuk left the courts a free man after arguing that his constitutional rights had been violated by the Crown. Madam Justice Wailan Low found that the Crown took far too long to disclose to defence lawyers the tapes, documents, and other evidence it had gathered. In response to this decision, Jim Leising, who supervises Crown prosecutors in the Toronto area, said the ruling sets 'an almost-impossible disclosure burden' for prosecutors. The result, he added, is that 'a very serious criminal case is not tried.' Just six months earlier, in September 2002, Paryniuk had successfully used the same argument in a case involving a different set of drug charges. Police had alleged that he planned to traffic about $4 million worth of seized Ecstasy and other drugs. In that case, the defendant also argued – unsuccessfully – that he was the victim of corrupt police officers. Police recorded seizing $664,000 from his safety-deposit box, but Paryniuk maintained in court-filed documents that more was there (Freeze, 2003a: A12).

In September 2003, an Edmonton judge threw out charges against eleven people accused of conspiring to sell cocaine and participating in a criminal organization, saying the lengthy delay in trying the case – chiefly because federal prosecutors and the RCMP were slow in disclosing evidence to the defence – violated their Charter rights (Mahoney, 2003). Law enforcement officials also complain that the disclosure requirements publicly expose informants, classified intelligence information, and law enforcement techniques. In Canada, police officers often divide law enforcement of the last fifty years into two periods: the pre-Charter era and the post-Charter era. While Charter rights make Canadian citizens the envy of many people throughout the world, they also have their costs. Many Charter advocates argue that these costs are reasonable and unavoidable. They argue that these and other Charter decisions have not necessarily restricted law enforcement powers, but have simply made it more time-consuming and labour intensive to carry out such powers.

Jurisdictional limitations, especially at the international level, also pose a major obstacle to effective organized crime and proceeds of crime enforcement. Criminal entrepreneurs increasingly operate across different jurisdictions, including international borders. Law enforcement, however, is largely carried out by local police forces. Even federal agencies with national jurisdictions are quite restricted in their ability to operate internationally. It is transnational organized crime that most exposes the debilitating jurisdictional barriers to a truly international approach to law enforcement. Criminal laws do not extend beyond national boundaries. There is no international police force, nor is there a fully functioning international criminal court that can be used to prosecute traditional organized crimes. International cooperation and coordination among police forces, while increasing in recent years, is still awkward and pales in comparison to the nature and scope of the international cooperation that exists within the criminal world. Many have called for the creation of international police forces (beyond the information-sharing mandate of Interpol). Despite the advances made by Europol, there is little hope that this will ever reach a stage where one police force can operate freely in diverse jurisdictions – and perhaps with good reason.

Resistance to the creation of international police forces and courts is premised on the contention that because these institutions would be granted certain international investigative and enforcement powers, countries would have to give up some political autonomy and sovereignty in order to participate. The sovereignty of countries continues to trump their willingness to participate in formal international law enforcement institutions. Gaining information from foreign jurisdictions remains an ongoing challenge. It is often said that while organized criminals are capable of operating transnationally, policing is *still* very jurisdictionally based. Under the present circumstances, then, where police forces are bound by their jurisdictions, there are two basic ways for the police to cooperate with law enforcement in other jurisdictions: police-to-police requests for assistance or via the more formal Mutual Legal Assistance Treaties (MLAT) arrangements.

The Mutual Legal Assistance in Criminal Matters Act serves as the primary vehicle for affording countries assistance in investigating or prosecuting offences, including terrorist financing offences. As of this writing, Canada had a network of approximately thirty bilateral Mutual Legal Assistance Treaties (MLAT) as well as fifty-one bilateral extradition treaties. In addition, Canada is party to a number of multi-lateral conventions allowing for legal cooperation against crime and terrorism, resulting in extradition for such offences. Canadian police authorities (acting primarily through the RCMP) have numerous bilat-eral arrangements relating to cooperation in the investigation of crimi-nal matters. There are also multilateral arrangements, notably through Interpol. These tools for cooperation are regularly used to assist foreign authorities and investigate terrorist offences and threats (DFAIT, 2001). The problem is that the response granted to these requests, in too many cases, tends not to be timely – or at least is not *predictably* timely. The MLAT agreements are actually seen by the police to be an obstacle to the pursuit of some criminal investigations. This criticism may be more valid in criminal rather than in terrorist-related cases.

MLATs are a treaty-based form of cooperation that imposes binding obligations on signatory countries. Responses to foreign requests for assistance under MLATs, a formal process subject to ministerial and court authorization in Canada, are performed under legislation which implements Canada's MLAT obligations: the Mutual Legal Assistance in Criminal Matters Act. The minister of justice plays a pivotal role as Canada's 'central authority' in the administration and exercise of pow-ers under MLATs. The minister of justice approves the sending of an MLAT request to a central authority in another jurisdiction. As Michael Sullivan and Josée Filion acknowledge, MLATs do not require that the conduct under investigation be the subject of a parallel investigation by Canada and the other jurisdiction. Neither does the conduct need to be illegal in both jurisdictions (dual criminality).

The minister of justice receives an MLAT request from another juris-diction and decides whether to grant the request and send it to the relevant investigative agency for action (to prepare the relevant documentation necessary to gain authorization from the courts in Canada to obtain the evidence requested) (Sullivan, 2004). Clearly the priorities in one jurisdiction may not be shared in a foreign jurisdiction and with limited resources, the demands of local law enforcement tend to take precedent over foreign requests.[17]

In addition to non-timely responses, some countries sign treaties but simply do not comply because of different laws and rules pertaining to how evidence must be collected in order to be of use in court. Law enforcement in some jurisdictions lacks the expertise to gather the evidence. In the face of these factors, the police often find the more direct and more informal 'police-to-police' assistance approach to be much more efficient – with the caveat that, once the information is obtained, it may be necessary to go the MLAT route in order to be able to use the information in Canadian courts. These police-to-police requests usually go by fax through the RCMP Foreign Liaison Officer (if there is one in the specific region) who then will contact the appropriate police officer in the foreign jurisdiction. Contact will then be made between the two operational police investigators. In summary, there are mechanisms that allow information to flow, but they are not always speedy and reliable.

All of these factors join to create a playing field that police and some prosecutors feel greatly benefits organized crime. From their perspective, law enforcement agencies are constrained in their actions by limited resources, jurisdictional obstacles, the lack of a truly concerted international effort, as well as constitutional and legal restrictions. In contrast, dominant organized crime groups have almost unlimited resources, are not bound by national sovereignty issues, freely cooperate and coordinate their actions with like-minded groups, and, by their very nature, can ignore laws and constitutional restrictions on their powers and operations. This sense of an uneven playing field inextricably contributes to a growing frustration and has spurred many to advocate the adoption, or at least the consideration, of alternative policy options that may stand a better chance of limiting the scope and power of organized crime in society.

Financial Intelligence Transaction Analysis Centre (FINTRAC)

The companion 'law enforcement' piece in the Canadian strategy against money laundering is the Financial Intelligence Transaction Analysis

Centre (FINTRAC). It was created in June 2000 and began operation in November 2001. Given its infancy, conclusions as to the efficacy of FINTRAC in particular, and Canada's financial transaction monitoring and reporting regime in general, are perhaps somewhat premature. While Canada's tardiness in implementing a mandatory reporting regime has been the subject of criticism by other G8 countries, this foot-dragging would, one might have hoped, have allowed the Canadian government to learn from the American, Australian, and British models. Amid some significant criticisms with their information technology systems, FINTRAC's 2005 Annual Report states that their 'next generation' of information technology applications will benefit from the information technology expertise such as is available in Australia at AUSTRAC (FINTRAC, 2005c).

According to its first annual report, tabled in Parliament on 5 November 2002, FINTRAC identified approximately $100 million in suspected illicit cash during its first year of existence, including half a dozen cases of possible terrorist financing. The report also states that between 8 November 2001 and 31 March 2002, the agency received 3,747 suspicious transaction reports involving more than 11,000 financial dealings. Of these, 161, or about 4 per cent, were passed on to law enforcement or intelligence agencies. About thirty were cases of suspected money laundering while the remaining reports were of possible terrorist financing schemes (FINTRAC, 2002). By the end of 2002–03, FINTRAC was receiving an average of 24,000 transaction reports each day, totalling more than 2 million for the year. As a result of these referrals to FINTRAC, approximately 100 disclosures to law enforcement and national security agencies were made (FINTRAC, 2003: 16). While the total number of referrals to FINTRAC has increased significantly, there has been little increase in the number of files passed on from FINTRAC.

During 2003–04 FINTRAC received approximately 10 million financial transaction reports (see fig. 4.2). Of this vast number, slightly less than 15,000 were Suspicious Transaction Reports (STRs) and 546 were Voluntary Information Reports (VIRs) from law enforcement and intelligence services. Of these 10 million, a mere 197 disclosures were made to law enforcement and other agencies. This is up from 103 the previous year when the total referrals received had been considerably fewer. By the end of 2004–05, from close to 11 million referrals received by FINTRAC, 142 cases were disclosed to the various reporting agencies. In total – from 2002 to 2005 – 442 cases were disclosed to the various

Figure 4.2: Financial transaction reports received by FINTRAC, 2001–05

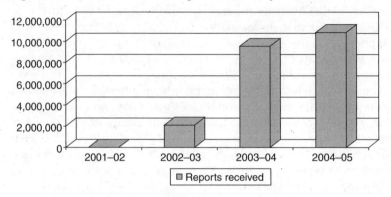

agencies by FINTRAC from over 22,000,000 referrals it had received (FINTRAC, 2005c: 13).

Of the 142 disclosures made in 2004–05, 110 were for suspected money laundering, 24 were for suspected terrorist activity financing and/or threats to the security of Canada, and 8 involved both suspected money laundering and terrorist activity financing and/or threats to the security of Canada. The Annual Report for 2004-05 points out that while the number of disclosures had decreased, the dollar value of the transactions disclosed had increased significantly. In addition, the report states that 'the percentage of our case disclosures involving transactions from six or more different reporting entities increased to 39 per cent in 2005 from 18 per cent in 2004. The average number of transactions per disclosure increased from 62 last year to 136 this year' (FINTRAC, 2005c).

While a great amount of rhetoric – and compliance costs on the part of the financial institutions – focus on 'suspicious transactions,' these transactions form a minute portion of all of the files that flow into FINTRAC (see fig. 4.3). Based on the 2004–2005 Annual Report, the break down of transactions indentified 7,077,65 electronic funds transfers; 3,658,462 large cash transactions; 19,113 suspicious transactions; and 75,821 cross-border currency reports, for a total of 10,831,071 transactions (FINTRAC, 2005c).

In listing FINTRAC's successes for the year, the Annual Report states, 'FINTRAC's case disclosures were unprecedented in the total value they represented and in the complexity of money laundering networks revealed. The Centre's financial intelligence product made a relevant

Figure 4.3: Types of transactions

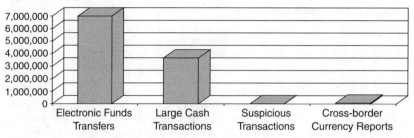

and meaningful contribution to the fight against money laundering and terrorist activity financing.'[18] This claim might be a little optimistic. The problem remains, as has been identified by an auditor's report, that it is virtually impossible to evaluate the success of FINTRAC.

Evaluating FINTRAC

FINTRAC has been set up in such a manner that any meaningful current evaluation is impossible. Due to what they claim is the need for privacy and the legislated requirement specifying the treatment of confidential information, the agencies that pass on information of 'suspicious transactions' receive no information back as to whether or not the information was of any use to either FINTRAC or the police – or if the information was even passed by FINTRAC to the police. The argument from FINTRAC is that if the reporting bodies were given any information on the outcome of their referrals, this would serve to inform reporting bodies (banks, for example) about the confidential status of potential police cases. Likewise, at the opposite end of the flow of financial information, law enforcement agencies do not feed back to FINTRAC information concerning the usefulness or conviction success stemming from FINTRAC information. Even when police or intelligence services *initiate* the exchange by submitting a VIR file, they will most often receive nothing back.[19]

The 2005 FINTRAC Annual Report states that 'tracking mechanisms will be put in place to demonstrate the extent to which their disclosures contribute to investigations and prosecutions,' however no information is provided as to how or when this will occur (FINTRAC, 2005c: 28). At this stage, FINTRAC is basically operating as a black hole – information of an unknown sort is fed in, and information of an unknown sort

Figure 4.4: Flow of financial information from reporting bodies via FINTRAC to enforcement agencies

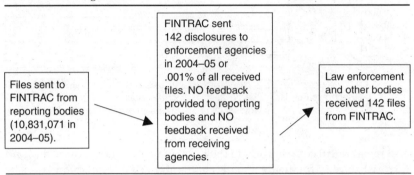

leaves with no record of impact! This is all carried out with considerable funding.

When FINTRAC refers a file to law enforcement, the information that is disclosed – without a production order – is so brief that it tends to be useless to law enforcement. Often, the information is sufficiently bare that it fails to provide any incentive for police to obtain a production order in order to secure more of the information that is held by FINTRAC. As stated in the critical 2004 Auditor General Report:

> Law enforcement officers told us that suspicious-transaction reports they receive directly from banks often contain more useful information than FINTRAC disclosures – they are more current and provide the reasons for suspicion. *This is a serious criticism of a system set up expressly to add value to the raw information provided by reporting entities.* (Office of the Auditor General, 2004: 12; emphasis added)

Law enforcement agencies can apply for a *production order* and then receive additional information from FINTRAC. However, only two had been requested at the time of the report in 2004 and both had been granted. The question remained as to why the police had not applied for more. According to the auditor's report:

> Law enforcement and security officers cited two basic reasons for the reluctance to apply for production orders. One is that the legislative threshold is high, the same as for a search warrant: the applicant must satisfy the court that there are 'reasonable grounds to believe' an offence

has been committed. A search warrant is preferable because FINTRAC provides only intelligence, whereas a search warrant provides direct access to a target and to information that could be used as evidence. Moreover, the information contained in FINTRAC disclosures is generally considered below the legislative threshold that a production order requires. (ibid.)

The Canadian government is attempting to rectify some of the legislative weakness while respecting the privacy and Charter rights (Department of Finance, 2005). The government proposes to expand the current list of designated information that FINTRAC can disclose to law enforcement and intelligence agencies to include

- additional publicly available information (including information from commercially available databases), such as
  - telephone numbers
  - names of related parties (e.g., partners or company directors), and
  - background information obtained from open sources (e.g., media articles)
- additional account information (e.g., type of account)
- Canada Revenue Agency-issued business numbers
- the type of transaction (e.g., asset or good purchased)
- the type of report (e.g., suspicious transaction report) from which the information disclosed is compiled, and
- the reasons for suspicion

The Auditor General's report identified a number of other failings related specifically to the usefulness of FINTRAC to law enforcement. Despite significant outreach efforts by FINTRAC over the past three years, police forces still are reluctant to share information and do not give much weight to unsolicited disclosures by FINTRAC. In addition to the limited information that FINTRAC provides, the police hesitate before giving FINTRAC voluntary information pertaining to ongoing cases for fear that their investigations will be compromised.

One might imagine that when the police *voluntarily* submit information to FINTRAC, they must have a fairly compelling reason for doing so – and yet of the 713 voluntary reports submitted to FINTRAC, only 113 resulted in disclosures back to the reporting agency, leaving 600 reports that resulted in no information. Given that FINTRAC has no turn-around time targets, the law enforcement agency is left to wonder about the status of the file. If FINTRAC has no information that meets the disclosure threshold, 'it simply sends nothing' (Office of the Auditor General, 2004: 13). Some law enforcement officers reported that they tend to submit voluntary information reports to FINTRAC only towards the end of an investigation, when about to close a file for lack of sufficient evidence. Others confirmed that they do not submit voluntary information reports because they expect little back from FINTRAC.

Despite the amount of research that went into setting up FINTRAC, there are already issues of incompatible software and an untimely backlog of files. Based on Canadian legislation, the Canada Border Services Agency can seize unreported cross-border transfers of monetary instruments with a value over $10,000. If the money is believed to be the proceeds of crime, the illicit proceeds can be seized and forfeited and reports are then sent to the Canada Border Services Agency (CBSA). CBSA must then enter the information into an automated system using data fields as specified by FINTRAC. Reports are then forwarded to FINTRAC. By the end of March 2004, CBSA had collected 60,000 reports and made 1,521 seizures, totaling $46 million. While those files that resulted in a seizure were processed expeditiously, the auditor's audit reported that incompatible software and 'security firewalls' between the two agencies caused a nine-month delay in data entry of all of the compliant reports (Office of the Auditor General, 2004: 15). To avoid the FINTRAC intelligence-gathering regime, criminals and terrorists need only comply with the cross-border reporting requirements, which appear, to date, to remove them from further scrutiny.

As we have found with other forms of intelligence systems, if the participants have little expectation of getting any valuable service, the effort and potential concerns related to the providing of information will result in little cooperation – which will further decrease the value of the intelligence function. Systems must be seen to be both legitimate and useful. Even before the mandatory transaction reporting became law, it came under vociferous attack. Civil libertarians denounced the legislation – and mandatory reporting requirements in general – as an infringement on the privacy rights of Canadians. Critics argued that banks and other companies would collect private personal and financial information on legitimate clients and lawful transactions. This data would then be shared with a government agency and would reside on a government database along with data on suspected and real criminals.

While fears regarding the passing of this information to Canadian agencies may not yet be an issue, a concern remains that the financial intelligence units (FIUs) have agreed to share information with each other internationally. Given international pressures to illustrate the compliance of Canadian officials, one might worry about the information that is shared 'out the back door' with foreign governments. As of 2004–05, FINTRAC had signed twenty memoranda of understanding to permit information sharing with foreign FIUs. This is particularly ironic given the dearth of real information that Canadian police have gained from FINTRAC so far.

Perhaps the most significant challenge facing Canada's new transaction reporting regime is ensuring a widespread compliance among the more than 100,000 reporting entities. FINTRAC's annual report acknowledges this challenge as a priority for 2003–04 (FINTRAC, 2003: 4). FINTRAC is mandated by legislation to carry out random compliance audits of entities covered by the reporting requirements. It appears, however, that much of this auditing function may be delegated to (self-) regulatory agencies responsible for individual sectors. In most cases these are bodies that traditionally have had a very different monitoring function that has focused on issues such as 'professionalism,' 'policy guidelines,' and issues arising from the direct complaints of clients or customers or the interest to their own members. These functions are extremely different from law enforcement compliance. FINTRAC's 2003 Annual Report acknowledges that it has 'met with over fifty regulatory bodies in various sectors' in order to 'initiate outreach approaches and other measures whereby regulators and FINTRAC can work together to further compliance' (FINTRAC, 2003: 15).

According to Sandra Brown, a senior FINTRAC official, the Ontario Securities Commission and other self-regulatory organizations will carry out compliance audits of brokerage firms and mutual fund dealers on behalf of FINTRAC. The Office of the Superintendent of Financial Institutions (OSFI) will be monitoring the compliance of the federally regulated financial institutions. The Mutual Fund Dealers Association (MFDA) of Canada, a self-regulatory agency, started conducting compliance audits of members in November 2002 and, by May 2003, the agency had completed twenty-six reviews of firms across the country, according to John Smeeton, Prairie Regional Director of the MFDA. As a result of these reviews, the MFDA uncovered a number of compliance deficiencies (Howlett, 2003). In addition to these groups, there are also all of the other non-regulated sectors that are meant to report to FINTRAC. Some of these groups, such as real estate agents and accoun-

Table 4.1: The national initiative to combat money laundering

Department Budget	2000–01	2001–02	2002–03	2003–04	Total
FINTRAC anti-money laundering	18.0	25.5	26.3	22.2	92.0
[FINTRAC anti-terrorist financing	*–*	*–*	*14.7*	*9.5*	*34.2]*
Canada Revenue Agency and					
Canada Border Services Agency	5.3	6.0	6.0	6.0	23.3
RCMP	2.6	4.9	4.9	4.9	17.3
Justice Canada	0.6	1.2	1.2	1.2	4.2
Citizenship and Immigration Canada[1]	0.0	0.7	0.7	0.7	2.1
Finance Canada	0.3	0.3	0.3	0.3	1.2
Totals anti-money laundering	26.8	38.6	39.4	35.3	140.1
[Plus anti-terrorist financing	*–*	*48.6*	*54.1*	*44.8*	*174.3]*

[1] Activities funded under the initiative were integrated into the Canada Border Services Agency with the reorganization of government departments (December 2003).
Source: Office of the Auditor General (2004): 5.

tants, have a licensing mechanism that may enforce a degree of compliance; other groups have little hanging over their heads to encourage any significant reporting to FINTRAC. The question remains: Will FINTRAC and other regulatory agencies have the capacity to comprehensively ensure compliance, especially if they are not provided with the additional resources and expertise to do so? An even more important question is, Will we ever know?

Shortcomings of any operation are often blamed on insufficient resources. This does not appear to be the case with FINTRAC, which is extremely well funded compared with other international FIUs, with the exception of the U.S. FinCEN operation. The entire budget for the National Initiative to Combat Money Laundering for 2000–01 to 2003–04 was $174.3 million. FINTRAC received $126.2 million of these resources for the fight against money laundering ($92 million) and anti-terrorist financing ($34.2 million) (Office of the Auditor General, 2004: 5).

Balancing costs with benefits is always difficult. The argument might be reduced to 'one terrorist attack being foiled.' However, although one must acknowledge that the system has only been in operation in Canada a relatively short time, to date, this 'enforcement' strategy has yet to prove itself. FinCEN in the United States has continually battled the problems that stem from the millions of non-relevant files that are collected on an ongoing basis. By 2005, FINTRAC had 23 million financial transaction reports in its database – and produced 142 disclosures in that year with unknown results. The math is not promising![20]

5 Compliance: Bankers and Lawyers

This chapter first examines the 'compliance' (or lack thereof) with the anti-money-laundering responsibilities by financial institutions and attempts to explain why one must expect an ambiguous commitment to continual reporting, despite what is now a legislated mandatory requirement. In the second section of this chapter, we look at the 'compliance' of lawyers. In speaking about the UK system, Gold and Levi state:

> Traditionally, few bankers (or, for that matter, auditors, company formation agents, or City lawyers) have seen it as their function to help to prevent crime by informing the police on their own initiative about suspicious behaviour ... Money-laundering regulations were intended to produce a very different approach to the social responsibilities of financial institutions and professionals ... (Gold and Levi, 1994: 4)

They make the point that, traditionally, the professions – bankers, accountants, and lawyers – were not in the business of assisting the police of their own volition. Yet these professions are important to launderers, both in terms of their services and in terms of their status and the sense of 'legitimacy' that they bring to transactions. In a recorded conversation from the transcript of one of the RCMP cases, Project Omerta, one suspect dictated to an accomplice what words should be used in a letter that was sent to the Bank of Nova Scotia on the suspect's lawyer's letterhead. The essence of the conversation was that the letterhead would provide legitimacy and credibility that would remove suspicion regarding the source of funds. Completing certain transactions through a lawyer – with letterhead – served to eliminate any hesitation by financial institutions. Throughout the international literature – such as that produced by the G7 Financial Action Task Force (FATF), the OECD, the EU, and studies such as the Gold and Levi (1994) examination of money laundering in the UK as well as our own analysis of the RCMP laundering cases – lawyers and accountants are seen to be the 'gatekeepers,' the 'intermediaries,' or the 'facilitators' of major money-laundering operations. Their actions have the potential to facilitate the movement of dirty money through a financial institution. The financial institutions, in turn, are important first steps in most laundering schemes.

While much of the field of enforcement (with respect to money laundering and more broadly) is based on legislatively defined and sanctioned behaviour, there are other forms of 'enforcement' that consist of various types of regulatory requirements, codes of conduct, guidelines, and agreements.[1] For this type of acquired information to enter into the more formal criminal justice process, it must be passed along to the police or to another enforcement body. In terms of transference of banking information about customers and their transactions to law enforcement agencies (i.e., transfer of knowledge), there are a number of basic procedures and combinations that involve variations of record keeping, suspicious transaction reporting (STR), and currency transaction reporting (CTR). To some extent, this list can be viewed as a continuum from the least to the greatest amount of intrusion into the transactions of customers. Stated differently, the continuum moves through an increasing degree of 'responsibilization' of the bank officials and of professionals such as lawyers. One ought not assume, however, that it is also a continuum towards the more likely detection of significant money laundering.

The range of alternative systems include

- *Record keeping*: All of a specific proscribed type of transaction records kept on file for a proscribed period of time for use on request by the police on a case-specific basis upon obtaining a warrant.
- *Voluntary suspicious transaction reporting*: Reporting to the police 'suspicious' transactions with some protections in law for the passing on of this information.
- *Combination of record keeping and voluntary suspicious transaction reporting*.
- *Mandatory suspicious transaction reporting*: Legal responsibility (with legal protections) to report 'suspicious' transactions.

- *Currency transaction reporting*: Reporting to a centralized agency of all transactions over a certain threshold.
- *Combination*: Mandatory reporting of suspicious transactions regardless of the amounts of money involved, together with the reporting of all transactions over a certain amount.

With the passing of the Canadian Proceeds of Crime (Money Laundering) Act, and later the Proceeds of Crime (Money Laundering) and Terrorist Financing Act, financial institutions, currency exchanges, casinos, and others organizations that act as financial intermediaries are required to report the following:

- *Suspicious transactions*: Any financial transaction about which there are reasonable grounds to suspect that it is related to a money-laundering or terrorist-financing offence.
- *Large cash transactions*: The receipt of monetary instruments in amounts of $10,000 or more.
- *Electronic fund transfers*: The transfer of funds of $10,000 or more from Canada to another country or from another country to Canada.
- *Terrorist property*: Cash, bank accounts, insurance policies, money orders, real estate, securities, and travellers' cheques and other types of assets known to be owned or controlled by a suspected terrorist group identified by the United Nations and listed by the Solicitor General.

In addition, organizations or individuals must verify the identity of new corporate clients and of directors of new corporations. Statements must be signed by the directors of new corporate clients and by new individual clients. It must be determined whether accounts are being opened on behalf of other parties, and specific details about the other parties must be documented. Records must be retained for five years.

The following individuals and organizations (hereafter 'reporting entities') are currently required to report suspicious and prescribed transactions:

- all banks
- credit unions, caisses populaires, cooperative credit associations and societies
- both domestic and foreign life insurance companies

- trust and loan companies
- persons engaged in the business of dealing in securities, including portfolio managers and investment counsellors
- foreign exchange dealers
- money service businesses which cash cheques, remit or transmit money, or redeem monetary instruments
- persons engaged in a profession (originally including lawyers and accountants)
- real estate brokers or sales representatives, and
- casinos

(Note: As will be discussed later in this chapter, lawyers are exempt from most of these mandatory requirements.)

A reporting entity that fails to report these transactions is committing an offence punishable by a fine of up to $2 million and/or imprisonment for up to ten years. It is also an offence for a reporting entity to disclose to its clients (whether money launderers or not) or anyone else that a report has been made if the intent of the reporting entity is to prejudice the criminal investigation or prosecution.

The proceeds of crime legislation also requires that any person who imports or exports $10,000 or more in cash or other liquid assets across the Canadian border must report to the Canada Border Services Agency. The CBSA will then forward the report to the Financial Transactions and Reports Analysis Centre. Currency can be seized if it is not declared, but will be returned after the person pays a fine unless the CBSA has reasonable grounds to suspect that it represents the proceeds of crime.[2]

Legislation alone does not always secure compliance. In speaking about the implications of the money-laundering reporting provisions in the UK, Gold and Levi referred to the fact that 'the "compliance culture" has to be established in areas of legal and accountancy professional practice which formerly saw themselves as entrepreneurial' (Gold and Levi, 1994: 23). This chapter touches on and begins to link several competing larger themes: the development of a language of compliance; the viability of a 'social contract' between corporations and the wider society; the consequences of assigning to institutions impossible or at least improbable compliance responsibilities; and, the impact of the international community and/or the U.S. on Canadian policymaking. This chapter examines what we can learn from Canadian anti-money-laundering research as well as other (non-money-laundering) regulatory research related to Canadian financial institutions and what we can learn from international literature and research.

In our study of RCMP proceeds of crime cases,[3] financial deposit-taking institutions plus an array of professionals were found to be involved, to varying degrees, in the money-laundering schemes of criminals under investigation. Aside from the banks, lawyers were the professionals most frequently found to have been used by launderers or knowingly involved with the proceeds of crime and money laundering. Lawyers were involved in 49.7 per cent of the cases. Of course, some lawyers work in real estate law and, on occasion, lawyers may serve as financial advisers. In these additional cases, lawyers also impact the tally of those other professional groups.[4]

Unless one is versed in the intricacies of international commerce, the manoeuvres of global banking operations are hard to monitor. When a scandal does arise, we get a glimpse of some of these transactions before the wall of confidentiality again descends. Following the investigation into Enron, SEC enforcement division director, Stephen Cutler, commented: 'Today's action demonstrated that neither financial institutions nor their executives can hide behind the technical complexities of structured transactions.'[5] While within some corporations the impact of unethical labour and polluting decisions may be geographically hidden (i.e., factories in less-developed countries or in rural, unpopulated regions), unethical commerce is more likely to be concealed by systemic veils of secrecy, interwoven incorporations, and confidentiality claims. In his introduction to the 2004 edition of Tom Naylor's *Hot Money and the Politics of Debt*, Michael Hudson states:

> Today, prestigious accounting firms and law partnerships busy themselves devising tax-avoidance ploys and creating 'veil of tiers' to provide a cloak of invisibility for the wealth built up by embezzlers, tax evaders, a few drug dealers, and arms dealers, and by government intelligence agencies for use in their covert operations. But the primary users are money managers and leading corporations concealing their profits (or losses, in the case of Enron and Parmalat dairy group) from oversight by the authorities in their countries. (Naylor, 2004: xviii)

We may think of professions such as the police, the military, or the prisons as operating within closed environments with relatively little exposure from the outside. Although quite different, in some ways, the 'white-collared' professions such as financial institutions, legal and accountancy firms operate with a similar degree of secrecy. The rhetoric for non-compliance (or exemptions) in each of these fields varies, but in every case it serves to protect the members. The 2004 Canadian Auditor General's review of FINTRAC concluded that the exemption of lawyers from the Canadian mandatory requirements to report suspicious financial transactions was 'widely regarded as a serious gap in the coverage of the anti-money-laundering legislation. It means that individuals can now do banking through a lawyer without having their identity revealed, bypassing a key component of the anti-money-laundering system' (Office of the Auditor General, 2004: 9).

Bankers and Financial Institutions

Banking is seen as a convergent point for illicit proceeds. Banking systems that deliberately attract illicit proceeds by facilitating money laundering provide a niche-market service to criminals. Typically, we think of offshore brass-plate banking services as being the laundering centres. Recently, however, the focus on banks and laundering activities reveals that some of the most prestigious banks in the world – in Switzerland, Monaco, United States, Britain, and so forth – are vulnerable or make themselves vulnerable.

In Canada, we take some comfort from the professionalism and regulation of our Big Five banks; yet Enron brought the reputations of at least two of these banks, the Canadian Imperial Bank of Commerce, and the Royal Bank of Canada, into question.[6] Beyond the 'facts' of these publicized cases that tell their own stories, this chapter examines the practicalities of compliance within the financial community. In order to examine the ethical conduct of financial institutions, the focus is on money laundering. The banks, domestically and internationally, had voiced their agreement in principle with the anti-laundering measures and committed themselves to full compliance (whatever form that might take). The literature on voluntary codes of conduct and ethical business protocols too often generalizes across sectors of the public and private corporate world and loses the context within which demands are being made on the operations. Far more than either the wording or the procedures used to formulate the agreements, it is the context that will determine the feasibility of relying on these measures. Understanding the emergence of specific codes of conduct serves as an entry into an understanding of local and international sensitivities and priorities. The context that gave rise to a given code reveals the potential array of agendas being met by the implementation, rhetoric of commitment, and conceivably compliance to voluntary regulatory regimes. Costs, risks (of compliance *as well as* for failure to comply), beliefs, and options are all relevant aspects of the probability of compliance.

The individual Canadian banks and their professional association, the Canadian Bankers Association, offered rhetorical support to the federal government's initiative to control money laundering via the agreed upon *voluntary* compliance mechanisms during the years leading up to the Act to Facilitate Combating the Laundering of Proceeds of Crime (1991) and the Regulations (1993). This voluntary regime was in lieu of legislated requirements that, as it turned out, were to come later. Given the rhetoric of support for the voluntary measures, it was felt that a study that looked at compliance patterns *prior* to mandatory reporting would tell us something about banking culture and provide an indication as to the likely degree of compliance that could be anticipated *after* the requirements were made mandatory by law. Therefore, research was carried out prior to the coming into force of the Proceeds of Crime (Money Laundering) Act that was enacted in 2000. Post–9/11, this legislation was changed to the Proceeds of Crime (Money Laundering) and Terrorist Financing Act (2001). After the passing of this legislation, the reporting of suspicious transactions was made mandatory. In addition, the legislation created a cross-border reporting requirement and created FINTRAC (Financial Transactions Reports Analysis Centre of Canada).

Two issues of legitimacy arise. Lessons from the study of deviance and criminology teach us that the success or failure of a compliance regime may rest in part on the legitimacy with which the policies are held. Where there is unanimous agreement as to the merit of a voluntary procedure, the argument holds that there is more likely to be a concerted effort to conform with the requirements (with the caveat that the more onerous or costly the requirements, the more compelling the 'need' may need to be). Where the merit is vague or debatable, coupled with low risk of detection and low negative risk of sanction or positive reward, compliance will be comparably less likely. The flip side of the legitimacy issue is the fact that the putting into place of 'publicized' codes of conduct may serve to legitimize ongoing (non-compliant) corporate procedures and dissuade governments from moving towards legislated controls.[7]

Separating the rhetoric of compliance from actual compliance becomes the difficult task. The rhetoric of compliance and the rhetoric of 'ethical conduct' originate from societal definitions; the strength of these definitions and the consensus surrounding them vary. These two bodies of discourse may be quite distinct. For example, the rhetoric of compliance can be very strong and serve to obfuscate a reality of neglect. Forceful compliance rhetoric may be the result of external pressures of one sort or another and may coexist with more ambivalent evaluations of the conduct in question. Understanding the rhetoric and the need for the rhetoric is part of the task of this chapter.

The Compliance of Financial Institutions: Results from the Voluntary Suspicious Transaction Study

The Canadian Big Five banks offered to participate in a Nathanson Centre research project (the *Suspicious Transaction Study: Referrals by Financial Institutions*), which studied the suspicious transaction reporting policies and practices that were in place.[8] Each bank had its own policies, training materials, and data collection systems. Our study of money laundering and suspicious reporting was intended to discover the degree of banking compliance, the diligence in their compliance, and the consequences of reporting. While the regime at the time of our research was 'voluntary' reporting, the banks had spoken out loudly regarding their desire to assist in enforcement efforts against money laundering. Some of their enthusiastic rhetoric may have been to ward off the legislation that would make their compliance mandatory! However, the fact remains that the banks were the first institutions to offer their verbal commitment to anti-money-laundering strategies. In a 19 February 1990 speech to the Canadian Club, then president of the Canadian Bankers Association, Helen Sinclair, stated:

> We don't want to be in the money-laundering business. We don't want to help or support the drug trade. We don't want to work with criminals or support criminal activity in any way, shape or form ... We *do not want* that kind of business. We are fighting it hard – and looking for ways to fight it harder. (Sinclair, 1990:2; emphasis in the original)

Words may not always translate into actions. Even prior to examining suspicious transaction files, there were indications that the banks were not prioritizing anti-money-laundering commitments. A tension exists within banking. A focus on profitability, fed in part by shareholders and CEOs with a vested interest in the competitiveness of each

financial institution, is juxtaposed against an increasingly strong philosophy of social responsibility in the 'fight' against money laundering.
As only one indication of which of these conflicting pressures is winning, it is relevant to compare the 'machinery' in the financial institutions that is in place to combat defalcations (frauds against the banks),
which often result in the bank losing money, compared with money
laundering where, depending on how long the illicit proceeds remain in
the bank and the quantity of these funds, the bank may in fact *make*
considerable money.

In an earlier confidential study of defalcations (Beare and Quellet,
1996) we concluded that, at times, profitability seemed to take precedence over security issues. We saw examples where a potential fraud
against the bank appeared to be a risk worth taking *if* there was a
possibility of a great enough profit.[9] Profit appeared to be the main
motivation. One would have to conclude that money-laundering prevention falls *third* in line behind profitability and behind the prevention
of risk from defalcations. While evidence of this 'ranking' is clearly
debatable, there are several indications of this prioritization. First, there
are sophisticated monitoring programs and technologies that are in
place to chart profitability and defalcations. By contrast, two of the five
banks merely placed suspicious files for referral to the police into a
bankers box with no computerized tally of the number or nature of
these referrals. Second, while all five banks stated that their employees
received training in the detection of suspicious transactions and money
laundering, it was acknowledged by at least one bank official that
training was given fairly low priority and that the turnover in staff
might mean that not everyone had adequate training. Third, while there
was a focus on aggressively sanctioning offenders/employees who cost
the banks, there was little evidence of any sanctioning of employees
who were not diligent in reporting suspected money-
laundering cases. Employees who were caught in even fairly minor
money offences against the banks, were always fired, informally blacklisted from employment at other banks, and were usually formally
charged.

Enforcement of money-laundering under these *voluntary* provisions
did not appear to produce this degree of sanctioning or indeed any
sanctioning. Similarly, a U.S. report prepared by the General Accounting Office questioned the U.S. Treasury Department as to why no high-
level bank official or major bank had ever been seriously sanctioned for
money laundering. Post–9/11 there have been charges, but these re-

main the exception. Officials have been criminally sanctioned in clear corruption cases but laundering cases remain in a more vague realm. Finally, the physical space within the headquarters of each financial institution that is devoted to each of these functions reflects the decreasing focus given to money-laundering prevention. For example, the money-laundering/suspicious transaction area within one of the financial institutions was slowly pushed aside by the bank's legal branch to the point that a photocopy room also served as a meeting room. These conditions cannot be considered an accident or merely a matter of circumstance; rather, they must be seen to reflect the level of importance assigned by senior management to money laundering.

Our findings indicated that compliance – or at least the banks' interpretations of what compliance entailed – varied greatly from bank to bank and that procedures fell far short of the expectations of the guidelines published by the Office of the Superintendant of Financial Institution (OSFI).[10] One could argue that there may be little reason to believe that the mandatory system of reporting will produce better results. Analysis of the files revealed wide discrepancy across the banks as to what was reported to the police as a 'suspicious transaction,' as can be seen in figure 5.1. The numbers of files from each of the separate banks varied greatly, from only fourteen cases in one bank to 169 in another. In some cases the data that we obtained posed more questions than answers. For example, what did this variation in the number of suspicious transactions across banks mean? It is not reasonable to assume that the clientele of the banks would be so different. The bank that provided us with the fourteen files also gave us a spread-sheet with 275 unusual-activity reports which, as the name would suggest, captured unusual activity but activity that was eventually deemed by the bank officials to not be related to money laundering and therefore was not referred to the police.

In the majority of cases it was only a deposit that was reported, not a true 'laundering' scheme (see fig. 5.2). The nature (i.e., the lack of any clear indication of suspiciousness) of these referrals may help to explain the limited feedback from the police to the banks and the lack of evidence that any of the referrals had resulted in a case being developed or a conviction made.

None of the banks had a computerized system in place that would have allowed for accurate ongoing monitoring of their suspicious transaction reporting. Likewise, the RCMP, from the bank's perspective, often failed to provide any information as to the outcome of the re-

Figure 5.1: Total number of referred files per the Big Five financial institutions

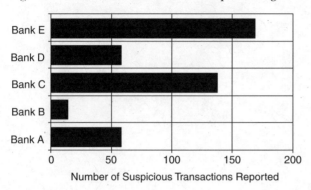

Source: M. Beare (2000b)

Figure 5.2: Type of financial transactions used in the 'suspicious' files referred to police

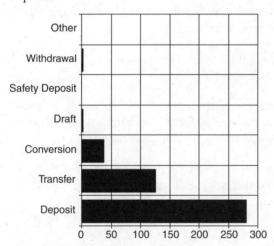

Source: M. Beare (2000b)

ported file and in many cases, there appeared to be no police follow-up.[11] At the time of our research, *none* of the referrals, based on the information that the banks had, was declared to be money laundering by the police, as can be seen in figure 5.3. The reasons the banks gave the police to explain the referrals were as vague as the profiles discussed in the

Figure 5.3: Stage of the investigation: Status of RCMP responses to the bank referrals

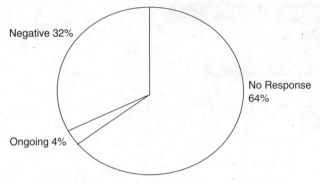

Negative 32%

No Response 64%

Ongoing 4%

Source: M. Beare (2000b)

international literature. Basically, in some of the banks, a hesitation by the customer to provide the banks with information or appearing to lie and dealing in cash or other large transactions were considered grounds for referring the file to the police (see fig. 5.4).

Looking for Explanations: The Banking Environment, Compliance, and Ethical Conduct

Four factors arguably determine the context within which one may explain the degree of compliance of Canadian banks with voluntary anti-money-laundering suspicious reporting guidelines:

1 The degree of contradiction between the *goals and culture* of the financial institutions and the 'law enforcement' roles that are assigned to the banks.
2 The *ability* of the financial institutions to comply meaningfully to the requirements.
3 The international evidence of the *merits* of complying.
4 The imperfect balance between the *costs versus gains* of adhering to anti-money-laundering strategies. At what point does compliance appear overly onerous?

Contradictory Goals and Mandates

The rhetoric of the financial institutions comes across as if all of the

Figure 5.4: Suspicious activity triggers, based on additional file and interview information

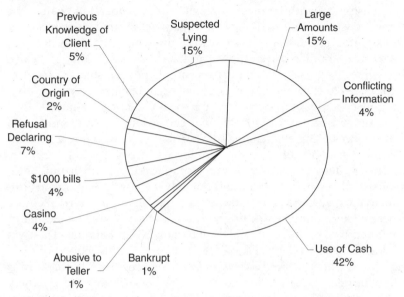

Previous Knowledge of Client 5%
Suspected Lying 15%
Large Amounts 15%
Country of Origin 2%
Conflicting Information 4%
Refusal Declaring 7%
$1000 bills 4%
Casino 4%
Abusive to Teller 1%
Bankrupt 1%
Use of Cash 42%

Source: M. Beare (2000b)

objectives of the bank are equal: profit, risk management, customer satisfaction, *and* a sense of societal/corporate responsibility towards the reduction of money laundering. In reality, these goals are often seen to be contradictory and are not given equal attention. As we have noted, a focus on profitability runs throughout the banking sector. Picking up on the 'what gets measured and gets rewarded, gets done' line of reasoning (Bogach and Gordon, 2000), it is important to consider the reward system within those institutions that have claimed to implement sound voluntary codes, especially where those codes might work against other rewarded objectives. During the U.S. Senate's 1999 review of the operations of private banking, one bank official stated that 'no one took the "know-your-customer" policies seriously until bonuses were threatened.' The internal study of bank defalcations within Canadian financial institutions revealed a maze of individual, departmental, and branch incentives that were offered based on performance. These individual and group rewards were so coveted that they were seen to be partially responsible for overzealous banking decisions (e.g., unwise loans and credit lines). Peer pressure from group incentives was particularly powerful. Hence any policy that resulted in the loss of customers – especially customers with large amounts of money – operated against the current reward structure. Banks are organized around the concept of attracting funds and few banks reward those who turn money away.

A study of fraud in corporations, authored by Peter C. Yeager (Pearce and Snider, 1995: 117–67), points to corporate policies that give contradictory cues to employees. For example, organizations may have policies that encourage employees to be personally 'innovative and creative' in the pursuit of profit (with the year-end results of these individual performances being evaluated and rewarded), while having a less tangible responsibility of assisting employees in being good corporate citizens by detecting *suspected* money laundering (with nebulous or non-existent personal rewards and possibly few for the banking institution). In the defalcation study, those situations that were seen to require 'inherent trust' and that seemingly could not be or were not audited or monitored proved to be the most vulnerable to exploitation. The twin notions of the 'calculated risk of detection' and the 'likelihood of swift negative sanctions' served as the main internal regulatory mechanisms within the financial institutions to protect the banks from fraud and theft.

Other studies have also concluded that wherever profitability is at stake, government policies cannot depend on voluntary measures. For example, the Mackay Task Force undertook a study on the future of the Canadian Financial Services Sector (CFSS). Entitled *Change Challenge Opportunity* (Department of Finance, 1993), it examined access to banking services. This report was critical of the fact that banks had not taken seriously the agreements that they had made with the government in 1997 to improve low-income citizens' access to banking services. The MacKay Task Force concluded that, if progress were not made, the government would need to legislate compliance. Research carried out by the Canadian Community Reinvestment Coalition (CCRC) in 1999, as well as a study commissioned by the Canadian Bankers Association (ACNielsen Canada study) concluded that compliance with the measures across the financial institutions was dismal.[12] The CCRC report found that not only were the guidelines that the financial institutions negotiated with the government (regarding the access of low-income people to banking services) *not* being adhered to by the banks, but also that,

in addition to successfully delaying government regulations in this area, the voluntary code negotiated with the government continues to benefit the banks by allowing them to boast that they have taken steps to making banking more accessible. As recently as May 1999, promotional material by the Canadian Bankers Association touted the 1997 promises of 'more flexible cheque-cashing and account-opening requirements' as well as an initiative of giving bank staff 'sensitivity training' to help them better meet the needs of low-income Canadians. (CCRC, 1999: 5)

One would have to assume that money-laundering prevention would fall into the same type of category – if not even lower in priority – as banking access by low-income customers. Profitability measures would lead, followed by prevention of defalcations, and finally those policies that have no direct gain for the financial institutions such as higher-risk access policies and the prevention of money laundering.

Much debate considers whether businesses such as the financial sector welcome voluntary regulations in order to prevent mandatory regulations. Some evidence would seem to support this contention. David McInnes, in an article entitled 'Can Self-regulation Succeed?' focused on consumer protection rather than on money laundering. Using bankers as his example, he justifies why the business community has a clear preference for voluntary measures rather than legislation: 'Bankers, for instance, are already weighted down by the Bank Act's 500 plus pages, as well as some 100 other federal and provincial statutes affecting their industry' (McInnes, 1996). The pressures of commercial expediency can place a premium on the flexibility of ethical standards rather than legislation. As G.P. Gilligan states: 'Compliance models of regulation are more malleable than those regimes based on instrumental models of control, so they provide more scope for renegotiation and reclassification of moral standards of behaviour' (1999: 71–2).

Competing Cultures

Related to the issue of contradictory goals and objectives, is the issue of competing cultures. Front-line banking officials are not police officers. A financial institution's objectives are to attract customers and make profits. Unless we were to alter our understanding of how banks operate, intensive training in money laundering *plus* an internal incentive and promotion system must be put in place to reward those bank officials who detect suspicious customers that result in positive referrals to the police. Effective suspicious transaction reporting requires a receptive police response to the referrals received from the banks. Problems arise when two quite different institutional cultures come together for anti-money-laundering enforcement. Gold and Levi cite the following barriers to police–bank harmony: first, some bankers, as a matter of principle, want to maximize the confidentiality of the affairs of their customers. By contrast, the police believe that bankers, like all citizens, have a moral obligation to provide them with any information relevant to the prevention and detection of crime. Second, the commercial interests of bankers may reflect a different sensitivity to different frauds. However, when the banks are victimized they want priority treatment from the police. Financial crimes seldom receive this type of treatment due to limited police resources. A lack of police response in this area may undermine the confidence of the banks regarding the likelihood that the police will respond to their 'suspicious' money-laundering referrals. In a revealing statement made during a public address, a vice-chair of the Bank of Montreal expressed concern at the 'emerging practice' whereby Canada's financial institutions provide financial assistance to the police in order to 'buy' more and quicker police attention (Chisholm, 1999).

The foundation of most partnerships – including those involving enforcement – is the relationship between people. People factors such as conflicts of personalities or departmental interests aggravated by poor training or job insecurity can undermine cooperation both within and between law enforcement agencies and financial services institutions (Gold and Levi, 1994). As Gold and Levi note: 'It is possible to imagine a world in which the interests of the police (including non-police regulators) in maximising intelligence collation and the interests of bankers coincide precisely. However, this is not the world in which we live' (ibid.: 5).

How Easily Accomplished Are the Recommended Reporting Responsibilities?

As one author suggests, detecting money launderers would be much easier if they wore stripy jumpers and carried bags labeled 'swag' (Willman, 2001). A researcher from the UK makes claims of a true story of reviewing suspicious referrals in one of the banks. Upon seeing what looked like a very normal transaction, he inquired as to why it was referred to the police. The explanation given was that the depositor 'had one glass eye and lived on a cul-de-sac'![13] This explanation serves to represent the more cynical view of the ability of front-line or managerial bank personnel to distinguish truly suspicious and significant behaviour from the merely unusual and irrelevant. To quote Gold and Levi (1994): '... the difference between "money movement facilities" and "money-laundering" is often a fine one, particularly when viewed from the perspective of the banker who wants to "do the deal" because ultimately, performing services for paying customers is the source of banking profitability' (4).

Add the fight against terrorism to the anti-money-laundering task and the expectations placed on front-line bank officials or others who are increasingly being held responsible for assuming a role in catching these criminals becomes quite impossible. As we discuss in chapter 6 ('Terrorist Financing'), the Financial Action Task Force (2002a) expressed doubts as to whether there would be any real indicators that would alert the financial institutions to the possible suspiciousness of terrorism-related funds, particularly given the fact that they may well have a legal source.[14]

After the 11 September 2001 terrorist attacks in the U.S., we read repeatedly that the tasks (in some cases, new tasks) being assigned to organizations such as banks were impossible. The response seems to have been 'But hey, let's do it with more of a vengeance!' All suspicious reporting, whether voluntary or mandatory, arguably rests on two essential principles: the 'know-your-customer' policies and the belief in an ability to profile suspicious transactions.

'Know-your-customer' policies are considered to be the base-level essential ingredient in any anti-laundering banking policy and, in fact, were assumed to be the basis of good banking practice. The absence of these policies indicates, more clearly than any rhetoric to the contrary, a disregard for money laundering at the domestic level. These policies have become, in many jurisdictions, a key ingredient behind the assumed ability to profile suspicious transactions. In Canada, the Office of the Superintendent of Financial Institutions (OSFI) issues 'best practices' documents confirming, among other anti-laundering strategies, the importance of the 'know-your-customer' policy. 'Know-your-customer' is one of the few policy links that go from the regulatory bodies to the financial institutions that they attempt to oversee. Once regulated institutions put these policies into operation, there is an expectation that a key defence against money laundering is at play. This expectation, however, takes for granted that the policy is actually being enforced by the financial institutions and that the financial institution sees it to their advantage (ethically or in terms of the risks that can occur) to comply.

The notion is that while there are millions of transactions that pass through financial institutions, a certain percentage are irregular in some respect (either in terms of the behaviour of the customer or the behaviour of the transaction that is being requested) and warrant greater – and more timely – scrutiny. Therefore, the belief in the merits of enforcing suspicious transaction reporting rests on three assumptions:

1 The assumption that suspicious transactions can be profiled by *any person* with unlimited training and innate abilities and that it is therefore possible to teach employees what characteristics ought to alert them to a potential criminal operation that can then be passed immediately to law enforcement (Goulet, 1998). In the wake of anti-terrorism recommendations, financial institutions are now asked to predict the *future* uses to which conceivably legally obtained money *might be* used.
2 The assumption that front-line tellers and personnel, untrained in wider law enforcement techniques, will be able to identify suspicious transactions.
3 If so, the assumption that they will be motivated to do so in a manner that neither ignores truly suspicious cases nor over-identifies cases that are unlikely to prove to be worthy of police investigations.

Few evaluations of suspicious-reporting regimes exist. Perhaps the most thorough was the previously referred to report by Michael Gold and Michael Levi (1994) in the UK. This study was not a full review of the process of financial investigations and it did not include a case analysis of the suspicious transaction reports. However, through interviews and observation they looked at some of the 'measures of impact' such as the triggering of new investigations; contributing substantially to existing investigations; and, the rendering of 'useful' information for future investigations. It is notable that they begin by hoping that their research will serve to inform the debate within financial, governmental, policing, and public circles about the future utilization of these inroads into the privacy of individuals. One might argue that the international community has seen a symbolic need for *mandatory* suspicious reporting, almost regardless of what researchers find. Unfortunately, Gold and Levi's findings were inconclusive. They found that there may be *some* deterrent, disruptive, and displacement effects from the suspicious-reporting anti-money-laundering measures. In addition, they found that these measures provide a more thorough audit trail once an investigation is underway. A concern throughout the report is that, to some extent, policies that rely on knowing your customer and profiling transactions might be moot. The trend towards automation and impersonality works against this suspicion-based model of detection.

The researchers noted, however, that a mandatory suspicion-reporting system would produce *more* but not necessarily *better* cases, resulting in defensive reporting without filtering. The number of disclosures could swamp the system and make it impossible for the police to adequately respond to the referrals that they receive:

> On the one hand, the more the disclosures, the more likely it is that one of them may produce a 'hit' on the routine checks. On the other hand, the more the disclosures, the less time they have left to do any 'real investigative work' on a) those cases that produce a 'hit' on names already known and b) ... those cases in which the circumstantial details on the disclosure make it plausible that an offence has been committed which is capable of leading to a prosecution. (Gold and Levi, 1994: 104)

With What Results Are These Initiatives Undertaken Internationally?

The intensive anti-money-laundering campaigns, multinational agreements, and diverse political pressures to conform, harmonize, and sanction methods have produced, at best, unreliable compliance and unverifiable results in terms of impact on money laundering. Given the international dimension to money laundering, the legal rules in one jurisdiction may reflect conditions elsewhere that are not necessarily relevant in the home jurisdiction. For example, in high-bank-secrecy locations, domestic laws may reflect the state's desire to compete with other offshore secrecy havens, or conversely, laws may reflect pressures from international groups such as FATF. In both of these situations, the imposed legislation may not seem particularly relevant to the domestic situation.

Both the rhetorical hype and the massive number of money-laundering banking cases involving negligence and/or corruption were extraordinary. Before and during the international hype against money laundering, there have been huge cases against large international banks rather than small unknown banking entities in offshore locations. It can be difficult for banks to decide whether capital moving through their centres is clean or part of some illegal operation, such as tax evasion or money laundering. However, the size and the nature of some of the high-profile cases present no such ambiguity. The optimism or the optimistic rhetoric that is attached to the current focus on criminal proceeds, as an alternative to more traditional law enforcement, may therefore not be warranted. An alternative interpretation is that the focus on money laundering is accomplishing exactly what is intended – a public relations exercise that speaks to a commitment to social responsibility without handicapping the flow of international finance.

During the 1980s, Swiss banks were embarrassed by their role in handling funds from the late Ferdinand Marcos of the Philippines. The French Parliament's task force into money laundering in Europe reported in the Montebourg Report in February 2001 that Switzerland's 372 banks made only 313 reports of suspected money laundering in the year 1999–2000. The Swiss countered that while France had referred 1,655 cases during that same period, Switzerland actually handed over more cases to the prosecutors (198 in Switzerland as compared with 129 in France). Aside from the name calling,[15] these results are paltry and hardly worth the machinery in place to supposedly target the launderers.

In 2001, British banks were found to have facilitated the looting of Nigeria by the late dictator General Sani Abacha – twenty-three UK banks were accused of having handled $1.3 billion. Despite repeated requests by the Nigerian government to freeze the funds held in British accounts and repatriate the money back to Nigeria, no action has been taken.[16] In another case, Citibank accounts in New York continued to do business with a Cayman Islands bank and allowed $300 million to pass through New York before finally closing the accounts. During a Senate inquiry into these laundering activities, U.S. Senator Carl Levin stated: 'They weren't just asleep at the switch – they were in a deep sleep on this one' (Golden, 2001). Citibank was also notorious for handling huge sums of money (over $87 million) for Raul Salinas. Raul Salinas de Gortari is the older brother of Mexico's former president, Carlos Salinas. In January 1999, he was convicted and sentenced to fifty years in prison for the murder of his ex-brother-in-law, Pepe Ruiz Massieu. (Six months later a Mexican appeals court reduced this sentence to twenty-seven and a half years.) He also has been accused of money laundering and 'inexplicable enrichment.' The Swiss government and courts have determined that the bulk of Raul's over $100 million in Swiss accounts is protection money paid by the drug cartels. Citibank facilitated the transfers and helped to hide the source of the funds.

The private banking sector is rife with potential money laundering, tax avoidance, and tax evasion opportunities. The use of multijurisdictional accounts and the movement of large sums (often at the advice of other professionals working for the same client for reasons that might not be clear to the banker) add to the problems of money-laundering detection. Quite naturally, over time, private bankers tend to be advocates for their clients.

The lengthy inquiry into the Salinas laundering affair (U.S. General Accounting Office, 1998) illustrated most of the things that can go wrong with accepting the premise that private banking officers will reliably care about voluntarily reporting money laundering. From that inquiry, we have the oft-quoted comment by Ms Amy Elliot, the official that handled the Salinas file. To a colleague in Switzerland, Ms Elliott stated: 'This account is turning into an exciting profitable one for us all. Many thanks for making me look good' (U.S. Senate, *The Minority Staff Report*, 1999: 14). In the private banking industry, compliance with anti-money-laundering procedures remains lax. Audits, compliance reviews, repeated deadlines, and bonus threats were all part of the maze of methods that were used to try to coax compliance. Interestingly, the fear by employees that they might lose their bonuses seemed to have the most direct results – which also speaks to performance-related bonuses that likely result in the low level of compliance in the first place. It is, therefore, unsurprising that behaviour that is rewarded is likely to be given priority by the employees. (This issue is more fully discussed later in this chapter in reference to Canadian banking.)

The amount of dirty money that moves around through international banks is obviously huge and the revenue is considerable. However, the rhetoric suggests that turning down dirty money might actually be good for business because of the enhanced reputation of the banks. Having a good reputation is claimed to generate more clean profits. The difficulty is in verifying this claim. The evidence that does exist tends to favour the opposing view. Banking is highly competitive. There would need to be real evidence of a detrimental impact from dirty money before accepting the claim that there is any redeeming *corporate* advantage to ethical behaviour aside from the sense of being a 'good corporate citizen' and, in the case of a mandatory regime, being a law-abiding one.

The main disincentive for the banks to allow money laundering within their financial institutions is claimed to be the adverse publicity and damage to one's reputation if a major scandal breaks; possibly, but not necessarily, changing an 'ethical good corporate citizen' issue into a 'loss of business and therefore loss of profits' issue. Banking rhetoric tells us that it does financial institutions no good to encourage money launderers to make use of their banking services. While there may be some disruption to financial trends in having large amounts enter and leave one's bank, there may also be a positive financial gain and possibly an incentive to attract international business, regardless of how dubious that business turns out to be in hindsight. While we hear that banking reputations are injured by high-profile cases involving money laundering, the reality is that the bank is in business to welcome money into its operation. Seemingly 'adverse' publicity does not necessarily damage a bank's reputation.

For the purposes of illustrating this point, let us look at the case of the Bank of New York scandal. While we repeatedly hear that banks will willingly comply with the anti-laundering mechanisms because their reputations are at stake, this may not necessarily be true. Perhaps the largest amount of negative publicity was aimed at the Bank of New York (BONY). BONY gained notoriety for accepting, depositing, and handling over $7 billion of suspicious Russian funds (Willman, 2001). The money was transferred from Russia through three accounts at a bank branch in New York between 1996 and 1999. This case drew enormous international attention due to the vast amounts involved and the obviously questionable routes and customers. If any scandal was going to actually hurt the bank financially, this ought to have been the one to do so. Regulatory monitoring ought to have detected 'non-normal' transactions. While the case involved actual corruption of officials, the amounts of the transitions ought to have been detected by some oversight mechanism. The question remains, however: Did the scandal hurt the Bank of New York? Several quotes capture the impact on BONY.

According to the chair and CEO of the Bank of New York, Thomas Renyi,

> Despite being at the center of an international money-laundering investigation, Bank of New York Co. remains on track for record earnings this year and has seen almost no impact on its business from the scandal ... the bank would [sic] post a record profit of $1.69 a share for 1999, up from $1.53 a share for 1998. (Beckett, 1999: 1)

The *Wall Street Journal* reported (Beckett, LeVine, and Cloud, 2000a, 2000b) that investors trusted the way that the bank responded. The paper acknowledged that the stock actually rose in value. The 3 October article quotes Robert Bissell (president of Wells Capital Management), as saying:

Figure 5.5: Climb in BONY share prices

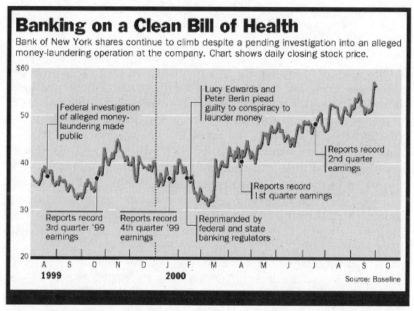

Banking on a Clean Bill of Health

Bank of New York shares continue to climb despite a pending investigation into an alleged money-laundering operation at the company. Chart shows daily closing stock price.

Source: Baseline

Source: *Wall Street Journal* (2000), 'Investors Are Betting that Bank of New York Will Emerge Unscathed from Investigation,' 3 October, retrieved 1 July 2006 from 'Redwash,' as published by Newswire: Official News Service of the U.S. /Russia Press Club, www. moscowtelegraph.com/redwash_foreword.htm.

'The stock price is telling you it is a controllable risk ... The market tries to figure out whether someone knowingly got involved in dirty business and the benefit of the doubt so far has gone to the Bank of New York ...

In response to the *rise* in the value of the stock, Chris Bingaman, analyst at Villanopva Capital (the asset management arm of Nationwide Financial Services), was quoted as saying:

That just says that the market is looking past the investigation and doesn't believe it is really material to the long-term outlook of the company. (ibid.: C1)

Figure 5.5, taken from the *Wall Street Journal*, traces the climb in BONY share prices. A scandal of this size was seen to be a housekeeping detail, something that needed to be handled appropriately and then forgotten. The following quote captures the nuisance status of the incident:

As a practical matter, it's a bit of an embarrassment and it's a public-relations nightmare to some extent, but from an investor's standpoint, it's behind them,' said Judah Kraushaar, bank analyst at Merrill Lynch and Co. of New York. (Beckett, 1999: 1)

In their attempt to explain the lack of anxiety on the part of investors, journalists concluded that there was a sense that the bank processed such vast volumes of transactions that it is expected that there would be problems, even to the tune of $7 billion. The only question becomes: How did the bank handle the problem once it surfaced? (Likewise, Canadian financial institutions caught in the Enron scandal continued to show profits during 2006 regardless of any 'entanglements.')

In terms of sanctions, the corrupt bank official Lucy Edwards was fired and pleaded guilty to laundering charges. No charges were brought against the Bank of New York, although Thomas Renyi was penalized. The bank's board of directors stated that it believed that Ranyi had 'no direct responsibility for the events,' but that the CEO 'does have ultimate responsibility for all matters that occur at the company.' Hence his salary was docked, as Beckett (2000) reported in the *Wall Street Journal*, 'Citing the impact of a massive Russian money-laundering probe, Bank of New York Co. lowered the compensation of Chairman and Chief Executive Thomas Renyi by about 11 per cent for 1999 ... Salary and bonus totaled $6.58 million in 1999, down from $7.38 million the prior year.'

This 'shortfall' was apparently made up to him in the year 2000 in the form of a $12.1 million bonus.[17] Jonathan Winer, former U.S. Deputy Assistant Secretary of State, gave a presentation in Toronto in 2000 during which he stated – even after the BONY fiasco – that Canadian banks were attractive to Russian organized crime because of the lack of money-laundering laws. When questioned as to what happened to the U.S. currency transaction reporting system during the BONY laundering period, Winer responded that the fault was with corrupt banking officials and not with the reporting system. The amounts of money in these high-profile cases are huge and the suspicious nature of the funds appears obvious. A number of the most atrocious cases do indeed involve corrupt officials. Therefore, it would seem that a self-regulatory mechanism that has no reliable bifurcated checks on corrupt or negligent officials is not a viable system of control. One might question whether it is even meant to be viable.

Since 11 September 2001, the picture has changed slightly, with more fines and therefore more consequences, although what remains constant is BONY's continuing preference for profit over due diligence. According to the *New York Times*, other actions are being taken against BONY:

> A federal appeals court revived a lawsuit accusing executives of the Bank of New York Company of looting assets from Inkombank, a Russian bank that is now defunct. The suit by Inkombank depositors claims that bank executives, Russian mobsters and a few Bank of New York employees systematically transferred money through the New York-based bank and caused the Russian bank to fail.[18]

In November 2004, a report in the *Wall Street Journal* indicated that BONY was negotiating to avoid an indictment for continuing to fail to report suspicious transactions. Following the Russian money scandal, BONY promised to comply with all money-laundering laws in order to avoid a criminal charge. This new case was therefore somewhat of an embarrassment. The article specified that BONY would pay $24 million in penalty with its continuing cooperation to be reviewed.[19]

New York is not the only jurisdiction where banks have illustrated an unwillingness to take money laundering and other financial offences seriously. The National Irish Bank has been fined a penalty of EUR64 million for an array of fraudulent and unethical manoeuvres. Similar to our research findings in Toronto, the inspectors in Ireland concluded:

> The branch network was target driven ... targets for fee income and deposits, but limited support by way of systems or training to enable the achievement of these targets. Managers felt under pressure to meet these targets, ... they feared criticism and possible humiliation before their fellow managers if they did not meet the targets set. (Kroll Inc., 2004: 9)

Different countries and different institutions tend to react in specific ways whenever a scandal occurs. The 'launching' of the Wolfsberg Principles may be a case in point. Much adverse publicity surrounded the various reports on the private banking industry in the U.S. and internationally. The result? High-profile adverse media attention; staunch resistance to the 'know-your-customer' plan proposed by the Federal Reserve; and those banks that were most criticized (i.e., Citigroup) signed on to the 'voluntary' series of the Wolfsberg Principles. There was a fair amount of press coverage of the release of these principles, which were claimed to be 'voluntary guidelines aimed at preventing private banking operations from being used to launder criminals' money' (Garver, 2000). In 1998, the U.S. Federal Reserve Board tried to introduce a 'know-your-customer' plan. The bank regulators withdrew these anti-laundering procedures in March 1999 because of the intense opposition from the banking industry and some members of the public. It is alarming that the banking regulators can be forced to withdraw their anti-laundering plans by those institutions that they are meant to be regulating. This, of course, speaks to the power of the banks. The Wolfsberg Principles consist of an enhanced form of the 'know-your-customer' policies.

Private banking 'is highly secretive and competitive,' and therefore it was considered to be 'no small feat' that eleven banks agreed to common procedures amid the fanfare of the launch of the Wolfsberg Principles.[20] Given the aggressive international stand that the U.S. has taken against money laundering, it is amazing that these policies were not taken for granted and implemented by all banks purporting to be concerned about money laundering. It is even more amazing that there was a *failed* forerunner to the Wolfsberg Principles.

It is acknowledged that some banks may have had some forms of 'know-your-customer' policies in place stemming from the U.S. Bank Secrecy Act, various U.S. General Accounting Office (GAO) reports, and reviews by the U.S. Federal Reserve Board (1999) that have been extremely critical of the anti-laundering efforts of the banks. However, private banking was found to be particularly open to laundering, tax evasion, capital flight, and looting by corrupt government officials. The argument is made that a culture of secrecy is combined with a culture of lax anti-money-laundering controls due, quite understandably, to competing agendas:

> It is the private banker who is charged with researching the background of perspective clients and it is the private banker who is asked in the first instance to monitor existing accounts for suspicious activity. But it is also the job of the private banker to open accounts and expand client deposits. (U.S. Senate, 1999: 5)

Bankers and lawyers are not the only professional groups that may capitalize on money movement. A new contingency fee market has developed in the United States and elsewhere whereby forensic accounting firms – comprised of bankers, lawyers, and accountants also known as 'financial engineers' – devise schemes to save large corporations taxes and then charge the corporations a percentage of the savings. The U.S. Treasury Department has identified corporate tax evasion as the nation's biggest tax enforcement problem and these shelters are seen to be the core of the problem. Charging a fee based on a percentage of taxes avoided is supposedly prohibited by ethics rules of the accounting industry. Hence, 'value pricing' becomes the substituted terminology. All of the former Big Five accounting firms (PricewaterhouseCoopers, Ernst and Young, Deloitte and Touche, KPMG, and the former Arthur Andersen) charged corporations based on savings from the tax shelters. While systems are in place to catch the suspicious depositor, an entire industry has grown up around assisting corporations in moving money around (Johnston, 2000). Arthur Anderson has since been put out of business as a result of its involvement in financial corruption. In addition, recent corporate scandals have resulted in new policies and laws restraining some of this behaviour.

Even if the policies are there and are adhered to, what is the impact of these policies in terms of the control of money laundering? In order to emphasize the shortcomings of the international initiatives, it is important to mention that this focus on money laundering is now well over a decade old. The FATF was established in 1989 and has become increasingly aggressive in the measures to enforce harmonization of anti-laundering strategies. This international pressure has been cumulative. Around the same time as the original FATF report, countries signed onto the Basle Committee on Banking Regulations and Supervisory Practices and produced a statement of principles entitled 'Prevention of Criminal Use of the Banking System for the Purpose of Money Laundering.'[21] Canada is a signatory to this 1988 document that encourages banks to

- verify the identity of the beneficial owners of accounts (know-your-customer)
- adopt an explicit policy of refusing significant transactions with customers who fail to provide evidence of their identity, and
- avoid transactions they believe are associated with money laundering (suspicious transactions)

Costs and Gains of Adhering to Anti-Money-Laundering Strategies

The question remains as to what might be the incentive to comply from the perspective of the financial institutions? Much of the compliance literature discusses of the viability of voluntary codes and often concludes, as does Harry Arthurs, that

230 Money Laundering in Canada

a modest body of research seems to suggest that they [corporations] can be responsible and profitable too. There is money to be made in 'ethical investment' and 'sustainable development'; social market policies do not seem to impair the efficiency and adaptability of workers; and economic prosperity may correlate positively with civic mindedness and progressive labour practices. (Arthurs, 2005: 195)

Arthurs's conclusion may be true when there is an additional product whose ethical production accounts for the profits – however, given the nature of money laundering, *what happens when the money is the product?* The key role of banking supervisors is to promote the overall financial stability and soundness of the bank. As stated by Ray Protti, president and CEO of the Canadian Bankers Association:

> Banks are profit-making institutions. If they're not profitable, employees don't have jobs. The marketplace has changed so dramatically and so quickly that our institutions have to show a tremendous amount of innovation, creativity and leadership to maintain their positions and profitability levels. (Protti, 2000: 21)

The business of financial institutions is the business of making money. There is no intermediary commodity, the production of which can be 'negotiated' to meet labour or environmental sensitivities. While regulators and best practices guidelines and other compliance mechanisms pressure financial institutions to assist with enforcement, the banks see themselves as being in a situation of increasing competition with the one objective being to attract funds (Willman, 2001).

Juxtaposed against this focus on profitability and competition is the fact that the banking industry is supposed to be one of the key institutions in the fight against money laundering. In the control of money laundering, the responsibility for detection rests in large part with the front-line tellers and private banking officials.[22] It may be argued that, in several important ways, holding the financial institutions accountable to 'ethical' standards in the detection of money laundering is different from other forms of corporate behaviour. While the profit motive is standard across corporations – providers of both goods and services – in most cases corporate decisions can be made via policies that set out clear tenets of acceptable business decisions. In banking, one may be less concerned with the more 'structural' decisions such as hiring and employment conditions or policies that affect the environment such as waste management than with the ability to hold the banks accountable for the ongoing case-by-case scrutiny of customers and transaction scenarios that may or not be suspicious, amid a sea of financial transactions deemed legitimate. Front-line banking staff are being asked to make spontaneous decisions that will work against the bank's interest in securing business, based on a fairly loose set of guidelines.

In the Canadian system, the *voluntary* suspicious transaction reporting system resulted in some of the financial institutions undertaking extensive investigative work in some of the cases and passing on to the police fairly large files. Theoretically, this can lead to the creation of a cadre of highly expert contact officers who would, over time, acquire a nuanced understanding of suspicious activity and possibly help secure a higher percentage of convictions. As Gold and Levi note (1994: 86), the 'skill' or commitment of compliance officers varies greatly and, as we see, the debate hardly matters. Driven by the work of the Financial Action Task Force (FATF),[23] the required uniform standard now expects *mandatory* reporting of suspicious transactions and reporting of large transactions. Whether the system works to any significant extent becomes immaterial. With the mandatory system, the financial institutions pass the simple STR/CTR forms on to FINTRAC and see that action as being the extent of their responsibilities. No longer do they take the initiative to investigate files at the bank level.

Perhaps more significantly, the form of detection enforced by FATF could result in the targeting of the most unsophisticated cases, where 'suspicious' literally takes the form of a hesitation to answer questions or unease in appearance – behavioural characteristics that may be absent from the truly professional launderer. One of the most pervasive complaints about transaction reporting schemes internationally is that they have generally failed to lead to the conviction of sophisticated money launderers. The clumsy novice is most often the criminal that is caught in what is seen by some critics to be a very expensive and intrusive web. Some research also indicates that there may be a class and/or racial aspect to reporting suspicion, as a certain appearance, presentation of self, or specific countries involved in financial transfers are seen to be more suspicious than other characteristics or jurisdictions. Geographical profiling is, of course, most likely to occur in the targeting of terrorist financing where typically the *only* suspicious indicator is the country of origin or destination of the financial transactions.

In conclusion, the mandatory status of suspicious reporting in Canada will not necessarily ensure that there is serious and diligent reporting by financial institutions unless the above barriers are replaced with incentives for compliance. The current system is set up to perpetuate these conditions. As the system now works, the financial institutions pass their referrals on to FINTRAC where officials make a decision as to whether or not to pass the referral on to law enforcement (following a strictly detailed procedure to protect the privacy of the information). However, there is no feedback mechanism whereby the banks learn whether or not their efforts have produced any results. Likewise, the police do not notify FINTRAC as to whether or not the referrals that they get have led to any successful cases, thus FINTRAC also has no idea of the impact it is having. The result is a system that cannot be evaluated in any real way. Any notion of 'compliance' will be interpreted in terms of numbers of files received or referred with no evidence of impact.

Debate continues as to whether a well-run voluntary suspicious transaction reporting system with some degree of centralized collection of financial intelligence might not prove to be more effective that a mandatory suspicious *and* large transaction regime. Based on the literature from other jurisdictions and from interviews that were held with Canadian banking officials, care must be taken to ensure that the regulations that accompany the now mandatory money-laundering requirements do not erode the few positive aspects of the voluntary system. An increase in reporting does not in and of itself add up to better surveillance of the movement of illicit proceeds or necessarily make us safer from terrorism.

Lawyers: The Relationship between the Legal Profession, Lawyers, and Money Laundering

*On 31 March 2005, Simon Rosenfeld was sentenced to **three years** in prison for money laundering (in Ontario) and attempting to possess the proceeds of crime. He was also ordered to pay a fine of $43,230 – his commission for laundering CDN$250,000 and U.S.$190,000 for drug profits. Rosenfeld is currently out on $1.95-million bail pending his appeal.*

In June 2004, the Toronto Proceeds of Crime Unit arrested Peter Shoniker and charged him with, among other offences, four counts of laundering the proceeds of crime. Mr Shoniker is a lawyer and financial consultant in Toronto.

Vancouver real estate lawyer Martin Chambers was sentenced to just over

15 years in a Florida state prison following his conviction in 2003 for laundering U.S.$700,000 in purported cocaine trafficking money.

Financial Action Task Force reports refer to professionals such as lawyers as 'gatekeepers' in the sense that when one looks at the type of assistance that these professionals provide, some of these functions are the gateway through which the launderer must pass to achieve his/her goals. Thus, according to the FATF, legal and accounting professionals have the ability to furnish access (knowingly or unwittingly) to the various functions that might help criminals who have funds to move or to conceal. Many if not all of these gateway services performed by lawyers lead into another stage. Banks, real estate agencies, accountants, and others who follow must also make decisions regarding the suspiciousness of a transaction. The lawyer, due to his/her status and position, serves to remove this suspicion.

In many of the police cases in our research, lawyers appear to have been unaware of the criminal source of funds provided by an offender and were unknowingly used to facilitate money laundering. However, the research also identified cases where a lawyer should have become suspicious of the circumstances surrounding a particular transaction, such as the use of a large amount of cash in small denominations to purchase real estate. Moreover, some lawyers appeared to offer services that were tailored expressly to satisfy the objectives of money laundering. This included converting substantial amounts of cash into less suspicious assets, concealing the criminal ownership of assets, incorporating numerous companies that carried out no commercial activities, fabricating or falsifying financial or legal documents, and transferring funds between bank accounts or between multiple trust account files established on behalf of clients and/or companies beneficially controlled by the client for no apparent commercial reason or financial gain.

At the time of this publication, lawyers in Canada have won a considerable victory: they are exempted from compliance with the mandatory suspicious transaction reporting requirement. Whether this decision was wise, and whether it will be permanent, remains to be seen. In the Supreme Court of British Columbia case between the Law Societies and the Attorney General of Canada, lawyers indicated[24] that little harm would be done to the investigation and prosecution of money launderers if lawyers were to be excluded from the mandatory reporting legislation because 'lawyers comprise a discrete class of persons who have historically occupied a unique position in the administration of justice for the benefit of society.'[25]

In reference to money laundering, lawyers are, indeed, a 'discrete class' and they *have* occupied a 'unique position.' Who they are and the services that they can offer, in fact, make them in many cases *essential* to sophisticated criminals with money to launder. As our analysis of the RCMP money-laundering cases illustrate, aside from financial deposit-taking institutions, lawyers are the professional group who come in contact with the proceeds of crime and money laundering most frequently (Schneider, 2004).

Based on our research into money laundering and money-laundering typologies, the exemption of lawyers leaves a significant gap that could frustrate the purpose of the money-laundering legislation. The evidence from money-laundering cases is clear:

> ... lawyers are utilized as part of particularly large-scale money laundering operations. The greater the quantity of cash generated by the criminal enterprise, the greater the need for increased sophistication in the laundering scheme. This increased sophistication in turn is facilitated by certain legal services to construct and maintain the laundering operation.[26]

While the argument is made that cash and other financial-related paperwork that passes through lawyers' offices may also cross into the domain of other institutions such as banks, businesses, or individuals who have to report, the role of the lawyer remains critical. To argue otherwise ignores the fact that a key service that a lawyer performs is to legitimate transactions.

As can be seen in our study, in some cases dirty money will be paid into the lawyer's trust account for the purchase of real estate in cash. While the financial institution will need to report, it is the lawyer who is in the position to judge the suspiciousness of the transaction. Therefore, lawyers provide not only services but also legitimacy to the larger laundering process. As the Law Society in the UK acknowledged with respect to the vulnerability of lawyers, 'solicitors are considered a soft target by fraudsters and money launderers because they lend legitimacy and respectability to illegal transactions.'[27]

In many cases, lawyers provide an unwitting service. However, our RCMP cases also reveal the entire range of lawyer involvement, from unwitting participants, to unconcerned facilitators, to partners in crime. While the FATF does refer at some length to the complicity of lawyers in laundering schemes, they also emphasize the additional need to 'develop a shield' that will protect 'vulnerable professions from influences of organized crime' (FATF, 1998a: para. 40). Mandatory reporting of suspicious transactions is seen to be part of this protection *for the lawyers*. The mandatory mechanism shifts what might be seen to be arbitrary reporting by those clients whose transactions are referred to as suspicious into a legislated requirement that protects the professional from accusations of bias.[28]

From a policing perspective, cases involving lawyers are extremely difficult to investigate. According to former chief superintendent Ben Soave, former head of the Combined Forces Special Enforcement Unit, 'Investigative tools that police could normally employ are extremely restricted when the subject of an investigation is a lawyer. The unfortunate consequence of these restrictions is that the legal profession can be exploited to cloak criminal activity' (RCMP, 2004). While recognizing that solicitor–client privilege is 'a needed, crucial and fundamental cornerstone of our justice system,' Soave argues that criminals

> go out of their way to engage, recruit, compromise, and corrupt lawyers and other members of the judicial system in order to further their criminal enterprises. The result is that criminals, with the assistance of a complicit lawyer, can hide behind the law, enabling them to shield their criminal activity from the legitimate scrutiny of law enforcement. (ibid.)

The Diverse Uses of Lawyers for Laundering Purposes

In recognition of the facilitation skills and attributes of lawyers, and in recognition of the potential new responsibilities falling on lawyers to assist in combating money laundering, a presentation given at a Canadian Bar Association Taking the Starch Out of Money Laundering Conference on 28 November 2000, outlined the unique ways in which lawyers could be used for laundering criminal proceeds (Wishart, 2000). The presentation outlined the importance of the following attributes of lawyers:

- unique expertise
- high social status
- credibility within the financial community
- solicitor–client privilege
- access to trust accounts

Because money-laundering transactions usually mimic business transactions, reputation and standing in the financial community is very
important. Together with legal/technical advice on the movement of
money, the social status of the lawyer is one of the most valuable
commodities that the criminal can buy.

There were four areas of law that were seen to be the most vulnerable:

1 corporate
2 commercial
3 real estate, and
4 *any* practice that involves the handling of large sums of money

In many cases the lawyer might be asked to perform what appears to be
a very ordinary service but that could have an ulterior laundering
purpose. For example:

- By assisting in the purchase of property in a way that will disguise
  the source of funds and/or the identity of the owner.
- By simply placing cash proceeds in trust accounts prior to settlement on the purchase of property.
- By establishing nominee companies and trusts for use by money
  laundering clients in Canada and overseas.
- By arranging false loans with other parties on behalf of clients.
- By holding funds in trust for clients and conducting transactions
  directly with financial institutions.
- By coordinating international transactions, including currency
  exchanges, and co-ordination of trans-border movement of funds.

The Financial Action Task Force (FATF) adds to this list:

- The creation of corporate vehicles or other complex legal arrangements (such as trusts).
- Financial and tax advice that involves complex financial schemes.
- Gaining introductions to financial institutions, thereby gaining a
  veneer of respectability.

Lawyers and Law Societies across Canada – Positions and Arguments

While they recognized how useful lawyers are to the laundering process, the most bitter and sustained criticism of the legislation came from

Canada's legal professionals. At the core of their opposition was the inclusion of lawyers under the reporting requirements of the legislation, which they contended would contravene the sacrosanct principle of solicitor–client privilege. Though it might be acknowledged that lawyers are fully protected by section 11 of the Act, which provides that legal counsel are *not* required to disclose any communication that is subject to solicitor–client privilege, lawyers maintained that the protection provided by 'privilege' falls short of the traditional 'confidential' nature of the solicitor–client relationship that they wish to maintain (para. 80).

'The protection of a client's interest is incompatible with the demand that a lawyer also act as an arm of the state,' stated Greg DelBigio, a Vancouver lawyer who studied the legislation on behalf of the Canadian Bar Association.[29] Equally alarming to lawyers are secrecy provisions built into the legislation that forbid lawyers from telling their clients they have had their transactions reported to FINTRAC. Eric Rice, the president of the Canadian Bar Association, said the legislation would quickly break down the openness and frankness between lawyer and client that ensures lawyers can perform their duties as officers of the court. 'This law creates a tremendous scope for one party to withhold information from the other and for distrust between solicitor and client.'[30]

Mr Jack Giles, lawyer for the Law Society of British Columbia, spoke in reference to the confidential relationship lawyers have with clients, stating,

> Today, without the intervention of this court, it becomes a crime for every lawyer in this country to fail to act as a secret agent for the government ... The lawyer's obligation to spy for the government becomes effective immediately ... the mere suspicion of money laundering is enough to trigger the report requirement, and a lawyer's whole body of knowledge is called upon – meaning the regulation applies retroactively to anything a lawyer knows about a client. If this regulation is not immediately postponed, the impact will not only be irreparable, but devastating. ... We are seeking to maintain what has been the status quo for over 700 years.[31]

Joseph Wood, representing the Federation of Law Societies of Canada compared the legislation to Nazism – claiming that no legislation had come so close to the orders that Adolf Hitler gave ordering lawyers to secretly inform on clients. He apologized but then insisted that the comparison was justified. Maurice Laprairie, president of the Federation of Law Societies, stated:

The legislation has nothing to do with money laundering or terrorist financing – it has to do with compromising the rights of any Canadian in need of a lawyer ... The legislation requires lawyers to submit details of their clients' confidential financial affairs to the federal government, contrary to our profession's ethical rules and contrary to the basic rights of all Canadians. Lawyers cannot be secret agents for the government. (Federation of Law Societies of Canada, 2002)

These quotes reveal the tone of the lawyers' opposition to the anti-money-laundering legislation. Their main argument related to the near-sacred position that solicitor–client privilege holds within the law profession – the right of a client to refuse to disclose an oral or documentary communication that passes between the client and his/her lawyer. As the debate evolved, the concept of privilege got deliberately blurred or genuinely confused with a looser, yet broader, notion of a lawyer's ethical rules concerning confidentiality. While both privilege and confidentiality are deemed important in order for there to be full and free communication between lawyer and client, 'privileged' information is of a higher order.

The requirement for lawyers to report suspicious transactions, lawyers claimed, violated the independence of the bar, solicitor–client confidentiality, and the duty of loyalty owed by lawyers to their clients. In the Supreme Court of British Columbia case between the Law Society of British Columbia and the Attorney General of Canada the main argument was that the requirement to note suspicion in the course of the lawyers' dealings with their clients – and having to report these suspicions in secret to the government – threatened the independence of the bar and solicitor–client confidentiality and created a conflict between the lawyers' duties to their clients and their obligations to report confidential information to the government.

The constitutional issue raised by the petitioners is whether certain provisions of the legislation that would have imposed duties on legal counsel were unconstitutional because they violated the protected right of an independent bar, the Constitutional Acts 1867 and 1982, and certain subsections of the Canadian Charter of Rights and Freedoms relating to fundamental rights, search and seizure, and the right to retain and instruct counsel without delay. The important question was whether or not the independence of the bar and the confidentiality of the lawyer–client relationship were in fact fundamental principles of justice that were deserving of the court's action and could not be infringed by legislation or by government action. While the independence of the bar may not be a right specifically protected by the Charter, lawyers argued this independence underlies other Charter rights that are without meaning unless lawyers are independent.[32] The lawyers argued that the state did not demonstrate that there would be dire consequences that warranted the infringement of rights if the lawyers were to be excluded, and that 'the state must show that its goals are reasonable and proportionate to the infringement of rights.'[33]

Particularly damaging to the state's argument was the case of *Lavallee et al. v. AG Canada* which, while recognizing that no right is absolute, continued on to say that 'the solicitor–client privilege must be as close to absolute as possible to ensure public confidence and retain relevance. As such, it will only yield in certain clearly defined circumstances, and does not involve a balancing of interests on a case-by-case basis.'[34] The lawyers argued that, even without the legislation, they are subject to codes of conduct and ethical obligations. Lawyers are also bound by provisions of the Criminal Code that prohibit them from engaging in criminal conduct such as money-laundering schemes or from becoming a party to any transactions with clients that conceal or convert property or proceeds that they believe to involve money laundering.[35]

Across the country, provincial law societies galvanized their opposition to the legislation through a number of legal challenges. In general, their requests for a judicial exemption from the reporting requirements met with success. On 20 November 2001, the Supreme Court of British Columbia exempted lawyers in that province from the reporting requirements. In her decision, Madam Justice Marion Allan said the bill 'authorizes an unprecedented intrusion into the traditional solicitor–client relationship.'[36] In the wake of the BC judgment, courts in Alberta, Ontario, Nova Scotia, and Saskatchewan also ruled that lawyers in those provinces were exempt from the reporting requirements. In Alberta, Court of Queen's Bench Justice Jack Watson issued a stay of a requirement lifting from lawyers any obligation to secretly report suspicious transactions made by their clients to a federal agency. Instead, they must report them to the Law Society of Alberta in sealed envelopes.[37] In response to these court decisions, Martin Cauchon, the Attorney General of Canada, agreed to exempt lawyers from the reporting requirements of the new proceeds of crime law.[38]

The Government Position

The government position with respect to money-laundering legislation appears to have been driven by diverse factors. A key issue was international pressure on Canada to pass this legislation; the inclusion of lawyers was part of the list of recommendations from the FATF.[39] Richard Lalonde, an officer of the Department of Finance, referred in some detail to various estimates regarding the amount of money laundering.[40] The Canadian government was convinced that money laundering was in fact serious, and available research indicated that lawyers were implicated in the most sophisticated schemes. The Crown pointed to a number of high-profile cases in which lawyers played a role in the development and proliferation of organized crime in North America, including Canada. The government claimed there was 'pressing and substantial concern' that lawyers knowingly assisted clients in laundering money. In recent years lawyers have increasingly moved away from traditional services to clients and often act as financial advisers equally or instead of their role as legal advisers. The role of financial adviser is often undertaken together with accountants in multidisciplinary partnerships. These partnerships could be seen to increase the facilitation of money laundering.

In light of the above arguments, why did the state then decide to repeal controversial parts of the regulations and offer at least a temporary exemption to lawyers? There were at least three reasons. First, the series of successful court challenges by the law societies across Canada had an impact on the Crown's perception of its position. Likewise, the cases involved prolonged discussion – somewhat unresolved – concerning the scope of privilege and the status of privilege in the administration of Canadian justice. Second, the *Lavallee* case in 2002 served to, if not confirm, then at least strengthen the position of those people who had previously advocated a broad interpretation of privilege. The conclusion in *Lavallee* stated, in part,

> Where the interest at stake is solicitor–client privilege, which is a principle of fundamental justice and a civil right of supreme importance in Canadian law, the usual exercise of balancing privacy interests and the exigencies of law enforcement is not particularly helpful because the privilege is a positive feature of law enforcement, not an impediment to it. Given that solicitor–client privilege must remain as close to absolute as possible to

retain its relevance, the Court must adopt stringent norms to ensure its protection.[45]

This decision potentially impacted the ability of FINTRAC to conduct compliance audits of law firms with respect to their reporting obligations under the PCMLTFA. Finally, perhaps even more important was the timing. The anti-terrorism legislation had just been passed and it was obvious that the same issues of disclosure and reporting would also apply to that legislation. It was argued that the criminal reporting and the terrorist-financing laundering cases would best be handled simultaneously since there were potentially the same legal arguments in both cases.

Requirements Specific to Lawyers (Prior to Their Exemption)

What follows is a discussion of various requirements that *would* have applied to lawyers under the Proceeds of Crime (Money Laundering) Act (PCMLA) and later under the Proceeds of Crime (Money Laundering) and Terrorist Financing Act (PCMLTFA) were it not for their exemption following their constitutional challenges.

- *Legislation includes lawyers*: Section 7 of the original PCMLA mandates the reporting of suspicious transactions by all specified persons and entities, which explicitly includes lawyers and law office staff. Lawyers were to report financial transactions that they suspected, on reasonable grounds, were related to the commission of a money-laundering offence.
- *Individual responsibility*: Section 5 of the PCMLA explicitly names lawyers as individuals, rather than law firms, as intended by the Act. For all intents and purposes, it is individual lawyers that are obliged to ensure that reports required on any matters that they are responsible for are made on a timely basis. The task of preparing and submitting the report can be delegated. Lawyers would have been required to commence reporting suspicious transactions on 8 November 2001.
- *Protection of privilege*: The Act's mandatory disclosure for solicitor–client communications (section 11) specifies, 'Nothing in this Part requires a legal counsel to disclose any communication that is subject to solicitor-client privilege.' The regulations expressly exempt

lawyers from having to report receipt of any funds received or paid
in respect of professional fees, disbursements, expenses, or bail.
- *Nature of suspicious transactions*: Because there is no threshold for
  determining a suspicious transaction, the process is more vague
  than the reporting of large cash transactions. Suspicious transactions
  may involve several factors that might seem individually insignificant, but that together raise suspicion that the transaction is related
  to the commission of a money-laundering offence:

  'As a general guide, a transaction may be connected to money
  laundering when you [the lawyer] think that it (or a group of
  transactions) raises questions or gives rise to discomfort, appre-
  hension or mistrust.'

  'As a reporting person or entity, or an employee of a reporting
  person or entity, you should evaluate transactions in terms of what
  seems appropriate and is within normal practices in your particular line of business. Thus, it is expected that individuals engaged in
  the practice of law will be in a good position to make such assessments with respect to the transactions they will deal with. The fact
  that transactions do not appear to be in keeping with normal
  industry practices may be a relevant factor for determining whether
  there are reasonable grounds to suspect that the transactions are
  related to money laundering.' (Law Society of Alberta, n.d.)
- *When does the mandatory reporting obligation take effect?* The requirement under section 7 to report a suspicious transaction applies *only
  when a transaction has been completed*.[42] In cases where the client or
  the reporting person or entity decides not to complete the transaction, there is no obligation to report. However, the indicators detected during an aborted transaction should be considered, where
  possible, in subsequent dealings with the client.
- *Reporting to FINTRAC*: In the event that a lawyer concludes that he/
  she is involved in a suspicious transaction on behalf of his/her
  client, the lawyer must submit a suspicious transaction report to
  FINTRAC.
- *Demonstrating compliance*: The legislation does not require a lawyer
  to keep a log of either suspicious transactions or of transactions that
  were considered but not reported. However, the existence of such a
  log could be helpful in demonstrating compliance were that ever in
  question.[43]
- *Reporting timelines*: Once a lawyer has determined that there are
  reasonable grounds to suspect that the transaction is related to the
  commission of a money-laundering offence, the lawyer's report,

including all required and applicable information, must be sent within thirty calendar days. The thirty days begin when the a lawyer or any of his/her employees or officers first detects a fact about a transaction that constitutes reasonable grounds to suspect that it is related to the commission of a money-laundering offence.

- *Liability in relation to reporting suspicious transactions to FINTRAC*: Section 75(1) of the PCMLA states that knowingly failing to report a suspicious transaction could lead to up to five years imprisonment and/or a fine of $2,000,000. However, section 75(2) states that 'no employee of a person or an entity shall be convicted of an offence under subsection (1) in respect of a transaction that they reported to their superior.' Thus, employees who report suspicious transactions to their superior cannot be held liable for failing to report the suspicious transactions to FINTRAC.
- *Protection from criminal and civil liability*: Section 10 states that those who make a suspicious transaction report in 'good faith' are protected from criminal and civil liability. This would protect someone who in good faith made too many reports or provided greater than the required information. However, over-reporting would be contrary to the Code of Professional Conduct.
- *Prohibited disclosure to clients*: Section 8 of the PCMLA states that no person or entity shall disclose that they have made a suspicious transaction report to FINTRAC under section 7, or disclose the contents of such a report, with the intent to prejudice a criminal investigation, whether or not a criminal investigation has begun. *Tipping off a client that a report has been made could result, upon conviction, in up to two years in jail.*[44]
- *Advanced warning to clients*: Lawyers were encouraged to have a communication strategy in place in order to fully disclose their obligations under the PCMLA to any potential client well in advance of any potential issues. Existing clients were likewise intended to be briefed on new and currently open matters. *'At the time you are retained you should disclose and confirm in writing to the client that you are bound by the* PCMLA,[45] *and outline your various obligations under the PCMLA.'*

Status: Self-Policing of Lawyers

Lawyers across the country remain exempt from obligations to record and report suspicious and large cash transactions under the federal government's money-laundering law. This situation will continue until a test case is resolved in the courts. The Federation of Law Societies of Canada reached an agreement in May 2004 with the Attorney General of Canada to proceed with a test case tried by the BC Supreme Court to decide the constitutionality of certain requirements in the Proceeds of Crime (Money Laundering) and Terrorist Financing Act.

As a result of the agreement between the Federation and the Attorney General, all lawyers and law firms in Canada will now be exempt until the BC challenge proceeds through the courts. The test case eliminates the need for the Federation and individual law societies to undertake the costly and time-consuming process of arguing the law's constitutionality province by province. Even if the constitutional challenge is eventually unsuccessful, it appears lawyers will not be required to report retroactively. The BC Supreme Court hearing on the merits, originally scheduled for 24 June 2002, was adjourned on consent. Negotiations between the Department of Finance and the Federation of Law Societies continue.

Without the mandatory reporting legislation, how likely is it that law societies will self-regulate their members with respect to money laundering? Will they even be able to do so, if they are so inclined? Obviously, this remains an open question. The Canadian Bar Association makes general rules followed by specific commentaries about the appropriate 'professional' conduct of Canadian lawyers. The Canadian Bar Association (2001) went through a process of modernizing its Code of Professional Conduct and released a consultative document. This document emphasizes that .the 'core values' of the legal profession include, among other points, respect for the confidentiality of client information; protection of solicitor–client privilege; independence of the legal profession; and the duty of loyalty to the client. The document does not mention changes brought about by international or global events and makes no mention of money laundering.

Provincial law societies are bodies to which all lawyers and law firms must belong. The law societies take responsibility for the education, licensing, supervision, and discipline of lawyers. They admit lawyers to the bar and in extreme cases can disbar a member. The main weakness of the provincial societies from the point of view of anti-money-laundering enforcement is the fact that disciplinary action of any sort tends usually to occur following an internal investigation carried out by the Complaints Branch, *and following a complaint from a client*. There will be no complaints from money-laundering clients. The best that might happen would be a complaint from another member of the profession, who is encouraged in the *Professional Conduct Handbook* of BC (at page 39) to inform the law society of any alleged wrongdoing by a fellow member.

The protection of the public appears to be the dominant objective of the law society's audit process; however, as noted by University of British Columbia law professor Wes Pue, an inherent conflict of interest exists because law societies are composed of and controlled by lawyers (Mucalov, 2004). The objective requires that lawyers maintain proper records for all funds received and disbursed. As the BC Law Society Rules (1998–2006) state:

> The Executive Director may at any time order an examination of the books, records and accounts of a lawyer for the purpose of determining whether the lawyer is maintaining and has been maintaining books, records and accounts in accordance with this Division and designate a chartered accountant or a certified general accountant to conduct the audit. (Law Society of British Columbia, 2006: sections 3–79, part 3)

The difficulty arises in that the majority of services that a lawyer might be offering to a money launderer will be legitimate services – it is only the money to finance these endeavours that will be tainted. Hence, the records may have a legitimate appearance for the audit process. The review of a lawyer's books and a formal audit by a designated chartered accounting process will not reveal the source of the funds nor the likely use to which the funds might be put. This information can only be revealed directly by lawyers as a result of their interactions with the clients. Therefore, the audit process will not advance the objectives of the anti-money-laundering initiative.

The BC law society's strategic plan for 2001–03 mentions the use of a random audit process as a method of ensuring honourable and ethical conduct. Although this is commendable, truly random audits still do not occur. Audits are intended to ensure that lawyers are maintaining records that comply with the law society's by-laws. These types of audits and the predictable timing of them expose no lawyer to discovery regarding complicity (willing or unwitting) in money-laundering schemes. Without a complaint, there is little oversight of operations of the type that would detect money laundering.

With the awareness that in several Commonwealth jurisdictions (Tasmania, Queensland and New South Wales in Australia, and growing discussions in the UK), the task of monitoring lawyers had been taken away from the law societies (or their equivalent) and given to bodies independent of the lawyers, Canadian law societies took action to protect themselves further from government intervention. In April 2004, the BC benchers passed a rule that has become a model for most of the law societies in Canada. Known as the 'no-cash rule,' it prohibits members of a law society from receiving for any purpose, other than retainers or bail, cash in excess of $10,000.

Clearly, part of the motivation for this action is to persuade the government that no further 'outside' intervention is required. As stated by the president of the Law Society of BC, 'To ensure that Canadian lawyers do not become the next target for a Clementi-like report, I think all law societies must carefully avoid any deficiencies in their regulatory processes that could draw criticism or interference.'[46]

In conclusion, lawyers are unique – as argued initially at the beginning of this section on lawyers. In reference to other sectors of the criminal justice process, we debate and endlessly attempt to solve such questions as to 'who will police the police?' In contrast, a similar question regarding lawyers is not framed in the same manner, but rather is discussed in very different 'legalized' terms. Cases are cited and judges are quoted as if it were an objective condition under discussion rather than a societal definition being assigned to a social issue. Rather than the transparent vested interests of the police shining through their rhetoric, the discussion pertaining to lawyers is transformed into a 'mere' legal question with justice and finance (government) lawyers on one side and the law societies on the other – all members of the same ideological 'legal community' – acting for and against greater accountability. One has to ask how committed government lawyers were as they found themselves in a situation that pitted them against their colleagues. The Federation of Law Societies and the Canadian Bar Association have been awarded full costs incurred to date, and are congratulating themselves on their victory.

Lawyers are a very powerful lobby group. Policymakers, who are often lawyers themselves, may share their institutional values. The question regarding the involvement of lawyers in suspicious transaction reporting has been potentially further complicated by the 2003 Recommendations of the FATF, namely, Recommendation 16 that states that 'lawyers ... are not required to report their suspicions if the relevant information was obtained in circumstances where they are subject to professional secrecy or legal professional privilege.' In a letter to the director of the Financial Sector Division of the Department of Finance, the chair of the Committee on Anti-Money Laundering for the Federation of Law Societies of Canada (2005) wrote confirming the Federation's commitment to its own devised 'no-cash rule':

> As negotiations between the Department of Finance and the Federation continue, in recognition of the importance of and to support the fight against money laundering, each law society has passed by-laws or rules of professional conduct prohibiting lawyers from receiving or accepting large amounts of cash from clients in respect of specified activities. These by-laws or rules are based on the Federation's Model Rule on Cash Transactions adopted in October 2004.

The Law Society of Upper Canada passed the following amendments to its Rules of Professional Conduct and By-Laws 18 and 19. The amendments include

- a prohibition on lawyers accepting large amounts of cash ($7,500 or more) from clients or third parties
- new record-keeping requirements with respect to receipt of cash, and
- new commentary to rule 2.02(5) on lawyers' responsibilities when their suspicions are raised about the legality of a transaction for which the lawyer receives instructions

The amendment notes that lawyers will not be required to report to FINTRAC, as is the law for other reporting bodies but that

> Beginning in 2006, as part of the 2005 Member's Annual Report, Ontario lawyers will be required to advise the Law Society if they have received cash, and if so, whether the receipt was in compliance with the by-laws. Through these amendments, the Law Society is enhancing its ability to regulate the profession in the public interest, which interest includes eradicating money laundering.[47]

Therefore, amid all of these 'concessions' being made by the law societies, the fact remains that to date, lawyers need not comply except via their internal process – and this may continue into the future. The rhetoric of willing voluntary compliance may serve to replace any mandated compliance.

6 Terrorist Financing and Its Enforcement

We will starve the terrorists of funding, turn them against each other, rout them out of their safe hiding places and bring them to justice.

President George W. Bush, 24 September 2001[1]

The terrorist attacks on the United States in 2001 renewed and intensified the attention paid to the financial underpinnings of serious crimes. In addition to the military front in the war on terror, a new complementary 'financial front' has been opened. As a former head of the money-laundering section at the U.S. Justice Department stated, 'A military success would not be sufficient without an attack on the financial infrastructure' of terrorist groups (Eichenwald, 2001: A1). This new front in the war on terror represents a reaffirmation and reinvigoration of the use of financial enforcement strategies to combat serious crimes while dramatically shifting the focus away from profit-oriented organized crime to the financing of terrorist activity.

On the surface, it would appear that terrorist financing fundamentally differs from the proceeds of organized criminal activities; the former involves funds to be used in *future* criminal activities while the latter entails revenues and profits generated from *past* criminal activities. Obtaining terrorist funds is a means to an end; a necessary operational requirement used by extremist groups to help advance their broader political and social goals. The proceeds of crime represents an end in itself; money constitutes the ultimate goal of organized criminal enterprises. This distinction also portends to the most deep-seated distinction between the goals of terrorism and that of organized crime: the former is concerned with political, social, and cultural change (at the mass society level) while the latter is consumed with the accumulation of wealth (at the individual or group level).

Despite these differences, there are several commonalities between terrorist financing and the proceeds of crime. As discussed later in this chapter, terrorist groups have used the proceeds of profit-oriented criminal ventures, such as drug trafficking, to fund their extremist operations. Under these circumstances, the proceeds of crime are now reconstituted as an input into terrorist operations (which is not necessarily unique, as ongoing entrepreneurial criminal activities also require the reinvestment of illegal revenue). Both terrorist funds and the proceeds of crime are subject to money laundering in order to facilitate their transport, storage, and use and to guard against detection and interdiction. Terrorist and organized crime groups both rely heavily on formal financial institutions and have capitalized on the globalization of finance, commerce, and trade. Intelligence information and other research also shows that terrorist and organized crime groups both use and even control legitimate organizations, such as companies and charities, for income generation, storage, transport, and money-laundering purposes.

Regardless of the differences or similarities between the proceeds of crime and terrorist funds, it was inevitable that the financial war on terror would borrow heavily from the nuts and bolts of organized crime theorizing (i.e., the creation of 'organizations' and 'structures' whether or not they actually exist) and from the proceeds of crime enforcement (i.e., identifying, blocking, freezing, and seizing money and assets). As such, efforts to identify and seize terrorist funds rely on the three most basic proceeds of crime enforcement strategies: (1) identification of terrorist 'organizations,' (2) an interdiction function carried out primarily by state agencies, which is focused on confiscating money and other assets, and (3) transaction reporting by the private sector (which ostensibly plays a supporting role for the former). A goal of this chapter is to examine the efficacy of adapting traditional proceeds of crime enforcement to terrorist-financing enforcement, and, by extension, analyze and critique the war on terrorist financing since 11 September. Included in this analysis is a conceptual and empirical overview of terrorist financing, which includes a description and analysis of the different sources of terrorist funds as well as the processes and techniques used to store, transport, and launder these funds.

Like proceeds of crime enforcement, there is little consensus on the philosophy or the effectiveness of terrorist-financing enforcement since 9/11. Western politicians, enforcement agencies, and their supporters are quick to point out their successes: tens of millions of dollars of *suspected* terrorist funds have been frozen, blocked, or seized throughout the world; the financial services sector has become more attuned to identifying such funds; and the measures thus far erected are claimed to have prohibited or at least hindered the ability of terrorist groups to raise, process, and transport their funds. Sceptics argue that the focus on terrorist funds, the adaptation of proceeds of crime enforcement to terrorist financing, and the vast apparatus erected in the public and private sectors to identify and seize terrorist funds are largely immaterial in the battle against terrorists. For, unlike organized crime, which is almost exclusively fuelled by the desire for financial gain, terrorist groups are not motivated as such, nor are their operations dependent upon large sums of money. Critics have also argued that a financial focus has been applied to combating terrorism, despite the lack of evidence that proceeds of crime enforcement has had any significant impact on the war on drugs or on organized crime. This argument is countered by the assertion that, like the war on drugs or organized crime, terrorist-financing enforcement must be viewed simply as one weapon in a larger, diversified arsenal.

While this counter-argument is valid, both the theory and practice of terrorist-financing enforcement raises a number of introspective and even troubling questions:

- Is this the best allocation of limited resources?
- Can and should proceeds of crime enforcement tactics be adapted to terrorist financing enforcement?
- Has too much burden been placed on the private sector, which has already been tasked with detecting the proceeds of crime?
- Has terrorist financing enforcement compromised civil, privacy, and due process rights?
- To what extent does terrorist financing enforcement incorporate ethno-economic profiling?

The last two questions are particularly significant in that terrorist-financing enforcement can be seen as a microcosm of the broader criticisms of the war on terror in the post–9/11 era – that is, it has become imbued with racial, ethnic, and religious profiling. Indeed, based on an analysis of available cases, one can easily argue that the enforcement attention paid to informal money transfer systems common to Muslim, Asian, and other developing societies is disproportionate to their use as conduits for terrorist financing.

The main difficulty with understanding both terrorism and terrorist financing is to differentiate among the various sources of information in order to weed out what has come to be accepted as 'fact' but happens to be wrong, the information that is deliberately presented as fact for political or career reasons but is wrong, from that information that is correct. The comparisons between organized crime and terrorism share this additional characteristic – what we know about both rely to a large extent on what is told to us by the police, security agencies, government, and by a group of 'experts' who appear following a crisis to pronounce on the nature of the event and make careers out of their on going analyses. Politics, racism, status or profile, and a grab for resources may all help to congeal a false understanding of the terrorist threat.

Combating Terrorist Financing in the Post–9/11 Period: American and Selective International Initiatives

Prior to 9/11, relatively little attention was paid to the issue of terrorist financing by most countries. Following the bombings of U.S. embassies in Kenya and Tanzania in 1998 by al Qaeda, the Clinton administration initiated the first significant effort to disrupt the network's financing. Beginning in 1999, President Clinton ordered the freezing of assets linked to al Qaeda and then sent federal officials to several Arab countries to gather information about charities that were purportedly used in financing the terrorist network. However, due to a lack of assistance from these countries, combined with the preoccupation over the attempt to impeach President Clinton, there were few policy or enforcement initiatives pursued, despite the considerable intelligence information collected. As Kurt Eichenwald wrote in the *New York Times*, 'When terrorists struck on Sept. 11, the assault on Al Qaeda's finances had largely fallen by the wayside. The American government had developed a good deal of information about Al Qaeda's finances, but it was not widely shared among agencies' (Eichenwald, 2001: A1).

Less than two weeks following the 9/11 attacks, President Bush announced to the world that terrorism financing would become a major part of the war on terror. On 24 September 2001, he signed Executive

Order 13224, entitled *Blocking Property and Prohibiting Transactions with Persons who Commit, Threaten to Commit, or Support Terrorism.*[2] The order expands the power of the Treasury Department to freeze the assets of groups or individuals suspected of committing, threatening to commit, or supporting terrorism and prohibits American citizens and entities from transacting with the same. Appended to this order was a listed of assets already frozen since 9/11. A few weeks later, President Bush unveiled an expanded list of individuals and organizations he claimed were associated with terrorist activities and their financing, and who would become the target of American and international 'asset blocking and freezing' efforts. (This list of individuals is overwhelmingly made up of names of Muslim and Arabic origin, which had led to numerous recriminations that Executive Order 13224 is nothing more than a 'regulatory jihad.') Since the initial list was released, it has been continually expanded; by 2005, it contained the names of approximately 400 individuals and entities allegedly linked to terrorism. By 2005, more than U.S.$200 million in assets connected to those on the list have been frozen by the United States and other countries (Wayne, 2005).

The Bush administration also created legislation to deal specifically with the funding of terrorism. Title III of the omnibus USA Patriot Act – The International Money Laundering Abatement and Anti-Terrorist Financing Act – significantly expanded the power of state agencies to investigate and prosecute the financing of terrorist activities. The Act also added terrorist financing provisions to the existing body of anti-money-laundering laws originally enacted under the Bank Secrecy Act and subsequent legislation. The amendments compel banks and other reporting entities to enhance customer due diligence measures by implementing strict procedures and controls for screening client lists and transactions against the government's list of suspected terrorists. Title III amends the Bank Secrecy Act to authorize the Treasury Department to impose penalties of up to $1 million for violations of new due diligence requirements. Not only did the new Act increase the regulatory burden on banks but it also broadened the scope of anti-money- laundering provisions to parts of the private sector that were previously unaffected by government-imposed transaction reporting, including those dealing in mutual funds, securities, credit cards, insurance, cheque cashing, and precious stones.

On the operational side, the Bush administration created at least three inter-agency groups dedicated to terrorist financing: the Foreign Terrorist Asset Tracking Center (a policy and strategy centre), Operation Green Quest (an investigative task force), and the Terrorism Financial Review Group (an intelligence gathering body). The creation of the Foreign Terrorist Asset Tracking Center (FTATC) was, in fact, announced a year prior to 11 September, but had not yet been implemented. In testimony to the Senate on 8 May 2001, Treasury Secretary Paul O'Neill announced that FTATC 'will develop government-wide strategies to counter terrorist financing and to incapacitate their financial holdings within the U.S., and to assist other countries to employ similar strategies' (Department of the Treasury, 2001a). According to a 26 September 2001 statement by Treasury Under-Secretary Jimmy Gurule, the FTATC is 'dedicated to identifying the financial infrastructure of terrorist organizations worldwide and curtail their ability to move money through the international banking system.'[3] Gurule indicated that the FTATC 'will ultimately be transformed into a permanent Foreign Terrorist Asset Tracking Center in the Treasury Department's Office of Foreign Asset Control.'

Created by the Treasury Department on 25 October 2001 and led by the U.S. Customs and Border Protection Agency, Operation Green Quest (OGQ) is a multi-agency financial enforcement task force mandated to 'freeze accounts, seize assets, and, where appropriate, bring criminal actions against individuals and organizations that finance terrorist groups.' Through its targeting and coordination centre in Washington, officials from various participating agencies collect, manage, and disseminate financial leads to investigative and intelligence agents around the country. According to a U.S. Customs and Border Protection (2002) press release, as of 2002, Operation Green Quest was conducting 300 ongoing investigations.

Under the supervision of the Department of Justice and headed by the FBI, the Terrorism Financial Review Group (TFRG) was formed with a twofold mission. 'First, it was designed to conduct a comprehensive financial analysis of the 19 hijackers to link them together and to identify their financial support structure within the United States and abroad. Second, it was designed as a template for preventive and predictive terrorist financial investigations.' Since its creation, the TFRG has been mandated to conduct ongoing financial analyses of terrorist suspects and has evolved into the financial component of the FBI's counterterrorism responsibilities (Mueller, 2002; see also Lehmkuhler, 2003).

In addition to these inter-agency initiatives, a number of federal enforcement and regulatory agencies had their mandates and resources expanded or reshaped to address terrorist financing. A summary of the mandate of the more relevant agencies with respect to terrorist-financing enforcement is presented in table 6.1.

Table 6.1: Agencies' roles in terrorist-financing enforcement

Department	Bureau/division/office	Role
Central Intelligence Agency		Leads gathering, analyzing, and disseminating intelligence on foreign terrorist organizations and their financing mechanisms; charged with promoting coordination and information-sharing between all intelligence community agencies.
Homeland Security	Bureau of Customs and Border Protection	Detects movement of bulk cash across U.S. borders and maintains data about movement of commodities into and out of the United States.
	Bureau of Immigration and Customs Enforcement (ICE – formerly part of the Treasury's U.S. Customs Service)	Participates in investigations of terrorist financing cases involving U.S. border activities and the movement of trade, currency, or commodities.
	U.S. Secret Service	Participates in investigations of terrorist financing cases, including those involving counterfeiting.
Justice	Bureau of Alcohol, Tobacco, Firearms, and Explosives (ATF)	Participates in investigations of terrorist financing cases involving alcohol, tobacco, firearms, and explosives.
	Civil Division	Defends challenges to terrorist designations.
	Criminal Division	Develops, coordinates, and prosecutes terrorist financing cases; participates in financial analysis and develops relevant financial tools; promotes international efforts and delivers training to other nations.
	Drug Enforcement Administration (DEA)	Participates in investigations of terrorist financing cases involving narcotics and other illicit drugs.
	Federal Bureau of Investigation (FBI)	Leads all terrorist financing investigations and operations; primary responsibility for collecting foreign intelligence and counterintelligence information within the United States.

Table 6.1: (*concluded*)

Department	Bureau/division/office	Role
National Security Council		Manages the overall interagency framework for combating terrorism.
State	Bureau of Economic and Business Affairs	Chairs coalition subgroup of a National Security Council Policy Coordinating Committee, which leads U.S. government efforts to develop strategies and activities to obtain international cooperation.
	Bureau of International Narcotics and Law Enforcement Affairs	Implements U.S. technical assistance and training to foreign governments on terrorist financing.
	Office of the Coordinator for Counterterrorism	Coordinates U.S. counterterrorism policy and efforts with foreign governments to deter terrorist financing.
Treasury	Executive Office for Terrorist Financing and Financial Crime	Develops U.S. strategies and policies to deter terrorist financing, domestically and internationally; develops and implements the National Money Laundering Strategy as well as other policies and programs to prevent financial crimes.

Source: U.S. General Accounting Office (2003), 8.

At the international level, the United Nations was also one of the first multilateral agencies to address the financing of terrorist activities. In 1999, the United Nations *Convention for the Suppression of the Financing of Terrorism* amalgamated and updated eleven previous UN conventions dealing with terrorism. The dual aim of this convention is to enhance the domestic measures of signatory countries to combat the financing of terrorism and to expand the legal framework for international cooperation in the investigation, prosecution, and extradition of individuals engaged in terrorist financing. Governments who sign the convention agree to make it a crime to finance terrorist activities, to introduce a reporting system for suspicious transactions, and assume legal powers to freeze terrorist assets (United Nations, 1999).

On 28 September 2001, the UN Security Council passed Resolution 1373, which calls upon member states to 'prevent and suppress the financing of terrorism,' to criminalize the willful provision or collection of funds that may be used to carry out terrorist acts, and to 'prohibit their nationals or any persons and entities within their territories from making any funds, financial assets or economic resources or financial or other related services available' for terrorist activities. Member states must also 'prevent those who finance, plan, facilitate or commit terrorist acts from using their respective territories for those purposes against other countries and their citizens.' Signatories are also required to enact measures to seize and freeze 'funds and other financial assets or economic resources of persons who commit, or attempt to commit, terrorist acts or participate in or facilitate the commission of terrorist' (United Nations, 2001).

Less than a month later, on 15 October 2001, the United Nations Security Council adopted Resolutions 1267 and 1333, which collectively imposed sanctions against the Taliban, Osama bin Laden, and al Qaeda and required any UN member state to freeze Taliban regime resources until bin Laden was in the custody of the proper authorities. The UN also founded the '1267 Sanctions Committee,' which maintains a list of individuals and entities subject to the sanctions spelled out in Resolution 1267. By 2005, the committee had compiled a list of more than 300 persons and 100 entities that are subject to sanctions (Wayne, 2005).

Prior to 9/11, the 2000–01 Financial Action Task Force (FATF) *Report on Money Laundering Typologies* (released in February 2001) discussed the issue of terrorist financing, but raised questions as to whether money-laundering countermeasures should be redefined to combat terrorist financing:

All experts agreed that terrorism is a serious crime which should be targeted along with other serious crimes that serve as the underlying offences for money laundering. *There was not agreement, however, on whether anti-money laundering laws could (or should) play a direct role in the fight against terrorism.* Some of the experts were of the opinion that terrorist related money laundering indeed constitutes a distinct subtype of money laundering and should therefore become a specific focus of anti-money laundering measures. Other experts remained unconvinced believing that the focus of money laundering counter-measures on serious crime (including terrorism) is sufficient and that further refinement of specific anti-terrorism measures should take place elsewhere. (FATF, 2001: 19–20; emphasis added)

The lack of consensus on the link between money laundering and terrorist financing was expressed in the report's conclusion. While some 'experts' saw money laundering as a useful approach to combat terrorism, others held the opposite view and believed that terrorism was best targeted under existing laws.

This debate was obviously significant enough that it could not be resolved and, hence, the lack of a consensus found its way into the final report (FATF, 2001: 28; see also Beare, 2003a). However, like most other open discussions, all debate ended after 9/11. This lack of consensus would be bridged in the wake of 9/11 and is reflected in what appears to be a united FATF front against the financing of terrorist activities through money laundering. Without engaging in meaningful debate about whether anti-money-laundering legislation could be effective against terrorist financing, the FATF embarked on an expansion of its own mandate.

In October 2001, the FATF convened a special session to assess its 'new' position on terrorist financing. The meeting resulted in a resolution that would shift the international agency's focus and resources towards terrorist financing. From this meeting (and a subsequent declaration in 2004), the FATF agreed to issue nine international standards for adoption by countries that 'set out the basic framework to detect, prevent and suppress the financing of terrorism and terrorist acts' (FATF, n.d.b). Through these standards, the FATF (2004) urges countries to:

- take immediate steps to ratify and implement the relevant United Nations instruments on terrorist financing

- criminalize the financing of terrorism, terrorist acts, and terrorist organizations
- freeze and confiscate terrorist assets
- report suspicious transactions linked to terrorism
- provide the widest possible range of assistance to other countries' law enforcement and regulatory authorities for terrorist financing investigations
- impose anti-money-laundering requirements on alternative remittance systems
- strengthen customer identification measures in international and domestic wire transfers
- ensure that entities, in particular non-profit organizations, cannot be misused to finance terrorism
- erect measures to detect, report, and seize currency and bearer negotiable instruments where there may be suspicions that such instruments are used for the financing of terrorism

In a wonderfully convoluted passage from the FATF document *Guidance for Financial Institutions in Detecting Terrorist Financing* (released in April 2002), financial institutions are strongly encouraged to take on a more active role in this regard:

> It should be acknowledged as well that financial institutions *will probably be unable to detect terrorist financing as such.* Indeed, the only time that financial institutions might clearly identify terrorist financing as distinct from other criminal misuse of the financial system is when a known terrorist or terrorist organisation has opened an account. Financial institutions are, however, in a position to detect suspicious transactions that, if reported, may later prove to be related to terrorist financing. It is the competent enforcement authority or the financial intelligence unit (FIU) then that is in a position to determine whether the transaction relates to a particular type of criminal or terrorist activity and decide on a course of action. For this reason, *financial institutions do not necessarily need to determine the legality of the source or destination of the funds. Instead, they should ascertain whether transactions are unusual, suspicious or otherwise indicative of criminal or terrorist activity.*[4]

In July 2002, the executive directors of the International Monetary Fund (IMF) proposed a joint IMF and World Bank plan to augment their efforts to combat money laundering and the financing of terrorism. Like the FATF, the IMF focused on transaction reporting by the private sector and pledged to develop strategies to assess compliance with financial supervisory principles as well as provide corresponding technical assistance, which includes expanding the IMF's involvement beyond anti-money laundering to efforts aimed at countering terrorism financing; providing funding to countries for technical assistance relating to anti-terrorism financing; enhancing the IMF's collaboration with the FATF; undertaking further research and analysis on issues related to money laundering and terrorist financing (IMF, 2001d: 2–4).

Terrorist Financing and Its Enforcement in Canada

Since at least 2000, a number of media articles, criminal and national security intelligence reports, as well as independent studies have accused Canada of being a haven for terrorist groups and their fund-raising fronts. The title of the 2001 Census Analysis released on 21 January 2003 by Statistics Canada is testimony to the incredible diversity that is Canada. *Canada's Ethnocultural Portrait: The Changing Mosaic* reports that there are more than 200 ethnic groups in Canada, and 13.4 per cent of the entire population of the country or almost 4 million individuals are visible minorities.[5]

The benefits of immigration are juxtaposed against the alternative opinion that sees the existence of the ethnic communities as potential bases for terrorist activity or, at the least, terrorist fund-raising and financing, which is evident in newspaper headlines like 'Safe Haven for Terror.'[6] The large amount of media coverage and the apparent tightening-up of immigration processes in some jurisdictions (pre- and post-September 11) requires serious study. What has tended to happen is for the 'policing' agencies and right-wing think tanks to define ethnic groups from a terrorism perspective. According to the Canadian Security Intelligence Service (CSIS), 'with the possible exception of the United States, there are more international terrorist organizations active in Canada than anywhere in the world' (CSIS, 2002). A 2005 Associated Press article (Duff-Brown, 2005) quotes a CSIS official who estimated that at least fifty terrorist groups have some presence in this country. Part of the Canadian activities of terrorist groups, writes CSIS in its 2002 report, is to raise money for their cause. The Mackenzie Institute, which counts as part of its focus the study of political extremism, asserts that, 'Canada is one of the most fertile grounds for insurgents, terrorist groups, and criminal cartels to operate – mostly by raising funds and laundering money' (Turlej, 2000).

How can the public evaluate the threats and distinguish 'real' threats from threat propaganda? Even before 11 September organized crime had been traditionally cloaked in secrecy. The same might now be said of actual terrorism-related facts. As is now widely known, the British government produced a report titled *Iraq: Its Infrastructure of Conceal-ment, Deception and Intimidation*, which it claimed was based on 'intelli-gence material' and was praised by Colin Powell as he tried to sell the international community on the necessity of war with Iraq. The report, in fact, was plagiarized from twelve-year-old material written and pub-lished by a postgraduate student and two additional authors in *Jane's Intelligence Review*.[7] As the *New York Times* reported:

> Critics of the British and American policy toward Iraq said the report showed how little concrete evidence the two governments actually have against Iraq, as well as how poor their intelligence sources were. 'Both governments seem so desperate to create a pretext to attack Iraq that they are willing to say anything,' said Nathaniel Hurd, a consultant on Iraq and a critic of the American position. 'This U.K. dossier, which decep-tively uses outdated material and plagiarizes, is just the latest example of official dishonesty.' Opposition politicians here attacked the report as the deceptive work of a bumbling government clutching at straws as it tries to make a case for war ... 'The document has been cited by the prime minister and Colin Powell as the basis for a possible war. Who is responsible for such an incredible failure of judgment?' (Lyall, 2003)

Voices are beginning to publicly question some of the more extreme anti-terrorist strategies. However, the 'war on terrorism' is, in part, a propaganda war and one does not want to mess with the desired tone of the message. In addition to the 'politics' of the messages there is a 'religious,' and some might argue a 'racism,' theme that runs through some of the rhetoric. Hence, 'knowing' what the real threats are be-comes even more impossible than at other times. The link that is cur-rently being made between organized crime, transnational crime, money laundering, and terrorism has ratcheted up the rhetoric machines!

The Liberation Tigers of Tamil Eelam (LTTE) – the principal force behind insurgency and civil war in Sri Lanka and which has as its objective the establishment of a separate state for its Tamil Hindu minority – has been the subject of a number of reports that claim it is raising large sums of money in Canada. Home to one of the world's largest Sri Lankan Tamil diaspora populations, Canada also hosts a number of expatriate political and charitable organizations that alleg- edly raise millions of dollars for the militant Tamil Tigers. Joe Turlej (2000) for the Mackenzie Institute claims that the LTTE fundraising machine in Canada is 'arguably the most sophisticated of any terrorist organization being undertaken on Canadian soil.' A report by Rohan Gunaratna, en- titled *Liberation Tigers of Tamil Eelam (LTTE) Organisation and Operations in Canada*, estimates that the LTTE raised more than $22 million in Canada in 1999 alone (Bell, 2000c). Donations to LTEE charitable organizations are voluntary, but may also be the result of coercion, via extortions and intimidation (Turlej and Thompson, 2003). According to CSIS, the group raises money through Canadian charities, front businesses, and criminal activities, including human smuggling, passport fraud, bank fraud, credit card fraud, theft, threats, extortion, and drug trafficking to raise money (Lak, 2000). The Canadian High Commissioner for Sri Lanka also con- firmed that the LTTE was actively raising funds in Canada that were being used for the purchase of arms in other countries (Bell, 2000c). Ac- cording to Human Rights Watch (2004), Sir Lankan Tamils living in Canada have participated in financing of the LITE (Cheran, 2002).

However, also over the course of almost two decades of civil war, Sri Lankan Tamils living in Canada have provided substantial resources for humanitarian relief to thousands of families displaced from the war-torn areas in Sri Lanka. These charitable donations assist in an array of non- military ways in the very poorest parts of Sri Lanka. As R. Cheran and S. Aiken emphasize:

> It must be emphasized that the Tigers are a multifaceted organization. Currently they govern a *de-facto* state in the north and eastern province and are head quartered in the Vanni region of Sri Lanka. The areas under their control have a separate judiciary, police service (Tamil Eelam Police Service), health authority (Tamil Eelam Health Services-TEHS), Tamil Eelam Administrative Service (TEAS), and Tamil Eelam Education Service (TEES). Their revenue department is elaborate and employs about 3,500 trained people. They also have a Planning and Development Secretariat (PDS) that is responsible for long-term planning and reconstruction. Everyone, including Sri Lankan government officers, is required to obtain permits to enter and exit the region. The LTTE 'government' operates all the hospi- tals in the region, employs pre-school, primary and secondary school teach- ers and manages these schools ... International non-government organizations, the World Bank, Asian Development Bank, UNICEF, UNDP

and several other international agencies coordinate their activities with the Tigers in the areas controlled by them. (Cheran and Aiken, 2005)

In the wake of a deadly suicide bombing in Sri Lanka in 2000, which killed a cabinet minister, his wife, and twenty-one bystanders, Canada's foreign minister told the House of Commons that he had 'no tolerance' for groups raising money in Canada for violence and would ensure that such practices were criminalized (Bell and Hunter, 2000). At that time, the federal government had signed the United Nations convention on terrorist fundraising, although it was not until December 2001 that it brought in legislation to codify into law the provisions of the UN treaty as well as post–911 United Nation Security Council resolutions. The Anti-Terrorism Act amended the Criminal Code to make it illegal to fund raise for a terrorist organization. The Anti-Terrorism Act also amended the Proceeds of Crime (Money Laundering) Act, not the least of which was to change its title to Proceeds of Crime (Money Laundering) and Terrorist Financing Act.

The legislation itself is a reflection of how proceeds of crime enforcement were simply adapted to combat terrorist financing; most changes to the Act merely amounted to the addition of 'the financing of terrorist activities' as an offence whereas 'money laundering' was previously the only offence listed. The amendments to the legislation extended the scope of transaction reporting by private sector individuals and organizations to include funds or transactions suspected of being linked to terrorist financing. Beginning on 12 June 2002, individuals and entities covered by the legislation were required to submit a Terrorist Property Report to FINTRAC 'without delay' if they had or suspected they had in their possession or control property that was 'owned, or controlled by, or on behalf of a terrorist or a terrorist group' (FINTRAC, n.d.a). The Anti-Terrorism Act also authorized the federal cabinet, upon the recommendation of the Solicitor General (who became Minister of Public Safety and Emergency Preparedness Canada), to create a list of individuals or entities suspected of terrorism. This list has been used as a basis to help reporting entities identify possible terrorist funds.[8] The legislation empowered the federal government to freeze and seize any assets belonging to those included on the list.

The legislative amendments also expanded the mandate of the Financial Transactions Reports Analysis Centre (FINTRAC) to receive and analyse the Terrorist Property Reports and to disclose information garnered from these reports to Canadian law enforcement and national security intelligence agencies as well as foreign governments. The extension of FINTRAC's mandate positioned it as a central agency in Canada's efforts to combat the financing of terrorist groups. Its expanded mandate also meant a substantial increase in its budget. According to the Auditor General of Canada, between 2001 and 2004, FINTRAC received an additional $34.2 million to detect and deter terrorist financing. This makes up the lion's share of the $45 million a year in supplemental funding provided to federal agencies by Canada's National Money Laundering Strategy (Office of the Auditor General, n.d.). According to its own figures, for the fiscal year 2003–04, FINTRAC made forty-four disclosures to enforcement and national security agencies related to *suspected* terrorist activity financing. The total value of the transactions involved in these cases was approximately $70 million. The average dollar values of FINTRAC's case disclosures related to suspected terrorist-activity financing was $1 million (involving three individuals, five businesses and twenty-nine transactions) (FINTRAC, 2004). In the fiscal year 2004–05, twenty-four cases involving suspected terrorist activity financing and/or threats to the security of Canada were disclosed. FINTRAC notes in their 2005 Annual Report that while fewer case disclosures were produced over fiscal year 2003–04, the value of the transactions included in disclosures of suspected terrorist activity financing rose to $180 million (FINTRAC, 2005a).

In the wake of 9/11, the RCMP formed the Anti-Terrorism Financing Group (ATFG). The ATFG is the RCMP unit designated to receive and investigate disclosures provided by FINTRAC (Ekos Research, 2004). It is mandated to

- detect and identify individuals and entities involved in raising and moving terrorist funds
- obtain evidence for prosecution
- provide support to national security investigations
- detect gaps or weaknesses in the financial system, and
- develop practices and make recommendations to prevent any abuse

Since 1996, the public reports of the Canadian Security Intelligence Service, which is mandated to collect and analyze information on national security threats to Canada, have all made reference to terrorist fundraising 'as a concern for the organization.' It also cites a 1997 report by its oversight body, the Security Intelligence Review Committee, which agreed that terrorist financing activities could be of interest to

CSIS (CSIS, 2002). The Anti-Terrorism Act mandated CSIS to receive Terrorist Property Reports from FINTRAC and to open an investigation if warranted (Ekos Research, 2004). In a *2002 Public Report*, CSIS (2003) states its 'intelligence is used in moving against terrorist financiers,' while its *2003 Public Report* notes that 'CSIS will continue working with partner agencies toward ... disrupting terrorist financing networks in Canada' (CSIS, 2004). Media articles as well as reports and statements publicly released by CSIS have indicated that it has gathered and analyzed information that has allowed it to identify terrorist groups raising funds in Canada.[9]

Terrorist Financing Sources, Methods, and Enforcement Targets

In general, the financing of terrorist activities involves four basic elements: (1) raising the funds, (2) storing the funds, (3) transporting the funds from the source to operatives undertaking terrorist activities, and (4) laundering the funds to conceal their source and purpose and to avoid reporting and seizure. As summarized in a report from a task force of the Council on Foreign Relations (2002), the more sophisticated terror networks, such as al Qaeda, use an amalgam of different sources and processes to raise, store, transport, and launder their funds:

> Al-Qaeda's financial network is characterized by layers and redundancies. It raises money from a variety of sources and moves money in a variety of manners. It runs businesses operating under the cloak of legitimacy and criminal conspiracies ranging from the petty to the grand. The most important source of al-Qaeda's money, however, is its continuous fund-raising efforts. Al-Qaeda's global fund-raising network is built upon a foundation of charities, nongovernmental organizations, mosques, websites, intermediaries, facilitators, and banks and other financial institutions ... Al-Qaeda moves its funds through the global financial system, the Islamic banking system, and the underground hawala system, among other money transfer mechanisms. It uses its global network of businesses and charities as a cover for moving funds. And it uses such time-honored methods as bulk cash smuggling and the global trade in gold and other commodities to move and store value.

This report clearly accepts the view that al Qaeda is a centrally run, transnational 'criminal organization' rather than a network of individuals with, at most, ad hoc associations.[10]

The amorphous depictions of nameless 'networks' of organized criminals, as identified by the UN, are harder to present to the public as posing a clear, understandable 'threat' than the sterotypical biker or Mafia operations. Likewise, there are advantages in seeing terrorism as operating within 'named' rigid structures with a global capability. The notion of an al-Qaeda structure and location of command suggests the need for military actions, enhanced anti-terrorism legislation, and massive terrorist-fighting resources. The assumed sophistication and purported financial base to this version of 'terrorism' also justifies why governments have been unsuccessful at defeating this omnipotent enemy.

Without specifying a criminal organizations perspective, in *What Is Terrorist Financing?*, FINTRAC (n.d.b) presents a picture of terrorists obtaining and moving money in the exact same manner that any other criminal or tax avoider might use. Of particular note is the acknowledgement that traditional banking centres remain the exit strategy of choice:

> Terrorist financing may involve funds raised from legitimate sources, such as personal donations and profits from businesses and charitable organizations, as well as from criminal sources, such as the drug trade, the smuggling of weapons and other goods, fraud, kidnapping and extortion. **Terrorists use techniques like those of money launderers to evade authorities' attention and to protect the identity of their sponsors and of the ultimate beneficiaries of the funds.** However, financial transactions associated with terrorist financing tend to be in smaller amounts than is the case with money laundering, and when terrorists raise funds from legitimate sources, the detection and tracking of these funds becomes more difficult. To move their funds, terrorists use the formal banking system, informal value-transfer systems, hawalas and hundis and, the oldest method of asset-transfer, the physical transportation of cash, gold and other valuables through smuggling routes. FINTRAC's analysts are finding that in their disclosures to date, funds suspected of being used for terrorist activities financing are moved out of Canada through traditional banking centers to countries with major financial hubs, in what is likely an effort to conceal their final destination.

In its analysis of methods used to earn, move, and store terrorist funds, the U.S. Government Accounting Office delineates terrorist financing 'mechanisms' into two categories: traditional and non-traditional. Traditional mechanisms include the services of 'legitimate' financial service providers and other private sector entities operating in the formal economy. Non-traditional (alternative and illegal) mechanisms include criminal activities, smuggling of legitimate commodities, charities, and informal banking systems:

> Terrorists, like other criminals, focus on crimes of opportunity in vulnerable locations worldwide and seek to operate in relative obscurity by taking advantage of close-knit networks of people and nontransparent global industry flows when earning, moving, and storing their assets. To earn assets, they focus on profitable crimes or scams involving commodities such as smuggled cigarettes, counterfeit goods, and illicit drugs and the use of systems such as charitable organizations that collect large sums. To move assets, terrorists use mechanisms that enable them to conceal or launder their assets through nontransparent trade or financial transactions such as charities, informal banking systems, bulk cash, and commodities such as precious stones and metals. To store assets, terrorists may use commodities that are likely to maintain their value over time and are easy to buy and sell outside the formal banking system. For example, terrorists may use precious stones and metals that serve as effective forms of currency. (U.S. General Accounting Office, 2003: 9–10)

The 'alternative financing mechanisms' that may be used in relation to earning, moving, and storing terrorist funds identified by the GAO are summarized in table 6.2.

Given the catalytic fallout following 9/11, it is important to remember the lack of 'sophistication' on the part of the hijackers but also the incompetence of the security network in the U.S. that appears to account for the terrorists' success in New York and Washington (Beare, 2003b). This information we now all know. According to a report issued on 11 October 2001, the INS commissioner James Ziglar, appearing before a congressional panel, said that

- ten of the hijackers had been in the U.S. legally at the time of the attacks
- of the four others who had been granted non-immigrant visas, at least three had overstayed those visas
- the INS said it had no conclusive records ... on the remaining six hijackers[11]

Table 6.2: Examples of alternative financing mechanisms that may be used to earn, move, and store terrorist assets

Alternative financing mechanisms	Earning	Moving	Storing
Trade in commodities			
Illicit drugs	X		
Weapons	X		
Cigarettes	X		
Diamonds	X	X	X
Gold		X	X
Systems			
Charities	X	X	
Informal banking		X	
Currency			
Bulk cash		X	X

Source: U.S. General Accounting Office (2003), 10.

When Paul Celluci (the former U.S. Ambassador to Canada) was governor of Massachusetts, he appointed his chauffeur to head security at Massport – the patronage-ridden authority that ran Logan Airport, the same airport that the terrorists flew out of on 9/11.[12] On March 2002, six months to the day *after* Mohamed Atta and Marwan Al-Sheh flew planes into the World Trade Center, the Immigration and Naturalization Service notified a Venice, Florida, flight school that the two men had been approved for student visas.[13] The report confirms that the visas were issued between 17 July 2001 and 9 August 2001. It is of importance to note that the four individuals working for the United States immigration agency, responsible for issuing the visas following the attacks, were not fired from their jobs. Rather, the INS says that 'four people had been named to various positions and the career employees in those posts will be moved to other jobs within the Justice Department.'[14]

The only illegal documentations possessed by the hijackers were driver licenses and various identification cards that they used to open bank accounts and purchase plane tickets. The identification cards were supplied by Abdel Rahman Omar Tawfiq Alfauru, a Jordanian man who, according to prosecutors, 'has been living illegally in the United States, in the New Jersey cities of Clifton and Paterson.'[15]

Two consequential events became apparent in the aftermath of 9/11. First, considering that most of the hijackers held legal status in the U.S. at the time of the attacks, it would be significant to inquire as to why and how the U.S. government had granted them their visas. According to a report in the *National Review* on 28 October 2002, sixteen of the 9/11 terrorists should have been denied visas under the then-existing law on the basis of their applications. According to an analysis of the terrorists' visa applications, conducted by six separate senior experts from Consular Affairs (CA), 'the forms were ... plagued with significant amounts of missing information – something that should have been sufficient grounds to deny many of the visas'. One officer declared the granting of these visas to 'amount to criminal neglect' (Mowbray, 2002: 2).

The carelessness with which the applications were filled out was, in fact, bizarre. Terrorists are trained to take the necessary steps to avoid detection and usually go about the correct routes of obtaining entry into the countries of their choice in order not to cause suspicion. For example, while all but one terrorist claimed to be employed or in school, only three of the applicants filled in the section marked 'Name and Street Address of Present Employer or School.' At the very least, as a Consular Affairs executive points out, 'the consular officers should not have ended the interview until the forms were completed.' Numerous other discrepancies should have been detected. For example, Abdulaziz Alomari 'claimed to be a student, but marked on his form that he would self-finance a two-month stay at the JKK Whyndham Hotel – and provided no proof, as required under law, that he could actually do so' (ibid.).

The most disturbing case, however, is that of Hani Hanjour, who was initially refused entry to the U.S. because he had originally stated that he wished for a three-year visa for the purpose of visiting. He included in his paperwork that he wished to find a flight school during the trip. On his subsequent application, Hanjour's answers were drastically changed. He stated that he wished entry for one year for the purpose of 'study.' His request was granted (ibid.: 3).

The mention of these failings within the United States is not intended to imply that Canadian officials are more diligent or that our border is fail proof; however, it would be hard to be worse.

In regards to the costs incurred by the terrorists, they demonstrated that extensive damages and deaths can be caused with minimal expense. The 1993 attack on the World Trade Center, which did U.S.$500 million in damages and killed six people, cost U.S.$400. The 2001 attacks are claimed to have cost in total less than U.S.$500,000. The hijackers stayed in cheap hotels, did their own laundry, and cooked their own meals while working in minimum-wage jobs.[16] Given these figures, a priority placed on 'terrorist financing' must be challenged.

The remainder of this section examines terrorist financing, focusing on its sources and the institutions and services used to process, transport, store, and launder these funds. Included in this section is a summary and analysis of enforcement strategies that are used at different stages of the terrorist-financing process.

Sources of Terrorist Financing

In both historical and contemporary terms, the main sources of funding for terrorist groups can be demarcated into the following categories: (1) state sponsorship, (2) legitimate fund-raising through charitable organizations (and to a lesser extent the collection of membership dues and subscriptions, speaking tours, cultural and social events, and so on), (3) legitimate companies, and (4) criminal activities.

State Sponsorship of Militant and Terrorist Groups

Since the end of the Second World War, a number of governments throughout the world have been involved in funding the foreign operations of terrorist groups, insurgents, counter-insurgents, guerillas, mercenaries, and other purveyors of violence and armed combat. During this period, the United States and the Soviet Union were perhaps the greatest source of funds for foreign militaries and militant groups as the two sides fought the Cold War, in part, by proxy in a number of developing countries.

However, it may have been the French government that pioneered the financing of foreign guerilla groups when it initiated its counter-insurgency strategy to fight the communists and nationalists in Indo-China during the late 1940s. In the immediate postwar years, France was eager to take back its south-east Asian colonies and to crush any nascent nationalist movements. To overcome its own resource limitations, the French government began to exercise this control through proxy militias. This 'counter-insurgency' or 'limited-war doctrine' would be a defining Cold War tactic of both the United States and the Soviet Union for decades to come. French authorities began by rearming captured Japanese troops who had invaded French Indo-China – and who were yet to be demobilized – to oversee the disarming of Viet Minh guerillas. In later years, France relied on small, elite militant units, composed of French soldiers and members of local populations, to quell the insurgency. When terrorist tactics were used against French civilians in Indo-China, the units responded in kind by targeting Vietnamese villages (Shafer, 1988).

The counter-insurgency strategy was soon emulated by other countries, most notably the United States, which began funding anti-communist guerrilla groups in Latin America, Asia, and Africa. In 1961, a secret group of Cuban exiles was formed and funded in part by the CIA – in direct violation of American laws – to invade Cuba and overthrow Fidel Castro. This invasion resulted in the Bay of Pigs fiasco, in which the Cuban invaders were captured and executed. This did not deter the U.S. government, which, as part of its protracted war in south-east Asia funded, trained, and organized Vietnamese troops and civilians into small commando units. The goal of these so-called death squads was to assassinate high-ranking Viet Cong officials, and within days of the launch of 'Black Eagle' in the mid-1960s, numerous leaders of the Viet Cong were killed. On their corpses, the assassins left a drawing of a human eye. The same image was found on the doors of the victims' homes, a warning to whoever supported them. Similar groups were trained in El Salvador during its civil war and, again, the human eye was used as a menacing calling card.

According to Loretta Napoleoni (2003: 13–14), psychological warfare – those tactics explicitly used to terrorize the enemy – became a central tenet of these counter-insurgency strategies. In the late 1970s and early 1980s, the Central Intelligence Agency was directing large sums of cash to the Mujaheddin, the Afghan rebels who were attempting to overthrow the Soviet-backed government in Afghanistan. Also in the early 1980s, the Reagan administration helped to create and fund the Contras in Nicaragua, an armed group used by the U.S. to destabilize the left-leaning Sandinista government, and which attacked civilian targets. In order to bridge the ever-widening gap between funding approved by Congress and the growing costs of the Contras, officials in the Reagan administration covertly began to raise money. This entailed an illegal fund-raising operation inside the U.S., headed by Colonel Oliver North and Donald Gregg, at the time the national security adviser to the vice president. The covert operation raised funds through secret donations, fraudulent insurance transactions, illegal bank loans, insurance fraud, and ultimately the sale of arms to Iran by the CIA – despite the embargo imposed by Congress on any dealings with that country. The proceeds were funnelled to the Contras, resulting in the well-publicized Iran-Contra affair that marred the second term of President Reagan (Brody, 1985).

The Soviet Union provided free training to Marxist militant groups from around the world and established a school of sabotage in Prague, where East German and Russian instructors trained foreign revolutionaries, including those belonging to the Palestinian militant group al Fatah (Napoleoni, 2003: 14–15). In the 1980s, the Soviet Union funnelled hundreds of millions of dollars to South American countries, via Cuba, to train Marxist guerilla groups.

More recently, Arab countries such as Libya, Iran, Syria, Saudi Arabia, and Afghanistan have been the most frequently cited state sponsors of international terrorist activities. In his book about the Hezbollah, Nizar Hamzeh (2004) claims this terrorist group receives two-thirds of its U.S.\$1-billion annual budget from Iran. After coming to power in 1969, Muammar Gaddafi began promoting anti-imperialist movements throughout the world and channelled money generated from oil sales to revolutionary groups, including the PLO, the IRA, the Angolan Liberation Movement, and the African National Congress in South Africa. The Libyan leader's generous support of numerous extremist groups earned him the nickname 'the godfather of terrorism' (Napoleoni, 2003: 18–19). In 2003, Gaddafi took formal responsibility for the 1988 bombing of an American airliner over the Scottish town of Lockerbie and agreed to pay U.S.\$2.7 billion in compensation to victims (Slevim, 2003: Sec. A).

'Legitimate' Fund-raising and Charitable Organizations

By the 1990s, the 'more-open' government sponsorship of foreign terrorist and militant groups began to decline, due in part to intense international pressure as well as the desire of these groups to escape the restrictions imposed by state sponsors. This funding void ushered in a new era of terrorist financing, characterized by a greater reliance on fund-raising and other revenue-generating activities from private sources, which Napoleoni (2003: 49) refers to as the 'privatization of political violence.'

Since 9/11, charitable organizations have come under particular scrutiny as a fund-raising conduit for terrorist activities. According to the Financial Action Task Force:

Community solicitation and fundraising appeals are one very effective means of raising funds to support terrorism. Often such fundraising is carried out in the name of organisations having the status of a charitable or relief organisation, and it may be targeted at a particular community. Some members of the community are led to believe that they are giving for a good cause. In many cases, the charities to which donations are given are in fact legitimate in that they do engage in some of the work they purport to carry out. Most of the members of the organisation, however, have no knowledge that a portion of the funds raised by the charity is being diverted to terrorist causes. For example, the supporters of a terrorist movement from one country may carry out ostensibly legal activities in another country to obtain financial resources. The movement's supporters raise these funds by infiltrating and taking control of institutions within the immigrant community of the second country. Some of the specific fundraising methods might include: collection of membership dues and/ or subscriptions; sale of publications; speaking tours, cultural and social events; door-to-door solicitation within the community; appeals to wealthy members of the community; and donations of a portion of their personal earnings. (FATF, 2002a: 4–6)

In its report on terrorist financing, the 9/11 Commission dismissed the initial speculation that al Qaeda was financed through Osama bin Laden's personal fortune or private businesses. 'Rather, al Qaeda was funded, to the tune of approximately $30 million per year, by diversions of money from Islamic charities and the use of well-placed financial facilitators who gathered money from both witting and unwitting donors, primarily in the Gulf region' (National Commission, n.d.: 4). The United Nations Group charged with monitoring sanctions against the Taliban and al Qaeda provided a similar and more detailed accounting of the use of charities by the latter:

> From its inception, Al-Qaida has relied heavily on charities and donations from its sympathizers to finance its activities. Charities provide Al-Qaida with a very useful international channel for soliciting, collecting, transferring, and distributing the funds it needs for indoctrination, recruitment, training, and logistical and operational support. These funds are often merged with and hidden among funds used for other legitimate humanitarian or social programmes. Al-Qaida supporters and financiers have also established front charity networks whose main purpose is to raise and deliver funds to Al-Qaida. The roots of these charity networks stem from the anti-Soviet jihad in Afghanistan during the late 1980s. During that time Al-Qaida could draw on the support of a number of State-assisted charities and other deep-pocket donors that supported the anti-

Soviet cause. Today, Al-Qaida continues to rely heavily on those charities to facilitate and mask the collection and movement of its funds. Activities range from collection boxes at mosques and Islamic centres to direct fund-raising and solicitations, the merging of funds for both legitimate relief purposes and terrorism, the misuse or embezzlement of legitimate chari-table funds, and the creation of front charities to channel funds from community collections or deep-pocket supporters. Al-Qaida has also ben-efited from, and relies heavily on, the activities of legitimate charities that support the propagation and teaching of more radical forms of Muslim fundamentalism.[17]

According to the *New York Times*, al Qaeda's operatives in Bosnia skimmed money from relief charities (Eichenwald, 2001). U.S. Treasury officials believe the charitable Muwafaq Foundation, which purport-edly promotes educational and social development programs in the Sudan, was used by wealthy Saudi businessmen to transfer millions of dollars to Osama bin Laden. The charity is believed to have been established by Yasin al-Qadi, whose assets were frozen by the Treasury Department. An investigation by the BBC shows that the UN was a donor to the Muwafaq Foundation.[18]

The International Islamic Relief Organization (IIRO), which is head-quartered in Saudi Arabia, has been accused of diverting funds to six al Qaeda training camps in Afghanistan prior to 9/11. Pakistan expelled two dozen people who worked for IIRO-sponsored organizations in that country, because of their alleged ties to al Qaeda. Allegations also surfaced in India and the Philippines that local IIRO officers and em-ployees were involved in terrorist activities carried out by al Qaeda.[19] Evidence produced by the Canadian government in its efforts to deport Mahmoud Jaballah, who had been deemed a terrorist by the federal government, linked IIRO funding directly to al Jihad, a purported asso-ciate group of al Qaeda, which was held responsible for the 1998 bomb-ings of the American embassies in Dar es Salaam and Nairobi.[20] In a September 2005 ruling, a U.S. court ruled that the IIRO could be sued by families of the 9/11 victims, effectively linking the charitable organi-zation to al Qaeda and the terror attacks on New York City.[21]

In 1998, the FBI seized U.S.$1.4 million in cash and property from a Chicago couple, allegedly destined for Hamas, a militant Palestinian organization which is outlawed in the U.S.[22] The seizure came after a U.S. attorney filed a civil forfeiture suit in federal district court against the assets of Mohammad and Azita Salah of the Illinois-based

Islamic literacy organization, Quranic Literacy Institute.[23] In December 2001, the assets of the Holy Land Foundation for Relief and Development – one of the largest Islamic charities in the United States – were frozen by the Treasury Department. The actions were taken based on an FBI report detailing links between the charity and the leaders of Hamas. The report described a 1993 meeting between officials of the charity, the Holy Land Foundation for Relief and Development, and Hamas leaders that was secretly recorded by the FBI. A year later, electronic surveillance by the FBI recorded a top Hamas leader, Mousa Abu Marzook, designating Holy Land as the main U.S. fundraiser for the Palestinian group. Bush administration officials said the group is used by Hamas to recruit suicide bombers, provide financial support for their families, and fund schools that indoctrinate children to become terrorists. The chair of the charity denied that it knowingly had any links to Hamas (Cohen and Franklin, 2001). An RCMP intelligence report alleges that charitable donations collected in Canada may be funding militant activities of Hamas and Hezbollah in Lebanon. Donors may believe their money is funding humanitarian work, but once in Lebanon, it is diverted partly for military purposes. A Hezbollah spokesperson quoted in the media stated that the money raised in Canada is used for humanitarian and not military purposes. He did admit, however, that some of the money goes to the families of suicide bombers (Bell, 2002a).

In March 2002, law enforcement officials raided fifteen organizations in north Virginia, all of which were suspected of laundering money for al Qaeda or other terrorist groups. One of these organizations, a Muslim charity called the SAAR Foundation, was suspected of moving money to front groups for Islamic terrorists. The money allegedly came from Saudis who support fundamentalist causes. The investigation revealed that several wire transfer from SAAR were made to Canada. In one such transfer in 1998, the Virginia charity sent close to U.S.$100,000 to the SAAR Foundation Canada in Quebec. Other transfers went to a Canadian Imperial Bank of Commerce account (Miller, 2002).

In the Gulf region, some fifty charities have reportedly been shut down and forty more came under official surveillance between 2001 and 2003. Saudi Arabia announced that it audited 245 domestic charities and froze their external offices, shut down twelve charities, and banned donation boxes at commercial stores and mosques (Comras, 2005).

Despite these international actions, targeting charities suspected of being used or abused for the purposes of supporting terrorism is difficult, precarious, possibly of limited value, and in many cases likely unjustified. The apparent legal source of donations provided to charities and funnelled to terrorist activities means 'there are few, if any, indicators that would make an individual financial transaction or series of transactions stand out as linked to terrorist activities' (FATF, 2002a: 4–6). It is even more difficult to identify charitable donations that have been made expressly for terrorist purposes, to prove that a donation to a legitimate charity was expressly made for terrorist purposes, or to identify individuals that expressly provide donations for such purposes. Regulators and investigators are also presented with the immense challenge of delineating funds used for terrorist financing from those used for legitimate purposes.

As we have noted, a related problem is that many of the charities accused of funnelling money to terrorist groups provide legitimate religious and humanitarian aid. There is a particular reticence among Arab and Muslim countries to act against charities, even if strong evidence is presented that they are involved in channelling funds to extremist groups. The fiscal structure of Islamic countries also makes it difficult to monitor charitable groups. In Saudi Arabia, for example, there is no tax system or internal revenue service, consequently the government is unable to audit the accounts and keep track of monetary inflows and outflows (Napoleoni, 2003: 123). Finally, many of the charities targeted by the United States are associated with Muslim or Arab causes, which contribute to the perception of religious and ethnic profiling. The targeting of Islamic charities by Western governments runs an exceptionally high risk of further alienating and infuriating Muslim populations.

Targeting Islamic charities has a profound effect, unrelated to the control of terrorism. There is an obligation under Islamic law to give up a portion of the wealth one may possess in order to 'purify' or legalize it so that the remainder may lawfully be used by the alms giver. Concern for the poor becomes a permanent and compulsory duty. This means an annual contribution of 2.5 per cent of one's income to public welfare, with a higher percentage applying to other types of wealth such as agricultural produce and jewellery:

It is incumbent on minors and adults, males and females, living or dead. Islamic law empowers the Islamic State or Community to collect such contributions and keep a separate account of them. The funds thus accumulated must be spent on the eight categories specified in the Qur'an (2:177) namely, the poor and the destitute, the wayfarer, the bankrupt, the needy, converts, captives, the collectors of *zakat*, and in the cause of God. The last category allows such funds to be used for the general welfare of the community – for the education of the people, for public works, and for any other need of the Muslim community. (Khan, n.d.)

Legitimate Companies

Loretta Napoleoni argues that the increased need to secure private sources of funding for terrorist activities in recent years has 'widened the range of legitimate businesses run by armed organizations.' This is often the case with operatives who inhabit terrorist 'sleeper cells' – they run legitimate businesses to ensure the cell is self-financing and to maintain a legitimate veneer. Napoleoni cites the case of twenty-four-year-old Mohammad Rashed Daoud al-Owhali, an al Qaeda operative who supported himself and his family by running a small fishing business in Mombasa, Kenya, before he received his instructions to bomb the U.S. embassy in Nairobi in 1998 (Napoleoni, 2003: 159; Burke, 2001). What this might mean is that future terrorists hold normal jobs while waiting to act.

Long before Osama bin Laden, the IRA and its members became involved in legitimate businesses in Northern Ireland and elsewhere. It owned two taxi companies that operated 350 cabs and employed 800 drivers in parts of Northern Ireland. 'In Dublin alone, the IRA is believed to own more than 20 pubs, as well as other businesses, such as cafes and restaurants.' The organization also owns businesses elsewhere in the country, including guesthouses, a security firm, video shops, courier services, and a haulage company (Silke, 2005). As with the debate around organized crime, whether it was the IRA as an organization or its individual members that owned the businesses is disputable. It has turned out that much of the talk of property 'owned ' by the Hells Angels, for example, has been found to be in the possession of individual members who bought and maintained these businesses through their individual criminal (or legitimate) pursuits.

Criminal Activities

There is considerable evidence that terrorists groups have turned to profit-oriented criminal activities to help finance their operations. Police cases and intelligence from around the world have linked numerous terrorist groups to such illegal activities as drug production and trafficking, counterfeiting, prostitution, auto theft, extortion, arms trafficking, and cigarette smuggling, among others.

The French government used proceeds from the production and sale of opium to help fund intelligence agents, saboteurs, and radio operators it was training to fight the communist insurgency in Indo-China in the postwar period. The *maquis,* as they were called, 'were the mirror image of the communist commandos; they fought using the same terror tactics as the enemy' (Napoleoni, 2003: 12–13). Palestinian extremist groups borrowed a page from organized crime when they began running 'protection rackets,' which involved extorting airlines out of millions of dollars in order to 'insure' them against hijackings (ibid.: 34). Since at least the 1970s, the IRA and its republican affiliates have relied on smuggling, prostitution, extortion, racketeering, drug trafficking, and armed robbery to finance their activities (R. Evans, 2002: 26–9). In 2001 alone, the IRA raised an estimated £7 million through criminal activities. The smuggling of tobacco products from Eastern Europe to England and the Irish Republic was one of the group's largest sources of illicit funding (Napoleoni, 2003: 32–3). There is a belief that the love of the cigarette-smuggling money has replaced their ideological zeal and rather than seeing the criminal activity as merely a fund-raising activity for their important political/terrorist activities, the criminal profits have become an end in themselves. The IRA is also the prime suspect behind the theft of £26.5 million from a Dublin bank on 20 December 2004.[24]

Officials with the U.S. Bureau of Alcohol, Tobacco, and Firearms say that Hezbollah, Hamas, and al Qaeda have all raised money by trafficking contraband cigarettes and counterfeit cigarette tax stamps. In one case, Lebanese nationals Mohammad Hammoud and his brother Chawki were arrested in 2000 and accused of smuggling U.S.$7.9 million worth of low-tax cigarettes out of low-tax north Carolina into high-tax Michigan, where they were resold through convenience stores linked to the brothers through family and religious ties. At their trial, the prosecution was able to prove that some of the U.S.$1.5 million profits accumulated by the smuggling operation were transferred to Hezbollah leaders (Roig-Franzia, 2002; U.S. General Accounting Office, 2003: 3). According to the U.S. Government Accounting Office, as of 20 August 2003, the ATF was investigating at least six similar cigarette smuggling cases with ties to terrorist groups (U.S. General Accounting Office, 2003: 16).

In Canada, a 1999 RCMP intelligence report alleged that a Lebanese-based auto-theft group operating in Quebec funnelled hundreds of thousands of dollars to a terrorist organization. A series of police raids in June of that year led to the dismantling of the crime ring, which stole millions of dollars worth of luxury cars for shipment overseas. As part of the investigation, police seized fifty-five luxury cars. The report claims the group made a profit of U.S.$3 million within a period of three months, 10 per cent of which was funnelled to an unnamed terrorist organization.[25]

The Tamil Tigers have also been accused of active involvement in criminal activities as part of their separatist fund-raising cause. A 2000 criminal intelligence report prepared by the RCMP states, 'Tamil criminal groups are involved in a variety of criminal activities including extortion, home invasion, thefts, sales of contraband cigarettes, the importation and trafficking of brown heroin, trafficking of other drugs, arms trafficking, fraud, production and sale of counterfeit passports, illegal migrant smuggling and attempted murders, bank and casino frauds and money laundering' (Bell, 2002b: A7). On 10 May 2004, two Sri Lankans of Tamil origin, residing in Montreal and Toronto, along with a Lebanese immigrant were arrested by the RCMP for their alleged involvement in counterfeiting Canadian money, credit cards, and passports. The investigation led to the seizure of CDN$284,000 in counterfeit bills, 92 documents of biographic data for Canadian passports, and more than 9,000 plastic cards that were to be used to make forged credit cards, social insurance cards, health insurance cards, and driver's licenses. The two Sri Lankan men were alleged to be close associates of the World Tamil Organization, which raises funds for LTTE operations in Sri Lanka under the guise of humanitarian assistance (Gamage, 2005).

In 1987, Veluppillai Pushpanathan, a Sri Lankan national, was among eight people arrested in Toronto who were accused of selling millions of dollars worth of heroin. Pushpanathan, who came to Canada in 1985 and was accepted as a permanent resident under a special humanitarian program, pleaded guilty and was sentenced to eight years in prison. At a deportation hearing held before the Immigration Review Board in 1993, police officials testified that Pushpanathan was involved in a drug trafficking organization controlled by the Tamil Tigers. The Board eventually ruled that Pushpanathan was 'closely associated in criminal activities with members of the LTTE in Canada.' Pushpanathan appealed the ruling to the Federal Court, arguing that the LTTE was not a terrorist organization and that he was not complicit in their activities. However, the Court ruled that he could not claim refugee status in Canada because of his 'crimes against humanity' in support of terrorism.[26]

In 2004, the secretary-general of Interpol told reporters in Brussels that there is 'a significant link between counterfeiting and terrorism in locations where there are entrenched terrorist groups.' Interpol found that some of the suspects involved in the sale of fake car brakes in Lebanon had links with terrorist groups. Militants in Northern Ireland and Colombia have also been linked to counterfeiting, according to Interpol (Moller, 2004).

While terrorist groups appear to use a wide range of criminal activities to help fund their causes, it is no surprise that illegal drug production and trafficking has emerged as perhaps the greatest single source of income for many extremist groups. In South America, groups such as the Revolutionary Armed Forces of Colombia (commonly known by their Spanish acronym FARC) and the *Sendero Luminoso* (the Shining Path) in Peru began their involvement in coca production and the cocaine trade by providing protection for coca farmers. Their profiteering from the coca trade continued to grow over the years; they provided escort and protection services during transportation; and in regions they controlled, they levied a tax on coca producers, charged rent and protection fees for laboratories, as well as tolls for the use of clandestine airstrips (Bronskill, 2002). A similar taxation system was used in relation to opium growers in parts of Afghanistan controlled by the Mujaheddin during its war against the Soviets (Napoleoni, 2003: 40, 83).

A 2001 intelligence report prepared by the RCMP entitled *Narcoterrorism and Canada*, contends, 'It is likely that terrorist elements in Afghanistan tax [drug] producers, thereby receiving a portion of the potential proceeds.' The report was released the same week that the warship HMCS *Toronto* discovered a shipment of drugs aboard a fishing vessel off the coast of Pakistan. The narcotics, either opium or hashish, were found in plastic bags marked with the phrase 'Freedom of Afghanistan.' The Canadian Department of Defence said an investigation was undertaken to determine 'possible links with al-Qaida or Taliban activities' (Millard, 2003: 161–2; Bronskill, 2002: A13).

The *New York Times* reported that militants associated with al Qaeda and the Taliban allegedly worked with Bosnian drug traffickers to smuggle heroin from Afghanistan into Europe through the Balkans. This operation proved so successful for al Qaeda operatives that it became a model for fund-raising and recruitment used by the terrorist organization in Kosovo, Albania, and Chechnya (Eichenwald, 2001: A1). The United Nations Group responsible for identifying terrorist-linked individuals, groups, and assets alleged in one report that the 'drug trade' is one source of funds for al Qaeda.[27] Saudi security sources claimed that Sunni insurgents in Iraq have been smuggling illegal drugs from that country to Saudi Arabia to finance insurgency attacks against coalition forces. 'In the space of one year, border police intercepted 10 tons of cannabis coming from Iraq,' according to a Saudi source quoted in the media. The security sources said revenues from the smuggling were being shared by al Qaeda operatives in Iraq and Saudi Arabia and that the money was being used to purchase weapons and finance attacks in both countries.[28] Despite these claims, in their report on terrorist financing, the 9/11 Commission wrote, 'No persuasive evidence exists that al Qaeda relied on the drug trade as an important source of revenue ...' (National Commission, n.d.: 4). It may be that the 'link' between drug trafficking and terrorism is too politically attractive to ignore. Claims that terrorists are *also* drug traffickers make their existence even more 'evil.' One has to question what al Qaeda or any other terrorist organization would do with all of the funds that are purported to swirl in their direction.

While the involvement of al Qaeda in drug trafficking may be in dispute, there is little argument that the Balkans became a major trafficking conduit for heroin beginning in the 1990s and that the Kosovo Liberation Army (KLA), a guerrilla group that battled the ruling Serbs, was heavily involved in the illicit Balkan drug traffic. In March 1999, the *Times of London* reported that the KLA was involved in narcotics trafficking. In the same month, the ITAR-Tass news agency reported that the chief of the Russian Armed Forces had sent a letter to NATO commanders detailing the involvement of 'Kosovo terrorists' in the drug trade in Europe. With the tacit support of the KLA, Kosovo became a primary conduit for heroin trafficking from Afghanistan via Turkey and the Balkans into Western Europe. The so-called Balkan Route also served as a conduit for illegal arms to the KLA, and drug organizations based in the Balkans were accused of helping the KLA funnel arms and cash into Kosovo for its guerrilla war. Other accusations emerged that Albanians from Kosovo living in Germany and Switzerland were skimming profits from inner-city heroin trafficking and sending the cash to the KLA. Czech police tracked down one Kosovo Albanian drug dealer who had escaped from a Norwegian prison where he was serving twelve years for heroin trafficking. A raid on his apartment turned up documents linking him with arms purchases for the KLA.[29]

Pierluigi Vigna, Italy's national anti-Mafia prosecutor, told reporters that Italian investigators have found evidence that the Camorra, one of Italy's main organized crime networks, has been implicated 'in an exchange of weapons for drugs' with 'Islamic terrorist groups.' He suggested the cooperation came about after a member of the Camorra converted to Islam and met in prison with Muslims who had been arrested in Italy.[30]

Because terrorist groups are motivated by cultural, political, and ideological goals rather than economic gain, they differ from organized crime groups in that the profit from illegal activities is a means to an end, not an end in itself. With that said, there is a natural symmetry between terrorist groups and organized criminal activities as well as a mutual attraction between organized crime and militant or terrorist groups. The latter can play the role of customer, for example, by purchasing arms or explosives, but can also play the role of supplier, such as providing armed protection to criminal groups operating in a certain area. Political extremist groups may 'contract out' profit-oriented activities to criminal entrepreneurs or may bypass them altogether and become directly involved in such activities, which include employing cells expressly for these purposes. As we have noted, attracted by the economic benefits of criminal activity and pushed by the achievement, irrelevancy, or unpopularity of their political agenda, militant groups like the IRA have been accused of evolving into organized crime groups whereby their political goals have become secondary to economic goals.

With respect to the investigation of terrorist funds and financing arrangements, the foray of extremist groups into criminal activities poses a particular enforcement challenge. Traditionally organized and proceeds of crime enforcement techniques are considerably weakened when used against terrorist groups. The cellular structure of terrorist networks makes it difficult for national security and law enforcement agencies to detect and interdict the full complement of terrorist operatives engaged in organized criminal activities. In addition, it is far more difficult to infiltrate or recruit informants or agents from terrorist cells relative to traditional criminal organizations. This is due in part to the ideological commitment of terrorist operatives to their cause, as well as the closeness, trust, shared purpose, and strong ethnic, family, and religious ties that bind members of political extremist groups. These factors combine to create a far more impenetrable barrier to traditional investigative and intelligence-gathering tactics compared with the profit-oriented motives of and less binding commercial relationships among criminal entrepreneurs.

There is also little doubt that terrorist groups have learned from the experience of criminal organizations in surreptitiously transporting and laundering their illicit funds, while evading the reporting of suspicious transactions. When terrorist groups undertake organized criminal activities or collaborate with organized crime groups, law enforcement and national security agencies are presented with the challenge of not only identifying, interdicting, and proving criminal activity among highly secretive and ideologically committed terrorist operatives but they also must prove a linkage between such criminal activities and terrorist motives.

Institutions and Services used to Process, Transport, and Launder Terrorist Funds

Once monies have been raised, extremists groups must then ensure the funds can be safely applied to their ultimate endeavours, which often means they must be transported across international borders. While a number of methods have been used, including the smuggling of cash and precious gems, this section focuses specifically on how terrorist groups transport funds internationally by capitalizing on the services of formal financial service providers as well as using what has been variously referred to as 'informal,' 'underground,' or 'alternative' banking systems and money transmitters.

Informal Money Transfer Systems

An informal money transfer system (IMTS) – also called alternative remittance services – refers to a network of individuals or organizations that send and receive money on behalf of customers for the purpose of making an equivalent value payable to a third party in another geographic location. Such transfers generally take place outside the conventional banking system through unregulated and undocumented businesses. A typical 'funds transfer' using an IMTS is as follows. An individual in Country 'A' provides an IMTS operator with money and instructions to deliver the equivalent value to a family member in Country 'B'. The IMTS operator in Country 'A' contacts a counterpart in Country 'B' via fax, e-mail, telephone, or another method and communicates the instructions. Then, through verification by some code passed from the sender to the recipient, the IMTS operator in Country 'B' delivers the equivalent value (in cash or an alternative monetary instrument or asset), less a transaction fee, to the recipient in that country. As indicated above, the cross-border transactions are accomplished without any physical or electronic transfer of funds, prompting Nikos Passas to label these networks 'informal value transfer systems.'[31] The relationship between different IMTS operators is based primarily on trust, and networks are often formed through family, cultural, or religious connections (although, increasingly, international transfer networks are being forged purely for commercial reasons and may be part of a multinational corporation or conglomerate). Often, the primary commercial activity of an IMTS operator is not the transmission of money; many are storeowners, importers or exporters, or even taxi drivers.

IMT networks pre-date the rise of the formal banking system for transferring funds and continues to be popular because it is flexible, reliable, operates twenty-four hours a day, provides greater anonymity for users, involves minimal paperwork, may not be subject to taxes or government regulations, and is often more efficient and less costly compared with conventional banking systems. Most importantly, some areas in the world are not served by formal banking systems; in fact, not all of the citizens in even the Western countries have access to the financial institutions within their own jurisdictions due to the lack of adequate identification. Although illegal in some countries, IMT networks are a cornerstone of the financial system in many parts of the developing world and are particularly favoured in countries where the formal banking system is under-developed. In some parts of south Asia, the system is called *hawala* or *hundi*. Among the Sri Lankan Tamils, it is popularly known as *undiyal* (literally 'piggy banking'). In southeast Asia, the system is known as *Fei Ch'ien* and *Chit*. Similar systems are used regularly to send money back to Mexico and other Latin American countries by migrant workers in the United States. In fact, IMT systems are said to be used overwhelmingly by expatriates – traders and immigrant laborers – to send money back to their home countries. In total, the United Nations estimates the turnover of the IMT systems at U.S.$200 billion a year.[32] This figure would need, however, to be seen as a mere guess since no reliable calculation could be possible.

There are a number of factors that have raised the fear in the West that terrorist organizations have turned to IMT networks and other forms of underground banking to help transfer and launder funds. Much of the concern appears to stem from geographical and cultural factors: IMT networks are common in Arab and Muslims societies. Heightening this risk is the unregulated and non-transparent nature of these systems, which stands in stark contrast to the ever-expanding litany of AML regulations that have been imposed upon the formal financial services sector in many countries. In its report on the use of informal banking systems by terrorist groups, the U.S. General Accounting Office aptly summarized the challenges facing and concerns of those engaged in the fight against terrorism: while such underground systems are used for legitimate purposes, they also 'entail a significant degree of nontransparency that terrorist groups and their supporters can exploit to move funds raised in the United States and elsewhere across borders' (U.S. General Accounting Office, 2003: 14).

Since 9/11, IMT networks have been singled out as a conduit used by extremist groups to transfer funds. According to the FATF, 'Money or value transfer systems have shown themselves vulnerable to misuse for money laundering and terrorist financing purposes' (FATF, n.d.c). The 2002 *National Money Laundering Strategy* report prepared by the U.S. Department of the Treasury and Department of Justice (2002: 14) states, 'There is also evidence that non-traditional money movement systems, such as *hawala* and other alternative remittance systems, have been used as links in the terrorist financial chain.' In his testimony before the U.S. Senate Judiciary Committee on 20 November 2002, U.S. Treasury Under-Secretary Jimmy Gurule (2002) claimed that terrorists have 'used hawalas and other informal value transfer systems as a means of terrorist financing.' Specific unsubstantiated allegations have also surfaced regarding the use of informal banking systems by al Qaeda and Osama bin Laden. The 9/11 Commission was particularly specific:

> After Bin Ladin relocated to Afghanistan in 1996, al Qaeda made less use of formal banking channels to transfer money, preferring instead to use an informal system of money movers or bulk cash couriers ... Al Qaeda moved much of its money by hawala before 9/11. In some ways, al Qaeda had no choice after its move to Afghanistan in 1996; the banking system there was antiquated and undependable. Hawala became particularly important after the August 1998 East Africa bombings increased worldwide scrutiny of the formal financial system. Bin Ladin turned to an established hawala network operating in Pakistan, in Dubai, and throughout the Middle East to transfer funds efficiently. (National Commission, n.d.: 4, 25)

Although there is no evidence that IMT networks in North America have been used to facilitate the transfer of terrorist funds, the USA

Patriot Act established greater regulatory oversight of informal banking businesses, including the requirement that all unlicensed money transmitters register with the Treasury Department. Further, the Act took the unprecedented step of making it a federal offence to operate a money transmitter business without an appropriate state license. The new offence carries a maximum sentence of five years imprisonment. The FATF quickly followed suit. As part of its nine anti-terrorism financing recommendations, the FATF required that member countries:

> take measures to ensure that persons or legal entities, including agents, that provide a service for the transmission of money or value, including transmission through an informal money or value transfer system or network, should be licensed or registered and subject to all the FATF Recommendations that apply to banks and non-bank financial institutions. Each country should ensure that persons or legal entities that carry out this service illegally are subject to administrative, civil or criminal sanctions. (FATF, n.d.b)

In a consultation paper released in June 2005, entitled 'Enhancing Canada's Anti-Money Laundering and Anti-Terrorist Financing Regime,' the Canadian government signalled that it would comply with the FATF recommendation by requiring any individuals or organizations 'engaged in the business of remitting or transferring funds by any means' to register their operations with FINTRAC. The proposed provision would also make it a crime to provide these services without a license. According to the consultation paper, 'The absence of licensing or registration in Canada makes the sector highly attractive to criminals looking for alternatives to the regulated banking sector to launder money or finance terrorism' (Department of Finance, 2005).

These measures have been proposed despite the fact that by 2005, not one alternative money transmitter in North America has been prosecuted for complicity in financing terrorist activities. IMT systems also appear to be the target of far more punitive sanctions relative to the formal financial services sector. Following the precedent set in the U.S. where informal money transmitters must register with FINCEN, the Canadian government has proposed that individuals and organizations offering such services register, not with an administrative or regulatory government agency, as is the norm with most financial service providers, but with FINTRAC, the federal agency concerned exclusively with criminal money laundering and terrorist financing, thereby unfairly casting an accusatory pall over all such businesses. Moreover, like the United States, the proposed 'enhancements' will mean that an IMTS operator can be criminally charged simply for operating without a license (a penalty that is practically unheard of in any other part of the financial services sector).

While there is evidence that *hawalas* have been used to facilitate the transfer of terrorist funds in other parts of the world, some have argued that they have been unfairly targeted. As described earlier, this may be due to the sheer *potential* risk they represent. Or, it can be blamed on overzealous and hasty enforcement actions that have become all too common in the shoot-first-ask-questions-later enforcement environment of the post–9/11 period. One can even go so far as suggest that the targeting of IMT networks is a reflection of the racial and cultural profiling that has inevitably accompanied the war on terror. This racial and cultural profiling has permeated two principal and overlapping anti-terrorist-financing strategies: (1) the freezing of assets of suspected terrorists, their supporters and financiers, and (2) the reporting of transactions that may be suspicious of terrorist financing.

In Canada, the Office of the Superintendent of Financial Institutions (OSFI) is responsible for circulating a list of names of suspected terrorists to private sector entities that are obligated to file Terrorist Property Reports. The contents of the list – which is derived primarily from United Nations sources and is published on the OSFI website – is populated with names that are almost exclusively of Arabic or Muslim in origin. OSFI (2004) advises reporting entities to regard with suspicion not only people whose names are on the list but also anyone whose name resembles the name of a listed person: '... if you have grounds for suspicion do not rely on different (but similar) spelling as grounds for deciding that a person is not intended to be covered by the list.' Commenting on this guideline, Reem Bahdi (2003: 302) writes: 'Bank managers and employees, working under the shadow of risk of financial and criminal sanction, are thus implicitly encouraged to regard Arabs and Muslims as especially suspect. In short, race and religion, through the use of names, becomes a proxy for risk.'

The most disquieting example of the frenzied targeting of a *hawala* in North America (that may or may not be based on racial profiling) began on 7 November 2001, when U.S. authorities added the names of sixty-two entities and people to its list of suspected terrorist associates. In a speech made that day, President Bush stated there was clear evidence showing the people on the list to be 'quartermasters of terror' (Robertson,

2001: A14). The new list targeted two IMT networks that were alleged to be transferring money for al Qaeda. One of the companies was al-Barakaat, a large Somalia conglomerate that operated an international network of informal remittance offices (and is also involved in telecommunications, electrical power generation, construction, banking, postal services, and money transfers). According to the U.S. Treasury Department, the network is controlled by al-Ittihad al-Islamiya, an extremist Somali militia that has been designated by the Bush administration as a terrorist organization. American intelligence accused al-Barakaat of siphoning a portion of its revenues to terrorists via its central headquarters in Dubai (Vaknin, 2001: 2). Specifically, U.S. Treasury officials estimated that al-Barakaat's central money exchange in Dubai receives U.S.$300 to $500 million globally per year, from which it provided al Qaeda a flat 5 per cent – or $15 to $20 million – annually (Eichenwald, 2001; Golden, 2002).

The FBI began gathering information on the al-Barakaat network in early 1999, and by 2000 had begun a criminal investigation. Around the time President Bush announced the addition of al-Barakaat to his list of terrorist supporters, the U.S. assets of the corporation were frozen and dozens of its American affiliates were raided by federal officials (National Commission, n.d.: 10). On 7 November 2001, the United Arab Emirates shut down al-Barakaat's Dubai office. On 13 November 2001, the European Union decreed that all banks would instantly freeze assets of, and prohibit financial dealings with, individuals and entities associated with al-Barakaat. In Canada, one al-Barakaat affiliate located in Ottawa – Massachusetts-based Barakaat North America Inc., which is run by Mohammed and Liban Hussein, both of whom are Canadian citizens – was raided by the RCMP. The American and Canadian assets of the Hussein brothers were frozen and Mohammed was arrested in Boston. Liban was jailed in Ottawa and proceedings were immediately undertaken to deport him to the U.S. to face charges.[33]

Despite these enforcement actions and a subsequent investigation into al-Barakaat and its affiliates by the FBI, no links to any terrorist groups could be established. Mohammed Hussein was convicted only of the charge of failing to have a license for his remittance office. The majority of assets frozen in the United States, Canada, and other countries were ultimately released. In June 2002, the Canadian Department of Justice announced it was discontinuing extrication proceedings against Liban Hussein and, after threats of a civil law suit, agreed to an out-of-court settlement. Only four criminal prosecutions were ever initiated from this investigation, and none involve charges of aiding terrorists.[34]

Like many other organizations and individuals, al-Barakaat is just one of the many innocent victims of the war on terror. The reputations of hundreds of al-Barakaat associates in North America, like Mohammed and Liban Hussein, were severely damaged. The temporary closing of al-Barakaat's foreign offices severed a vital channel through which much-needed funds could be sent to poverty-stricken and war-torn Somalia. 'This was literally a lifeline for our people,' according to Osaman Shardeed, assistant director for Somali Community of Minnesota. 'No way will our people survive without this business' (Robertson, 2001: A14). International relief officials in Somalia say the impact of blocking al-Barakaat has been devastating to Somalia's largest company – and by extension the country's economy – resulting in company layoffs, the disruption in business for thousands of companies that deal with the corporation, and a lack of access to deposits by its customers (Golden, 2002).

The al-Barakaat case represents the most cogent example of the charges levelled by critics that informal transfer systems, in particular those associated with Arab or Muslim societies, have been unfairly singled out and made the subject of unwarranted accusations, misguided enforcement actions, and ethnic or religious profiling. This case also provides some indication as to the immense challenges inherent in investigating or regulating IMT systems. The abundance of informal money transfer networks globally, their popularity in the developing world, and the sheer volume of funds transferred through these networks, makes eliminating or even regulating IMT systems nearly impossible. From an investigative perspective, these networks are difficult to detect and penetrate because, by their very nature, they are underground and operate through relationships that are based on trust as well as ethnic, religious, and family ties. This lack of transparency severely undermines the ability of government agencies to access and monitor the clients and transactions of IMT systems.

Another component of this non-transparency is the absence of transaction records or indecipherable records. This lack of a paper trail greatly limits the ability of investigators to track suspected terrorist funds or to apprehend those involved in terrorist financing. Cracking down on informal money transfer services in the name of fighting terrorism may also have the counterproductive result of driving the businesses further underground (Cheran and Aiken, 2005). IMT systems are also a microcosm of one of the most significant challenges facing anti-terrorism enforcement: identifying a drop of terrorist funds in an ocean of legitimate money and transactions, while avoiding the type of imprudent targeting that was so evident in the case of al-Barakaat.

Perhaps the most reasonable conclusion regarding the highly charged debate over the role of IMT networks in the financing of terrorism can be drawn by comparing the findings of two seemingly contradictory studies, both of which were prepared for the United Nations. While the UN agency responsible for compiling international lists of terrorists observed that a large proportion of the Taliban resources moved to al Qaeda via *hawalas*, a discussion paper prepared for the United Nations Department of Economic and Social Affairs concluded that 'there is no evidence that *hawalas* have become the *preferred* vehicle for the movement of funds by contemporary terrorist organizations or criminal networks' (Leonides and Gorbunov, 2002: 1; emphasis added). A most prudent observation was made by the United States General Accounting Office (2003), which rightly points out, 'the extent of terrorists' use of alternative financing mechanisms is unknown, owing to the criminal nature of terrorists' use of alternative financing mechanisms and the lack of systematic data collection and analysis of case information.'

Based on a juxtaposition of these observations, one can reasonably conclude that while it may be entirely appropriate to target IMT networks as a conduit for terrorist financing, the scope and nature of this attention by policymakers and law enforcement officials must be more commensurate with the extent to which they are actually used to such ends (which could be estimated through more rigorous empirical research). Further, according to R. Cheran and S. Aiken (2005), existing anti-terrorist financing laws and policies may be 'fully adequate to address criminal concerns,' but many of these laws and policies should be implemented in a manner that is more sensitive to the actual users of the system and to the cultural context in which these systems operate.

Banks and Other Formal Financial Service Providers

While much controversy surrounds the extent to which informal banking systems are used to transfer terrorist funds, there is little disagreement regarding their more formal cousin. An ample number of cases suggest that it is the formal financial service sector, and banks in particular, that are the main vehicles for storing, processing, and transporting terrorist money.

In its report on terrorist financing, an independent task force sponsored by the Council on Foreign Relations wrote that 'al Qaeda operatives and supporters in the West and other banking centers freely used the international financing system.' Fund-raisers for the terrorist network used banks to store and move their money, which may have been facilitated by corrupt individuals working for these banks (National Commission, n.d.: 24–5). The use of chartered banks by al Qaeda cells became abundantly clear when the dust settled following the 9/11 attacks: all of the hijackers relied on banks to hold, move, and retrieve money that was used to pay the expenses associated with the coordinated airborne assault. Of the U.S.$400,000 to $500,000 it cost to run the hijacking operation, $300,000 was deposited in U.S. bank accounts of the nineteen hijackers. The *New York Times* reported that approximately U.S.$238,000 was sent to the American bank accounts of the hijackers in more than a dozen wire transfers from the United Arab Emirates (Eichenwald, 2001; see also Council on Foreign Relations, 2002). The 9/11 Commission concluded that there were 'three primary and unexceptional means' by which funds were brought into America: (1) wire transfers from overseas, (2) the physical transport of cash or traveller's checks, and (3) accessing funds held in foreign financial institutions by debit or credit cards. 'Once here, all of the hijackers used the U.S. banking system to store their funds and facilitate their transactions' (National Commission, n.d.: 13).

On 16 September 2001, the *Sunday Times* of London described how an account with Barclays Bank in the name of the Advice and Reformation Committee, a charitable organization believed to be a front for Osama bin Laden, had received tens of millions of dollars from correspondent banks in Sudan, Dubai, and the United Arab Emirates. From Barclays, the money was transferred to the accounts of al Qaeda operatives in Western cities, including Geneva, Chicago, and London. The signatory for the Barclay's account was Khalid al-Fawaaz, a Saudi dissident with a home in north London, who was suspected of heading Osama bin Ladin's operations in Britain. Fawaaz was also implicated in the bombing of the American embassies in Nairobi and Dar-es-Salaam. By 19 September Barclays had frozen the account. Seven days later, French finance minister Laurent Fabius announced that his government had blocked approximately U.S.$3.9 million in bank accounts linked to al Qaeda.

Not only were al Qaeda cells using banks to transfer funds, Osama bin Ladin himself was said to have invested heavily in at least one Islamic bank. On 14 August 1996, the U.S. State Department issue a 'Fact Sheet on Bin Laden,' which stated that he had invested U.S.$50 million in Al-Shamal Islamic Bank, based in Sudan. During a U.S. Senate Banking Committee hearing on money laundering and the funding of terrorist activities held on 26 September 2001, Senator Carl Levin claimed that the Al-Shamal Islamic Bank was founded by Osama bin Laden and was still controlled by him in 2000. At the hearing, Senator Levin pointed to the website of the Al-Shamal Bank, which at the time listed an extensive correspondent network in the U.S., including Citibank, American Express, and the Arab American Bank.[35] During the same committee hearings, Senator John Kerry alleged that bin Laden once held accounts at the notorious Bank of Credit and Commerce International (BCCI), which was shut down in 1991. BCCI was a British-Pakistani bank that was implicated in international fraud and money laundering, which included financing arms sales to terrorist groups, such as the Mujaheddin (which was supported by bin Laden in its battle against Soviet troops in Afghanistan). The money funnelled through BCCI to the Mujaheddin came from the CIA and Saudi intelligence agencies (although there is no evidence that CIA funds were directly provided to bin Laden or deposited in his accounts at BCCI). The BCCI was also used on a regular basis by the CIA to fund its international covert operations and was an intermediary for the U.S. National Security Council when it funnelled money, generated from arm sales to Iran, to the Contras in Nicaragua.[36]

In its extensive fund-raising in Canada, the Tamil Tigers is said to rely heavily on Canadian banks. At one time, the group allegedly transferred money out of the country through forty 'feeder' Canadian bank accounts. The funds were sent to twenty different accounts at banks in Europe and Asia, which were then debited to pay for the purchase of weapons (Bell, 2000c). A Singapore bank account opened by a Canadian of Sri Lankan origin was purportedly used to purchase 60 tonnes of explosives by Tamil insurgents for the 1996 bombing of the Central Bank of Sri Lanka in Colombo, which killed eighty-six people and injured 1,400 (Bell, 2000a).

According to a deputy director of Europol, a typical scheme to transfer funds by Middle Eastern terrorists begins with the deposit of a small amounts of money in various local banks. Then, 'they'll look for a weak link in the [global] financial system.'[37] This reference to 'weak links' is a euphemism for countries that are attractive to those wishing to hide legitimate (untaxed) revenue, the proceeds of crime, and terrorist funds. These non-conformist countries include 'underregulated jurisdictions, places with limited bank supervision, no anti-money-laundering laws, ineffective law enforcement institutions, and a culture of no-questions-asked bank secrecy' (Council on Foreign Relations, 2002: 8–9). According to a terrorism financing task force of the Council on Foreign Relations, to find such weak links, Middle Eastern terrorist groups like al Qaeda do not have to look far.

> The regional banking centers of the Middle East – Dubai and other emirates of the United Arab Emirates (UAE), Kuwait, Bahrain, and (in its day) Lebanon – have each over the years generally ignored repeated calls by the international community to build anti-money laundering regimes consistent with international standards. Similarly, banking systems that have been major recipients of al Qaeda's funds – most notably in Pakistan while the Taliban ruled neighboring Afghanistan – have also had weak or nonexistent anti-money laundering regimes. (Council on Foreign Relations, 2002: 8–9)

As with criminal organizations looking to launder funds, al Qaeda operatives moved funds through other jurisdictions long known for providing bank secrecy, in particular Liechtenstein and the Bahamas (ibid.).

The formal banking system is also drawn into the web of terrorist financing because it is used in conjunction with other formal and informal financial intermediaries, including informal money transfer networks, charitable organizations, and legitimate businesses. According to the terrorist financing report of the 9/11 Commission: 'Hawaladars associated with al Qaeda (like hawaladars generally) relied on banks as part of their hawala operations. One bank, for example, had 1,800 to 2,000 branches in Pakistan, making it relatively easy for a hawaladar to use the bank to move funds. In addition to hawaladars, charities such as Wafa Humanitarian Organization had accounts at banks, which served as a means to move money for terrorists' (National Commission, n.d.: 24–5).

Given the mounting evidence about the role of formal financial services industry in facilitating the financing of terrorism, it came as no surprise following 9/11 that it would now be mandated to detect funds that may be associated with terrorist groups. There was also little shock when the anti-terrorism-financing measures simply copied the two-pronged approach used in existing anti-money-laundering strategies: ensuring that adequate due diligence is carried out on clients and transaction reporting. The only substantive difference was that the anti-terrorism-financing regime required the development of profiles and indices of clients and transactions that are specific to terrorists and their financing activity. However, the problem, according to the 9/11 Commission, is that 'no effective financial profile for operational terrorists located in the United States exists.' The New York Clearinghouse, a private consortium of large banks, 'attempted to put together such a profile in partnership with government investigators. After two years, they concluded it could not be done' (National Commission, n.d.: 56).

The inability to develop a profile of a typical terrorist or a financial transaction supporting terrorism means that private sector entities now must refer to a list of names, compiled by the U.S. Treasury Department and the United Nations, of individuals and organizations suspected of being associated with terrorist groups. Of course, relying so heavily on such a cursory list of information is fraught with limitations and problems. Individuals on the list can easily open accounts under an assumed identity or use a nominee. Moreover, the list most likely excludes hundreds if not thousands of persons associated with terrorist groups, including those who reside in unactivated sleeper cells. And as previously mentioned, the fact that these lists are almost exclusively populated by names of individuals from Arabic, North African, and Muslim backgrounds 'creates a risk that financial institutions could rely primarily on religious, geographic, or ethnic profiling in an attempt to find some criteria helpful for identifying terrorist financing' (National Commission, n.d.: 57).

Another limitation in adapting anti-money-laundering measures to anti-terrorist-financing stems from the amount of terrorist funds circulating within the legitimate economy. In theory, transaction reporting that targets the proceeds of organized criminal activities has a chance of realizing at least minimal success due to the sheer volume of cash generated from drug trafficking and other criminal activities. Given the comparatively small amount of terrorist funds that moves through the legitimate economy, the chance that any financial institution will be exposed to such funds, let alone detect them, is equally small. Financial transactions associated with terrorist financing tend to be in amounts not large enough to trigger existing reporting thresholds. An FBI analysis of the events surrounding 9/11 indicated that the hijackers each opened accounts with a single cash or wire transfer deposit in the average amount of U.S.$3,000 to $5,000. The analysis also showed that they made numerous withdrawals in small amounts by using mostly debit cards (Canada, Office of the Auditor General, 2003). Terrorist operatives also live modestly, thereby avoiding detection based on conspicuous spending and consumption (FINTRAC, n.d.b).

Detecting transactions that may involve terrorist funds is made even more difficult given that the source of funds may come from legitimate businesses and fund-raising. These legal sources eliminate the risk indicators that often make transactions conducted with the proceeds of crime conspicuous. The use of private fund-raising can also avoid one of the red flags of transaction reporting – a large amount of cash in small denominations – by requesting all donations be made by monetary instrument or even electronically. Further, the type of 'suspicious' terrorist financing activity that prompts the filing of a terrorist property report remains nebulous and highly subjective. The head of FinCEN has been quoted as saying the decision by a regulated entity to report will often come down to 'a hunch' (Lynden, 2003: 233). Even the FATF cast suspicions over the ability of the financial services sector to detect terrorist funds. In its 2002 document *Guidance for Financial Institutions in Detecting Terrorist Financing*, the international agency acknowledged 'that financial institutions will probably be unable to detect terrorist financing as such. Indeed, the only time that financial institutions might clearly identify terrorist financing as distinct from other criminal misuse of the financial system is when a known terrorist or terrorist organisation has opened an account.'[38]

In conclusion, one has to seriously question whether the small amount of terrorist funds that can possibly be detected by the new reporting regime is worth the burden being placed on the private sector. The application of transaction reporting to terrorist financing represents the proverbial shotgun approach to killing flies. On a global scale, these new anti-terrorist-financing measures will surely cost the financial services sector hundreds of millions if not billions of dollars to implement. This does not include money lost due to stricter screening (and rejection) of clients, accounts, and correspondent banks. The increased burden will also create concerns among financial institutions in heavily regulated countries as to their ability to compete against institutions in countries that have not adopted similar regulations. Ironically, increased measures to regulate the legitimate financial services sector may very well serve to drive terrorists' funds into the unregulated informal financial sectors, which exponentially decreases the chances that these funds can be detected.

The commitment of the private sector to these new responsibilities, and the extent to which affected entities comply with the new transaction reporting laws, is also hindered by the sheer complexity of implementing prevention and compliance measures that must simultaneously try to identify the proceeds from drug trafficking and the funding for terrorist groups. Developing policies and programs, designating compliance personnel, training staff, adapting anti-money-laundering systems to terrorist funds, attempting to red flag one or two highly nuanced transactions within the midst of hundreds of millions of transactions, and the constant need to adapt reporting systems to new types of suspicious transactions and ever-expanding lists of suspected terrorists all represent considerable challenges and costs to private sector firms. This enhanced burden on banks and other members of the financial services industry comes on the heels of a decade of intense lobbying against stiffer money-laundering regulations. Not to be outdone, professional groups representing lawyers in Canada and the United States have waged a determined battle to escape even the most basic due diligence and reporting requirements with respect to both the proceeds of crime and terrorist funds. All of the above contributes to a healthy scepticism about the extent to which banks and other reporting entities will comply with the spirit and letter of these new due diligence and transaction reporting regulations.

To help ensure compliance, the new anti-terrorist-financing laws include provisions that severely penalize regulated entities if they fail to enhance due diligence efforts, implement a terrorist financing reporting regime, or actually detect terrorist funds. These penalties include substantial fines and even criminal sanctions. Thus, while the enhanced regulations are expected to have only a minimal impact on the contribution that regulated entities can make in the overall war on terror, they are being held accountable to protect society from national security threats (and to be far more accountable than the politicians and policymakers who have pushed these new regulations).

7 Conclusion: Full Speed Ahead on a Runaway Horse

This book has called for a serious and honest appraisal of the objectives and practicalities related to some of the policies that are presented as anti-money laundering and anti-terrorism strategies. We have been interested in dissecting where policies have come from and who has benefited the most from them. Policies that spring from, and whirl through, the international non-state agencies can be as compelling as domestic policies but less 'democratically' accountable and conceivably less relevant to local conditions. As this book goes to press, it has just been announced that Toronto, Canada, will become the permanent home for the Egmont Secretariat and, that beginning in July 2006, Canada will serve for the coming year as the president of the Financial Action Task Force. Newspaper claims of putting Canada into the centre core of the 'battle' against money laundering and references to putting criminals and terrorists 'out of business' followed these announcements.[1]

No one is arguing that criminals should be allowed to maintain their illegally gained wealth or that everything should not be done to combat terrorism. We have attempted to ask the following pertinent (or possibly impertinent) questions:

- Do we know that going after the money is the most appropriate strategy – or are there more costs than gains? Simply stated, is it a realistic strategy in terms of impacting criminal conduct or terrorism to any significant degree?
- Are international organizations being set up that resist being displaced due to the power and perks that come to their members – and will continue to come to them as long as there is a unquestioned belief in the efficacy of these international strategies?

- Could perhaps a better use of our resources be to build up what appears to be decrepit community-based intelligence networks, better- resourced traditional police work, and the political will to 'problem-solve' in some of the most troubled areas of our cities and within foreign jurisdictions?

Answers to these questions might provide 'better' strategies that could reduce our sense of insecurity and risk. The same tactics now used to combat terror have been used in the war on drugs and drug trafficking, yet drug use, drug purity, and drug profits are all flourishing despite fifteen years of increasing pressure on bankers to identify 'suspicious transactions' and integrated policing anti-money-laundering policies that theoretically should lead law enforcement agents to drug barons (Hughes, 2001). The concern is not just with the lack of a 'track record' of these appropriated strategies. Of greater concern is the fact that the targeted 'enemies' might be quite different and require different approaches. The various links between money laundering and terrorism must be scrutinized given the ethical implications for the human rights of those who fall within the radar of over-zealous agencies hunting for terrorist financiers.

These 'global prohibition regimes' (Nadelmann, 1990) entail a combination of economic, and social interests, which are often packaged in part as moral interests. Who among us would choose to support drug traffickers? Who would value his/her own selfish rights to privacy over the need to 'stop' terrorists from killing? This morality aspect was perhaps best exploited by President George W. Bush. To criticize U.S. policy was to be anti-American, and in Bush's terminology, you are 'with us or *with the terrorists.*'[2] In his address to Congress on 20 September 2001, Bush launched what was to be a continuing series of 'fear' speeches that told the American people and the world that there was much to be afraid of, and that the answer lay in amassing power and being able to pre-emptively destroy whatever appeared to have the potential of being, *or of becoming,* a threat to the United States. He outlined a vision for a strong American leadership in the world, a leadership that would project America's power and influence in a fear-ridden world.

Canada has not been immune to current or past foreign pressures – from the 1989 passing of Proceeds of Crime Legislation that, in part, was introduced in order to bring Canada into compliance with the United Nations *Convention Against Illicit Traffic in Narcotic Drugs and Psychotropic*

Substances, to the 2000 Proceeds of Crime (Money Laundering) Act that brought Canada into line with the international community's call, via the Financial Action Task Force, for mandatory reporting of financial transactions. As with anti-money-laundering provisions adopted in the late 1990s, the more recent amendments codified into law through the Proceeds of Crime (Money Laundering) and Terrorism Financing Act are a reflection of American enforcement priorities and approaches. One would be hard-pressed to identify any aspect of Canada's terrorist financing enforcement philosophy that is original to Canada.

What's New?

Money laundering is not new. What is new is the international preoccupation with the rhetoric of fighting laundering and terrorist financing. 'Money laundering' as a concept serves to conjure up images of tangible and nefarious criminal processes. The various dangers associated with money laundering can then be effectively communicated and sold to policymakers, the public, the private sector, and other countries as a means to gain their support for powerful, intrusive, and far-reaching anti-laundering laws and enforcement initiatives.

Ironically, one now must expect *more* laundering rather than *less*. As long as enforcement targets illicit proceeds, there will be and has to be money laundering. In other words, enforcement actually promotes more sophisticated forms of money laundering. Even given the significant new legislation and additional policing powers and policies, there is almost no difference between the type of 'money-laundering' cases documented in our 1990 *Tracing of Illicit Finds Report* as compared to the cases in our most recent RCMP money-laundering case analysis. The majority of these cases were simple deposits into financial institutions and only a minority of the 'laundering' cases actually involved 'laundering.' Juxtaposed against the strict 'full' definition of money laundering, our empirical analyses of police cases reveal that the proceeds of crime are usually deposited into formal banks and 'used' in the exact same manner as other people spend their pay cheques. The large sophisticated schemes, as before, involved a critical role played by white-collar professionals, including accountants and lawyers.

Along with corruption and violence, money laundering has come to be seen as an integral tactical imperative of criminal entrepreneurs and has produced widespread demand for such services in both the criminal underworld and within the legitimate economy. Money laundering not only reflects but has also helped to fuel a division of labour that has been emerging among organizations and networks of criminal entrepreneurs in recent years, whereby specialized criminal tasks are carried out by individuals or groups with the appropriate expertise or connections.

However, unlike other criminal tasks that are a necessary part of the integrated chain of profit-oriented criminal activities, a good majority of money laundering is carried out (wittingly and unwittingly) by those in the legitimate economy. Indeed, what distinguishes money laundering from most other profit-oriented or tactical criminal activities is that it is firmly rooted in the legitimate economy and carried out by professionals therein. Thus, money laundering represents a nexus between the underground and legitimate economies and, as such, should not be seen as an economic aberration; it thrives on the very same commercial and financial transactions that are conducted by most Canadian citizens and companies. Far from being perversions of capitalism, drug trafficking, money laundering, and other entrepreneurial crimes may be interpreted as the continuation of the free market economy, the laws of supply and demand, and the pursuit of profit maximization (Fabre, 2003: 67).

Policies from Where?

In 1975, Kettil Bruun and his co-authors (1975) wrote *The Gentlemen's Club*, which is about a small clutch of powerful men representing both themselves and equally powerful nations. They noted that the concept of power is necessary to an understanding of all international systems (113). While they were discussing a different time and different circumstances, there are, we would argue, parallels with the current situation regarding money laundering and terrorism. As they state:

> The first failure is simply that the goal of eliminating the 'evil,' be it cannabis use, coca-leaf chewing, or the opium habit has not been achieved. It may of course be said that the expression of such as goal is mere rhetoric and idealism, and serves only as a spur to action – that such expressions are no more than political maneuvers. Yet there are those within the establishment in whom an acceptance of tactical necessity is combined with at least a partial commitment to this rhetorical goal, and who are thereby led to subscribe to utterly unrealistic expectations and operations. (274)

When we question the motives that lurk behind policies, it is too easy to take a conspiratorial view that is restricted to a concern with the vested interests of only the key policymakers. As Bruun and co-authors outline above, policies may reflect political manoeuvring, or reflect mere rhetoric and idealism, or a sense of tactical necessity (i.e., something has to be done!), mixed with an actual commitment to the rhetorical goals – however unrealistic those goals might be.

Anti-money-laundering campaigns highlight the effect of internationally driven, non-democratically created policies on Canadian laws, practices, and policies. Issues of accountability are paramount to our understanding of the issues surrounding the responses to money laundering. A relatively small group of policymakers, many of whom worked at one stage at the U.S. FinCEN agency, wield considerable power over this initiative. There is also the very real possibility that Canadian officials *use* the international community as the justification for changes that might prove unacceptable if openly debated within Canada. The vested interests of our own officials may be no more 'pure' than those abroad.

The massive anti-laundering campaign is not a neutral activity; rather, it has been carried out at considerable expense in terms of resources, impact of the sanctions imposed on certain of the more vulnerable nations, and possibly even on the way in which criminals conduct their businesses (while not reducing the amount of crime). Likewise, the global war on terrorist financing is being pursued through a foreign policy approach that places intense pressure on countries around the world – both bilaterally and through multilateral institutions like the FATF, the IMF, and the UN – to stop the funding of various ethnic communities via established charities and to enact laws and regulations that force the private sector to play a role in detecting these 'suspicious' terrorist funds. The difficulty of separating terrorism from non-terrorism purposes, means that nationalities, jurisdictions, or even just appearances can be deemed 'suspicious' along with a growing list of organizations. All wars are waged in the pursuit of the interests of the major combatants, which invariably means that there is 'collateral damage' to lesser players or bystanders.

The U.S.-led war on terrorist financing continues an American legislative and enforcement trend that had begun long before 9/11: a creeping extraterritoriality of American criminal laws. Section 317 of the International Money Laundering Abatement and Anti-Terrorist Financing Act provides U.S. courts with 'long-arm' jurisdiction over foreign persons and foreign financial institutions that commit money laundering acts that take place in the United States, or, in the case of a financial institution, that maintains a bank account at a financial institution in the United States. Section 319 of the Act vests in the Secretary of the Treasury and the Attorney General the power to summon and subpoena records of foreign banks that have correspondent accounts in the United States, and request records relating to such accounts, including records maintained outside the United States relating to the deposit of funds into a foreign bank. Thus, this section provides U.S. authorities with the power to circumvent mutual legal assistance treaties and other procedures dependent on cooperation of foreign governments (Lyden, 2003: 219).

Kirk Munroe (1996: 505) refers to the 'swaggering attitude' and reach of extraterritorial legislation used in the 'wars' against drugs and money laundering (and now terrorism). He cites as an example of this 'reach' the charging and conviction of a Luxembourg bank, with no office in the U.S., that was charged and convicted of money laundering in the U.S. because U.S. dollar cashier's cheques had to be cleared through the Luxembourg bank's correspondent bank in New York City. No one at the Luxembourg bank had been bribed. No one 'knew' the true source of the funds (Colombian drug money) and yet the bank pled guilty based on the 'willful blindness of the account manager' (Munroe, 1996: 522). This early example has been replayed many times over in different jurisdictions. The 2006 controversy over the *New York Times'* articles, outlining the use by the U.S. of the intelligence generated from access to Swift, which consists of data from over 7,800 financial institutions, provides another hint of their surveillance reach into financial matters within foreign jurisdictions in the name of 'fighting terrorism' (Rich, 2006: 10).

Pillar-Talk

Valsamis Mitsilegas (2003) takes the reader though the 'securitization' process that resulted in the European Union's three pillars in the fight against money laundering. These measures constitute what he calls a 'new paradigm of security governance,' which are now integral to the dictates of the Financial Action Task Force. The three pillars are: *criminalization*, consisting in the emergence of new criminal offences; *responsibilization*, consisting in the mobilization of the private sector in the fight against money laundering; and the emphasis on the administration of knowledge via *centralization*, through the establishment of new institutions, the financial intelligence units, with extensive powers to administer a wide range of information provided by the private sector. As we have described in this book, these same changes have become the Canadian approach to 'fighting' money laundering.

Within the past ten years, new laws have been passed, greater mandated 'policing' responsibilities have been assigned to the private sector (banks, businesses, casinos, and so on), and all of this information/intelligence is now supposed to flow into our Financial Transactions and Reports Analysis Centre (FINTRAC) in Ottawa. Rather than an abdication of direct state intervention, this form of responsibilization, with all of the mandated requirements and sanctions to be applied for failure to comply equates to an expanded state role *at the domestic level* – even though new players have been forced into the enforcement game. *Internationally*, the driving forces behind the policies that have the greatest impact on domestic policy are non-state bodies such as the FATF, UN, IMF, and the World Bank.

A tremendous burden has fallen upon the shoulders of the private sector, which is now deputized to combat both money laundering and terrorist financing and, by extension, organized crime, drug trafficking, and terrorism. As such, they have had forced upon them detection and prevention mandates that are deemed critical to the safety and security of the societies in which they operate. This is no small point, given the impossibility of these mandates and the fact that the purpose of the private sector is to generate wealth, not to police criminal activity or play a national security role.

A number of ironies have emerged when considering the efficacy of the anti-money laundering and anti-terrorist financing responsibilities placed on the financial and legal private sectors. First, regarding the financial institutions, the banking and investment systems are structured to efficiently expedite legal and illegal transactions rather than to regulate or prevent them. This burden is being thrust upon the private sector during a time that has seen a number of high-profile cases involving unethical and illegal activity by large corporations, facilitated by our major financial institutions. In other words, private sector organizations now have the mandate to protect society from organized criminals and terrorists during a period when its ability and commitment to regulate and prevent internal malfeasance has been seriously questioned. Under even the best of conditions, assigning private sector institutions, such as financial institutions, enforcement responsibilities traditionally carried out by the state, will predictably encompass numerous limitations. Different institutional cultures, different mandates, the profit-oriented and cost-reduction goals of financial institutions, and, hence, different priorities will obstruct any real compliance with the anti-laundering requirements.

Second, regarding the role of lawyers, Canadian lawyers are free to claim proceeds of crime for their professional fees *and* are exempt from the mandatory reporting requirements. Domestic power politics can be detected in the legislative decisions related to money laundering. These two significant 'inconsistencies' pertaining to the role of lawyers in the national strategy against laundering speak to the power of the legal lobby – and possibly the fact that the Department of Justice policymakers are themselves lawyers. We have discussed both of these issues in this book; however, to emphasize the point, even U.S. lawyers are forbidden to take their professional fees from the proceeds of crime.

In Canada, the principle, *ex turpi causa non oritur action* – the wrong-doer cannot accrue benefit to him/herself through the commission of a crime (Kroeker, 1995: 871) – is argued to be pitted against the right to counsel, and loses. This priority appears to hold even given the 2005 legislation (Bill C-53) that creates a reverse onus mechanism that facilitates even wider confiscation of criminal proceeds. However, whether this is an 'actual' collision of rights is questionable. As Kroeker argues:

> To suggest that the profit earning 'racketeer' has the right to use the proceeds of crime to retain the 'Rolls Royce' of attorneys is offensive when juxtaposed with the fact that a large number of those in conflict with the law must 'settle' for counsel retained on a legal aid basis due to their socio-economic status. (872–3)

He makes it clear that if the argument is that legal aid lawyers are incapable of defending someone charged with sophisticated/ complex laundering schemes, then the legal aid system must be changed, rather than abandoning the fundamental principles of justice.

We have discussed at some length the exception of lawyers from the mandatory reporting of suspicious transactions. This was a long, hard fight by the law societies across Canada and accountability for compliance now rests with those societies. Banks, insurance institutions, the brokers, and so on initially resisted the mandatory reporting regime. Only the lawyers prevailed. As our study of the RCMP launder-ing cases illustrated, lawyers are important, and in some schemes es-sential, partners in money laundering. *If* the government cares about money laundering, the exclusion of lawyers is an aberration. The exclusion of lawyers from mandatory suspicious reporting and the right of defence lawyers to benefit from criminal proceeds throws into question the sincerity of those in government who push the anti-money-laundering initiative.

Looking for the Harm – at What Cost?

Despite its reach into the country's numerous economic sectors, and despite the oft-repeated mantra that 'the infusion of billions of dollars from organized crime into money laundering schemes poses a significant threat to countries on both a micro- and macro-economic level,' (Bell, 2000), there is little empirical evidence that money laundering, *in and of itself*, has any substantial negative repercussions for the Canadian economy or society as a whole. It could even be argued that money laundering has some benefits for society in that at least a portion of the funds are transferred from the underground economy (where they are untaxed) and expended in the legal economy, where the money can contribute to producing legitimate and taxable wealth.

With this said, one cannot look at the impact of money laundering in isolation from the destructive criminal activities from which it is derived. The desire to ensure that criminals do not benefit from their criminality is a valid objective – how realistic it is as a prime enforcement strategy is what is in doubt, and there is even less evidence that criminals will be 'put out of business' via these strategies. While we are not refuting that organized criminal activities like drug trafficking have a serious impact on society, the evidence is less strong that the criminal proceeds derived from these activities pose a significant *additional* harm nor that the limited ability – regardless of the resources used in the effort – to deprive criminals of their profits will reduce the amount of these types of criminal operations. More attention needs to be focused on the laundering of funds derived from those crimes where the money comes directly from the pockets and pensions of the victims. In order to find empirical evidence of direct harm that is derived *exclusively* from money laundering, we must look to the laundering of funds from the large-scale financial frauds, corporate criminal conduct, and political scandals – not the laundering of the more traditional organized crime proceeds.

To the extent that enforcement has any influence on criminal operations, enforcement activities may ensure that criminals remain outside legitimate operations and thus make no positive contribution and,

therefore, only use legitimate businesses to further their criminal operations or to hide their proceeds before moving them elsewhere. In summary: anti-laundering policies and laws are invasive and expensive with
little evidence of success and with numerous and significant 'costs.' A return to a focus on the criminal and his/her criminal activities that resulted
in the illicit proceeds may be the next enforcement shift, with only a secondary attempt to take away the criminal earnings. With adequate and
timely record-keeping in place, these documents may be sufficient to forfeit criminally derived proceeds upon the completion of criminal trials.

Given the dearth of empirical information regarding the impact of
laundering, the size of the laundering operations, or the impact of
enforcement on the laundering operations, one must look for alternative motives or different agendas to explain the international commitment of the network of non-government/inter-government agencies
that meet frequently around the globe to pass their recommendations
and inflict sanctions on non-member states (non-G8 members). The
allure of seized dollars, the political sway over non-compliant states,
and the related focus on fleeing tax dollars or capital flight all make
these anti-laundering campaigns attractive. The international push for
anti-laundering initiatives is also an extension of American hegemony,
which includes forcing U.S. enforcement priorities and strategies on the
international community.

Ten Years of Legislation – What Consequences?

Based upon a longitudinal analysis of money-laundering cases in Canada,
one could argue that deterrence derived from increased security imposed
on transaction reporting within the private sector has failed to materialize. Like organized crime in general, money laundering will continue to
prove to be extremely resilient, adaptive, sophisticated, and resistant to
law enforcement measures. Enforcement ultimately results in the mere
displacement of organized criminal activity, not in its eradication.

While it is widely acknowledged that Canada's Schedule 1 banks have
been at the forefront of anti-money-laundering measures, the results of the
survey of police cases indicate that they are still overwhelmingly used to
launder the proceeds of crime and continue to be the main portal through
which illicit cash finds its way into the legitimate economy.

In one of the few rigorous evaluations of the American CTR system,
Joseph Benning argues, 'although the CTR regime produced a large
quantity of reports, it yielded little useful information' (Benning, 2002),

in part because launderers simply circumvent the reporting threshold by structuring deposits in increments less than $10,000 and also because of the other methods by which money can be moved – simply smuggling the money out of the country being perhaps the easiest. These observations speak volumes about how the doctrine of deterrence is almost irrelevant when applied to chronic offenders and sophisticated, profit-driven organized and entrepreneurial criminals.

One notes that after all of the pressure that was put on countries to replicate the U.S. CTR regime, in September 2005 the U.S. government introduced a bill that would excuse U.S. banks from filing reports for 'seasoned business customers.' 'Seasoned' is defined as having been a customer for twelve months or more. Surely, any capable or serious criminal can devise a way onto this exemption list. Quoting from Steve Bartlett, president and CEO of Financial Services Roundtable,

> To ensure that a seasoned customer exemption is fully utilized, we suggest that it be made automatic: once a customer has had an account opened with a financial institution for twelve months, that customer automatically should be deemed 'seasoned' and the institution accordingly should be exempt from CTR requirements with respect to that customer.[3]

The impact of the enhanced and more punitive enforcement measures that include the seize and freeze laws, transaction reporting legislation, as well as augmented enforcement resources, is reflective of the impact of organized crime enforcement in general: there are measurable successes, but money laundering is a constant and remains largely unencumbered. It would be fair to use a tired cliché that is applicable to all sorts of organized crime enforcement: law enforcement has won some important battles, but it is far from making any significant impact on money laundering or organized crime in general. History clearly demonstrates that early successes in organized crime enforcement are often followed by diminishing returns as criminal entrepreneurs continuously adapt to the increased enforcement efforts.

The ever-increasing preoccupation of governments with the financial aspects of organized and terrorist crimes is not surprising. Attacking the financial power base and the profit-motivated raison d'étre of organized crime represents a common-sense approach that complements other supply-side enforcement tactics. The added bonus is that the forfeited revenue can theoretically accrue to government coffers. How-

ever, it has become clear that the original lofty expectations that preceded the enactment of the seize-and-freeze laws in Canada have never
been realized.

The government predictions – fuelled by an enthusiastic RCMP desir-
ous of additional resources – that saw the upfront costs of the proceeds of
crime units serving to 'prime the pump,' which would gush money into
the government reserve, failed to materialize. At the macro level, the value
of proceeds of crime forfeitures has been modest at best, especially when
compared with the value of seizures. These disappointing results are also
reflected at the global level. Fabre estimates that 'less than one percent of
the 100 billion narco-dollars laundered annually are seized by specialized organizations, which are almost powerless in the face of criminal
groups who are prepared to sacrifice up to 40 percent of their profits to
recycle their gains in the legitimate economy' (2003: 71).

Proceeds of crime enforcement has failed to live up to its expectations
in every jurisdiction. However, in Canada, the importation of this American enforcement philosophy has been further restricted by the emphasis
on due process by the judiciary within the post-Charter era. In other
words, by attacking money laundering through the criminal courts (and
by building in such legislative provisions as allowing criminal defence
lawyers access to seized funds), combined with the inherent secretive
nature of money laundering, the onus of proof that lies on the shoulders
of the Crown creates a significant barrier to forfeiting the accumulated
wealth of organized criminals. What has been most successful in the
United States in combating money laundering and organized criminality
are the civil (forfeiture) sanctions enacted through statutes like RICO,
which shifts at least part of the burden of proof onto the defendant and
creates a lesser legal standard to force an accused to forfeit his/her
assets.

The obstacles that the criminal onus represents to an efficient system
of proceeds of crime enforcement has been recognized through the
ongoing pressure being placed on federal policymakers to introduce
laws that shift the burden of proving seized assets were acquired legitimately onto defendants. While many legal experts have consistently
stated that this reverse onus would never survive a Charter challenge in
Canada (because it abrogates the due process rights of defendants), it
has not stopped law enforcement officials and some parliamentarians
from pursuing this avenue. In 2004, all three opposition parties joined
forces to push through a Bloc Québécois-proposed bill (C-53) that makes
it easier for the Crown to forfeit the proceeds of crime. As we discussed,

this legislation forces defendants to prove that their assets were acquired honestly, a measure that reverses the burden of proof that normally requires the prosecution to make a case of guilt rather than the accused to prove innocence. Even the New Democratic Party, which has long been a strong advocate for the sanctity of due process within the criminal justice system, threw its support behind the bill because, according to NDP MP Joe Comartin, 'it's a logical extension of some of the work we've already done around gangsterism and organized crime' (Tibbetts, 2004: A9).

This infringement on the due process of defendants, according to the Canadian Bar Association, is reflective of the 'invasions of privacy and fundamental rights' that have been 'creeping into Canadian law over the past few years' and which are part of the 'dramatically expanding state powers' that followed the 2001 terrorist attacks on the United States (quoted in Geddes, 2004: 32).

'Fighting' Terrorism

Globalizing the war on terror financing is key to the U.S. terrorist strategy in that much of the funds used to finance political extremism is raised and stored outside of U.S. borders. As part of this international strategy, the United States, through its embassies, has formally approached governments internationally to freeze the assets of individuals and entities designated by the U.S. It has also supported changing national laws, regulations, and regulatory institutions around the world to better combat terrorist finance and money laundering. This has been accomplished, in part, by placing 'pressure on difficult countries via its Non-Cooperating Countries and Territories (NCCT) program, which provides for listing countries that are non-cooperative with respect to internationally accepted anti-money-laundering practices' (Wayne, 2005). Assistant Secretary E. Anthony Wayne acknowledged the quick progress that has been made in ensuring international uniformity in national terrorist financing enforcement standards and laws. His quote makes no mention of the actual *impact* on terrorism:

> ... we have witnessed considerable progress on the part of countries around the world to equip themselves with the instruments they need to clamp down on domestic terrorist financing. Since 9/11, about 90 countries in every region of the world, including the Middle East and South Asia, have either adopted new laws or regulations to fight terrorist financing or

are in the process of doing so ... We have seen substantial progress in securing countries' commitment to strengthen their anti-money laundering laws and regulations, which is inextricably linked to combating the financing of terrorism. In large part due to FATF's focus and our technical assistance and diplomatic pressure, governments pass amendments to improve their ability to combat terrorist financing. (ibid.)

Terrorist financing fundamentally differs from the proceeds of crime in a number of ways, and yet identical anti-money-laundering strategies are being applied to each. These differences are not simply academic; they have significant implications and pose particular challenges for terrorist financing enforcement. The first difference reflects the fundamental distinction between terrorism and organized crime: terrorist financing is ultimately concerned with promoting political, social, and cultural change, while the proceeds of crime represent the culmination of the capital accumulation goal explicit in drug trafficking and other organized criminal activities. Thus, terrorist financing affects at the mass societal level, while the proceeds of crime ostensibly benefits the individual (i.e., the accumulation of wealth by individual criminal entrepreneurs). And while those situated at the top of political extremist groups have been known to siphon off funds for their own personal enrichment, the fact that the funds are not raised for material purposes indicates that terrorist operatives are less concerned with money and more concerned with the end goals of their mission.

Terrorist financing is a means to an end, while the proceeds of crime is an end in itself. Given this, efforts to deprive extremist groups of funding may be inconsequential for at least two reasons. First, as described earlier, terrorist attacks, especially those involving suicide attacks, do not necessarily require large sums of money. Second, members of terrorist groups (especially those willing to sacrifice their lives) are not motivated by personal enrichment, and hence, depriving them of funds may offer little incentive to engage in terrorist activities.

Terrorist financing can also be distinguished from the proceeds of crime in that the former involves funds *to be used in future* criminal activity while the later entails revenues *generated from past criminal activities*. Put another way, terrorist financing is an *input* into the criminal process, while the proceeds of crime is an *output*. This poses an immense challenge to proceeds of crime enforcement, which traditionally focuses on and reacts to criminal outputs (i.e., a criminal event and the proceeds thereof). In general, criminal investigative units spend little time identifying and interdicting criminal inputs or anticipating and preventing future criminal actions. The reactive nature of proceeds of crime enforcement is also a product of the due process and burden of proof requirements of criminal cases: the confiscation of the proceeds of crime through a criminal court can only be affected once there is proof that a defendant has profited from a predicate criminal offence. In short, unlike the proceeds of crime that can be linked to past criminal activities, terrorist financing is much more difficult to identify and characterize as such because the money is an input to criminal actions that have not yet taken place.

In terms of the 'responsibilization' of the private sector in the anti-laundering initiatives, identifying and seizing funds that may be linked to terrorism is even more difficult when those funds are derived from sources that are legitimate and legal (e.g., a charitable donation, earned salary, or investment incomes). While terrorist groups may be involved in criminal activity in order to raise funds, much of their resource base will consist of legitimate non-criminal proceeds. The legal sources for the terrorist funds represents another important distinction with the proceeds of crime, which by definition, are generated from sources that are illegal in nature.

The ability of terrorist groups to capitalize on the global inter-connectivity of the financial services sector illustrates the centrality of the international free market system in helping to finance terrorism. Despite the new terrorism financing laws, despite the creation of new agencies and units, despite the additional funding and unprecedented and intrusive powers provided to these agencies and units, and despite the many accusations that Canada is awash with terrorists and their money, few arrests or seizures of terrorist funds have been made in Canada (or any other country for that matter).

The reaction to the limited enforcement results has been to propose even more intrusive laws. In June 2005, the Department of Finance released a consultation paper on how they would abide by the FATF terrorist financing recommendations, which include increased information collection by the private sector on its clients and the application of criminal sanctions to unlicensed money transmitters. In August of the same year, the Canadian justice minister announced that the federal government would introduce legislation that would give police and national security agencies new powers to eavesdrop on cell-phone calls and monitor the Internet activities of Canadians. The law would force Internet service providers to retain records on the Internet use of its clients in such a way that they could be easily retrieved by police (in some instances without a judicially approved search warrant), doing away with the need in many cases to seize an individual's computer as part of an investigation.

In submission to the government for 2005, Privacy Commissioner Jennifer Stoddart concluded that the federal government and the police have not provided enough justification to warrant such a law. Her reports states: 'We remain skeptical about the need for these potentially intrusive far-reaching measures' (Curry, 2005). The extraordinary powers granted to the federal government through Security Certificates and terrorist financing legislation must be scrutinized given the ethical implications for the human rights of those who fall within the radar of overzealous agencies hunting for terrorists and their financiers. According to William Fisher, critics say the U.S. government's anti-terror-financing campaign is a product of the paranoid Islamophobia that has had its desired effect: to scare Muslim-Americans into abandoning one of the premier tenets of Islam – giving to those in need (Fisher, 2005). Fisher quotes from OMB Watch:

> Once a charitable organization is so designated, all of its materials and property may be seized and its assets frozen. The charity is unable to see the government's evidence and thus understand the basis for the charges. Since its assets are frozen, it lacks resources to mount a defense. And it has only limited right of appeal to the courts. So the government can target a charity, seize its assets, shut it down, obtain indictments against its leaders, but then delay a trial almost indefinitely. (ibid.)

OMB Watch makes the point that Halliburton Corporation (the giant defence contractor with high-level-government connections) has been under investigation by the U.S. Treasury Department and the Department of Justice since 2001 for doing business with Iran, which is listed as a 'sponsor of terrorism.' But rather than seizing and freezing assets 'pending an investigation,' Treasury's Office of Foreign Assets Control (OFAC) and the Department of Justice sent an inquiry to Halliburton requesting 'information with regard to compliance.' After four years of refusal to produce the required documents, the U.S. government took action:

> In Sept. 22, 2005, the Progressive Caucus in the House of Representatives wrote to President George W. Bush, asking that Halliburton be suspended from hurricane relief contracts for a host of reasons, including 'dealing

with nations that sponsor terrorism.' The White House took no action and Halliburton received no-bid contracts valued currently at $61.3 million, and growing ...' (ibid.)

To date, Halliburton has received more than $12 billion in contracts in Iraq, many of them on a no-bid basis. This example, only one of many, serves to justify the scepticism that some of the most vulnerable sectors of the society feel towards the anti-terrorist-financing schemes – that, in fact, they might be nothing but 'schemes.' As Mary Robinson of the UN High Commission for Human Rights noted in December 2001, 'The purpose of anti-terrorism measures is to protect human rights and democracy, not to undermine these fundamental values of our societies' (Robinson, 2001).

These potential and real abuses of civil rights, human rights, and due process rights would not have been tolerated by the courts or the public in August 2001. But, of course, as has been recited ad nauseam, 9/11 changed everything. One of these 'changes' has been the acceptance of aggressive strategies to target funds associated with criminal and politically extremist activity as a means to combat such activity. The 9/11 Commission writes that terrorist financing enforcement has 'had a significant impact on al Qaeda's ability to raise and move funds, on the willingness of donors to give money indiscriminately, and on the international community's understanding of and sensitivity to the issue.' However, the report acknowledges this conclusion is only tentative as 'definitive intelligence is lacking' (National Commission, n.d.: 16).

Therefore, while there are some overlap and commonalities between the proceeds of crime and terrorist funds, significant differences exist. Each involves the use of proceeds – illicit or licit. Each now must launder their funds, either to 'cleanse' them or simply to 'move' them. Each continues to use legitimate businesses and to rely on the formal financial services sector. Also in common is the low 'success rate' of enforcement in both areas. Although supporters will argue that some success has been achieved and that financial enforcement is simply another tool to combat criminal activity and terrorism, this additional tool comes with a very hefty price tag as far as due process rights are concerned.

The Future?

For one seeking to predict how money laundering will be conducted in the future, one simply has to look to the trends that are occurring in the legitimate economy. The increased blurring of the once clearly demarcated sectors of Canada's financial services industry means that criminal entrepreneurs will increasingly use financial service providers, such as insurance companies or brokerage firms, as quasi-deposit institutions.

The globalization of trade and commerce has greatly benefited money laundering and the transfer of illicit capital across national borders and has made the concept of 'offshore financial centres' pointless, since the globalization of financial markets means that all financial markets are 'offshore' (Pratt, 2002: 130). To further complicate matters, while organized crime and money laundering have become increasingly international in scope, and have realized numerous partnerships and intergroup cooperation, law enforcement remains instrumentally bound by local, regional, and national jurisdictions, while international enforcement cooperation and coordination continues to be severely limited. Mechanisms such as Mutual Legal Assistance Treaties (MLATs) remain limited in number, scope, and effectiveness.

The largely unregulated Internet, complete with its multitude of banking and financial intermediary services, will surely be increasingly used for laundering purposes. The underground *hawala* system that provides services to many jurisdictions will continue to accommodate the financial transactions associated with anyone seeking to avoid transaction reporting. These informal systems are essential in many parts of the world for absolutely legitimate financial transactions – often where there is no alternative 'formal' financial infrastructure or segments of the populations have no access to it, if it does exist. One must acknowledge, however, that the same routes can be used to move criminal proceeds, evade taxes, or fund terrorist activities.

One should also anticipate an increase in internal conspiracies and corruption within the financial services industry and other sectors that are mandated to report suspicious transactions, as organized criminals attempt to circumvent such laws. Thus, like the so-called war on drugs, one of the repercussions of augmented anti-money-laundering laws will be increased corruption. Like the battle against drug trafficking, transnational organized crime, and money laundering, a central pillar of the American government's foreign policy on terrorist financing is to ensure other countries adopt made-in-America policies, priorities, and approaches, which are characterized by a punitiveness, extreme sanctions, and an increasing disregard for due process. And while a tough enforcement approach may be needed to combat violent criminality, there appears to be little effort and an absence of political willingness to address the underlying causes.

Other than the rhetoric of various successes, no evidence can link the enforced new policies and legal enhancements to an expectation of greater security. At the very least, there is an urgent need for empirical research – as well as more reliable strategic and tactical intelligence – to determine whether *any* policy that prioritizes the targeting of funding has any likelihood of enhancing security or reducing crime.

Greater care must be taken to ensure that laws be enforceable before they are introduced. Louder, more united voices must demand that a priority be put on protecting rights. If all political parties wish to stand behind 'get-tough' policies, then they should vote for adequate funds for both traditional law enforcement *and* a viable legal aid system. Finally, Canadian sovereignty should continue to include 'made-in-Canada' laws, policies, and enforcement practices.

Notes

Preface

1 United Nations, Office on Drugs and Crime (n.d.), 'The Money Laundering Cycle,' retrieved November 2005 from www.undoc.org/undoc/
money_laundering_cycle.html.

1. Canadian Money-Laundering History

1 Catherine Wismer (1980); *Hamilton Spectator* (1970), 'The Family that
Works Together Can Sometimes Kill Together?' 6 June; *Hamilton Spectator*
(1974), 'Hamilton Men at Crime Summit: Shulman,' 20 November; Peter
Moon (1971: 9).
2 The CBC programs, aired June 1977, became the subject of libel suits and
the tapes have since been pulled from archives and libraries.
3 William Marsden, 'How Canadian Banks Are Used to "Launder" Narcotics Millions: Cash Floods Bahamas Branches,' *Montreal Gazette*, 21 December 1985: A1; 'Why a Drug Dealer Needs a Friendly Bank,' *Montreal
Gazette*, 23 December 1985: A1; and 'Scotia Bank stonewalled U.S. Drug
Smuggling Probes,' *Montreal Gazette*, 24 December 1985: A4.
4 Canada, Department of Finance (2005b), *Year Five Evaluation of the National
Initiatives to Combat Money Laundering and Interim Evaluation of Measures to
Combat Terrorist Financing: Objectives of the Act*, retrieved 7 June 2006 from
www.fin.gc.ca/activity/pubs/nicml-incba_1e.html#Executive.
5 Canada, Department of Finance (2005b), *Year Five Evaluation of the National
Initiatives to Combat Money Laundering and Interim Evaluation of Measures
to Combat Terrorist Financing: Appendix B*, retrieved 7 June 2006 from
www.fin.gc.ca/activity/pubs/nicml-incba_3e.html#AppB.

6 Canada, Department of Finance (2005b), *Year Five Evaluation of the National Initiatives to Combat Money Laundering and Interim Evaluation of Measures to Combat Terrorist Financing: Executive Summary, Background*, retrieved 7 June 2006 from www.fin.gc.ca/activity/pubs/nicml-incba_3e.html #Background.

2. The Evil that Dirty Money Does

1 Jimmy Buffett, 'A Pirate Looks at Forty,' *Jimmy Buffett's Greatest Hits*, lyrics by Jimmy Buffett 1974, MCA [CD].
2 See works listed in the bibliography by Tom Naylor, Petrus Van Duyne, Michael Levi, Margaret Beare, Nigel Morris-Cotterill, John Braithwaite, and Brent Fisse and David Fraser.
3 These designations are somewhat arbitrary – 'dirty money in' means criminal proceeds used to buy into the business. 'Clean money out' merely means that the profits are earned in a legitimate (although possibly exploitive) business. Clean in this sense does not mean 'laundered.'
4 See Peter Lupsha (1981), 'Individual Choice, Material Culture, and Organized Crime.' He rejected these claims and saw instead that certain individuals or groups 'chose' the criminal route because it was seen to be more exciting, had more potential for quick wealth, and appeared to be relatively easy.
5 Chicago Crime Commission, 'Spotlight on Legitimate Business and the Hoods – Part II,' in 'Remarks of Senators Charles Percy,' *Congressional Record*, vol. 114 (June 24, 1968), 18354–18356, cited in Jester (1974), 14.
6 New Jersey Public Hearing, 'Statutory and Regulatory Controls over Casino Credit and Casino Industry Credit Practices,' Trenton, NJ, 1–4 March 1983, 8. See also the prepared statement by Lt. Col Justin Dintino, 3–4. The concept of a 'mutual exploitive' relationship was first introduced by J. Dintino and F. Martens in 1983.
7 G. Robert Blakey (1998), 'Inside the Tobacco Deal,' interview with G. Robert Blakey, *Frontline Online*, retrieved December 2005 from www.pbs.org/wgbh/pages/frontline/shows/settlement/interviews/blakey.html.
8 G. Robert Blakey (1998), 'Amway Expert Opinion Report,' *The Procter & Gamble Company, et al. v. Amway Corporation, et al.*, Case No. H-9723 84 (S.D. Texas, Houston Division), retrieved December 2005 from www.ratbags.com/rsoles/comment/amwayblakeyreport.htm.
9 See, for example, FinCEN's website http://www.treas.gov/FinCEN/af_faqs.html#problem. See also J. McDowell and G. Novis (2001), available online from http://usinfo.state.gov/journals/ites/0501/ijee/state1.htm.

10 I am indebted to the following students of the Osgoode Hall Law School course International Criminal Law and Regulation, Part II (Summer 2002) whose research was drawn upon extensively in this chapter. Amy Barkin; Carol-Ann Bauman; Michael Brown; Paul Burstein; David Carruthers; Stacey Christ; Chris Chorney; Louisa Collins; Steve Coroza; Joseph DiLuca; C.E. John Ecclestone; Clara Greco; Aston J. Hall; John Hanbidge; Peter Harte; William Hewitson; Antoine Issa; Leo Kinalan; William Lightfoot; David Muttart; Patricia Neal; Alfred O'Marra; Joanna Opalinski; Jennifer Katrina Penman; Steven Scharger; Elaine Strosberg; Cara Sweeny; and Leane Towsend.

11 See Financial Action Task Force (n.d.), *More About the FATF and Its Work*, retrieved 30 May 2006 from www1.oecd.org/fatf/AboutFATF_en.html.

12 See David Scott (1995). See also Financial Action Task Force (n.d.), *More About the FATF and Its Work*.

13 Attempts to find out the 'costs' of a country's participation in FATF were unsuccessful. Numerous officials fly several times per year to fairly exotic locations for their meetings and then have other officials/bureaucrats meet to respond to the demands of the FATF in terms of the collection of information and the pressuring for new legislation.

14 Personal correspondence with New Zealand produced a good attempt at determining the number of days that senior NZ government officials would spend at FATF-related meetings per year: two delegates (although sometimes three or four) each spend a minimum of five days at each of five annual meetings, plus preparation and secretarial-type duties.

15 Financial Action Task Force (2005) *55 Jurisdictions Agree to Fight Money Laundering*, retrieved August 2005 from www.fatf-gafi.org/dataoecd/41/27/34988026.pdf.

16 Financial Action Task Force (2005b), *55 Jurisdictions Agree to Fight Money Laundering*, retrieved 16 June 2006 from www.fatf-gafi.org/dataoecd/41/27/34988026.pdf.

17 FATF, *More About the FATF and Its Work*.

18 Foreword by the FATF president in FATF (2005a), *Annual Report 2004-2005*, 4, retrieved August 2005 from www.fatf-gafi.org/dataoecd/41/25/34988062.pdf.

19 Ibid.

20 At its second meeting (in November 1996), the Egmont Group established the following standard definition of a Financial Intelligence Unit: 'A FIU is a central, national agency responsible for receiving (and, as permitted) requesting, analyzing and disseminating to the competent authorities, disclosures of financial information: (1) Concerning suspected proceeds of crime, or (2) Required by national legislation or regulation, in order to

counter money laundering.' During the Egmont Group annual plenary meeting in Monaco, 6–7 June 2002, Canada joined the Egmont Group of FIUs.

21 Egmont Group (2006), *Financial Intelligence Units of the World*, retrieved December 2006 from www.egmontgroup.org/list_of_fius.pdf.

22 FinCEN (2003), *FinCEN Follows the Money*, retrieved 1 June 2006 from www.fincen.gov/followme.pdf.

23 See Financial Action Task Force web site at www1.oecd.org/fatf; and also *FATF-IX Annual Report 1997–98*, ss.37–40, available online from www.treas.gov/FinCEN/pub_external_reports.html.

24 Ibid. For a thorough review of FINTRAC and the new provisions of Bill C-22, see Karen Hauser (2001), 'New Money Laundering Legislation: Will You Be Compliant?'

25 Steve Coroza (2002), 'Money Laundering and Canada (FIUs – FINTRAC).' See note 10.

26 See the PCML&TFA, specifically sections 54(d), 54(c), 55(3), 55(7), and 56.

27 See United Nations Office of Drugs and Crime Prevention, retrieved 30 May 2006 from www.odccp.org/organized_crime.html.

28 Council of Europe (n.d.), *Greater and Smaller Europe: An Overview*, available online at www.coe.int/T/E/Communication-and-research/Contacts-with-the-public/.

29 Council of Europe (1990), *Convention on Laundering, Search, Seizure and Confiscation of the Proceeds From Crime*, retrieved 30 May 2006 from www.conventions.coe.int/Treaty/en/Treaties/Html/141.htm. European Committee on Crime Problems Select Committee of Experts on the Evaluation of Anti-Money Laundering Measures (March 21, 2002), *A Review of the Anti-Money Laundering Systems in 22 Council of Europe Member States 1998–2001*, 2. The work has continued through conferences and seminars with new member states.

30 William Drozdiak (2001), 'An Anxious Countdown to New Cash,' A1.

31 For the FATF/IMF's estimates see the address by Michael Camdessus (February 10, 1998), 'Money Laundering: The Importance of International Countermeasures,' retrieved 30 May 2006 from www.imf.org/external/np/speeches/1998/021098.htm. He claims that '2–5% of GDP would be a consensus range' for the amount laundered globally. This number is not attributed to any study. For the Quirk estimate, see Peter Quirk (1997) 'Money Laundering: Muddying the Macroeconomy,' in which he refers to his other paper, 'Macroeconomic Implications of Money Laundering,' IMF Working Paper 96/99 (1999). The Walker estimate is quoted in John Walker (2002b), *Modeling Global Money Laundering Flows*.

32 Affidavit of R. Lalonde, quoted in the Ontario Superior Court of Justice, Federation of Law Societies of Canada and the Attorney General of Canada, 9 January 2002, Court File No. 01-CV-222041, quoted in Paul Burstein (2002), 'Federation of Law Societies of Canada v. Canada.' See note 10.

33 Address by Michel Camdessus, 'Money Laundering: The Importance of International Countermeasures,' presented at the IMF, Paris 10 February 1998, retrieved 16 June 2006 from www.img.org/external/np/speeches/ 1998/021098.htm.

34 See ODCCP website at www.odccp.org/money_laundering.html.

35 IMF (2001b), 'Financial System Abuse, Financial Crime and Money Laundering – IMF Background Paper, 10, quoted in Michael Brown (2002), 'Money Laundering Research Report: FATF – Financial Action Task Force on Money Laundering,' 6. See note 10.

36 IMF (2001b), Financial System Abuse, Financial Crime and Money Laundering, 10, quoted in Elaine Strossberg (2002), 'International Monetary Fund.' See note 10.

37 Financial Action Task Force (1990), FATF-I Annual Report 1990, 6, quoted in DiLuca (2002: 13).

38 IMF (2001e), Financial System Abuse, Financial Crime and Money Laundering – IMF Background Paper, 10, quoted in Brown, 'Money Laundering Research Report,' 6–7.

39 These reports are available on FinCEN's website www.treas.gov/ FinCEN/pub_external_reports.html.

40 For example, in its online FAQ section, FinCEN admits that 'many believe that it is simply not possible to pinpoint the amount [of money laundering].' But it maintains that 'the problem is serious' and that 'the profits of crime that creep into the United States' financial system each year are staggering and detrimental by any calculation. Drug trafficking alone generates tens of billions of dollars a year.' See www.treas.gov/FinCEN/ af_faqs.html.

41 See FinCEN, www.treas.gov/FinCEN/fininfosources.html.

42 See FinCEN (2000b), The National Money Laundering Strategy for 2000, 79 (the report was co-released by the U.S. Treasury Department and the Attorney General) and FinCEN (2000a), FinCEN's 2000-2005 Strategic Plan, 12–13.

43 E-mail communication between Ms Solongo and Jennifer Katrina Penman, quoted in Jennifer K. Penman (2002), 'United Nations and Money Laundering,' 6–7. See note 10.

44 J. Walker (2000a), Foreword to AUSTRAC – Estimates of the Extent of Money

Laundering In and Throughout Australia quoted in David Carruthers (2002, 'Money Laundering Down Under,' 3). See note 10.

45 J. Walker (2000a), *Estimates of the Extent of Money Laundering In and Throughout Australia*, chap. 13, summary and conclusions.

46 Quoted in Carruthers (2002: 6), 'Money Laundering Down Under.'

47 John Walker (Nov. 30, 1998), *Proposed Methodology for Estimating Global Money Laundering*, retrieved August 2005 from www.uplink.com.au/ lawlibrary/Documents/Docs/Doc50.html, and quoted in Penman (2002: 9), 'United Nations and Money Laundering.'

48 John Walker (1999), 'Measuring the Extent of International Crime and Money Laundering,' 13–14, 15–16, available online at www.members .ozemail.com.au/~born1820/Budapest.html. It is interesting to note how difficult it is to get figures with regard to how much is laundered in such classic bank-secrecy jurisdictions as Luxembourg, Hungary, Switzerland, and the Cayman Islands.

49 J. Walker (2000b), *'Modeling Global Money Laundering Flows: Some Findings.'* For this part of the model, Walker notes that the index of attractiveness to money launderers is 'scored based on a very simple formula derived from publicly available information and the researchers' own intuition as to the relative importance of the various factors, most of the country rankings appear to be quite logical' (7).

50 *Canadian Press Newswire* (1997), 'Canada Looks Good to Money Launderers: Police,' 15 July.

51 From RCMP's 13 April 2004, *Money Laundering: Impact of Money Laundering on Society*, available online at www.rcmp-grc.ca/html/launder.htm.

52 Quoted in Daniel P. Murphy, *Canada's Anti Money Laundering Regime*, 'Analysis of RCMP Proceeds of Crime Units and Similar Joint Police Force Policing Operations Nationally.' Resource Material Series No. 58 pp. 286– 302. www.unakei.or.sp/english/pdf/PDF_ms/no58/58-23.pdf.

53 IMF (2001d), *Public Information Notice: IMF Executive Board Discusses Money Laundering*; FinCEN (1998), *1997–2002 Strategic Plan*, 3, available online at www.treas.gov/FinCEN/pub_FinCEN_reports.html. See also FinCEN (2000), *The National Money Laundering Strategy for 2000*. The State Department site makes it clear that the integrity of financial institutions of whole nations are at risk. See FinCEN (2001), *International Narcotics Control Strategy Report*, available online at www.state.gov/g/inl/rls/nrcrpt/2000/959.htm.

54 *FinCEN* (2000a), *2000–2005 Strategic Plan*, quoting Deputy Secretary of the Treasury Stuart Eizenstat.

55 See Michael Camdessus (1998), address to the Plenary Meeting, 10 February 1998.

56 Walker (2000a). No evidence to support the validity of this claim is provided.

57 'ODCCP Counters Money Laundering,' Press Release provided to Jennifer Katrina Penman (2002), 'United Nations and Money Laundering,' in e-mail exchange with Ms Solongo.

58 FinCEN (1998), *1997–2002 Strategic Plan.*

59 See United Nations, 'Political Declaration and Action Plan Against Money Laundering,' adopted at the 20th special session of the general Assembly at New York, 10 July 1998 under the heading 'Countering Money Laundering.'

60 See FinCEN (1998), *1997–2002 Strategic Plan*, 5. See also the U.S. Department of State (2000), *International Narcotics Control Strategy Report*, available online from www.state.gov/g/inl/rls/nrcrpt/2000/959.htm.

61 FATF quoted in FinCEN (1998), *FinCEN Advisory* 1(4): 13.

62 FinCEN (2000a), *2000–2005 Strategic Plan*, 1.

63 See FinCEN (2003), *FinCEN Follows the Money.*

64 See, for example, FATF (1998), *FATF-IX Annual Report, 1997–98*, available through the FinCEN website at www.treas.gov/FinCEN/pub_external _reports.html.

65 E-mail communication between Ms Solongo and Jennifer Katrina Penman, quoted in Penman (2002: 16), 'United Nations and Money Laundering.'

66 See UN Global Program Against Money Laundering at www.imolin.org, retrieved 31 May 2006.

67 J. Walker (2000b), *Modeling Global Money Laundering Flows*. Retrieved 10 August 2004 from www.ozemail.com.au/~born1820/mlmethod.htm. Two additional charts illustrate the misplaced focus on 'offshore' laundering islands: 'Top 20 Destinations of Laundered Money' and the 'Top 20 Origins of Laundered Money.'

68 Hungary was also blacklisted by the FATF in the early 1990s as a bank haven attractive to money launderers. To remove itself from the blacklist, Hungary had to introduce anti-money-laundering legislation – partly a response to the 9/11 crackdown on Terrorism (9/11 being used as an excuse to increase surveillance). See John Horvath (2002: 2–3), *Big Brother Is Back*, retrieved 30 May 2006 from www.towardfreedom.com/ mar02bigbro.htm.

69 See Beare (2001: 13–14). Anti-money-laundering efforts have also been seen to have a taxation component. For example, FinCEN is starting to concede that one reason for its intrusive data gathering is to combat tax evasion. See FinCEN online from www.treas.gov/FinCEN/af_faqs.html. See also Beare (2002).

70 See FinCEN online from www.treas.gov/FinCEN/int_fius.html.

71 See FinCEN online from www.treas.gov/FinCEN/int_fius.html. See also
   the U.S. State Department (2000), *International Narcotics Control Strategy
   Report*, online from www.state.gov/g/inl/rls/nrcrpt/2000/959.htm:
   'Overall anti-money laundering efforts in the year 2000 made progress
   across two broad fronts. The international community demonstrated its
   resolve to confront money laundering by showing a strong commitment to
   work collectively to address the problem while seeking to isolate those
   countries and jurisdictions that lack this commitment. In this regard, the
   year 2000 marked a milestone in international cooperation on fighting
   money laundering as the Financial Action Task Force (FATF) publicly
   released a list of 15 countries and territories that were found to be non-
   cooperative in the international fight against money laundering. At the
   conclusion of its June 2000 plenary meeting, the FATF published a report
   that stated that these countries and territories had "serious systemic
   problems with money laundering controls and that they must improve
   their rules and practices as expeditiously as possible of face possible
   sanctions." Following publication of this report, the United States, its G-7
   partners and other FATF members issued advisories, notices or other
   various communications alerting the financial institutions in their countries about the money laundering risks they face in the "non-cooperating"
   jurisdictions.' Quoted in David Muttart (2002), 'The Case of the Tentative
   Trillion.' See note 10.
72 The acting deputy assistant secretary, enforcement policy, of the U.S.
   Department of Treasury wrote: 'Another, more controversial initiative that
   FATF has developed to enhance international cooperation is publication of
   a list of non-cooperative countries and territories (NCT) – jurisdictions
   that lack a commitment to fight money laundering.' Following the June
   2000 publication of the first such list, a number of the fifteen NCCT jurisdictions have acted quickly to implement FATF standards. See J. Myers
   (2001), 'International Standards and Cooperation in the Fight Against
   Money Laundering,' retrieved 30 May 2006 from http://usinfo.state.gov/
   journals/ites/0501/ijee/treasury.htm.
73 Juan G. Ronderos (2002), 'The War on Drugs and the Military: The Case of
   Colombia.' See also P. Knox (2002a), 'War Without End, Amen,' *Globe and
   Mail*, 24 May: A17, and P. Knox (2002b), 'Hardliner Sweeps Colombian
   Election,' *Globe and Mail*, 27 May: A10.
74 'By filing these forms, financial institutions aid law enforcement authorities in the fight against money laundering. These forms also impose real
   costs on these institutions and on legitimate customers. FinCEN estimated

that reporting and record-keeping costs associated with BSA compliance in 1999 totaled $109 million, which does not include the costs of training and monitoring personnel, modifying computer programs to enable compliance, and inconveniencing legitimate customers. There is also concern that a disproportionate share of these costs may fall on smaller institutions.' P. Bauer (2001), 'Understanding the Wash Cycle,' retrieved 31 May 2006 from http://usinfo.state.gov/journals/ites/0501/ijee/clevelandfed.htm. The article contains a useful history of U.S. anti-money-laundering legislation.

75 A.T. Vitale (2001), 'U.S. Banking: An Industry's View on Money Launder-ing,' retrieved 31 May 2006 from http://usinfo.state.gov/journals/ites/0501/ijee/vitale.htm. Beare is quoted as noting problems with reliance on banking/financial institutions to conduct anti-money laundering enforce-ment tasks: 'Front-line banking officials are not 'police' officers. A finan-cial institution's objectives are to attract customers and make profits. Unless we were to alter our understanding of how banks operate, inten-sive training in ML plus an incentive/promotional system internal to the banks must be put in place to reward those bank officials who detect the suspicious customers that result in 'positive' referrals to the police.' Quoted in Leane Towsend (2002: 15), 'Financial Institutions and Their Fight against Money Laundering.' See note 10.

76 See G.R. Chaddock (2001), 'How Authorities Will Be Monitoring Your Money,' retrieved 31 May 2006 from www.csmonitor.com/2001/1026/p3s1-uspo.html; V de Rugy (2001), 'Privacy Punished, Not Terrorism,' retrieved 31 May 2006 from www.cato.org/dailys/10-26-01.html.

77 In correspondence between David Muttart and J. Byrne, senior counsel and compliance manager of the ABA, Byrne advised that he was unsure of where the number came from: 'We have never offered such statistics.' The only reliable figure for the annual cost to the banking industry that Byrne was aware of was $109 million.

78 Exhibit 18 to Affidavit of R. Lalonde, p. 1620, quoted in Paul J. Burstein (2002: 18), 'Federation of Law Societies of Canada v. Canada.' See note 10.

79 Naylor (2002), *Wages of Crime*, quoted in Aston J. Hall (2002: 11–12), 'International Criminal Law and Regulation.' See note 10.

3. Money-Laundering Cases

1 Pierre Tremblay and Richard Kedzier (1986: 7), 'Analyzing the Organiza-tion of Crime in Montreal 1920, to 1980: A Canadian Test Case.' The

examples of money laundering included in this study are therefore skewed towards those that have been identified and investigated by the POC Sections and the IPOC Units. As such, this study must be viewed as an analysis of money laundering as filtered through the enforcement priorities and capacities of the police, and the RCMP in particular.

2 The limitations inherent in examining money laundering, combined with the problems encountered with the sampling methodology employed for this study, may adversely affect the reliability and universality of the research findings. With that said, however, the findings do parallel those of past studies into money laundering in Canada. See, for example, Rod Stamler and Robert Fahlman (1983); Gary Lamphier (1986); Bruce Bowie (1988); Margaret Beare and Stephen Schneider (1990); Mario Possamai (1992); Canada, Department of Justice and Solicitor General Canada (1998).

3 Criminal Code of Canada, R.S., 1985, c. 42 (4th Supp.), s. 462.3 and s. 462.31; Controlled Drugs and Substances Act, R.S. 1996, c. 19, s. 8 and 2. 9; Customs Act, R.S., 1985, c. 1 (2nd Supp.), s. 163.1 and s. 163.2; Excise Act R.S 1985, c. E-14, s. 126.1 and s. 126.2.

4 While most POC cases examined for this study were concluded by 1998, some investigations were concluded in 2000.

5 The Expert Witness Program includes members of the RCMP, as well as provincial and municipal police agencies assigned to the Integrated Proceeds of Crime Units, who caredesignated as experts in money laundering for court purposes.

6 Theft or fraud offences are considered a lower priority for POC investigations, which explains why, statistically, there are only a few POC cases where these offences constituted the source of the criminal proceeds.

7 This figure is skewed upward because included in the random sample were at least ten cases involving undercover currency exchange companies set up by police.

8 For the purposes of this study, the definition of a deposit institution is taken from that of the Federal Office of the Superintendent of Financial Institutions, and includes Schedule 1 and 2 chartered banks, trust companies, loan investment companies, and cooperative credit societies (credit unions and caisse populaires). Schedule 1 banks are those that have been incorporated in Canada. Schedule 2 are subsidiaries of foreign banks.

9 *Vancouver Sun* (2002), 'Brand-new Homes Used to Grow Pot, RCMP Claim: Upscale Surrey Houses Are Then Sold to "Launder" Cash.' 9 October: A1; *Vancouver Sun* (2002), 'Surrey Bunker Used for Growing Pot: First One Discovered in Underground Shelter,' 9 October: A3.

10 *New York Times* (1990), 'Racketeering Held to Persist at New York's Fish Market,' 9 August: B12. The era of corruption at the fish market may not end, but will be at least temporarily disrupted when the Fulton Fish Market moves to the Bronx during the Summer of 2005. *New York Times* (2005), 10 July.

11 Neal Hall (1996), 'Charges Follow Massive Hashish Seizure: Counts Laid against Four Vancouver Residents and Nearly a Dozen Companies,' *Vancouver Sun*, 10 January: A2; Neal Hall (1997a), 'Lawyer Acquitted of Money-laundering: Judge Accepts Vancouver Man's testimony He Didn't Know Client's $8 Million Came from Drugs,' *Vancouver Sun*, 18 April: B3; Neal Hall (1997b), 'B.C. Bust Ended One of World's Biggest Drug Empires,' *Vancouver Sun*, 26 April: A1.

12 See, for example, Alan Phillips (1963a), 'The Inner Workings of the Crime Cartel,' *MacLean's*, 5 October: 72; Alan Phillips (1963b), 'Organized Crime's Grip on Ontario,' *MacLean's*, 21 September: 58; Peter Edwards (1990: 72); Walter (1971: 1–6); Quebec Police Commission Inquiry on Organized Crime (1977: 148).

13 'Caller Says BioChem Animal Rights Target: But Expert Suggests Tuesday's Bombings Were Too Sophisticated for Animal Liberation Front,' *Financial Post*, 28 November 1997: 4.

14 *Financial Post*, 27 May 1998.

15 *Vancouver Sun*, 26 April 1997.

16 *Business Week*, 'The Mob on Wall Street,' 16 December 1996: 92–3.

17 Several papers covered this story, see, for example, Knight Ridder/Tribune Business News, 17 June 1999; *Globe and Mail*, 17 June 1999; Dow Jones News Service, 2 July 1999; Associated Press, 2 March 2000.

18 *Canadian Business*, 15 November 2002.

19 The FATF defines derivatives as securities with no intrinsic value but which derive their value from an underlying financial instrument or asset. The three primary types of derivative contracts are forward contracts, futures, and options. The report says the instruments 'in simple terms, are contracts sold as a hedge against the future risk of fluctuations in commodity prices, time differentials, interest rates, tax rates, foreign exchange rates, etc.' (FATF, 1999: 19).

20 *Globe and Mail* (1999), 'Russian Mob Set Up YBM Office with Stolen Goods, Sold Weapons. Court Documents also Cite Money Laundering,' 21 December.

21 *National Post* (1999), 'YBM Was Urged to Consider Liquidation – Then Raised $100 Million – Warned of "Lack of Inventory," Possible "Cooked Books,"' 10 December: C1.

22 *Globe and Mail* (1999), 'Russian Mob Set Up YBM Office ...'
23 *Globe and Mail* (2001), 'YBM Officers Pocketed Millions, U.S. Says,' 26 April.
24 *Globe and Mail* (1999), 'Mob Boss Picked Canadian Exchanges for YBM Scam. Court Told Russian Selected Canada for Alleged Money-Laundering Plan because He Thought Market Had Lax Rules,' 8 June.
25 Background research conducted for Beare and Schneider (1990).
26 Ibid.
27 *United Press International*, 23 December 1999; *Chicago Sun-Times*, 13 December 1999.
28 To counter this laundering technique, some casinos have enacted a policy that gamblers purchasing chips with a large amounts to cash will be provided the same cash back when cashing in their chips.
29 *New York Times* (2000), 'Police Search the Cash Boxes of Betting Clerks for Evidence of Money Laundering,' 29 September.
30 *Times* (London) (2000), 'Cleaning Up Filthy Lucre – Money Laundering – Investigation,' 30 March.
31 *Times* (London) (2000), 'Racing: Concern Over Money Laundering,' 24 October.
32 The number of cases where automobile dealerships came into contact with the proceeds of crime is most likely underestimated. The RCMP case files often had little information as to where cars were purchased.
33 See *Lavallee, Rackel and Heintz v. AG Canada* [2000] A.J. No. 159 (C.A.) 143 C.C.C. (3d) 187.
34 *Globe and Mail* (1995), 'Lawyer Jailed for 13 Years,' 30 June: A2.
35 *Vancouver Sun* (1997), 'Lawyer Acquitted of Money-Laundering: Judge Accepts Vancouver Man's Testimony He Didn't Know Client's $8 Million Came From Drugs,' 18 April: B3.
36 *Montreal Gazette* (2002), '"Hells" Bought Cocaine in Bulk,' 18 July: A4; *Globe and Mail* (2002), 'Judges Win New Rules after Failed Biker Trial,' 12 August.

4. Enforcement

1 *Toronto Star* (1988), 'Police Set to Seize Drug Assets Bonanza,' 4 December: A19.
2 The Access to Information process involved a two-year-long delay while we waited for the Department of the Solicitor General and other government officials to produce the documents. These evaluation documents were originally intended to be public documents that would serve to

provide the public and wider policymakers with empirical information pertaining to organized crime and the enforcement of money laundering.

3 See M.E. Beare (1996) for a fuller discussion of recognized limitations in other jurisdictions that prompted a similar search for broader seizure powers.

4 Fraud and other white-collar crime offences, which are prosecuted provincially, received a very low priority among the new units. This was due in part to the reluctance of provincial governments to prosecute proceeds of crime offences, due to the 'under-taking' provision of the 1989 legislation, which requires that the federal or provincial government with jurisdiction over a particular case guarantee any assets seized by the police. This means that if the courts order the asset returned to the owner, the government must pay any damages. Another reason why so few proceeds of crime investigations have been conducted into fraud or theft cases is that, unlike drug-trafficking cases, the former often have a victim, which means that forfeited assets accrue to the victim and not to government coffers.

5 Project Eyespy was in fact an undercover sting operation, whereby the Vancouver IADP Section operated a bogus currency exchange business. This undercover operation generated a number of separate proceeds of crime and drug investigations. Project Exceed was a multidefendant investigation that targeted hundreds of millions of dollars generated from an ongoing hashish importation conspiracy in British Columbia.

6 *Chronicle-Herald* (Halifax) (2002), 'Police Made $160-million Coke Bust on Eastern Coast of Cape Breton – RCMP,' 15 July; *Ottawa Citizen* (2003), 'Police Raid $20M Ecstasy Operation: One of the Largest Busts Involving the Drug in Canadian history. Chemicals Could Have Produced a Million Pills,' 8 January: C1; *Globe and Mail* (2003),'Canada's Drug War a Bust, Study Says. Fund Treatment Instead, Researchers Urge,' 21 January: A2; 'High-Seas Takedown Nets 1.5 Tons Cocaine and Five Local Arrests,' *RCMP Press Release*, 21 May 2003; 'CCRA and RCMP Seize Record Amount of Ecstasy,' *Canada Customs News Release*, 11 December 2003.

7 The increase in predatory, victim-based criminal activities poses a particular challenge to the Proceeds of Crime Sections. The sections have long avoided investigating fraud, in part because few provincial governments, which have jurisdiction over prosecuting Criminal Code-based predatory crimes, have committed any prosecutorial resources to proceeds of crime cases. Indeed, the survey of RCMP proceeds of crime cases indicated that of the 149 cases examined, theft and fraud accounted for only 11 (7.4 per cent) of all the predicate offences.

8 Charles Levendosky (1999), 'Civil Forfeiture Laws Have Turned Police into Pirates,' *New York Times*, 14 July; R.T. Naylor (2000a), 'Civil Forfeiture in the U.S. Led to Police Profiteering and the Miscarriage of Justice. Do We Want that Here?' *Globe and Mail*, 29 August; Marian R. Williams (2002: 321–9); Margaret Beare (1992).

9 Solicitor General Canada, Press Release, 28 August 1996.

10 Canada, Parliamentary Debates (Hansard), 37th Parliament, 2nd Session, no. 066 (February 24, 2003), retrieved 31 May 2006 from www.parl.gc.ca/37/2/parlbus/chambus/house/debates/066_2003-02-24/han066_1440-e.htm.

11 Lindsay Kines (1996), 'Business People Laundered Cash: Police Said the "Main Player" for the Companies Will Be Arrested Shortly,' *Vancouver Sun*, 26 January: B3; *Edmonton Journal* (1996), 'Mounties' Sting Store Laundered Drug Money,' 25 January: A1; Janet Steffenhagen (1996), 'Police Sting Operation Bags 120 for Drugs, Money-Laundering,' *Montreal Gazette*, 25 January: A12; Andy Ivens (1996), 'Police Spring Trap in Massive Drug Sting,' *Vancouver Province*, 25 January: A5.

12 William Marsden and Geoff Baker (1994), 'RCMP Traces Cash in Huge Money-Laundering Case,' *Montreal Gazette*, 16 October: A1; Geoff Baker (1995), 'Lawyer Handed 13-year Prison Sentence for Overseeing Money-Laundering Scheme,' *Montreal Gazette*, 30 June: A4; *Globe and Mail* (1995), 'Lawyer Jailed for 13 years,' 30 June: A2. For a thorough discussion on the Rizzuto family, see Lamothe and Humphreys (2006).

13 Canada, Parliamentary Debates (Hansard), 37th Parliament, 2nd Session, no. 066 (24 February 2003).

14 See U.S. Senate Committee on the Judiciary, Subcommittee on Criminal Laws and Procedures (1978); Jay Albanese (1982); Margaret Beare (1996); Stephen Mastrofski and Gary Potter (1987); Embassy of Colombia (1998); Kathryn Meyer and Terry M. Parssinen (1998); Donald Liddick (1999); Richard M. Stana et al. (2000); Robert J. MacCoun and Peter Reuter (2001); U.S. General Accounting Office (2002).

15 See Stephen Flynn (1993); Tullis LaMond (1995); Criminal Intelligence Service Canada (1997); Ian Mulgrew (1998), 'Police Specialize in Public Relations Crackdowns,' *Vancouver Sun*, 17 October: B5; Anne McIlroy (2003), 'Canada's Drug War a Bust, Study Says. Fund Treatment Instead, Researchers Urge,' *Vancouver Sun*, 21 January: A2; RCMP (2003).

15 See Stephen Flynn (1993); LaMond Tullis (1995); Criminal Intelligence Service Canada. (1997); Ian Mulgrew (1998), 'Police Specialize in Public Relations Crackdowns,' *Vancouver Sun*, 17 October: B5; McIlroy (2003); RCMP (2003).

16 Colin Nickerson (2000), 'A Northern Border Menace Boom in Marijuana Trafficking Mars Canada's Image,' *Boston Globe*, 26 April: A1; Emma Poole (2003), 'Police Seize $60M Drug Truck: Cocaine, Pot Headed for United States,' *Calgary Herald*, 14 January: A1; Chris Turner (2003), 'Grass Routes: It's Bigger than Wheat, Dairy or the Fishery,' *National Post*, August; Adrian Humphreys and Stewart Bell (2003), 'Violence Grows as Marijuana Profits Rise Suburban "Epidemic,"' *National Post*, 29 October; Colin Freeze (2003b), 'High, Neighbour!' *Globe and Mail*, 31 May.

17 Unpublished Research carried out by Juan Ronderos through the Nathanson Centre for the May 2001 meeting of CSCAP held in Sydney, Australia.

18 FINTRAC (2005), 'Striving for Excellence,' *2005 Annual Report*, 9, retrieved 2 July 2006 from www.canada.gc.ca/publications/annualreport/2005/AR_E.pdf.

19 The RCMP and FINTRAC are currently working out some agreement whereby the police will attempt to keep some record of the results stemming from FINTRAC information.

20 FINTRAC (2005c), 'The First Five Years,' *2005 Annual Report*, 2.

5. Compliance: Bankers and Lawyers

1 There is a vast literature regarding voluntary codes of conduct. The general agreement is that voluntary codes are 'compatible with the neo-liberal model of trade liberalization, privatization, deregulation, cost-cutting, labour flexibility and global competitiveness' (Jeffcott and Yanz, 1999).

2 Please see http://laws.justice.gc.ca/en/P-24.501/SOR-2001-317/165755.html for the full details of the *Proceeds of Crime (Money Laundering) and Terrorist Financing Suspicious Transaction Reporting Regulations*.

3 Schneider (2004: 67). The source of primary data was the RCMP proceeds of crime (POC) case files. The final number of cases included in the sample totaled 149. These were all cases that had been successfully closed between 1993 and 2000 – closed by the RCMP following the forfeiture of assets resulting from either a conviction or plea bargain. A standardized coded questionnaire was used to gather data from the case files for a quantitative and qualitative analysis; 72.4 per cent of the predicate offences involved some form of drug trafficking.

4 In chapter 3 of this book we present the chart with the breakdown of sectors involved in money laundering. See especially fig. 3.9.

5 *Washington Post* (2003), 'CIBC Settles Enron-Linked Fraud charges,' 22 December.

6 For CIBC's involvement, see K. Drawbaugh (2003), 'CIBC Enron-Linked

Fraud Charges,' *Reuters*, 22 December; and Channel Newsasia (2003), 'CIBC Settles Charges in Enron Fraud for US$80 Million,' 23 December. Available online from www.channelnewsasia.com/stories/afp_world_ business/view/63192/1/html. On 22 December 2003, CIBC agreed to pay $80 million to settle charges that it helped Enron Corp. in its accounting fraud. In addition, three current or former CIBC executives have been sued. On 4 December the report of the bankruptcy examiner, Harrison Goldin, concluded that the Royal Bank of Canada knew of the fraud that they helped Enron set up. Likewise, the report concluded that Enron's accounting firm, KPMG LLP, committed 'negligence' in the work that they did for Enron.

7 Following the announcement that CIBC would pay $80 million to the SEC following the Enron collapse, the chief executive officer, John Hunkin, was quick to respond that the bank had already implemented strict policies and procedures to ensure that these types of actions will not happen again. *Reuters* (2003), 'Find Law: Legal News and Commentary,' 22 December, retrieved June 2006 from www.cnn.com/2003/BUSINESS/ 12/22/cibc.cnron.reut/.

8 Canadian Bankers Association offered not only their support and access but also financial assistance to the project.

9 Agreeing to provide high-risk loans or certain mortgaging schemes are examples where employees feel pressured to produce even when there are obvious risks of potential fraud involved.

10 Whatever flaws there may be in the approaches to suspicious transactions taken by the Big Five banks, it must be emphasized that the banks were the only sector that made any real effort to comply with anti-laundering guidelines.

11 The working relationship between the banks and the RCMP was guided in part by the 'Operational Guidelines for Proceeds of Crime Investigations between the Canadian Bankers Association and the Royal Canadian Mounted Police,' signed in 1994. The signatories to this MOU are the director of economic crime and the director of security for the Canadian Bankers Association. The offences specified include enterprise crime offences, designated drug offences, or customs and excise offences. These are the offences that are covered by the proceeds of crime legislation. It is the RCMP/Bankers Suspicious Transaction Referral form that is currently being filled in by most of the banks. A similar MOU is in place between the RCMP and the credit unions. This agreement, titled the 'Operational Guidelines for Proceeds of Crime Investigations between the Canadian Credit Union System and the Royal Canadian Mounted Police,' was

signed in 1996. As with the banks, an RCMP/Credit Union Suspicious Transaction referral form is used by the credit unions to pass the suspicious transactions information to the police.

12 However, the CBA suggested in 2000 that the government's decision not to let the banks offer car lease financing and retail insurance was 'strongly anti-consumer' because the Mackay Task Force had indicated 'that low-income Canadians have no life, health or home insurance, a market the banking industry could serve through branch sales.' Conceivably these are the same low-income Canadians who are not allowed to have access to traditional banking from the banks! (Protti, 2000: 27).

13 Rowan Bosworth-Davies, interview with Margaret Beare, 2000.

14 Again, little evidence is offered to link charitable organizations to money laundering, although two examples of cases under investigation are cited. Tom Naylor notes, 'To be sure, an Islamic charity could, on occasion, be used in a scam or have its funds diverted to illicit purposes, included financial terrorism. But so too could the Salvation Army' (Naylor 2002: 298).

15 Last year's report from the same task force characterized Liechtenstein as 'Europe's most dangerous tax haven' and criticized Monaco's anti-laundering efforts. See *Financial Times*, 21 February 2000.

16 *London Times*, 9 March 2001.

17 Newswire: The Official News Service of the US/Russia Press Club, foreword to 'Redwash: The Untold Story of the Bank of New York Global Money Laundering and Financial International Terror,' retrieved 1 July 2006 from www.moscowtelegraph.com/redwash_foreword.htm.

18 *New York Times* (2002), 'Bank of New York Suit Revived,' 15 January.

19 *Wall Street Journal* (2004), 'Money Laundering Problems at Bank of New York,' 30 November.

20 Editorial, *New York Times* (2000), 'Banks Are ABN-Amro, Banco Santander, Barclays, Citigroup, Chase Manhattan Corp, Credit Suisse Group, Deutsche Bank, HSBC Holdings, J.P. Morgan, Societe General, UBS,' 11 June.

21 The Basel Committee comprised representatives from Belgium, Canada, France, Germany, Italy, Japan, Netherlands, Sweden, Switzerland, United Kingdom, United States, and Luxembourg. The name changed from 'Basle' to 'Basel' in June 1993.

22 As we have seen, these enforcement responsibilities are either 'voluntarily' secured (with legislative protections against liability for confidentiality violations) or 'mandated' by law.

23 The Financial Action Task Force (FATF) is a body that was created in 1989 by the G7 countries to address money laundering. Each year an annual report is produced. The forty recommendations made by the FATF serve

as guidelines for the appropriate response to money laundering. This 'consensus' oriented body has turned to 'name and shame' techniques to encourage countries to adhere to their recommendations.

24 In this report, the Federation of Law Societies of Canada and the Canadian Bar Association is referred to as 'the lawyers' (vs. the Crown, government, or state).

25 *The Law Society of B.C. v. A.G. Canada; Federation of Law Societies v. A.G. Canada*, 2001 BCSC 1593, para. 100.

26 Beare and Schneider (1990: 310). This is of course relevant to Canada where lawyers have been exempted from the new mandatory suspicious transaction reporting requirements due to privacy and confidentiality considerations.

27 Law Society, UK, '*Fraudsters, Money Launderers and Scams,*' available online from www.lawsoc.org.uk/des/fourth_tier, cited in Andrew Campbell (2001) (unpublished).

28 Some of the EU governments appreciated the importance of having the lawyers included. Ottaviano del Turco, an Italian minister who had been involved in the anti-Mafia campaign told the EU ministers that he had never come across a case of money laundering that did not involve lawyers. Germany was most vocally opposed. It was acknowledged that the consensus was eventually forged mainly because the EU would have suffered a loss of face if they – supposedly the leaders in the global fight against money laundering – could not agree on the role of lawyers and hence an enhanced anti-money-laundering directive. Perhaps quite rightly, Bruce Zagaris stated in his Report to the House of Delegates: 'Once the EU enacts legislation, they will increasingly insist that the US act to ensure a level playing field. Similarly, other jurisdictions that are already the target of economic sanctions or threatened sanctions already subject professionals to anti-money-laundering due diligence (e.g., the U.K., the Cayman Is., Bermuda, Switzerland). They not surprisingly believe that the country most active in the anti-money-laundering rhetoric – the U.S. – should match its words with actions' (Zaggaris, 2002: 7–8).

29 *National Post* (2001), 'War on Terrorism: Legislation Changes to Anti-crime Law Likely to Face Constitutional Challenge: Lawyers Required to Secretly Report on Clients' Finances,' 11 October: A10.

30 *National Post* (2001), ' Lawyers Warn of Threat to Privacy: "An Enormous Surprise,"' 6 November: A1.

31 *National Post* (2001), 'Ottawa Approach Akin to Nazis, Judge Charges Money Laundering Bill,' 9 November: 4.

32 *The Law Society of BC v. A.G. Canada; Federation of Law Societies v. A.G. Canada*, para. 62 and 71.

33 Ibid., para. 107.
34 *Lavallee, Rackel & Heintz v. Canada (Attorney General); White, Ottenheimer & Baker v. Canada (Attorney General); R. v. Fink,* [2002] 3 S.C.R. 209, 2002 SCC 61.
35 Ibid., para. 104.
36 *The Law Society of B.C. v. A.G. Canada; Federation of Law Societies v. A.G. Canada,* 2001.
37 *Canadian Press* (2001), 'Alberta Lawyers Win Partial Victory Involving New Money Laundering Law,' 6 December.
38 *Canadian Press* (2001), 'Clients' Secrets Safe with Lawyers – for Now: Attorney General Grants Exemption to Proceeds of Crime Law,' 16 May: A6.
39 See the discussion of the 2003 FATF Recommendations in the conclusion of this book.
40 Affidavit of R. Lalonde, quoted in Ontario Superior Court of Justice, Federation of Law Societies of Canada and Attorney General of Canada, 9 January 2002, Court File No: 01-CV-222041.
41 *Lavallee et al.* (2002).
42 This point acknowledges that lawyers may lose clients when it is made clear that to go further might result in a report being filed with FINTRAC.
43 The possibility of an audit by FINTRAC, as to the compliance of the lawyers, remained a serious concern to the law societies.
44 This requirement NOT to tell the client that a report was being submitted to FINTRAC remained one of the most contentious aspects of the PCMLA.
45 We see in some jurisdictions – i.e., the UK – a policy whereby the lawyers have signs on their walls outlining their obligations regarding the reporting of money-laundering activities.
46 Ralston Alexander (2005: 1–2). Sir David Clementi (a CA and MBA from Harvard, career banker, and later deputy governor of the Bank of England) reported on the results of his two-year consultation and study into the regulation of law-related service providers in Great Britain noting the difficulties inherent in 'self-governing' models.
47 The Law Society of Upper Canada, 'Update on Money Laundering,' retrieved 3 July 2006 from www.lsuc.on.ca/news/a/hottopics/update-on-money-laundering-legislation.

6. Terrorist Financing and Its Enforcement

 1 The White House (2001), 'Fact Sheet on Terrorist Financing Executive Order,' 24 September: 1, retrieved 25 June 2006 from www.whitehouse.gov/news/releases/2001/09/20010924-4.html.

2 U.S. Department of the Treasury, Executive Order 13224, *Blocking Terrorist Property* and a Summary of the *Terrorism Sanctions Regulations* (Title 31 Part 595 of the U.S. Code of Federal Regulations). Available online from www.Treasury.gov/offices/enforcement/ofac/sanctions/terrorism.html.
3 Jakarta, Embassy of the United States of America (2001), 'Treasury's Gurule on Strategy Against Money Laundering,' 26 September, available online from www.usembassyjakarta.org/treasury.html.
4 FATF (2002a), 3–4. Emphasis added. It is extremely relevant to note that no evidence of the efficacy of financial institutions' participation in successfully curbing money laundering is given.
5 Indeed, the visible minority population is growing much faster than the total population, largely due to immigration patterns – in the period 1991 to 1996, the visible minority population increased by 27 per cent, while the total population rose by 6 per cent. The government recognizes the crucial role that immigration plays in the growth and prosperity of Canada. It has however tightened its screening of immigrants and refugees including entering into a pact with the U.S. concerning asylum seekers.
6 *ABC News World* (2001), 'Safe Haven for Terror,' 14 January; *Guardian Unlimited* (2001), 'Canada under Fire as Haven for Terrorists,' 19; *NewsMax* (2002), 'Canada Wide Open for Terrorists,' 10 July.
7 E-mail from Ibrahim Marashi, author of the original material that described the build-up to the 1991 Gulf War, and the *BBC News* (2003), 'Iraq Dossier "Solid" Downing Street,' 7 February.
8 The 'Keeping Canadians Safe' list of terrorist organizations numbered thirty-nine as of June 2006. The list can be found at www.psepc-sppcc.gc.ca/prg/ns/le/cle-en.asp.
9 Duff-Brown (2005); CSIS (2000); and Lak (2000).
10 R.T. Naylor (forthcoming) argues via an analysis of trial transcripts and government documents that relationships among militant factions are temporary alliances of convenience.
11 *CNN.com* (2001), 'INS Release Legal Status of Alleged Hijackers.'
12 Michael Crowley (2001). Likewise, on 11 December, authorities in Salt Lake City indicted forty-five airport workers for having lied on their job applications as to their status as illegal aliens, criminals, etc. Obviously no previous checks had been made.
13 *CNN.com* (2002), 'Six Months after Sept. 11, Hijackers' Visa Approval Letters Received.'
14 *ABC Online* (March 2002), 'U.S. Agency Moves Staff after Sept 11 Hijackers Issued Posthumous Visas.'
15 *CNN.com* (2002), 'N.J. Man Charged with Helping Hijackers Get IDs.'

16 *Wall Street Journal*, 20 September 2001; *Financial Times September*, 24 September 2001 quoted in Naylor (2006).

17 Personal correspondence from UN official, extracted from unspecified United Nations classified report.

18 *BBC News* (2001), 'Bin Laden "Received UN Cash," Charities Worldwide Responded to the Sudan's Famine,' 20 October.

19 *Associated Press* (2001), 'Pakistan Deporting 89 Arab Aid Workers,' 6 October.

20 *Canada (Minister of Citizenship and Immigration) v. Jaballah*, [2003] F.C.J. No. 1274 (F.C.A.), available online from http://recueil.cmf.gc.ca/fc/src/shtml/2005/pub/v1/2005fc35032.shtml.

21 *PR Newswire* (2005), 'U.S. Court Rules Saudi Charity to Remain in 9-11 Terrorist Lawsuit,' 22 September.

22 Regardless of the status given to Hamas by the U.S., the party has been gaining wider support in Palestine. The Islamic Resistance Movement (Hamas) launched in Gaza City the campaign for the Palestinian legislative elections that took place on 25 January 2006 and in which Hamas won a majority. Even before the Hamas victory, the director of Israeli homeland security intelligence, Shin Bet, cautioned that Israel would be in 'deep trouble' if Hamas won the elections.

23 *Dow Jones News Service* (1998), 'FBI Seizes $1.4M in Assets Destined for Hamas Terrorists,' 9 June.

24 *BBC News* (2005), 'Police Say IRA Behind Bank Raid,' 7 January, available online from http://news.bbc.co.uk/1/hi/northern_ireland/4154657.stm.

25 Judy Mogck and Josée Therrien (1998); *Montreal Gazette* (1999), 'Terrorists Netted Car-Theft Cash: RCMP,' 2 March: A11; Stewart Bell (2002a: 18).

26 Stewart Bell (2002b: A7); Office of the Commissioner for Federal Judicial Affairs (1999), *Veluppillai Pushpanathan (Applicant) v. The Minister of Citizenship and Immigration (Respondent)*. Indexed as *Pushpanathan v. Canada (Minister of Citizenship and Immigration) (T.D.)*, Trial Division, Sharlow J: Toronto, 13 May; Ottawa, 10 June.

27 Personal correspondence from UN official, extracted from unspecified United Nations classified report.

28 *Worldtribune.com* (2005), 'Cannabis New Drug of Choice to Finance Al Qaida,' 26 September.

29 *Globe and Mail* (2000), 'NATO in Kosovo: In Bed with a Scorpion. The KLA is Running Drugs and Refuelling Conflict,' 9 August; Roger Boyes (1999: B1); Michel Chossudovsky (1999).

30 *Reuters* (2004), 'Islamic Terrorists Linked to Italy Mafia Group,' 19 April.

31 Nikos Passas (1999); Sam Vaknin (2001); United States General Accounting

Office (2003: 18); Rajiv Chandrasekaran (2001); R. Cheran and Sharryn Aiken (2005). See also a series of papers on informal banking on the Nathanson Centre website www.yorku.ca/nathanson.
32 United Nations, Security Council Committee pursuant to resolution 1267 (1999), 22 September 2002: 15, quoted in Napoleoni (2003: 124).
33 *Canadian Press* (2001), 'Canada on the List as U.S. Moves against Islamic Money Exchanges in Crackdown on al-Qaida Finances,' 7 November; Colin Freeze (2001); J. Pasternak and S. Braun (2002).
34 National Commission (n.d.: 10); T. Cambanis (2002b); Tim Golden (2002); *Ottawa Citizen* (2003), 'Government Pays Off Victim of Smear. Ottawa Man Was Arrested, His Business Ruined,' 2 October: A1.
35 *CNN.com* (2001), 'Bin Laden's Global Financial Reach Detailed,' 26 September.
36 M. Potts, N. Kochan, and R. Whittington (1992); *Sacramento Bee* (2001), 'Follow the Money – through U.S. Banks: Stop the Global System of Money-Laundering that Global Terrorists Use,' 23 September; Loretta Napoleoni (2003: 82).
37 *Neewsweek* (2001), 'Storming the Fortress. Investigators Are Rushing to Crack Open the Bank Secrecy that Allows Terrorists to Hide Their Money Trail,' 8 October.
38 Financial Action Task Force (2002a: 4–6). No evidence of the efficacy of transaction reporting and other measures in curbing money laundering is provided in this document.

7. Conclusion: Full Speed Ahead on a Runaway Horse

1 Steven Chase, 'Top Sleuths to Set Up Home in Toronto,' *Globe and Mail*, 8 July 2006: A1, A4. See also Deloitte, 'A Month in Money Laundering' (September 2005), 4, retrieved 12 July 2006 from www.deloitte.com/dtt/cda/doc/content/UK_FS_AMonthinMoneyLaundering_Sep05(2).pdf.
2 *Globe and Mail* (2001), 21 September: A1.
3 Letter to The Honorable Spencer Bachus, The United States House of Representatives, Washington, DC, 18 May 2006, retrieved 12 July 2006 from www.fsround.org/pdfs/SpencerBauchusCTRLetter.pdf. The full range of CTR 'exemption' categories can be found at www.ffiec.gov/bsa_aml_infobase/pages_manual/OLM_009.htm, the site for the Federal Financial Institution Examination Council: Bank Secrecy Act/Anti-Money Laundering InfoBase.

References

Abadinsky, Howard. (2000). *Organized Crime*. New York: Wadsworth Publishing.

ABCsolutions. (2002). 'The Future of IPOC: Progress or Peril.' January 10. Document obtained under Access to Information Act.

Albanese, Jay. (1982). *Organizational Offenders: Why Solutions Fail to Stop Political, Corporate, and Organized Crime*. Niagara Falls, NY: Apocalypse.

Alexander, Ralston. (2005). 'President's View: Lawyer Independence in the Balance.' *Benchers Bulletin*, no. 2 (April–May). Retrieved 31 May 2006 from www.lawsociety.bc.ca/publications_forms/bulletin/ 2005/ 05-05-01-Pres-independ.

Alexander, Shana. (1988). *The Pizza Connection: Lawyers, Money, Drugs, Mafia*. London, UK: Weidenfeld and Nicolson.

Alford, D.E. (1991). 'Anti-Money Laundering Regulations: A Burden on Financial Institutions.' *North Carolina Journal of International Law and Commercial Regulation* 19: 437–68.

Antoine, Rose-Marie Belle. (2002). *Confidentiality in Offshore Financial Law*. Oxford: Oxford University Press.

Arthurs, Henry. (2005). 'Private Ordering and Workers' Rights in the Global Economy: Corporate Codes of Conduct as a Regime of Labour Market Regulation.' In Wesley Cragg, ed., *Ethics Codes, Corporations and the Challenge of Globalization*, 194–211. Boston, MA: Edward Elgar Publications.

Australia. (1992). *Taken to the Cleaners: Money Laundering in Australia*. Canberra: A.C.T.

Bahdi, Reem. (2003). 'No Exit: Racial Profiling and Canada's War Against Terrorism.' *Osgoode Hall Law Journal* 41(2 & 3): 293–317.

Baker, Geoff. (1995). 'Lawyer Handed 13-year Prison Sentence for Overseeing Money-Laundering Scheme.' *Montreal Gazette*, 30 June: A4.

Bartlett, Steven. (2006). 'Letter to the Honourable Spencer Bachus.' Retrieved 24 July 2006 from www.fsround.org/pdfs/SpencerBachusCTRletter.pdf.

Bauer, P. (2001). 'Understanding the Wash Cycle.' *Economic Perspectives* 6(2). Retrieved 31 May 2006 from http://us.info.state.gov/journals/ites/0501/ijee/clevelandfed.html.

Beare, Margaret. (1992). *International Drug Enforcement: Tracing Illicit Funds and the Politics of Sharing the Proceeds of Crime*. Ottawa: Solicitor General Canada.

– (1996). *Criminal Conspiracies: Organized Crime in Canada*. Scarborough: Nelson Canada.

– (2000a). 'Russian (East European) Organized Crime Around the Globe.' Paper presented at the Transnational Crime Conference convened by the Australian Institute of Criminology in association with the Australian Federal Police and Australian Customs Service, Canberra, Australia, 9–10 March.

– (ed.) (2000b). 'Suspicious Transaction Study: Referrals by Financial Institutions.' Paper prepared for the Canadian Bankers' Association. Toronto: Nathanson Center for the Study of Organized Crime and Corruption.

– (2001). 'Critique of a Compliance-Driven Enforcement Strategy: Money Laundering and the Financial Sector.' Paper presented at the Transparency International Conference, Toronto, ON.

– (2002). 'Searching for Wayward Dollars: Money Laundering or Tax Evasion – Which Dollars Are We Really After?' *Journal of Financial Crime* 9: 259–67.

– (2003a). 'Full Speed Ahead on A Run-Away Horse.' Paper presented at the International Symposium on Economic Crime, Jesus College, Cambridge University, Cambridge, UK, September.

– (2003b). 'Policing with a National Security Agenda.' Paper prepared for Heritage Canada and presented at the Canadian Heritage National Forum, Policing in a Multicultural Society, Ottawa, ON, 27 February.

– (2005). 'Case Study – "Voluntary" Ethical Conduct: Anti-Money Laundering Compliance and the Financial Sector.' In Wesley Cragg, ed., *Ethics Codes: The Regulatory Norms of a Global Society*, 154–93. Boston, MA: Edward Elgar Press.

Beare, Margaret, and Stephen Schneider. (1990). *Tracing of Illicit Funds: Money Laundering in Canada*. Working Paper #1990-05. Ottawa: Solicitor General Canada.

Beare, M.E., and E. Quellet. (1996). 'Bank Defalcation Study.' Internal report prepared for the Canadian Bankers' Association.

Beckett, P. (1999). 'BONY Is on Track to Post Record Profit for Year.' *Wall Street Journal*, 17 December 17: 1.

- (2000). "Bank of New York CEO's Pay Is Cut in Wake of Money-Laundering Probe.' *Wall Street Journal*, 3 April: Who's News Section.
Beckett, P., S. LeVine, and D. Cloud. (2000a). 'Investors Are Betting that Bank of New York Will Emerge Unscathed from Investigation.' *Wall Street Journal*, 3 October: C1.
- (2000a). 'USA: Bank of New York Weathers Inquiry.' *Wall Street Journal*, 4 October.
Beddoes, Z.M. (1999). 'A Survey of Global Finance.' *The Economist*, 30 January: 1–18.
Bell, Daniel. (1965). *The End of Ideology*. New York: Free Press.
Bell, R.E. (2000). *Prosecuting the Money Launderers Who Act for Organised Crime*. The Hague, Netherlands: International Association of Prosecutors. Available online from www.iap.nl.com/journal/papers/article_prosecution .html.
Bell, Stewart. (2000a). 'Canadian Financed Terror Bombs, Sri Lankans Say.' *National Post*, 9 March: A1.
- (2000b). 'Tamil Street Gangs Expanding Illegal Activities, Report Says.' *National Post*, 18 May: A1.
- (2000c). 'Canadian Cash Flow Confirmed as Tigers Kill 21 Terrorist Suicide Bomber: Money Collected in Canada May Pay for Tamil Weapons.' *National Post*, 8 June: A1.
- (2002a). 'Supporting Hezbollah.' *National Post*, 13 February: A15, A18.
- (2002b). 'Sri Lankan to be Extradited for "Narco-Terrorism": Sold Drugs for Tigers.' *National Post*, 5 October: A7.
Bell, Stewart, and Justine Hunter. (2000). 'Axworthy to Stanch Terror Funds Flow. Government on the Defensive in Wake of Tigers' Deadly Bomb.' *National Post*. 9 June: A1.
Benning, Joseph F. (2002). 'Following the Dirty Money: Does Bank Reporting of Suspicious Activity Pose a Threat to Drug Dealers?' *Criminal Justice Policy Review* 13(4): 337–55.
Bercu, S.A. (1994). 'Toward Universal Surveillance in an Information Age Economy: Can We Handle Treasury's New Police Technology.' *Jurimetrics Journal* 34: 394–401.
Bers, Melvin K. (1970). *The Penetration of Legitimate Business by Organized Crime*. Washington, DC: U.S. Department of Justice, Law Enforcement Assistance Administration, National Institute of Law Enforcement Criminal Justice.
Blakey, G. Robert. (1998a). 'Inside the Tobacco Deal: Interview Frontline Online.' Retrieved July 2006 from www.pbs.org/wgbh/pages/frontline/shows/settlement/ interviews/blakey.html.

– (1998b). 'Amway Expert Opinion Report.' *The Procter & Gamble Company, et al. v. Amway Corporation, et al.* Case No. H-9723 84 (S.D. Texas, Houston Division). Retrieved December 2005 from www.ratbags.com/rsoles/comment/amwayblakeyreport.htm.

Blatchford, Christie. (2004). 'Shoniker's Bail Conditions Set.' *Globe and Mail,* 16 June: A14.

Blickman, Tom. (1997). 'The Rothschilds of the Mafia on Aruba.' *Transnational Organized Crime* 3(2): 50–89.

Bogach, H., and L. Gordon. (2000). 'The Role of Social Audits.' *The Corporate Ethics Monitor* (May–June): 46.

Bonner, Robert. (2001). 'Speech to the Egmont Group of FIUs.' Available online from www.customs.ustreas.gov/about/speeches.

Bourque, M.J., and C. Senechal. (1988). 'Project Pilgrim.' RCMP Montreal Anti-Drug Profiteering Unit. Unpublished intelligence report in possession of the authors.

Bowie, Bruce. (1988). 'Money Laundering Techniques.' Ottawa: Royal Canadian Mounted Police, Drug Enforcement Directorate. Unpublished paper in possession of the authors.

Boyes, Roger. (1999). 'Drug Money Linked to KLA.' *Montreal Gazette,* 24 March: B1.

Bradley, C.M. (1980). 'Racketeers, Congress, and the Courts: An Analysis of RICO.' *Iowa Law Review* 65: 837–97.

Braithwaite, John. (1993). 'Following the Money Trail to What Destination? An Introduction to the Symposium.' *Alabama Law Review* 44, no. 3 (Spring): 657–68.

British Columbia. Coordinated Law Enforcement Unit (CLEU). (1974). *Initial Report on Organized Crime in British Columbia.* Victoria: CLEU, Ministry of the Attorney General.

British Columbia. Ministry of the Attorney General. (1980). *Business of Crime: An Evaluation of the American R.I.C.O. Statute from a Canadian Perspective.* Victoria: Ministry of the Attorney General.

Brody, Reed. (1985). *Contra Terror in Nicaragua: Report of a Fact-Finding Mission: September 1984–January 1985.* Boston, MA: South End Press.

Bronskill, Jim. (2002). 'Canada's Hashish Trade "Funds Terrorists": RCMP Believe Extremists Get Millions from Drugs.' *Vancouver Sun,* 16 February: A13.

– (2003). 'Proceeds of Crime Units Are Shackled.' *National Post,* 3 June: A7.

Bruun K.L. Pan, and I. Rex, eds. (1975). *The Gentlemen's Club: International Control of Drugs and Alcohol.* Chicago: University of Chicago Press.

Buffett, Jimmy. (1974). 'A Pirate Looks at Forty.' *Jimmy Buffett's Greatest Hits.* [C.D.] MCA Label.

Burke, Jason. (2001). 'Dead Man Walking.' *The Observer [Manchester Guardian]*, 5 August. Retrieved 25 June 2006 from http://observer.guardian.co.uk/life/story/ 0..532626,00.html.

Cambanis, T. (2002a). 'Trial Opens in Money Wiring Case.' *Boston Globe*, 22 April: B2.

– (2002b). 'Somali Guilty of Running Unlicensed Money Firm: Verdict a First Under New Federal Antiterror Law.' *Boston Globe*, 1 May: B3.

Camdessus, Michael. (1998). 'Money Laundering: The Importance of International Countermeasures.' Address to the Plenary Meeting of the Financial Action Task Force on Money Laundering, Paris, France, 10 February. Available online from www. imfg.org/external/np/speeches/1998/021098.htm.

Campbell, Andrew. (2001). 'Solicitors and the Prevention of Money Laundering.' Paper presented at the Nineteenth Cambridge Symposium, The Hiding of Wealth, International Symposium on Economic Crime, Jesus College, Cambridge, UK, September.

Canada. Department of Finance. (1998). *Change Challenge Opportunity, Task Force on the Future of the Canadian Financial Services Sector*. Ottawa: Department of Finance.

– (2001). 'FINTRAC Receives Increased Funding to Combat Terrorism.' *Department of Finance News Release*. Media Room Ref. No. 2001-094. 25 October.

– (2005a). 'Enhancing Canada's Anti-Money Laundering and Anti-Terrorist Financing Regime. Consultation Paper.' Ottawa: Department of Finance. Available online from www.fin.gc.ca/activty/pubs/enhancing_e.pdf.

– (2005b). *Year Five Evaluation of the National Initiatives to Combat Money Laundering and Interim Evaluation of Measures to Combat Terrorist Financing*. Ottawa: Department of Finance. Available online from www.fin.gc.ca/activity/pubs/nicml-incba_a2_e.gif.

– (n.d.). *National Initiative to Combat Money Laundering. Evaluation of Program – Year Three. Terms of Reference*. Ottawa: Department of Finance.

Canada. Department of Foreign Affairs and International Trade (DFAIT). (2001). *Report of the Government of Canada to the Counter-Terrorism Committee of the United Nations Security Council on Measures Taken to Implement Resolution 1373 (2001)*. Ottawa: DFAIT. Available online from www.dfait-maeci .gc.ca/anti-terrorism/resolutions1373-en.asp.

Canada. Department of Justice. (1983). *Enterprise Crime Study Report*. Ottawa: Department of Justice.

– Evaluation Section. (1998). *Proceeds of Crime Prosecutions: Preliminary Findings and Baseline Measures of Workload Pressure*. Prepared for Strategic Prosecutions Police Section, Criminal Law Branch, Department of Justice.

– and Solicitor General. (1998). *Electronic Money Laundering: An Environmental Scan*. Ottawa: Solicitor General Canada.

Canada. Office of the Auditor General. (2003). 'Canada's Strategy to Combat Money Laundering.' 8 April. *Office of the Auditor General of Canada News Release*. Retrieved 2 June 1006 from www.oag-bvg.gc.ca/domino/reports.nsf/html/20030403ce.html.

– (2004). *Report of the Auditor General of Canada to the House of Commons and to the Ministers of Finance and National Revenue*. Ottawa: Office of the Auditor General.

– (n.d.). 'Implementation of the National Initiative to Combat Money Laundering.' *Office of the Auditor General of Canada News Release*. Available online from www.oag-bvg.gc.ca/domino/reports.nsf/html/20041102.ce.html.

Canada. Office of the Superintendent of Financial Institutions. (2004). 'Consolidated List of Names Subject to the Regulations Establishing a List of Entities Made under Subsection 83.05(1) of the Criminal Code or the United Nations Suppression of Terrorism Regulations. PART A – INDIVIDUALS.' Available online from www.osfi-bsif.gc.ca/eng/documents/advisories/docs/indstld.txt.

Canadian Bar Association. (2001). 'Modernizing the CBA Code of Professional Conduct — A Consultation Paper.' Available online from www.cba.org.

Canadian Community Reinvestment Coalition (CCRC). (1999). *Access Denied: The Failure of Voluntary Measures to Improve Banking Services, National Survey Report*. Ottawa: CCRC.

Canadian Security Intelligence Service (CSIS). (2000). 'International Terrorism: The Threat to Canada.' *Perspectives: A Canadian Security Intelligence Service Publication*. Report #2000/04. Ottawa: CSIS. Retrieved 2 June 2006 from www.csis-scrs.gc.ca/eng/miscdocs/20004_3.html.

– (2002). *Operational Programs: Counter-Terrorism*. Ottawa: CSIS. Available online from www.csis-scrs.gc.ca/eng/operat/ct_e.html.

– (2003). *2002 Public Report*. Ottawa: CSIS.

– (2004). *2003 Public Report*. Ottawa: CSIS.

Carrington, Ian. (2000). 'Countering Abuses of the Banking System – Where Do We Stand?' Paper presented at the Rule of Law in the Global Village: Issues of Sovereignty and Universality Symposium, UN Global Programme Against Money Laundering, Palermo, Italy, 12–14 December.

Carroll, Lisa C. (n.d.). *Alternative Remittance Systems Distinguishing Sub-Types of Ethnic Money Laundering in Interpol Member Countries on the Asian Continent*. Available online from www.interpol.int/Public/FinancialCrime/Money Laundering/EthnicMoney.htm.

Chaddock, G.R. (2001). 'How Authorities Will Be Monitoring Your Money.'

Christian Science Monitor. Retrieved 31 May 2006 from ww.csmonitor.com/ 2001/1026/p3s1-uspo.html.

Chandrasekaran, Rajiv. (2001). 'Muslim World Moves Money Without Trace.' *Washington Post Foreign Service*, 10 November: A20.

Chase, Steven. (2006). 'Top Sleuths to Set Up Home in Toronto.' *Globe and Mail*, 8 July: A1, A4.

Cheh, Mary M. (1994). 'Can Something This Easy, Quick and Profitable also Be Fair?' *New York Law School Law Review* 39(1-2): 1–48.

Cheran, Rudhramoorthy. (2002). *The Sixth Genre: Memory History and the Tamil Diaspora Imagination*. Colombo, Sri Lanka: Marga Institute.

Cheran, Rudhramoorthy, and Sharryn Aiken. (2005). *The Impact of International Informal Banking on Canada: A Case Study of Tamil Transnational Money Transfer Networks (Undiyal), Canada/Sri Lanka*. Ottawa: Law Commission of Canada, and Toronto: The Nathanson Centre for the Study of Organized Crime and Corruption (York University). Retrieved 2 June 2006 from www.lcc.gc.ca/ research_project/cheran-main-en.asp.

Chisholm, Jeffrey S. (1999). 'Banks and Police: A Practical Partnership.' Speech presented to the Canadian Association of Chiefs of Police Conference, 24 August. Retrieved 20 January 2006 from www.cba.ca/eng/Media_ Centre/Speeches/ 990824-a.htm.

Chrétien, Jean. (1994). *Government Action Plan on Smuggling*. Ottawa: House of Commons.

Chossudovsky, Michel. (1999). *Kosovo 'Freedom Fighters' Financed by Organised Crime*. Retrieved 2 June 2006 from www.wbenjamin.org/balkan_archives .html#chossudovsky.

Cohen, Laurie, and Stephen Franklin. (2001). 'FBI Report Helped Shut Down Hamas-Linked Local Charity.' *Chicago Tribune*, 6 December.

Comras, Victor. (2005). 'Al Qaeda Finances and Funding to Affiliated Groups.' *Strategic Insights* 4(January). Retrieved 2 June 2006 from www.ccc.nps.navy .mil/si/2005/Jan/comrasJan05.asp.

Consulting and Audit Canada. (2002). 'IPOC Evaluation for Years 4 and 5 1999–2000 and 2000–2001.' Completed for the Solicitor General of Canada. Document obtained under Access to Information Act.

Council of Europe. (1990). *Convention on Laundering, Search, Seizure and Confiscation of the Proceeds From Crime. Preamble*. Retrieved 31 May 2006 from www.conventions.coe.int/Treaty/en/Treaties/Html/141.htm.

– (2001). *Multidisciplinary Group on International Action against Terrorism*. Retrieved 31 May 2006 from www.coe.int/T/E/Legal_Affairs.

– (n.d.). *Greater and Smaller Europe: An Overview*. Available online from www.coe.int/T/E/Communication-and-research/Contacts-with-the-public/.

Council on Foreign Relations. (2002). *Terrorist Financing Report*. Prepared by the Independent Task Force Sponsored by the Council on Foreign Relations. Washington, DC: Council on Foreign Relations.

Cressey, D. (1969). *Theft of the Nation*. New York: Harper and Row.

Criminal Intelligence Service Canada. (1997). *Annual Report on Organized Crime in Canada, 1997*. Ottawa: CISC.

– (2002). *Annual Report on Organized Crime in Canada, 2002*. Ottawa: CISC.

Crowley, Michael. (2001). 'Into the Breach: Why They Chose Logan.' *The New Republic*. 1 October. Available online from www.freerepublic.com/focus/f-news/529165/posts.

Cruise, David, and Alison Griffiths. (1987). *Fleecing the Lamb*. Toronto: Douglas and McIntyre.

Curry, Bill. (2005). 'Ottawa to Give Police More Power to Snoop.' *Globe and Mail*, 19 August. Retrieved 25 June 2006 from www.theglobeandmail.com/servlet/story/RTGAM. 20050819.wx.

Day, K. (2000). 'USA: Citigroup Called Lax on Money Laundering.' *Washington Post*, 30 November.

Delaney, Adam Vai. (2002). 'The Island Nations Engagement with the OECDE's Harmful Tax Practices Initiative.' Unpublished paper in the possession of the authors.

Demont, John. (1988). 'A Dangerous Trail: Police Pursue the Profits from Drug Sales.' *Maclean's*, 31 October: 40.

de Rugy, V. (2001). 'Privacy Punished, Not Terrorism.' *The Cato Institute*, 26 October. Retrieved 31 May 2006 from www.cato.org/dailys/10-26-01.html.

Desjardins, Josee. (2002). 'The Proceeds of Crime (Money Laundering) and Terrorist Financing Act.' Unpublished paper in the possession of the authors.

DiLuca, Joseph. (2002). 'Money Laundering Ghostbusters: A Review of the Nature, History and Claims of the Financial Action Task Force.' Unpublished paper in the possession of the authors.

DiManno, Rosie. (1989). 'New Law's Long Arm Seizes Suspects' Assets. Tough Measure that Takes Effect Today Is Aimed at Big-Time Criminals but Critics Say It Erodes Basic Rights.' *Toronto Star*, 1 January: A3.

Dintino, Justin J., and Frederick T. Martens. (1983). *Police Intelligence Systems in Crime Control: Maintaining a Delicate Balance in a Liberal Democracy*. Springfield, IL: Charles C. Thomas Publishers.

Drozdiak, William. (2001). 'An Anxious Countdown to New Cash.' *Washington Post*, 20 August: A3.

Duff-Brown, Beth. (2005). '50 Terror Groups Believed to Be in Canada.' *Associated Press*, 4 July.

Edwards, Peter. (1990). *Blood Brothers: How Canada's Most Powerful Mafia Family Runs Its Business*. Toronto: Key Porter.

Egmont Group. (2006). *Financial Intelligence Units of the World. Operational Units (Meeting the Egmont Definition) Status as of June 2006*. Retrieved December 2006 from www.egmontgroup.org/list_of_fius.pdf.

Eichenwald, Kurt. (2001). 'Terror Money Hard to Block, Officials Find.' *New York Times*, 10 December.

EKOS Research Associates. (2004). *Questionnaire Pertaining to the Year Five Evaluation of the National Initiatives to Combat Money Laundering and Interim Evaluation of Measures to Combat Terrorist Financing. Final Report*. Submitted to Finance Canada. Toronto: EKOS.

Embassy of Colombia. (1998). *Colombia's War on Illegal Drugs: Actions and Results for 1997*. Washington, DC: Embassy of Colombia.

Embassy of U.S.A. in Jakarta. (2001). Treasury's Gurule on Strategy Against Money Laundering. Retrieved 2 June 2006 from www.usembassyjakarta.org /treasury.htm.

European Committee on Crime Problems. Select Committee of Experts on the Evaluation of Anti-Money Laundering Measures. (2002). *A Review of the Anti-Money Laundering Systems in 22 Council of Europe Member States 1998-2001*. Strasbourg: John Ringguth.

Evans, John. (1995). 'International Money Laundering: Enforcement Challenges and Opportunities.' Paper presented to the Southwestern University School of Law Symposium on the Americas: Eradicating Transboundary Crime, Vancouver, BC, 10 March. Available online from www.icclr.law .ubc.ca/Publications/Reports/Enforcement_Challenges.pdf.

– (1997). 'The Proceeds of Crime: Problems of Investigation and Prosecution.' Paper prepared for the Government of Canada. In the possession of the authors.

– (2002). 'Organised Crime and Terrorist Financing in Northern Ireland.' *Jane's Intelligence Review* 14 (9 September): 26–9.

Fabre, Guilhem. (2003). *Criminal Prosperity: Drug Trafficking, Money Laundering, and Financial Crises after the Cold War*. London: RoutledgeCurzon.

Federation of Law Societies of Canada. (2002). 'Lawyers and Federal Government Agree to have Test Case on Money Laundering.' *Federation of Law Societies of Canada Press Release*. 15 May. Available online from www.flsc.ca/ en/pdf/FLSCCom_15May02.pdf.

– (2005). *Submission in Response to Finance Canada's Enhancing Canada's Anti-Money Laundering and Anti-Terrorist Financing Regime Consultation*. 30 September. Montreal: FLSC.

Financial Action Task Force. (1990). *FATF-I Annual Report of 1990*. Paris: FATF.

– (1996). *FATF-VII Report on Money Laundering Typologies*. Paris: FATF.
– (1997). *1996–1997 Report on Money Laundering Typologies*. Paris: FATF.
– (1998a). *Report on Money Laundering Typologies, 1997-1998*. Paris: FATF.
– (1998b). *FATF-IX Annual Report, 1997-98*. Paris: FATF.
– (1999). *1998–1999 Report on Money Laundering Typologies*. Paris: FATF.
– (2000). *Report on Non-Cooperative Countries and Territories*. Paris: FATF.
– (2001). *FATF Report on Money Laundering Typologies 2000-2001*. Paris: FATF.
– (2002a). *Guidance for Financial Institutions in Detecting Terrorist Financing*. Paris: FATF.
– (2002b). *Review to Identify Non-Cooperative Countries or Territories: Increasing the Worldwide Effectiveness of Anti-Money Laundering Measures*. Paris: FATF.
– (2004). *Special Recommendations on Terrorist Financing*. Retrieved 30 May 2006 from www.fatf-gafi.org/dataoecd/8/17/34849466.pdf.
– (2005a). *Annual Report 2004-2005*. Paris: FATF. Available online from www.fatf-gafi.org/dataoecd/41/25/34988062.pdf.
– (2005b). *55 Jurisdictions Agree to Fight Money Laundering*. Paris: FATF. Available online from www.fatf-gafi.org/dataoecd/41/27/34988026.pdf.
– (n.d.a). *More about the FATF and Its Work*. Paris: FATF. Retrieved 30 May 2006 from www1.oecd.org/fatf/AboutFATF_en.html.
– (n.d.b). *Terrorist Financing* and *Special Recommendations on Terrorist Financing*. Paris: FATF. Retrieved 30 May 2006 from www1.oecd.org/fatf/ TerFinance_en.htm.
– (n.d.c). *Interpretative Note to Special Recommendation VI: Alternative Remittance*. Paris: FATF. Retrieved 30 May 2006 from www1.oecd.org/fatf/pdf/ INSR6_en.pdf.
– (n.d.e). *Special Recommendations on Terrorist Financing*. Paris: FATF. Available online from www1.oecd.org/fatf/SRecsTF_en.htm#VI.%20Alternative.
Financial Crimes Enforcement Network (FinCEN). (1998). *1997–2002 Strategic Plan*. Washington, DC: FinCEN. Available online from www.treas.gov/ FinCEN/pub_FinCEN_reports.html.
– (1998). *FinCEN Advisory* 1(4). Washington, DC: FinCEN.
– (2000a). *2000–2005 Strategic Plan*. Washington, DC: FinCEN. Retrieved 2 June 2006 from www.fincen.gov/finstrategicplan2000.pdf.
– (2000b). *The National Money Laundering Strategy for 2000*. Washington, DC: FinCEN.
– (2001). *International Narcotics Control Strategy Report*. Washington, DC: FinCEN. Available online from www.state.gov/g/inl/rls/nrcrpt/2000/ 959.htm.
– (2003). *FinCEN Follows the Money*. Washington, DC: FinCEN. Retrieved 1 June 2006 from www.fincen.gov/followme.pdf.

Financial Transactions Report and Analysis Centre of Canada. (2002).
   FINTRAC Annual Report, March 31 2002. Ottawa: FINTRAC.
– (2003). *FINTRAC Annual Report, 2003.* Ottawa: FINTRAC.
– (2004). *Annual Report, 2004.* Ottawa: FINTRAC. Retrieved 31 May 2006 from
   www.fintrac.gc.ca/publications/annualreport/2004/AR_E.pdf.
– (2005a). *Highlights of FINTRAC's 2004-2005 Annual Report.* Ottawa:
   FINTRAC. Retrieved 31 May 2006 from www.fintrac.gc.ca/publications/
   nr/Highlights2005-11-04_e.asp.
– (2005b). *Departmental Performance Report 2004-2005.* Treasury Board of
   Canada. Available online from www.tbs-sct.gc.ca/rma/dpr1/04-05/
   FINTRAC-CANAFE/FINTRAC-CANAFEd4501_e.asp.
– (2005c). *Annual Report 2005.* Ottawa: FINTRAC. Available online from
   www. fintrac.gc.ca/publications/nr/Highlights2005-11-04_e.asp.
– (n.d.a). *What Must Be Reported? Terrorist Property.* Ottawa: FINTRAC. Available online from www.fintrac.gc.ca/reports/terrorist_e.asp.
– (n.d.b). *What Is Terrorist Financing?* Available online from
   www.fintrac.gc.ca/fintrac-canafe/definitions/terrorist_e.asp.
Fisher, William. (2005). 'Opinion: Anti-Terrorism Financing Laws Unequally
   Applied.' *Scoop Independent News*, 21 Friday. Retrieved 3 July 2006 from
   www.scoop.co. nz/stories/HL0604/S00257.htm.
Fisse, Brent, and David Fraser. (1993). 'Some Antipodean Skepticism about
   Forfeiture, Confiscation of Proceeds of Crimes and Money Laundering
   Offenses.' *Alabama Law Review* 44, no. 3 (Spring): 737–62.
Flynn, Stephen. (1993). 'World Wide Drug Scourge: The Expanding Trade in
   Illicit Drugs.' *Brookings Review* (Winter): 6–11.
Freeze, Colin. (2001). 'Barakaat Outlets under Heavy Scrutiny.' *Globe and Mail*,
   10 November: A14.
– (2003a). 'Disclosure Standard Too High, Crown Says.' *Globe and Mail*,
   27 March: A12.
– (2003b). 'High, Neighbour!' *Globe and Mail*, 31 May.
Gamage, Daya. (2005). 'Canadian Police Arrest Two Tamils of Sri Lankan
   Origin Connected with LTTE Front Group WTO for Counterfeiting.' *Asian
   Tribune*, 12 May. Available online from www.asiantribune.com/show
   _news.php?id=14417.
Garland, David. (2001). *The Culture of Control: Crime and Social Order in Con-
   temporary Society.* Chicago: University of Chicago Press.
Garver, R. (2000). 'Laundering Plan Back; New Names, Sponsors.' *American
   Banker*, 6 November.
Geddes, John. (2004). 'Are We Safe Enough? A Mandatory Review of
   Post-9/11 Security Could Set Off Fireworks in Ottawa.' *Maclean's*, 25 Oc-
   tober: 32.

Gilligan, G.P. (1999). *Regulating the Financial Services Sector*. The Hague, Netherlands: Kluwer Law International.

Gilmore, William C. (1999). *Dirty Money: The Evolution of Money Laundering Countermeasures*. 2d ed. Belgium: Council of Europe Publishing.

Gold Michael, and Michael Levi. (1994). *Money-Laundering in the UK: An Appraisal of Suspicious-Based Reporting*. London: Police Foundation and the University of Wales College of Cardiff.

Golden, Tim. (2001). 'Citibank Criticized for Slow Response to Money Laundering Scheme.' *New York Times*, 27 February.

– (2002). '5 Months After Sanctions Against Somali Company, Scant Proof of Qaeda Tie.' *New York Times,* 13 April: A10.

Goulet, L. (1998). 'Position Paper – Suspicious Transaction Reporting.' Ottawa: Royal Canadian Mounted Police.

Gurule, Jimmy. (2001a). 'Statement of Jimmy Gurule, Under-Secretary for Enforcement U.S. Department of the Treasury for the Senate Committee on Banking, Housing, and Urban Affairs Domestic and International Money Laundering.' Embassy of the United States of America, Jarkarta, Indonesia, 26 September. Available online from www.usembassyjakarta.org/treasury.html.

– (2001b). 'Remarks at the Launch of Operation Green Quest,' 25 October. Available online from http://usinfo.org/wf-archive/2001/011025/epf410.htm.

Hall, Neal. (1996). 'Charges Follow Massive Hashish Seizure: Counts Laid against Four Vancouver Residents and Nearly a Dozen Companies.' *Vancouver Sun*, 10 January: A2.

– (1997a). 'B.C. Bust Ended One of World's Biggest Drug Empires.' *Vancouver Sun*, 26 April: A1.

– (1997b). 'Lawyer Acquitted of Money Laundering: Judge Accepts Vancouver Man's Testimony He Didn't Know Client's $8 Million Came from Drugs.' *Vancouver Sun*, 18 April: B3.

Haller, Mark. (1971–72). 'Organized Crime in Urban Society." *Journal of Social History* 5: 210–34.

– (1976). 'Bootleggers and American Gambling 1920–1945: An Overview.' Unpublished paper. A final version became part of the Commission on the Review of the National Policy Toward Gambling, titled *Gambling in America*, Appendix 1. Washington, DC: U.S. Government Printing Office.

Hamzeh, A. Nizar. (2004). *In the Path of Hizbullah*. Syracuse: Syracuse University Press.

Hauser, Karen. (2001). 'New Money Laundering Legislation: Will You Be Compliant?' *National Banking Law Review*, 20(9).

Helleiner, Eric. (2000). 'The Politics of Global Financial Reregulation: Lessons from the Fight against Money Laundering.' In L. Taylor and J. Eatwell, eds., *International Capital Markets*. Oxford: Oxford University Press.

Hetzer, Wolfgang. (2003). 'Money Laundering and Financial Markets.' *European Journal of Crime, Criminal Law and Criminal Justice* 11(3): 264–77.

Horvath, John. (2002). *Big Brother Is Back – In Europe, Terrorism Provides the Excuse for More Surveillance*. Retrieved 31 May 2006 from www.towardfreedom.com/mar02bigbro.htm.

Howlett, Karen. (2003). 'Financial Industry under Fire. Complaints up 50 Per Cent: Ombudsman.' *Globe and Mail*, 13 May.

Hughes, J.E. (2001). 'Elusive Terror Money Slips Through Government Traps.' *USA Today*, 27 November.

Human Rights Watch. (2004). *Living in Fear: Child Soldiers and the Tamil Tigers in Sri Lanka*. Retrieved 25 June 2006 from www.hrw.org/report/2004/srilanka1104/.

Humphreys, Adrian, and Stewart Bell. (2003). 'Violence Grows as Marijuana Profits Rise.' *National Post*, 29 October.

Hunt, C.W. (1988). *Booze, Boats, and Billions: Smuggling Liquid Gold*. Toronto: McClelland and Stewart.

Ianni, Francis. (1972). *A Family Business*. New York: Russell Sage Foundation.

International Monetary Fund. (2001a). *Annual Report 2001*. Washington, DC: IMF.

– (2001b). *Financial System Abuse, Financial Crime and Money Laundering – IMF Background Paper*. Washington, DC: IMF.

– (2001c). *Public Information Notice: IMF Executive Board Discusses Money Laundering*. Washington, DC: IMF.

– (2001d). *Public Information Notice: IMF Board Discusses the Fund's Intensified Involvement in Anti-ML and Combating the Financing of Terrorism*. Washington, DC: IMF.

– Monetary and Exchange Affairs & Policy Development & Review Departments. (2001e). *Financial System Abuse, Financial Crime and Money Laundering – Background Paper*. Washington, DC: IMF. Available online from www.imf.org/external/np/ml/2001/eng/021201.pdf.

International Monetary Fund and the World Bank. (2001). *Enhancing Contributions to Combating Money Laundering: Policy Paper*. Washington, DC: IMF and WB.

Ivens, Andy. (1996). 'Police Spring Trap in Massive Drug Sting.' *Vancouver Province*. 25 January: A5.

Jeffcott, B., and L. Yanz. (1999). *Voluntary Codes of Conduct: Do They Strengthen or Undermine Government Regulation and Worker Organizing?* Retrieved 21 June 2006 from www.laborrights.org/projects/globalecon/jeffcott.html.

Jensen, N.J. (1993). 'International Funds Transfer Instructions: Australia at the

Leading Edge of Financial Transaction Reporting.' *Journal of Law and Information Science* 4(2): 323.

Jester, Jean. (1974). 'An Analysis of Organized Crime's Infiltration of Legitimate Business.' *Criminal Justice Monograph* 5, no. 1.

Johnston, D.C. (2000). 'Tax Shelters for Businesses Flourish as IRS Scrutiny Fades.' *New York Times*, 19 December.

Kelly, Robert. (1986). 'The Nature of Organized Crime and Its Operations.' In Herbert Edelhertz, ed., *Major Issues in Organized Crime Control*, 5–43. National Institute of Justice Symposium Proceedings, 25–26 September, Washington, DC.

Khan, Maulana Wahiduddin. (n.d.). *The Concept of Charity in Islam*. Retrieved January 2006 from www.alrisala.org/Articles/mailing_list/charity.html.

Kines, Lindsay. (1996). 'Business People Laundered Cash: Police Said the "Main Player" for the Companies Will Be Arrested Shortly.' *Vancouver Sun*, 26 January 26: B3.

Knox, P. (2002a). 'War Without End, Amen.' *Globe and Mail*, 24 May: A17.

– (2002b). 'Hardliner Sweeps Columbian Election.' *Globe and Mail*, 27 May: A10.

KPMG. (1999). *1998/99 Performance and Accountability Review of the Anti-smuggling Initiative*. Vol. 1, *Technical Report*. Prepared for the Department of the Solicitor General. Toronto: KPMG.

Kroeker, Robert G. (1995). 'The Legal and Ethical Propriety of Allowing Accused to Use the Proceeds of Crime to Retain Counsel.' *The Advocate* 53, Part 6 (November): 865–77.

Kroll Inc. (2004). 'When Irish Banks Aren't Smiling.' *Report on Fraud* 7(3): 9.

Lak, Daniel. (2000). 'Canada's Tamils Under Scrutiny.' *BBC News*, 16 June. Retrieved 25 June 2006 from http://news.bbc.co.uk/1/hi/world/south_asia/793625.stm.

Lamothe, Lee, and Adrian Humphreys. (2006). *The Sixth Family: The Collapse of the New York Mafia and the Rise of Vito Rizzuto*. Toronto: John Wiley.

Lamphier, Gary. (1986). 'Dirty Money, Dirty Deals.' *Toronto Life*, January: 29.

Landesco, John. (1968). 'Organized Crime in Chicago.' In Illinois Association for Criminal Justice, *Illinois Crime Survey*, 825–1100. Newark, NJ: Patterson Smith Publishing.

Law Society of Alberta. (n.d.). *PCMLA Guide*. Edmonton: LSA.

Law Society of British Columbia. (2006). *Law Society Rules 1998–2006*. Vancouver: Law Society of British Columbia. Accessed June 2006 from www.lawsociety.bc.ca/ publications_forms/rules/rules_part03.

Lehmkuhler, Sina. (2003). *Countering Terrorist Financing: We Need a Long-Term Prioritizing Strategy*. Available online from www.homelandsecurity.org/journal/Articles/Lehmkuhler.html.

Leonides, Buencamino, and Sergei Gorbunov. (2002). 'Informal Money Transfer Systems: Opportunities and Challenges for Development Finance.' Discussion Paper of the United Nations Department of Economic and Social Affairs. No. ST/ESA/2002/DP/26.

Levendosky, Charles. (1999). 'Civil Forfeiture Laws Have Turned Police into Pirates.' *New York Times*, 14 July.

Levi, Michael. (1991). *Customer Confidentiality, Money Laundering and Police Bank Relationships: English Law and Practise in a Global Environment*. London: Police Foundation.

– (2001a). 'Money Laundering and Its Regulation.' *Future Governance Paper* 6 (November).

– (2001b). 'Money Laundering: Private Banking Becomes Less Private.' In Robin Hodess et al., eds., *Global Corruption Report*. New York: Transparency International.

– (2002). 'Money Laundering and Its Regulation.' *Annals of the American Academy of Political and Social Science* 582 (July): 181–94.

Levi, Michael, in collaboration with Mark Pieth and Bill Gilmore. (2003). 'Controlling the International Money Trail: A Multi-level Cross-National Public Policy Review. Future Governance Research Initiative. Final Report.' Paper available from Cardiff University.

Levy, Leonard. (1996). *A License to Steal*. Chapel Hill: University of North Carolina Press.

Liddick, Donald. (1999). *Empirical, Theoretical, and Historical Overview of Organized Crime*. Lewiston, NY: Edwin Mellen Press.

Lupsha, Peter. (1981). 'Individual Choice, Material Culture, and Organized Crime.' *Criminology* 19(1): 3–24.

Lyall, Sarah. (2003). 'Britain Admits that Much of Its Report on Iraq Came from Magazines.' *New York Times*, 8 February. Retrieved 25 June 2006 from http:// luts.cc.utexas.edu/~rhart/courses/materials/plagiarism/plagiarizedreport.html.

Lyden, George. (2003). 'The International Money Laundering Abatement and Anti-terrorist Financing Act of 2001. Congress Wears a Blindfold while Giving Money Laundering Legislation a Facelift.' *Fordham Journal of Corporate and Financial Law* 8(1): 201–243.

MacCoun, Robert J., and Peter Reuter. (2001). *Drug War Heresies: Learning from Other Vices, Times, and Places*. Cambridge, UK: Cambridge University Press.

Mahoney, Jill. (2003). 'Alberta Judge Quashes Charges in Mega-Trial.' *Globe and Mail*, 10 September.

Marini, Regina. (2000). *Italian Organized Crime: Money Laundering Techniques*. RCMP Toronto Integrated Proceeds of Crime Unit. Unpublished paper in possession of the authors.

Marsden, William. (1985). 'How Canadian Banks Are Used to "Laundering" Narcotics Millions: Cash Floods Bahamas Branches.' *Montreal Gazette*, 21 December: A1; 'Why a Drug Dealer Needs a Friendly Bank,' *Montreal Gazette*, 23 December: A1; and 'Scotia Bank Stonewalled U.S. Drug Smuggling Probes,' *Montreal Gazette*, 24 December: A4.

– (1994). 'Following the Money Trail: New Law and Sting Operation Help RCMP Seize Drug Profits.' *The Vancouver Sun*, 6 September: A4.

Marsden, William, and Geoff Baker. (1994). 'RCMP Traces Cash in Huge Money-Laundering Case.' *Montreal Gazette*, 16 October: A1.

Martin, David J. (1996). 'I spy … a Police Sting that Broke the Law.' *Vancouver Sun*, 13 February: A17.

Mastrofski, Stephen, and Gary Potter. (1987). 'Controlling Organized Crime: A Critique of Law Enforcement Policy.' *Criminal Justice Policy Review* 2(3): 269–301.

McCarthy, Shawn. (1993). 'Foreign Drug Money Cleaned in Canada, U.S. Report Says.' *Toronto Star*, 17 June: B1.

McDowell, J., and G. Novis. (2001). 'The Consequences of Money Laundering and Financial Crime.' *Economic Perspectives* 6(2). Retrieved 31 May 2006 from http://usinfo.state.gov/journals/ites/0501/ijee/state1.html.

McIlroy, Anne. (2003). 'Canada's Drug War a Bust, Study Says. Fund Treatment Instead, Researchers Urge.' *Vancouver Sun*, 21 January: A2.

McInnes, D. (1996). 'Can Self-Regulation Succeed?' *Canadian Banker* 103(2) (March–April).

McIntosh, Andrew. (1998a). 'How the RCMP Helped "Push" $2 Billion Worth of Cocaine.' *Ottawa Citizen*, 11 June: A1, A7.

– (1998b). 'RCMP's Sting Aided Drug Lords: Organized Crime Imported 5,000 Kilograms of Cocaine.' *Ottawa Citizen*, 11 June: A1.

– (1998c). 'RCMP Sting Sparks Call for Inquiry. Opposition Demands Details on Undercover Drug Operation.' *Ottawa Citizen*, 21 June: A1.

– (1998d). 'Government Defies Court Order to Open Files on "Illegal" Drug Sting.' *Ottawa Citizen*, 13 June: A1.

– (1998e). 'Mounties Didn't Have Government's OK for Covert Drug Sting. RCMP Laundered Cash for Five Months before Getting Cabinet Approval.' *Ottawa Citizen*, 14 June: A1.

– (1998f). 'RCMP Sting Broke U.S. Laws. Mounties Changed U.S. Criminals' Cash for Months without U.S. Authorization.' *Ottawa Citizen*, 15 June: A1.

– (1998g). 'Mounties' Botched Currency Exchange Lacked Resources, Report Says: Montreal Probe: Organized Crime Laundered $141M through Operation.' *National Post*, 14 December: A6.

Meyer, Kathryn, and Terry M. Parssinen. (1998). *Webs of Smoke: Smugglers,*

Warlords, Spies, and the History of the International Drug Trade. Lanham, MD: Rowman and Littlefield.

Mikuriya, Kunio. (2002). 'The Challenges of Facilitating the Flow of Commerce in a Heightened Security Environment.' Speech delivered during the United Nations, International Forum on Trade Facilitation, New York City, 29–30 May.

Millard, George. (2003). 'The Forgotten Victims of Narco-Terrorism.' In Dilip Das and Peter C. Kratcoski, eds., *Meeting the Challenges of Global Terrorism: Prevention, Control, and Recovery*, 159–70. Boulder: Lexington Books.

Miller, Judith. (2002). 'Raids Seek Evidence of Money-Laundering.' *New York Times*, 21 March: 19.

Mitchell, Daniel J. (2002). 'U.S. Government Agencies Confirm that Low-Tax Jurisdictions Are Not Money-Laundering Havens.' *Prosperitas* 2(1).

Mitsilegas, Valsamis. (2003). *Money Laundering Counter-Measures in the European Union: A New Paradigm of Security Governance Versus Fundamental Legal Principles.* The Hague, Netherlands: Kluwer Law International.

Moffat, Carol. (1991). 'Properties Linked to Drug Ring Homes, Firms Seized, 7 Charged in Money-Laundering Probe.' *Toronto Star*, 22 April: A2.

Mogck, Judy, and Josée Therrien. (1998). 'Project Sparkplug.' Ottawa: Royal Canadian Mounted Police. Unpublished Intelligence Report.

Moller, Marie-Louise. (2004). 'Interpol: Counterfeiting Used to Finance Terrorism.' *Reuters*, 25 May.

Moon, Peter. (1971). 'The Mob. Part V: A Foothold in Ontario.' *Canadian Magazine*, 17 February: 9.

Morris-Cotterill, Nigel. (2001). 'Think Again: Money Laundering.' *Foreign Policy* (May/June). Retrieved 31 May 2006 from www.foreignpolicy.com.

Mowbray, Joel. (2002). 'Visas that Should Have Been Denied.' *National Review*, 9 October. Retrieved 25 June 2006 from http://national review.com/mowbray/Mowbray100902.asp.

Mucalov, Janice. (2004). 'Walking the Tightrope: Law Societies and Lawyer Self-Protectionist Ways.' *Magazine for Canadian Lawyers* (October). Retrieved 2 January 2006 from www.justice4you.org/lawyers_self_protectionist.html.

Mueller, Robert S. (2002). 'Statement for the Record of Robert S. Mueller, III, Director, Federal Bureau of Investigation before the Committee on Financial Services, United States House of Representatives, September 19, 2002.' Available online from http://financialservices.house.gov/media/pdf/091902rm.pdf.

Mulgrew, Ian. (1998). 'Police Specialize in Public Relations Crackdowns.' *Vancouver Sun*, 17 October: B5.

Munroe, Kirk. (1996). 'Surviving the Solution: The Extraterritorial Reach of the United States.' *Dickinson Journal of International Law* 14, no. 3 (Spring): 505-24.

Myers, J. (2001). 'International Standards and Cooperation in the Fight against Money Laundering.' *Economic Perspectives* 6(2). Retrieved 30 May 2006 from http://usinfo.state.gov/journals/ites/0501/ijee/treasury.htm.

Nadelmann, Ethan A. (1990). 'Global Prohibition Regimes: The Evolution of Norms in International Society.' *International Organization* 44, no. 4 (Autumn): 479–526.

Napoleoni, Loretta. (2003). *Modern Jihad: Tracing the Dollars behind the Terror Networks.* London: Pluto Press.

National Commission on Terrorist Attacks Upon the United States. (n.d). *Monograph on Terrorist Financing. Staff Report to the Commission.* Washington, DC: The Commission. Available online from http://counterterror .typepad .com/ the_counterterrorism_blog/files/ 911_TerrFin _Monograph.pdf.

National Governors' Association et. al. (1998). *State Laws and Procedures Affecting Drug Trafficking Control: A National Overview.* GAO Report HR-99-1. Washington, DC: General Accounting Office.

National Institute of Justice, Bureau of Justice Assistance. (1998). *Lessons Learned from the Organized Crime Narcotics (OCN) Trafficking Enforcement Program Model.* Rockville, MD: National Institute of Justice.

Naylor, R. Tom. (1999a). 'Follow-the-Money Methods in Crime Control Policy.' Study prepared for the Nathanson Centre for the Study of Organized Crime and Corruption, York University. Retrieved 31 May 2006 from www.yorku.ca/nathanson/Publications/washout.html.

– (1999b). 'Wash-Out: A Critique of the Follow-the-Money Methods in Crime Control Policy.' *Crime, Law and Social Policy* 32: 1–57.

– (2000a). 'Civil Forfeiture in the U.S. Led to Police Profiteering and the Miscarriage of Justice. Do We Want that Here?' *Globe and Mail,* 29 August.

– (2000b). 'Pursuing Money Rather than Criminals Creates More Problems than It Solves.' *Globe and Mail,* 13 April: A19.

– (2002). *Wages of Crime: Black Markets, Illegal Finance, and the Underworld Economy.* Ithaca, NY: Cornell University Press, and Montreal: McGill-Queen's University Press.

– (2004). *Hot Money and the Politics of Debt.* 2d ed. Montreal: McGill-Queen's University Press.

– (2006). *Satanic Purses: Money, Myth and Misinformation in the War on Terror.* Montreal: McGill-Queen's University Press.

Newman, Peter. (1978). *Bronfman Dynasty.* Toronto: McClelland and Stewart.

Nicaso, Antonio, and Lee Lamothe. (2000). *Bloodlines: The Rise and Fall of Mafia's Royal Family*. Toronto: Harper Collins.

Nickerson, Colin. (2000). 'A Northern Border Menace Boom in Marijuana Trafficking Mars Canada's Image.' *Boston Globe*, 26 April: A1.

Nkechi, Taifa. (1994). 'Civil Forfeiture vs. Civil Liberties.' *New York Law School Law Review* 39(1-2): 95–115.

Noble, Kimberly. (1996). 'A Drug Lord's Comedown.' *Globe and Mail*, 20 April: B2.

Ouston, Rick. (1998). 'Illegal Money-Laundering Sting Jeopardizes Massive Drug Busts.' *Vancouver Sun*, 6 February: B1.

Passas, Nikos. (1999). *Informal Value Transfer Systems and Criminal Organizations*. Boston: College of Criminal Justice, Northeastern University, and The Hague: Wetenschappelijk Onderzoek-en Documentatiecentrum. Available online from www.minjust.nl:8080/b_organ/wodc/publications/rapportenlijst-engels.htm.

Pasternak, J., and S. Braun. (2002).'Emirates Looked Other Way while al Qaeda Funds Flowed.' *Los Angeles Times*, 20 January: A1.

Pearce, F., and L. Snider, eds. (1995). *Corporate Crime: Contemporary Debates*. Toronto: University of Toronto Press.

Peel, Michael. (2000). 'World Economy – Global Policy Challenges – G7 Clamps Down on Hot Money.' *FT.Com*, 20 September.

Phillips, Alan. (1963a). 'Organized Crime's Grip on Ontario.' *MacLean's*, 21 September: 15.

– (1963b). 'The Inner Workings of the Crime Cartel.' *MacLean's*, 5 October: 24.

Poole, Emma. (2003). 'Police Seize $60M Drug Truck: Cocaine, Pot Headed for United States.' *Calgary Herald*, 14 January: A1.

Porteous, Samuel. (1998a). 'Final Report: Organized Crime Impact Study.' (Confidential Report.) Prepared for the Solicitor General of Canada.

– (1998b). 'Organized Crime Impact Study: Highlights.' (Confidential Report.) Prepared for the Solicitor General of Canada.

Possamai, Mario. (1989). 'Canada "Washes" Billions in Drug Money.' *Vancouver Sun*, 13 October: A11.

– (1992). *Money on the Run: Canada and How the World's Dirty Profits Are Laundered*. Toronto: Viking.

Potts, M., N. Kochan, and R. Whittington. (1992). *Dirty Money: BCCI – The Inside Story of the World's Sleaziest Bank*. Bethesda, MD: National Press Books.

Pratt, Richard. (2002). 'Global Financial Business and the Implications for Effective Control of Money Laundering in Offshore Centers.' *Journal of Financial Crime* 10(2): 130–2.

Pritchett, Jennifer. (2003). 'Proceeds of Crime: A System Shrouded in Secrecy.' *Kingston Whig-Standard*, 5 April: 1–2.

Protti, R. (2000). 'Interpreting Bill-38.' *Canadian Banker: Third Quarter*. Available online from www.cba.calen/magazine/getArticle.asp?at _id=196.

Public Safety and Emergency Preparedness Canada. (2006). 'Keeping Canadians Safe.' Available online from www.psepc-sppcc.gc.ca/prg/ns/le/cle-en.asp.

Quebec Police Commission Inquiry on Organized Crime. (1977). *Report of the Commission of Inquiry on Organized Crime and Recommendations: Organized Crime and the World of Business*. Quebec: Quebec Police Commission.

Quirk, Peter. (1997). 'Money Laundering: Muddying the Macroeconomy.' *Finance and Development* (March). Retrieved 30 May 2006 from www.worldbank.org/fandd/english/0397/articles/0110397.htm.

– (1999). 'Macroeconomic Implications of Money Laundering.' IMF Working Paper 96/99. Washington, DC: International Monetary Fund.

Ragano, Frank, and Selwyn Raab. (1994). *Mob Lawyer*. New York: Charles Scribner's Sons.

Reuter, Peter, and Edwin M. Truman. (2004). *Chasing Dirty Money: The Fight against Money Laundering*. Washington, DC: Institute for International Economics.

Rich, Frank. (2006). 'Op-Ed Can't Win the War? Bomb the Press.' *New York Times*, Sunday Week in Review, 2 July: 10.

Robertson, Tatsha. (2001). 'Somalis Decry Closing of Money Centers.' *Boston Globe*, 9 November: A14.

Robinson, Mary. (2001). Multidisciplinary Group on International Action against Terrorism, Council of Europe, Joint Statement UN High Commissioner for Human Rights, Walter Schwimmer, Secretary General of the Council of Europe, and Ambassador Gerald Stoudmann, Director of the OSCE Office for Democratic Institutions and Human Rights, 3 December. Retrieved 2 June 2006 from www.coe.int/T/E/Legal_Affairs.

Roig-Franzia, Manuel. (2002). 'Man Convicted of Using Smuggling to Fund Hezbollah.' *Washington Post*, 23 June.

Ronderos, Juan G. (2002). 'The War on Drugs and the Military: The Case of Columbia.' In M.E. Beare, ed., *Critical Reflections on Transnational Organized Crime, Money Laundering and Corruption*, 207–36. Toronto: University of Toronto Press.

Royal Canadian Mounted Police. Drug Enforcement Directorate. (1988). *National Drug Intelligence Estimates: 1987/88*. Ottawa: Minister of Supply and Services.

– (1991). *RCMP National Drug Intelligence Estimate 1991*. Ottawa: Minister of Supply and Services.
– (1993). *RCMP National Drug Intelligence Estimate 1993*. Ottawa: Ottawa: Minister of Supply and Services.
– (2001a). *RCMP Fact Sheets 2000/01*. Ottawa: Ministry of Public Works and Government Services Canada. Retrieved 31 May 2006 from www.rcmp-grc.gc.ca/pdfs/facts-english.pdf.
– (2001b). *2000/2001 Performance Report*. Ottawa: RCMP. Retrieved 31 May 2006 from www.rcmp-grc.gc.ca/dpr/performance01e.pdf.
– (2002). *2001/2002 Performance Report*. Ottawa: RCMP. Retrieved 31 May 2006 from www.rcmp-grc.gc.ca/dpr/performance02e.pdf.
– Organized Crime Analysis Section, Criminal Intelligence Directorate. (2003). *Drug Situation in Canada – 2002*. Ottawa: RCMP.
– (2003). 'High-Seas Takedown Nets 1.5 Tons Cocaine and Five Local Arrests.' *RCMP Press Release*, 21 May.
– (2004). 'Two Arrested on Money Laundering Charges.' 14 June. Retrieved 2 January 2006 from www.rcmp-grc.gc.ca/on/press/2004/2004_june_14_e.htm.
– (2004/2005). *Money Laundering: Impact of Money Laundering on Society*. Ottawa: RCMP, 2004, revised January 2005. Retrieved 16 June 2006 from www.rcmp-grc.ca/html/launder.htm.
Royal Commission on Customs and Excise (Canada). (1982). *Interim Reports (Nos. 1 to 10)*. Ottawa: F.A. Acland.
Salerno, Ralph. (1968). 'Organized Crime's Growing Threat to American Business.' *Business Management* 35 (November): 57–9.
Schneider, Stephen. (1997a). 'IADP Evaluation: Financial Impact Assessment, Fiscal Years 1992/93 to 1995/96.' Report submitted to the Department of the Solicitor General of Canada.
– (1997b). 'IADP Pilot Project Evaluation: 1997 Focus Groups.' Report submitted to the Solicitor General Canada.
– (2004). *Money Laundering in Canada: An Analysis of RCMP Cases*. Toronto: Nathanson Centre for the Study of Organized Crime and Corruption.
Schneider, Stephen, and Jean Sauvageau. (1996).' IADP Evaluation: Focus Group Sessions, 1996. Final Report.' Report submitted to the Solicitor General of Canada.
Schneider, Stephen, with Margaret Beare, and Jeremy Hill. (2000). *Alternative Approaches to Combating Transnational Crime*. Ottawa: Solicitor General Canada.
Scott, David. (1995). 'Money Laundering and International Efforts to Fight It.'

Public Policy Journal: Investment Climate and Globalization (May). Retrieved 2 July 2006 from http://rru.worldbank.org/PublicPolicyJournal/Investment.Climate-Globalization.

Selick, Karen. (2000). 'Ontario Wants to Put Grab on Property Rights.' *National Post*, 7 December: C19.

Shafer, D. Michael. (1988). *Deadly Paradigms: The Failure of U.S. Counterinsurgency Policy*. Princeton, NJ: Princeton University Press.

Silke, Andrew. (2005). 'Endgame? Unravelling the IRA's Financial Empire.' *The Sunday Business Post*, 9 October. Retrieved 2 June 2006 from http://archives.tcm.ie/businesspost/2005/10/09/story8653.asp.

Sinclair, Helen K. (1990). 'Dirty Business.' Notes for remarks to the Canadian Club. Presented at the Canadian Bankers' Association, Toronto, ON, 19 February.

Slevin, Peter. (2003). 'Libya Takes Blame for Lockerbie Bombing; Letter about Flight 203 Is Bid to Lift Sanctions.' *Washington Post*, 16 August 2003: A Section.

Solicitor General Canada. Policing and Law Enforcement Directorate. (1997). *Evaluation Framework for the Integrated Proceeds of Crime (IPOC) Initiative*. Ottawa: Solicitor General Canada.

– (1999). *House of Commons Book. Issue: Release of the Year 3 (1998–1999) Evaluation Report*. Ottawa: Solicitor General Canada.

– Policing and law Enforcement Directorate. (2002). *IPOC Evaluation Report, Years 4 and 5 1999–2000; 2000–2001: Toward Effective Horizontal Management*. Ottawa: Solicitor General Canada.

Stamler, Rod, and Robert Fahlman. (1983). 'The Profits of Organized Crime: The Illicit Drug Trade in Canada.' *Bulletin on Narcotics* 35(2): 61–70.

Stana, Richard M. et al. (2000). *Alien Smuggling: Management and Operational Improvements Needed to Address Growing Problem*. Washington, DC: General Accounting Office.

Steffenhagen, Janet. (1996). 'Police Sting Operation Bags 120 for Drugs, Money-Laundering.' *Montreal Gazette*, 25 January: A12.

Sullivan, Michael. (2004). 'The Basics of International Cartel Enforcement in Canada.' Paper prepared for the Osgoode Hall Continuing Legal Education Program and presented at Canada's Competition Regime: Thinking Strategically: A Practical Guide for Business, Osgoode Hall Law School, York University, 14 January. Retrieved 31 May 2006 http://competition.ic.gc.ca/epic/internet/incb-bc.nsf/en/ct02790e.html.

TCI Management Consultants. (2003). 'Methodologies for Measuring the Impacts of Organized Crime-Related Money Laundering Activities on

Canada.' A report prepared for the Solicitor General of Canada. Obtained through the Access to Information Act.

Thomas, Gwyn. (1974). 'Crime Cash in Metro, Police Say.' *Toronto Star*, 4 April.

Thoumi, Francisco. (2003). *Illegal Drugs, Economy, and Society in the Andes.* Washington, DC: Woodrow Wilson Center Press.

Tibbetts, Janice. (2004). 'Organized Crime Opposition Unites on Bloc Bill. First Joint Initiative: Rare Support from All Three Parties Gives Bill Solid Chance.' *National Post*, 26 October: A9.

Towsend, Leane. (2002). 'Financial Institutions and their Fight against Money Laundering.' Unpublished paper in the possession of the authors.

Tremblay, Pierre, and Richard Kedzier. (1986). 'Analyzing the Organization of Crime in Montreal 1920 to 1980: A Canadian test case.' In R.J. Kelly, ed., *Organized Crime: A Global Perspective*, 78–94. Totowa, NJ: Rowman and Littlefield.

Tullis, LaMond. (1995). *Unintended Consequences: Illegal Drugs and Drug Policies in Nine Countries.* Boulder, CO: L. Rienner.

Turlej, Joe. (2000). 'Turning a Blind Eye to Terrorism.' Paper prepared for the Mackenzie Institute, Toronto. Retrieved 25 June 2006 from www.mackenzieinstitute.com/2000/2000_04_Tigers_Terrorism.html.

Turlej, Joe, and John Thompson. (2003). 'Other People's Wars: A Review of Overseas Terrorism in Canada.' A Mackenzie Institute Occasional Paper. Retrieved 25 June 2006 from www.mackenzieinstitute.com/ Overseas_ Terrorism_In_Canada.pdf.

Turner, Chris. (2003). 'Grass Routes: It's Bigger than Wheat, Dairy or the Fishery.' *National Post*, 5 August.

United Nations. (1988). *United Nations Convention Against Illicit Traffic in Narcotic Drugs and Psychotropic Substances.* E/CONF.82/15. Vienna: United Nations.

– (1999). *International Convention for the Suppression of the Financing of Terrorism.* Adopted by the General Assembly of the United Nations in Resolution 54/109 of 9 December. Available online from www.un.org/law/cod/ finterr.htm.

– (2001). 'Security Council Unanimously Adopts Wide-Ranging Anti-Terrorism Resolution; Calls For Suppressing Financing, Improving International Cooperation Resolution 1373 (2001) Also Creates Committee to Monitor Implementation.' *United Nations Press Release*, 28 September. Available online from www.un.org/News/Press/docs/2001/sc7158.doc.htm.

– Office on Drugs and Crime. (n.d.). 'The Money Laundering Cycle.' Retrieved 25 November 2005 from www.unodc.org/unodc/money_ laundering_cycle.html.

U.S. Congress. (1950–51). *Special Committee to Investigate Organized Crime in Interstate Commerce.* Washington, DC: U.S. Government Printing Office.

– (1957). *Special Committee on Improper Activities in the Labor and Management Field.* Washington, DC: U.S. Government Printing Office.

U.S. Customs and Border Protection. (2002). 'Operation Green Quest overview.' *U.S. Customs and Border Protection Press Release*, 26 February. Retrieved 2 June 2006 from www.cbp.gov/xp/cgov/newsroom/press_releases/archives/legacy/2002/22002/02262002.xml.

U.S. Department of State. Bureau for International Narcotics and Law Enforcement Affairs. (1998). *International Narcotics Control Strategy Report, 1997.* Washington, DC: Department of State. Retrieved 30 May 2006 from www.state.gov/www/global/narcotics_law/1997_narc_report/money.html.

– Bureau for International Narcotics and Law Enforcement. (2000). *International Narcotics Control Strategy Report.* Washington: U.S. Department of State.

U.S. Department of the Treasury. (2001a). 'Testimony of Paul H. O'Neill Secretary of the Treasury before the Senate Committee on Appropriations.' *U.S. Treasury Department Press Release*, 8 May. Retrieved 31 May 2006 from www.treas.gov/press/releases/po361.htm.

– Office of Public Affairs. (2001b). *Under Secretary Jimmy Gurule Speech Before the ABA Money Laundering Conference*, 22 October. Available online from www.treas.gov/press/releases/po707.htm.

U.S. Department of the Treasury and the Department of the Attorney General. (2000). *The National Money Laundering Strategy for 2000.* Washington, DC: United States Department of the Treasury and the Department of the Attorney General.

U.S. Department of the Treasury and Department of Justice. (2002). *The National Money Laundering Strategy, 2002.* Washington, DC: Department of the Treasury and Department of Justice.

U.S. Federal Reserve Board. (1999). Testimony of Richard A. Small: 'The Vulnerability of Private Banking to Money Laundering Activities.' Washington, DC: U.S. Federal Reserve Board.

U.S. General Accounting Office. (1998). *General Accounting Office Report to the Ranking Minority Member, Permanent Subcommittee on Investigations, Committee on Governmental Affairs, US Senate Private Banking: Raul Salinas, Citibank, and Alleged Money Laundering,* Washington, DC: General Accounting Office October.

– (2002). *Identity Theft: Available Data Indicate Growth in Prevalence and Cost.* Washington, DC: General Accounting Office.

– (2003). *Terrorist Financing. U.S. Agencies Should Systematically Assess Terrorists' Use of Alternative Financing Mechanisms*. Washington, DC: General Accounting Office. Retrieved 2 June 2006 from www.gao.gov/new.items/d04163.pdf.

U.S. Presidential Commission on Organized Crime. (1984). *The Cash Connection: Organized Crime, Financial Institutions and Money Laundering*. Washington, DC: Presidential Commission on Organized Crime.

U.S. Presidential Commission on Law Enforcement and the Administration of Justice. (1967). *The Challenge of Crime in a Free Society: A Report*. Washington, DC: U.S. Government Printing Office.

U.S. Senate Committee on the Judiciary. Subcommittee on Criminal Laws and Procedures. (1978). *Racketeering in the Sale and Distribution of Cigarettes: Hearing, October 21, 1977, on S. 1487*. Washington, DC: U.S. Government Printing Office.

U.S. Senate. The Permanent Subcommittee on Investigations. (1999). *The Minority Staff Report for Hearings on Private Banking and Money Laundering: A Case of Opportunities and Vulnerabilities*. Retrieved 2 June 2006 from www.senate.900/ ~900-aff /110499_psipress.htm.

Vaknin, Sam. (2001). 'Hawalas: The Bank that Never Was.' *Critical Mass Economics*, 15 November. Retrieved 2 June 2006 from www.e-venthorizon.net/macroeconomics/Hawala.html.

Valverde, Mariana. (2002). 'Governing Security through Security.' In Ronald J. Daniels, Patrick Macklem, and Kent Roach, eds., *Security of Freedom: Essays on Canada's Anti-Terrorism Bill*, 83-92. Toronto: University of Toronto Press.

Van Dyne, P.C. et al. (2003). *Criminal Finances and Organized Crime in Europe*. The Hague, Netherlands: Wolf Legal Publishers.

– ed. (2004). *Threats and Phantoms of Organized Crime and Terrorism: Critical European Perspectives*. The Hague, Netherlands: Wolf Legal Publishers.

Vitale, A.T. (2001). 'U.S. Banking: An Industry's View on Money Laundering.' *Economic Perspectives* 6(2). Retrieved 2 July 2006 from http://usinfo.state.gov/journals/ites/0501/ijee/vitale.htm.

Walker, Chris. (1996). 'Year Four Evaluation Report. Integrated Anti-Drug Profiteering Initiative. Vancouver, Toronto, and Montreal Pilot Units.' Report prepared for the Solicitor General Canada.

Walker, John. (1999). 'Measuring the Extent of International Crime and Money Laundering.' Paper presented at the KriminálExpo, Budapest, Hungary, 9 June. Available online from http://members.ozemail.com.au/~john.walker/crimetrendsanalysis/Budapest.html.

– (2000a). *AUSTRAC – Estimates of the Extent of Money Laundering In and Throughout Australia, Executive Summary*. Sydney: Government of Australia.

Retrieved 31 May 2006 from www.austrac.gov.au/text/publications/
moneylaundestimates/chap11.html.
– (2000b). *Modelling Global Money Laundering Flows: Some Findings*. Available
online from www.ozemail.com.au/born1820/m/method.htm.
Walter, R. (1971). 'Organized Crime.' *Canadian Securities* (May): 1–6.
Wayne, E. Anthony. (2005). 'Money Laundering and Terrorist Financing in the
Middle East and South Asia.' Testimony before the Senate Committee on
Banking, Housing, and Urban Affairs Washington, DC, 13 July, *U.S. State
Department Press Release*, 14 July. Retrieved 2 June 2006 from
www.state.gov/e/eb/rls/rm/2005/49564.htm.
White House, The. (2001). 'Fact Sheet on Terrorist Finances Executive Order.'
White House Press Release, 24 September. Retrieved 2 June 2006
www.whitehouse.gov/news/releases/2001/09/20010924-4.html.
Williams, Marian R. (2002). 'Civil Asset Forfeiture: Where Does the Money
Go?' *Criminal Justice Review* 27(2): 321–9.
Willman, J. (2001). 'The Electronic Age Has Made It Much Harder for Banks to
Recognize Suspect Funds.' *Financial Times*, 19 April.
Wishart, Caron. Lawyers' Professional Indemnity Company. (2000). 'Money
Laundering – A Growing Claim's Exposure: Understanding the Lawyer's
Risks and Responsibilities.' Paper presented at the Taking the Starch Out of
Money Laundering CBA Conference, Toronto, ON, 28 November.
Wismer, Catherine. (1980). *Sweethearts*. Toronto: James Lorimer.
Woodiwiss, Michael. (2001). *Organized Crime and American Power*. Toronto:
University of Toronto Press.
Yeager, Peter Cleary. (1995). 'Management, Morality, and Law: Organizational
Forms and Ethical Deliberations.' In F. Pearce and L. Snider, eds., *Corporate
Crime: Contemporary Debates*, 147–67. Toronto: University of Toronto Press.
Zagaris, Bruce. (2002). 'Report to the House of Delegates.' American Bar
Association, Criminal Justice Section, Washington, DC, February.

Statutes and Legal Cases

Affidavit of R. Lalonde, quoted in Ontario Superior Court of Justice, Federation of Law Societies of Canada and Attorney General of Canada , January
9, 2002 Court File No: 01-CV-222041.
Canada (Minister of Citizenship and Immigration) v. Jaballah, [2003] F.C.J. No.
1274 (F.C.A.). Retrieved 2 June 2006 from http://recueil.cmf.gc.ca/fc/src/
shtml/2005/pub/v1/2005fc35032.shtml.
Controlled Drugs and Substances Act, R.S. 1996, c. 19, s. 9.
Criminal Code of Canada, R.S., 1985, c. 42 (4th Supp.), s. 462.31.

Customs Act, R.S., 1985, c. 1 (2nd Supp.), 163.2.

Excise Act, R.S. 1985, c. E-14, s. 126.2.

Federation of Law Societies v. A.G. Canada, 2001 BCSC 1593 (Federation of Law Societies of Canada v. Canada).

Lavallee, Rackel & Heintz v. Canada (Attorney General); White, Ottenheimer & Baker v. Canada (Attorney General); R. v. Fink, [2002] 3 S.C.R. 209, 2002 SCC 61.

R. v. Campbell and Shirose, April 1999. Supreme Court of Canada [1999] 1 S.C.R. 565. File #25780.

Veluppillai Pushpanathan (Applicant) v. The Minister of Citizenship and Immigration (Respondent). Indexed as: Pushpanathanv. Canada (Minister of Citizenship and Immigration) (C.A.). Court of Appeal, Stone, Strayer and Linden JJ.A. 'Toronto, November 15; Ottawa, December 19, 1995. Available online from http://reports. fja.gc.ca/src/shtml/1996/pub/v2/1996fca0086.shtml. Reference [1996] 2 F.C. 49.

Index

2 to 5 per cent estimate, 49, 57, 59, 318n31
11 September 2001: 9/11 Commission, 272, 280; costs to terrorists, 268; impact on anti-money-laundering legislation, xiv, 19–20, 28, 248, 252, 257–8; security failures, 266–8
$10,000 threshold, 17, 26, 44, 84, 95, 198–202, 205–6, 293, 306

Abachi, General Sani, 222
ABCsolutions, 164, 184
Abramo, Philip, 115–16
Access to Information Act, 150, 326–7n2
accountants: auditing lawyers, 245; contact with proceeds of crime, 135-136, 298; contingency fee market/tax evasion, 228–9; forensic, 151, 157, 159; as gatekeepers, 204, 233, 240; criminal operations and, 143–5; as professional launderers, 6; reporting entities, 206
account transfers, 92–3
Act to Facilitate Combating the
Laundering of Proceeds of Crime, 1991 (Bill C-9), 16
advance/loan funding initiative, 153, 162–6, 174
adverse publicity, 223–7
Advice and Reformation Committee, 290
Afghanistan, 270–1, 279
Aiken, S., 261–2
Albania, 42–3, 48
al-Barakaat case, 287–8
Alberta Stock Exchange, 121
alcohol smuggling. See smuggling
Alfauru, Abdel Rahman Omar Tawfiq, 267
al-Fawaaz, Khalid, 290
al-Ittihad al-Islamiya, 287
al Jihad, 273
Allan, Madam Justice Marion, 239
Alomari, Abdulaziz, 268
al-Owhali, Mohammad Rashed Dauod, 276
al-Qadi, Yasin, 273
al Qaeda: banking industry, 290–1; charitable organizations, 272–3; Clinton administration, 251; drug trafficking, 279–80; financial

handling, 236; 'no-cash rule,' 246–
7; transactions, 95, 104–6, 205
casinos, 33, 103, 132–3, 206, 326n28
Castro, Fidel, 270
Cauchon, Martin, 239
Cayman Islands, 42–3, 70, 117, 222
cell-phone calls, 310
Celluci, Paul, 267
Cencan Investments, 107
Census Analysis, 2001 (Canada), 259
Centorrino, Mario, 125
Central Bank of Sri Lanka, bombing,
291
CEO salaries, 226
certified cheques, 91–2
*Challenge of Crime in a Free Society,
The,* 5–7
Chambers, Martin, 232
Change Challenge Opportunity, 216–17
Channel Islands, 121–2
charitable organizations: and bank-
ing industry, 291–2; as conduit for
terrorist financing, 271–4; links to
money laundering, 331n14; Tamil
Tigers, 260–2; targeting Islamic,
111, 274–6; targeting of, 300
chartered banks, 88–9. *See also*
banking industry
Charter of Rights and Freedoms,
189, 191–2, 199, 238–9, 307
Chase Manhattan, 70
Cheney, Rob, 142
cheque cashing operations, 101–2
Cheran, R., 261–2
Chicago Crime Commission, 1970,
32–3
Chile, 42–3
China, 70
Chit. See informal money transfer
systems

CIA (Central Intelligence Agency),
254, 270, 291
CIMM (Centre International
Monetaire de Montreal), 167, 169
Citibank, 70, 222, 291
Citizen and Immigration Canada, 19
civil forfeiture, 15, 31, 188–90, 273–4,
307–8
Clinton administration, 251
cocaine: cartels, 9–11, 15, 104–5, 168–
9, 182; FATF estimates of global
sales, 51; Hells Angels, 143, 169;
horse racing, 134; imported to
Canada, 12–14; laundering profits
from, 82–5, 91, 93, 97–102, 110–13,
117, 132, 140–1; Project Eyespy,
168; seizures, 169–70, 185; Shining
Path (Peru), 279; statistics, 80, 162;
terrorist financing, 279. *See also*
proceeds of crime enforcement
code of silence, 13
codes of conduct, 329n1
Cold War, 269
Colombia, 12, 42, 64–5
Colombian cartels, 9–11, 15, 168–9,
182
Comartin, Joe, 308
commingling of funds, 82, 106, 109
Committee on Anti-Money Laundering for the Federation of Law
Societies of Canada, 247
companies. *See* criminally controlled
companies
compliance: banking industry,
16, 24, 74, 212–18, 223, 229–31,
330n10–330n11; Canada and,
297–8 (*see also* Canada); costs of,
73–5, 322–3n74; factors affecting,
208–9; with FATF standards, 68–9;
Halliburton Corporation, 311–12;

382   Index

Remedies for Organized Crime and Other Unlawful Activities Act (Ontario), 188–9

Renyi, Thomas, 224, 226

repatriation of funds, 7, 107, 112–13, 141

reporting entities, 206–7. *See also* banking industry; FATF; financial services industry; FinCEN; FINTRAC (Financial Transactions Reports Analysis Centre of Canada)

reporting requirements. *See* mandatory transaction reporting

Report on Money Laundering Typologies, 256–7

responsibilization strategy, 28–9, 301–2, 310

restaurants, 103–7, 109–112, 276

restraint orders, 15

Reuter, Peter, 57, 66

revenue property, 98

reverse onus. *See* onus of proof

Reverse Onus Forfeiture Provisions, 2005 (Bill C-53), 26

'reverse sting' operations, 164, 167–74

Revolutionary Armed Forces of Colombia, 279

Richardsons Greenshields, 117–18

RICO (Racketeer Influenced and Corrupt Organizations Act) U.S., 189

risk management approach, 186

Rizzuto crime family, 168–9

Robinson, Mary, 312

Rockers, 143

Rolfe, Basil, 111, 138

Romania, 42–3, 48, 70

Rosegarden Construction, 107

Rosen, John, 188–9

Rosenfeld, Simon, 232

Royal Bank of Canada, 8, 10, 117, 151, 208, 330n6

Royal Bank of Scotland, 121

Royal Canadian Mounted Police. *See* RCMP (Royal Canadian Mounted Police)

Royal Commission on Certain Sectors of the Building Industry in Ontario, report of, 7

Ruby, Clayton, 15

Russia, 42–3, 70, 224

Russian crime groups, 115, 120–3

Russian Federation, 38, 48

SAAR Foundation, 274

safe-haven countries, 89, 124, 259

safety deposit boxes, 91, 93, 213

Saint-Pierre and Miquelon, 4

Salah, Mohammad and Azita, 273–4

salaries, fictitious, 114

Salerno, Ralph, 32

Salinas, Carlos, 222–3

Salinas, Raul, 222–3

Sandanista government, 270

San Marino, 42–3, 48

Santa Rita Import-Export Ltd., 104

Saskatoon, 83

Saudi Arabia, 271

Sauvageau, Jean, 160, 164

Savard, Francois, 129–30

savings/chequing accounts, 91–2

scandals, 223–7

Schneider, Stephen, ix, xi, 78, 156, 160, 164

Scotiabank, 4, 8

Seagram, 4

'seasoned customer exemption,' 306